75
READINGS:
AN ANTHOLOGY

75
READINGS:
AN
ANTHOLOGY

Third Edition

McGRAW-HILL, INC.
New York   St. Louis   San Francisco   Auckland   Bogotá
Caracas   Hamburg   Lisbon   London   Madrid   Mexico   Milan
Montreal   New Delhi   Paris   San Juan   São Paulo
Singapore   Sydney   Tokyo   Toronto

In special appreciation
Santi Buscemi
Middlesex County College

This book was set in Times Roman by the College Composition Unit
in cooperation with Waldman Graphics, Inc.
The editors were Lesley Denton and James R. Belser;
the production supervisor was Richard A. Ausburn.
The cover was designed by Joan E. O'Connor.
Cover illustration by Jane Moorman.
Arcata Graphics/Fairfield was printer and binder.

75 READINGS: AN ANTHOLOGY

1 2 3 4 5 6 7 8 9 0 FGR FGR 9 5 4 3 2 1 0

ISBN 0-07-046677-7

Acknowledgments appear on pages 415–420, and on this page by reference.

Library of Congress Cataloging-in-Publication Data

75 readings: an anthology.—3rd ed.
    p.   cm.
  Includes index.
  ISBN 0-07-046677-7
  1. College readers.   2. English language—Rhetoric.   I. Title:
Seventy-five readings.
PE1417.A23   1991
808'.0427—dc20   90-6393

CONTENTS

THEMATIC CONTENTS   **ix**
PREFACE   **xv**

CHAPTER 1
Narration

George Orwell: *A Hanging*   1
Langston Hughes: *Salvation*   6
Maya Angelou: *Grandmother's Victory*   9
Akira Kurosawa: *Crybaby*   14
William Zinsser: *The Transaction*   23
Luz Alicia Herrera: *Testimonies of Guatemalan Women*   26
Richard Selzer: *The Discus Thrower*   37
Olive Schreiner: *Somewhere, Some Time, Some Place*   40

CHAPTER 2
Description

Margaret Laurence: *Where the World Began*   46
Joan Didion: *The Metropolitan Cathedral in San Salvador*   52
William Least Heat Moon: *Tuesday Morning*   54
Peter Schjeldahl: *Cyclone! Rising to the Fall*   59
Mordecai Richler: *Main Street*   64
Virginia Woolf: *The Death of the Moth*   73
Peter Freundlich: *The Crime of the Tooth: Dentistry in the
   Chair*   76
Doris Lessing: *My Father*   84

CHAPTER 3
Process

Benjamin Franklin: *Attaining Moral Virtue*   93
Alexander Petrunkevitch: *The Spider and the Wasp*   97
Rachel Carson: *The Grey Beginnings*   102
Euell Gibbons: *How to Cook a Carp*   112
Jessica Mitford: *Behind the Formaldehyde Curtain*   115
Mary Wollstonecraft Shelley: *Introduction to
    Frankenstein*   125
Richard Howey: *How to Write a Rotten Poem with Almost
    No Effort*   130

CHAPTER 4
Definition

Bruno Bettelheim: *The Holocaust*   133
Susan Sontag: *Beauty*   136
Joseph Epstein: *The Virtues of Ambition*   139
Barbara Grizzuti Harrison: *Moral Ambiguity*   145
Jo Goodwin Parker: *What Is Poverty?*   150
Tom Wolfe: *Pornoviolence*   154
Dorothy Parker: *Good Souls*   161

CHAPTER 5
Division and Classification

William Golding: *Thinking as a Hobby*   167
Erika Ritter: *Bicycles*   175
American Friends Service Committee: *Struggle for Justice*   178
James David Barber: *Presidential Character and How to
    Foresee It*   197
David M. Ludlum: *The Climythology of America*   203
Robert Brustein: *Reflections on Horror Movies*   211
Susan Allen Toth: *Cinematypes*   221

CHAPTER 6
Comparison and Contrast

Bruce Catton: *Grant and Lee: A Study in Contrasts*   225
Cynthia Ozick: *On Permission to Write*   229
Murray Ross: *Football Red and Baseball Green*   235
Mark Twain: *Two Views of the Mississippi*   244
May Sarton: *The Rewards of Living a Solitary Life*   246
Marie Winn: *Viewing vs. Reading*   247
Ralph Waldo Emerson: *Conservatives and Liberals*   255

CHAPTER 7
Example and Illustration

Ann Hodgman: *Backwater Cuisine*   259
William F. Buckley, Jr.:   *Why Don't We Complain?*   262
Richard Rodriguez: *Does America Still Exist?*   268
Joyce Maynard: *I Remember...*   273
Robertson Davies: *A Few Kind Words for Superstition*   277
Stephen Jay Gould: *Were Dinosaurs Dumb?*   279
Peter Farb and George Armelagos: *The Patterns of
    Eating*   285

CHAPTER 8
Cause and Effect

Marya Mannes: *How Do You Know It's Good?*   291
Isaac Asimov: *The Villain in the Atmosphere*   298
Norman Cousins: *Pain Is Not the Ultimate Enemy*   303
E. M. Forster: *My Wood*   307
Ellen Goodman: *Watching the Grasshopper Get the
    Goodies*   310
Jonathan Schell: *Nuclear Holocaust*   312
Lewis Thomas: *The Iks*   328
Nadine Gordimer: *Art and the State in South Africa*   331

CHAPTER 9
Analogy

Plato: *The Myth of the Cave*   338
Horace Miner: *Body Ritual among the Nacirema*   343
Annie Dillard: *Transfiguration*   349
James C. Rettie: *"But a Watch in the Night": A Scientific Fable*   352
Loren Eiseley: *The Cosmic Prison*   358
Barry Lopez: *My Horse*   361
Farley Mowat: *The Perfect House*   368
Albert Camus: *The Myth of Sisyphus*   373

CHAPTER 10
Argument

Jonathan Swift: *A Modest Proposal*   377
Lindsy Van Gelder: *The Great Person-Hole Cover Debate: A Modest Proposal for Anyone Who Thinks the Word "He" Is Just Plain Easier...*   385
Arthur E. Lean: *The Farce Called "Grading"*   388
H. L. Mencken: *The Penalty of Death*   394
Thomas Jefferson: *The Declaration of Independence*   397
Martin Luther King, Jr.:   *I Have a Dream*   401
Alan Paton: *Eight Signposts to Salvation*   406
Walter Murdoch: *On Rabbits, Morality, Etc.*   409

ACKNOWLEDGMENTS   415

THEMATIC CONTENTS

Perspectives on Existence

Albert Camus: *The Myths of Sisyphus*   373
Rachel Carson: *The Grey Beginnings*   102
Loren Eiseley: *The Cosmic Prison*   358
Stephen Jay Gould: *Were Dinosaurs Dumb?*   279
Luz Alicia Herrera: *Testimonies of Guatemalan Women*   26
Plato: *The Myth of the Cave*   338
James C. Rettie: *"But a Watch in the Night": A Scientific Fable*   352
May Sarton: *The Rewards of Living a Solitary Life*   246
Olive Schreiner: *Somewhere, Some Time, Some Place*   40
Virginia Woolf: *The Death of the Moth*   73

Growing Up, Growing Old

Maya Angelou: *Grandmother's Victory*   9
Norman Cousins: *Pain Is Not the Ultimate Enemy*   303
Benjamin Franklin: *Attaining Moral Virtue*   93
William Golding: *Thinking as a Hobby*   167
Langston Hughes: *Salvation*   6
Akira Kurosawa: *Crybaby*   14
Doris Lessing: *My Father*   84
Richard Selzer: *The Discus Thrower*   37

Life in America

William F. Buckley, Jr.: *Why Don't We Complain?* 262
Euell Gibbons: *How to Cook a Carp* 112
Ellen Goodman: *Watching the Grasshopper Get the Goodies* 310
William Least Heat Moon: *Tuesday Morning* 54
Ann Hodgman: *Backwater Cuisine* 259
Barry Lopez: *My Horse* 361
Jessica Mitford: *Behind the Formaldehyde Curtain* 115
Jo Goodwin Parker: *What Is Poverty?* 150
Peter Schjeldahl: *Cyclone! Rising to the Fall* 59
Mark Twain: *Two Views of the Mississippi* 244

Canadian Voices

Robertson Davies: *A Few Kind Words for Superstition* 277
Margaret Laurence: *Where the World Began* 46
Farley Mowat: *The Perfect House* 368
Mordecai Richler: *Main Street* 64
Erika Ritter: *Bicycles* 175

Power and Politics

American Friends Service Committee: *Struggle for Justice* 178
James David Barber: *Presidential Character and How to
 Foresee It* 197
Bruce Catton: *Grant and Lee: A Study in Contrasts* 225
Joan Didion: *The Metropolitan Cathedral in San Salvador* 52
Ralph Waldo Emerson: *Conservatives and Liberals* 255
Nadine Gordimer: *Art and the State in South Africa* 331
Barbara Grizzuti Harrison: *Moral Ambiguity* 145
Luz Alicia Herrera: *Testimonies of Guatemalan Women* 26
Thomas Jefferson: *The Declaration of Independence* 397
Martin Luther King, Jr.: *I Have a Dream* 401
Alan Paton: *Eight Signposts to Salvation* 406
Richard Rodriguez: *Does America Still Exist?* 268

Olive Schreiner: *Somewhere, Some Time, Some Place* 40
Lewis Thomas: *The Iks* 328

Problems, Solutions, and Consequences

Isaac Asimov: *The Villain in the Atmosphere* 298
Euell Gibbons: *How to Cook a Carp* 112
Barbara Grizzuti Harrison: *Moral Ambiguity* 145
Arthur E. Lean: *The Farce Called "Grading"* 388
H. L. Mencken: *The Penalty of Death* 394
Farley Mowat: *The Perfect House* 368
Walter Murdoch: *On Rabbits, Morality, Etc.* 409
Jonathan Schell: *Nuclear Holocaust* 312
Mary Wollstonecraft Shelley: *Introduction to* Frankenstein 125
Jonathan Swift: *A Modest Proposal* 377
Lewis Thomas: *The Iks* 328

Territory and Competition

Joseph Epstein: *The Virtues of Ambition* 139
E. M. Forster: *My Wood* 307
Ann Hodgman: *Backwater Cuisine* 259
Arthur E. Lean: *The Farce Called "Grading"* 388
Alexander Petrunkevitch: *The Spider and the Wasp* 97
Murray Ross: *Football Red and Baseball Green* 235

Cultural Rules of Form and Behavior

Peter Farb and George Armelagos: *The Patterns of Eating* 285
Benjamin Franklin: *Attaining Moral Virtue* 93
Ellen Goodman: *Watching the Grasshopper Get the Goodies* 310
Nadine Gordimer: *Art and the State in South Africa* 331
Akira Kurosawa: *Crybaby* 14
Marya Mannes: *How Do You Know It's Good?* 291
Horace Miner: *Body Ritual among the Nacirema* 343

George Orwell: *A Hanging*   1
Dorothy Parker: *Good Souls*   161
Lewis Thomas: *The Iks*   328

The Evolution of Science and Technology

Isaac Asimov: *The Villain in the Atmosphere*   298
Peter Freundlich: *The Crime of the Tooth: Dentistry in the Chair*   76
David M. Ludlum: *Climythology*   203
Jessica Mitford: *Behind the Formaldehyde Curtain*   115
James C. Rettie: *"But a Watch in the Night": A Scientific Fable*   352
Jonathan Schell: *Nuclear Holocaust*   312
Mary Wollstonecraft Shelley: *Introduction to* Frankenstein   125
Marie Winn: *Viewing vs. Reading*   247

Fear and Exhilaration

Robert Brustein: *Reflections on Horror Movies*   211
Norman Cousins: *Pain Is Not the Ultimate Enemy*   303
Robertson Davies: *A Few Kind Words for Superstition*   277
Peter Freundlich: *The Crime of the Tooth: Dentistry in the Chair*   76
Peter Schjeldahl: *Cyclone! Rising to the Fall*   59
Richard Selzer: *The Discus Thrower*   37
Mary Wollstonecraft Shelley: *Introduction to* Frankenstein   125

On Media

Robert Brustein: *Reflections on Horror Movies*   211
Barbara Grizzuti Harrison: *Moral Ambiguity*   145
Joyce Maynard: *I Remember...*   273
Susan Allen Toth: *Cinematypes*   221

Marie Winn: *Viewing vs. Reading*   247
Tom Wolfe: *Pornoviolence*   154

On Language and the Writing Process

Bruno Bettelheim: *The Holocaust*   133
Annie Dillard: *Transfiguration*   349
Richard Howey: *How to Write a Rotten Poem with Almost No Effort*   130
Marya Mannes: *How Do You Know It's Good?*   291
Cynthia Ozick: *On Permission to Write*   229
Susan Sontag: *Beauty*   136
Lindsy Van Gelder: *The Great Person-Hole Cover Debate: A Modest Proposal for Anyone Who Thinks the Word "He" Is Just Plain Easier...*   385
William Zinsser: *The Transaction*   23

PREFACE

75 Readings: An Anthology is designed to introduce students to a broad variety of both traditional and contemporary essays, as well as topical pieces by international, ethnic, and women writers. The anthology has been compiled by an editor-composition instructor team whose purpose has been to provide a wide range of supplementary essays at a low price to the students. The primary aim has been to expose students to a variety of rhetorical purposes, writing styles, and subject matter, while retaining maximum pedagogical flexibility for the instructor. While the essays are organized by rhetorical mode, they can be used in other configurations as well; a thematic table of contents suggests other ways for clustering the essays.

The third edition features twelve new readings. Most of these address some current issue, so that the anthology now has essays on abortion, the greenhouse effect, nuclear war, and racial and gender issues. There is also an essay based on documented research which, in addition to addressing racial and gender issues, can provide a model for researched papers.

A comprehensive instructor's manual, prepared by Professors Santi Buscemi of Middlesex County College and Charlotte Smith of New York University, provides brief author biographies, discussion questions, and journal and paper assignments for each essay in the anthology.

Special thanks are due to those instructors who reviewed the anthology and gave us their suggestions for the third edition: Paula Gibson, Cardinal Stritch College; Eric Hibbison, J. Sargeant Reynolds Community College; Dale Ross, Iowa State University; and Deborah Spencer, Cabrillo College.

In addition, the following people at McGraw-Hill helped to bring this project to fruition: Lesley Denton, James R. Belser, and Richard Ausburn.

75
READINGS:
AN ANTHOLOGY

1

Narration

A Hanging

George Orwell

It was in Burma, a sodden morning of the rains. A sickly 1
light, like yellow tinfoil, was slanting over the high walls into the
jail yard. We were waiting outside the condemned cells, a row of
sheds fronted with double bars, like small animal cages. Each
cell measured about ten feet by ten and was quite bare within except for a plank bed and a pot of drinking water. In some of them
brown silent men were squatting at the inner bars, with their
blankets draped round them. These were the condemned men,
due to be hanged within the next week or two.

One prisoner had been brought out of his cell. He was a 2
Hindu, a puny wisp of a man, with a shaven head and vague liquid eyes. He had a thick, sprouting moustache, absurdly too big
for his body, rather like the moustache of a comic man in the
films. Six tall Indian warders were guarding him and getting him
ready for the gallows. Two of them stood by with rifles and fixed
bayonets, while the others handcuffed him, passed a chain
through his handcuffs and fixed it to their belts, and lashed his
arms tight to his sides. They crowded very close about him, with
their hands always on him in a careful, caressing grip, as though
all the while feeling him to make sure he was there. It was like

1

men handling a fish which is still alive and may jump back into the water. But he stood quite unresisting, yielding his arms limply to the ropes, as though he hardly noticed what was happening.

Eight o'clock struck and a bugle call, desolately thin in the 3 wet air, floated from the distant barracks. The superintendent of the jail, who was standing apart from the rest of us, moodily prodding the gravel with his stick, raised his head at the sound. He was an army doctor, with a grey toothbrush moustache and a gruff voice. "For God's sake hurry up, Francis," he said irritably. "The man ought to have been dead by this time. Aren't you ready yet?"

Francis, the head jailer, a fat Dravidian in a white drill suit 4 and gold spectacles, waved his black hand. "Yes sir, yes sir," he bubbled. "All iss satisfactorily prepared. The hangman iss waiting. We shall proceed."

"Well, quick march, then. The prisoners can't get their 5 breakfast till this job's over."

We set out for the gallows. Two warders marched on either 6 side of the prisoner, with their rifles at the slope; two others marched close against him, gripping him by arm and shoulder, as though at once pushing and supporting him. The rest of us, magistrates and the like, followed behind. Suddenly, when we had gone ten yards, the procession stopped short without any order or warning. A dreadful thing had happened—a dog, come goodness knows whence, had appeared in the yard. It came bounding among us with a loud volley of barks, and leapt round us wagging its whole body, wild with glee at finding so many human beings together. It was a large woolly dog, half Airedale, half pariah. For a moment it pranced round us, and then, before anyone could stop it, it had made a dash for the prisoner, and jumping up tried to lick his face. Everyone stood aghast, too taken aback even to grab at the dog.

"Who let that bloody brute in here?" said the superinten- 7 dent angrily. "Catch it, someone!"

A warder, detached from the escort, charged clumsily after 8 the dog, but it danced and gambolled just out of his reach, taking everything as part of the game. A young Eurasian jailer picked up a handful of gravel and tried to stone the dog away, but it dodged the stones and came after us again. Its yaps echoed from the jail walls. The prisoner, in the grasp of the two warders, looked on incuriously, as though this was another formality of the hanging. It was several minutes before someone managed to catch the dog. Then we put my handkerchief through its collar and moved off once more, with the dog still straining and whimpering.

It was about forty yards to the gallows. I watched the bare **9** brown back of the prisoner marching in front of me. He walked clumsily with his bound arms, but quite steadily, with that bobbing gait of the Indian who never straightens his knees. At each step his muscles slid neatly into place, the lock of hair on his scalp danced up and down, his feet printed themselves on the wet gravel. And once, in spite of the men who gripped him by each shoulder, he stepped slightly aside to avoid a puddle on the path.

It is curious, but till that moment I had never realised what **10** it means to destroy a healthy, conscious man. When I saw the prisoner step aside to avoid the puddle, I saw the mystery, the unspeakable wrongness, of cutting a life short when it is in full tide. This man was not dying, he was alive just as we were alive. All the organs of his body were working—bowels digesting food, skin renewing itself, nails growing, tissues forming—all toiling away in solemn foolery. His nails would still be growing when he stood on the drop, when he was falling through the air with a tenth of a second to live. His eyes saw the yellow gravel and the grey walls, and his brain still remembered, foresaw, reasoned— reasoned even about puddles. He and we were a party of men walking together, seeing, hearing, feeling, understanding the same world; and in two minutes, with a sudden snap, one of us would be gone—one mind less, one world less.

The gallows stood in a small yard, separate from the main **11** grounds of the prison, and overgrown with tall prickly weeds. It was a brick erection like three sides of a shed, with planking on top, and above that two beams and a crossbar with the rope dangling. The hangman, a grey-haired convict in the white uniform of the prison, was waiting beside his machine. He greeted us with a servile crouch as we entered. At a word from Francis the two warders, gripping the prisoner more closely than ever, half led, half pushed him to the gallows and helped him clumsily up the ladder. Then the hangman climbed up and fixed the rope round the prisoner's neck.

We stood waiting, five yards away. The warders had formed in a rough circle round the gallows. And then, when the noose was fixed, the prisoner began crying out on his god. It was a high, reiterated cry of "Ram! Ram! Ram! Ram!", not urgent and fearful like a prayer or a cry for help, but steady, rhythmical, almost like the tolling of a bell. The dog answered the sound with a whine. The hangman, still standing on the gallows, produced a small cotton bag like a flour bag and drew it down over the prisoner's face. But the sound, muffled by the cloth, still persisted, over and over again: "Ram! Ram! Ram! Ram! Ram!" 12

The hangman climbed down and stood ready, holding the lever. Minutes seemed to pass. The steady, muffled crying from the prisoner went on and on, "Ram! Ram! Ram!" never faltering for an instant. The superintendent, his head on his chest, was slowly poking the ground with his stick; perhaps he was counting the cries, allowing the prisoner a fixed number—fifty, perhaps, or a hundred. Everyone had changed colour. The Indians had gone grey like bad coffee, and one or two of the bayonets were wavering. We looked at the lashed, hooded man on the drop, and listened to his cries—each cry another second of life; the same thought was in all our minds: oh, kill him quickly, get it over, stop that abominable noise! 13

Suddenly the superintendent made up his mind. Throwing up his head he made a swift motion with his stick. "Chalo!" he shouted almost fiercely. 14

There was a clanking noise, and then dead silence. The prisoner had vanished, and the rope was twisting on itself. I let go of the dog, and it galloped immediately to the back of the gallows; but when it got there it stopped short, barked, and then retreated into a corner of the yard, where it stood among the weeds, looking timorously out at us. We went round the gallows to inspect the prisoner's body. He was dangling with his toes 15 pointed straight downwards, very slowly revolving, as dead as a stone.

The superintendent reached out with his stick and poked 16 the bare body; it oscillated slightly. *"He's* all right," said the superintendent. He backed out from under the gallows, and blew out a deep breath. The moody look had gone out of his face quite suddenly. He glanced at his wrist-watch. "Eight minutes past eight. Well, that's all for this morning, thank God."

The warders unfixed bayonets and marched away. The dog, 17 sobered and conscious of having misbehaved itself, slipped after them. We walked out of the gallows yard, past the condemned cells with their waiting prisoners, into the big central yard of the prison. The convicts, under the command of warders armed with lathis, were already receiving their breakfast. They squatted in long rows, each man holding a tin pannikin, while two warders with buckets marched round ladling out rice; it seemed quite a homely, jolly scene, after the hanging. An enormous relief had come upon us now that the job was done. One felt an impulse to sing, to break into a run, to snigger. All at once everyone began chattering gaily.

The Eurasian boy walking beside me nodded towards the 18 way we had come, with a knowing smile: "Do you know, sir, our friend (he meant the dead man), when he heard his appeal had been dismissed, he pissed on the floor of his cell. From fright.— Kindly take one of my cigarettes, sir. Do you not admire my new silver case, sir? From the boxwallah, two rupees eight annas. Classy European style."

Several people laughed—at what, nobody seemed certain. 19

Francis was walking by the superintendent, talking garru- 20 lously: "Well, sir, all hass passed off with the utmost satisfactoriness. It wass all finished—flick! like that. It iss not always so— oah, no! I have known cases where the doctor wass obliged to go beneath the gallows and pull the prisoner's legs to ensure decease. Most disagreeable!"

"Wriggling about, eh? That's bad," said the superinten- 21 dent.

"Ach, sir, it iss worse when they become refractory! One 22

man, I recall, clung to the bars of hiss cage when we went to take him out. You will scarcely credit, sir, that it took six warders to dislodge him, three pulling at each leg. We reasoned with him. 'My dear fellow,' we said, 'think of all the pain and trouble you are causing to us!' But no, he would not listen! Ach, he wass very troublesome!"

I found that I was laughing quite loudly. Everyone was 23 laughing. Even the superintendent grinned in a tolerant way. "You'd better all come out and have a drink," he said quite genially. "I've got a bottle of whisky in the car. We could do with it."

We went through the big double gates of the prison, into the 24 road. "Pulling at his legs!" exclaimed a Burmese magistrate suddenly, and burst into a loud chuckling. We all began laughing again. At that moment Francis's anecdote seemed extraordinarily funny. We all had a drink together, native and European alike, quite amicably. The dead man was a hundred yards away.

1931

Salvation
Langston Hughes

I was saved from sin when I was going on thirteen. But not 1 really saved. It happened like this. There was a big revival at my Auntie Reed's church. Every night for weeks there had been much preaching, singing, praying, and shouting, and some very hardened sinners had been brought to Christ, and the membership of the church had grown by leaps and bounds. Then just before the revival ended, they held a special meeting for children, "to bring the young lambs to the fold." My aunt spoke of it for days ahead. That night I was escorted to the front row and placed on the mourners' bench with all the other young sinners, who had not yet been brought to Jesus.

My aunt told me that when you were saved you saw a light, 2 and something happened to you inside! And Jesus came into your life! And God was with you from then on! She said you could see and hear and feel Jesus in your soul. I believed her. I had heard a great many old people say the same thing and it seemed to me they ought to know. So I sat there calmly in the hot, crowded church, waiting for Jesus to come to me.

The preacher preached a wonderful rhythmical sermon, all 3 moans and shouts and lonely cries and dire pictures of hell, and then he sang a song about the ninety and nine safe in the fold, but one little lamb was left out in the cold. Then he said: "Won't you come? Won't you come to Jesus? Young lambs, won't you come?" And he held out his arms to all us young sinners there on the mourners' bench. And the little girls cried. And some of them jumped up and went to Jesus right away. But most of us just sat there.

A great many old people came and knelt around us and 4 prayed, old women with jet-black faces and braided hair, old men with work-gnarled hands. And the church sang a song about the lower lights are burning, some poor sinners to be saved. And the whole building rocked with prayer and song.

Still I kept waiting to *see* Jesus.   5

Finally all the young people had gone to the altar and were 6 saved, but one boy and me. He was a rounder's son named Westley. Westley and I were surrounded by sisters and deacons praying. It was very hot in the church, and getting late now. Finally Westley said to me in a whisper: "God damn! I'm tired o' sitting here. Let's get up and be saved." So he got up and was saved.

Then I was left all alone on the mourners' bench. My aunt 7 came and knelt at my knees and cried, while prayers and songs swirled all around me in the little church. The whole congregation prayed for me alone, in a mighty wail of moans and voices. And I kept waiting serenely for Jesus, waiting, waiting—but he didn't come. I wanted to see him, but nothing happened to me. Nothing! I wanted something to happen to me, but nothing happened.

I heard the songs and the minister saying: "Why don't you 8

come? My dear child, why don't you come to Jesus? Jesus is
waiting for you. He wants you. Why don't you come? Sister
Reed, what is this child's name?"

"Langston," my aunt sobbed.   9

"Langston, why don't you come? Why don't you come and   10
be saved? Oh, Lamb of God! Why don't you come?"

Now it was really getting late. I began to be ashamed of my- 11
self, holding everything up so long. I began to wonder what God
thought about Westley, who certainly hadn't seen Jesus either,
but who was now sitting proudly on the platform, swinging his
knickerbockered legs and grinning down at me, surrounded by
deacons and old women on their knees praying. God had not
struck Westley dead for taking his name in vain or for lying in the
temple. So I decided that maybe to save further trouble, I'd better
lie, too, and say that Jesus had come, and get up and be saved.

So I got up.   12

Suddenly the whole room broke into a sea of shouting, as   13
they saw me rise. Waves of rejoicing swept the place. Women
leaped in the air. My aunt threw her arms around me. The minister took me by the hand and led me to the platform.

When things quieted down, in a hushed silence, punctuated   14
by a few ecstatic "Amens," all the new young lambs were
blessed in the name of God. Then joyous singing filled the room.

That night, for the last time in my life but one—for I was a   15
big boy twelve years old—I cried. I cried, in bed alone, and
couldn't stop. I buried my head under the quilts, but my aunt
heard me. She woke up and told my uncle I was crying because
the Holy Ghost had come into my life, and because I had seen
Jesus. But I was really crying because I couldn't bear to tell her
that I had lied, that I had deceived everybody in the church, that
I hadn't seen Jesus, and that now I didn't believe there was a
Jesus any more, since he didn't come to help me.

1940

Grandmother's Victory
Maya Angelou

"Thou shall not be dirty" and "Thou shall not be impu- 1
dent" were the two commandments of Grandmother Henderson
upon which hung our total salvation.

Each night in the bitterest winter we were forced to wash 2
faces, arms, necks, legs and feet before going to bed. She used to
add, with a smirk that unprofane people can't control when venturing into profanity, "and wash as far as possible, then wash
possible."

We would go to the well and wash in the ice-cold, clear wa- 3
ter, grease our legs with the equally cold stiff Vaseline, then tiptoe into the house. We wiped the dust from our toes and settled
down for schoolwork, cornbread, clabbered milk, prayers and
bed, always in that order. Momma was famous for pulling the
quilts off after we had fallen asleep to examine our feet. If they
weren't clean enough for her, she took the switch (she kept one
behind the bedroom door for emergencies) and woke up the offender with a few aptly placed burning reminders.

The area around the well at night was dark and slick, and 4
boys told about how snakes love water, so that anyone who had
to draw water at night and then stand there alone and wash knew
that moccasins and rattlers, puff adders and boa constrictors
were winding their way to the well and would arrive just as the
person washing got soap in her eyes. But Momma convinced us
that not only was cleanliness next to Godliness, dirtiness was the
inventor of misery.

The impudent child was detested by God and a shame to its 5
parents and could bring destruction to its house and line. All
adults had to be addressed as Mister, Missus, Miss, Auntie,
Cousin, Unk, Uncle, Buhbah, Sister, Brother and a thousand
other appellations indicating familial relationship and the lowli-
ness of the addressor.

Everyone I knew respected these customary laws, except 6
for the powhitetrash children.

Some families of powhitetrash lived on Momma's farm land 7

behind the school. Sometimes a gaggle of them came to the Store, filling the whole room, chasing out the air and even changing the well-known scents. The children crawled over the shelves and into the potato and onion bins, twanging all the time in their sharp voices like cigar-box guitars. They took liberties in my Store that I would never dare. Since Momma told us that the less you say to white-folks (or even powhitetrash) the better, Bailey and I would stand, solemn, quiet, in the displaced air. But if one of the playful apparitions got close to us, I pinched it. Partly out of angry frustration and partly because I didn't believe in its flesh reality.

They called my uncle by his first name and ordered him 8 around the Store. He, to my crying shame, obeyed them in his limping dip-straight-dip fashion.

My grandmother, too, followed their orders, except that 9 she didn't seem to be servile because she anticipated their needs.

"Here's sugar, Miz Potter, and here's baking powder. You 10 didn't buy soda last month, you'll probably be needing some."

Momma always directed her statements to the adults, but 11 sometimes, Oh painful sometimes, the grimy, snotty-nosed girls would answer her.

"Naw, Annie..."—to Momma? Who owned the land they 12 lived on? Who forgot more than they would ever learn? If there was any justice in the world, God should strike them dumb at once!—"Just give us some extra sody crackers, and some more mackerel."

At least they never looked in her face, or I never caught 13 them doing so. Nobody with a smidgen of training, not even the worst roustabout, would look right in a grown person's face. It meant the person was trying to take the words out before they were formed. The dirty little children didn't do that, but they threw their orders around the Store like lashes from a cat-o'-nine-tails.

When I was around ten years old, those scruffy children 14 caused me the most painful and confusing experience I had ever had with my grandmother.

One summer morning, after I had swept the dirt yard of 15 leaves, spearmint-gum wrappers and Vienna-sausage labels, I raked the yellow-red dirt, and made half-moons carefully, so that the design stood out clearly and mask-like. I put the rake behind the Store and came through the back of the house to find Grandmother on the front porch in her big, wide white apron. The apron was so stiff by virtue of the starch that it could have stood alone. Momma was admiring the yard, so I joined her. It truly looked like a flat redhead that had been raked with a big-toothed comb. Momma didn't say anything but I knew she liked it. She looked over toward the school principal's house and to the right at Mr. McElroy's. She was hoping one of those community pillars would see the design before the day's business wiped it out. Then she looked upward to the school. My head had swung with hers, so at just about the same time we saw a troop of powhite-trash kids marching over the hill and down by the side of the school.

I looked to Momma for direction. She did an excellent job 16 of sagging from her waist down, but from the waist up she seemed to be pulling for the top of the oak tree across the road. Then she began to moan a hymn. Maybe not to moan, but the tune was so slow and the meter so strange that she could have been moaning. She didn't look at me again. When the children reached halfway down the hill, halfway to the Store, she said without turning, "Sister, go on inside."

I wanted to beg her, "Momma, don't wait for them. Come 17 on inside with me. If they come in the Store, you go to the bedroom and let me wait on them. They only frighten me if you're around. Alone I know how to handle them." But of course I couldn't say anything, so I went in and stood behind the screen door.

Before the girls got to the porch I heard their laughter 18 crackling and popping like pine logs in a cooking stove. I suppose my lifelong paranoia was born in those cold, molasses-slow minutes. They came finally to stand on the ground in front of Momma. At first they pretended seriousness. Then one of them wrapped her right arm in the crook of her left, pushed out her mouth and started to hum. I realized that she was aping my grandmother. Another said, "Naw, Helen, you ain't standing like her. This here's it." Then she lifted her chest, folded her

arms and mocked that strange carriage that was Annie Henderson. Another laughed, "Naw, you can't do it. Your mouth ain't
pooched out enough. It's like this."

I thought about the rifle behind the door, but I knew I'd   19
never be able to hold it straight, and the .410, our sawed-off shotgun, which stayed loaded and was fired every New Year's night,
was locked in the trunk and Uncle Willie had the key on his
chain. Through the fly-specked screen-door, I could see that the
arms of Momma's apron jiggled from the vibrations of her humming. But her knees seemed to have locked as if they would
never bend again.

She sang on. No louder than before, but no softer either.   20
No slower or faster.

The dirt of the girls' cotton dresses continued on their legs,   21
feet, arms and faces to make them all of a piece. Their greasy
uncolored hair hung down, uncombed, with a grim finality. I
knelt to see them better, to remember them for all time. The
tears that had slipped down my dress left unsurprising dark
spots, and made the front yard blurry and even more unreal. The
world had taken a deep breath and was having doubts about continuing to revolve.

The girls had tired of mocking Momma and turned to other   22
means of agitation. One crossed her eyes, stuck her thumbs in
both sides of her mouth and said, "Look here, Annie." Grandmother hummed on and the apron strings trembled. I wanted to
throw a handful of black pepper in their faces, to throw lye on
them, to scream that they were dirty, scummy peckerwoods, but
I knew I was as clearly imprisoned behind the scene as the actors
outside were confined to their roles.

One of the smaller girls did a kind of puppet dance while   23
her fellow clowns laughed at her. But the tall one, who was almost a woman, said something very quietly, which I couldn't
hear. They all moved backward from the porch, still watching
Momma. For an awful second I thought they were going to throw
a rock at Momma, who seemed (except for the apron strings) to
have turned into stone herself. But the big girl turned her back,
bent down and put her hands flat on the ground—she didn't pick
up anything. She simply shifted her weight and did a hand stand.

Her dirty bare feet and long legs went straight for the sky. 24
Her dress fell down around her shoulders, and she had on no
drawers. The slick pubic hair made a brown triangle where her
legs came together. She hung in the vacuum of that lifeless morning for only a few seconds, then wavered and tumbled. The other
girls clapped her on the back and slapped their hands.

Momma changed her song to "Bread of Heaven, bread of 25
Heaven, feed me till I want no more."

I found that I was praying too. How long could Momma 26
hold out? What new indignity would they think of to subject her
to? Would I be able to stay out of it? What would Momma really
like me to do?

Then they were moving out of the yard, on their way to 27
town. They bobbed their heads and shook their slack behinds
and turned, one at a time:

"'Bye, Annie."   28
"'Bye, Annie."   29
"'Bye, Annie."   30

Momma never turned her head or unfolded her arms, but 31
she stopped singing and said, "'Bye, Miz Helen, 'bye, Miz Ruth,
'bye, Miz Eloise."

I burst. A firecracker July-the-Fourth burst. How could 32
Momma call them Miz? The mean nasty things. Why couldn't
she have come inside the sweet, cool store when we saw them
breasting the hill? What did she prove? And then if they were
dirty, mean and impudent, why did Momma have to call them
Miz?

She stood another whole song through and then opened the 33
screen door to look down on me crying in rage. She looked until
I looked up. Her face was a brown moon that shone on me. She
was beautiful. Something had happened out there, which I
couldn't completely understand, but I could see that she was
happy. Then she bent down and touched me as mothers of the
church "lay hands on the sick and afflicted" and I quieted.

"Go wash your face, Sister." And she went behind the 34
candy counter and hummed, "Glory, glory, hallelujah, when I
lay my burden down."

I threw the well water on my face and used the weekday 35

handkerchief to blow my nose. Whatever the contest had been out front, I knew Momma had won.

I took the rake back to the front yard. The smudged foot- **36** prints were easy to erase. I worked for a long time on my new design and laid the rake behind the wash pot. When I came back in the Store, I took Momma's hand and we both walked outside to look at the pattern.

It was a large heart with lots of hearts growing smaller in- **37** side, and piercing from the outside rim to the smallest heart was an arrow. Momma said, "Sister, that's right pretty." Then she turned back to the Store and resumed, "Glory, glory, hallelujah, when I lay my burden down."

1970

Crybaby
Akira Kurosawa

It was in the second or third term of my second year in **1** school that I transferred to this school. Here everything was so entirely different from Morimura Gakuen that I was astounded. The schoolhouse itself was not painted white, but was an un-adorned, humble wooden building rather in the style of a Meiji-era military barracks. At Morimura all the students had worn smart European-style uniforms with lapels; here they wore Japanese clothing with the wide trousers called hakama. At Morimura they had all worn "Landsel," German-style leather knapsacks for their books; here they carried canvas bookbags. At Morimura they had worn leather shoes; here they wore wooden clogs.

Above all, their faces were different. They should have **2** been, because while at Morimura students had all let their hair

grow long, here they had their hair shaved close. And yet I think
that the Kuroda students may have been even more surprised by
me than I was by them.

Imagine someone like me suddenly appearing among a   3
group that lives by purely Japanese customs: a haircut like a
sheltered little sissy's, a belted, double-breasted coat over short
pants, red socks and low, buckled shoes. What's more, I was still
in a wide-eyed daze and had a face as white as a girl's. I immediately became a laughingstock.

They pulled my long hair, poked at my knapsack, rubbed   4
snot on my clothes and made me cry a lot. I had always been a
crybaby, but at this new school I immediately got a new nick-
name on account of it. They called me Konbeto-san ("Mr. Gum-
drop") after a popular song that had a verse something like this:

> Konbeto-san at our house,
> He's so much trouble, so much trouble.
> He's always in tears, in tears.
> Blubber blubber, blubber blubber.

The idea was that the crybaby's tears were as big as gum-drops.   5
Even today I can't recall that name, "Konbeto-san," without a
feeling of severe humiliation.

But at the same time I entered the Kuroda Primary School,   6
my older brother also arrived. He conquered them all straightaway with his genius, and there is no doubt in my mind that this
"Konbeto-san" cried all the more because his brother did not
lend his dignity to back him up. It took a full year for me to find
a place for myself. At the end of that year I no longer cried in
front of people, and no one called me "Konbeto-san" any more.
I was now very respectably known as "Kuro-chan." The
changes that occurred during that year were in part natural. My
intelligence began to bud and blossom, growing with such speed
that I caught up with my peers. Spurring my remarkable progress
there were three hidden forces.

One of these hidden forces was my older brother. We lived   7
near Ōmagari, which was the center of the Koishikawa district,
and every morning I would walk along the banks of the Edogawa
River with my brother on the way to school. Since I was in a

lower grade, school ended earlier for me and I would have to make my way back home alone in the afternoon. But every morning I went side by side with him. Every morning my brother would deride me thoroughly. The vast number of different expressions he found to abuse me with was in itself amazing. He did this not in a loud or conspicuous way, but in a very soft voice that was barely audible even to me. None of the passers-by could hear him. If he had been loud, I could have shouted back, or cried and run away, or covered my ears with my hands. But he spoke in a subdued patter so that I could never retaliate while he was continually showering me with scathing insults.

I thought of complaining to my mother and older sister   8
about the way my brother was treating me, but I couldn't do it. As soon as we got close to the school, my brother would say, "I know you're a dirty little rotten sissy coward, so I know you'll go straight to Mother and our sisters and tell them about me. Well, just you try it. I'll despise you even more." I found myself unable to lift a finger to stop his needling me like this.

Nevertheless, this very same mean and nasty brother of   9
mine always turned up at recess time when I needed him. Whenever I was being teased by the other children, he would appear from somewhere—I don't know how he happened to be watching. He was the center of attention for the entire school, and those pestering me were younger than he, so without exception they would shrink back when he arrived on the scene. Not even bothering to look at them, he would command, "Akira, come here a minute." Relieved, I would happily run up to him and say, "What is it?" but he'd only reply, "Nothing" and walk briskly away.

As this same sequence of events occurred over and over   10
again, my fogged brain began to think a little: My brother's behavior on the way to school was different from his behavior in the schoolyard. Gradually his abuse on the way to school every morning became less hateful to me, and I began to listen in silent appreciation. Looking back on it now, I feel that this was the time when I began to grow from a baby-level intelligence toward the thinking capacity of a normal school-age child.

There is one more incident I would like to relate about my   11 brother. When I was still in my "Konbeto-san" period, my father suddenly decided to start taking us all to the Suifuryū practice pool, which was built out into the Arakawa River. At this time my brother was already wearing a white bathing cap with a black triangle pattern on it and swimming around the practice pool with a first-rate over-arm crawl stroke. I was put in the charge of the Suifuryū teacher, who was apparently a friend of my father.

Because I was the youngest child, my father spoiled me. 12 But how irritated he must have been to see me carrying on like a girl, playing patty-cake and cat's cradle with my older sisters. He said if I learned to swim and got tanned by the sun—even if I just got a suntan without learning to swim—he would give me a reward. But I was afraid of the water, and I never entered the practice pool. It took many days of scolding by the swimming teacher for me even to get wet up to my navel.

My older brother also accompanied me whenever we went 13 to the pool, but as soon as we arrived, he would abandon me. He would swim straightaway to the diving raft out in the deepest part of the river, and he never came back till it was time to go home. I spent many a lonely and frightened day.

Then one day, when I was finally learning how to kick my 14 feet along with the other beginners, holding on to a log floating in the river, my brother appeared. He came rowing up to me in a boat and offered me a ride. Rejoicing, I reached out my hand and let him pull me up into the boat. As soon as I was on board, he began rowing vigorously out toward the middle of the river. Just when the flag and the reed blinds of the poolside hut began to look very small, he suddenly pushed me into the river.

I flailed with all my strength to keep afloat and reach the 15 boat with my brother in it. But as soon as I came close, he rowed away from me. After he repeated this action several times, my strength drained from me. When I could no longer see the boat or my brother and had already sunk below the surface, he grabbed me by my loincloth and pulled me up into the boat.

Shaken and surprised, I found there was nothing wrong 16 with me except that I had swallowed a little water. As I sat gasping and wide-eyed, my brother said, "So you can swim after all,

Akira." And sure enough, after that I wasn't afraid of the water any more. I learned to swim, and I learned to love swimming.

On the way home that day my brother bought me some   17
shaved ice with sweet red-bean sauce. As we ate, he said, "Akira, it's true that drowning people die smiling—you were." It made me angry, but it had seemed that way to me, too. I remembered having felt a strangely peaceful sensation just before I went under.

A second hidden force that aided my growth was that of the   18
teacher in charge of Kuroda Primary School, Tachikawa Seiji. Some two years after I transfered to Kuroda, Mr. Tachikawa's progressive educational principles came into direct conflict with the conservatism of the school principal, and my teacher resigned. He was subsequently invited to teach at Gyōsei Primary School, where he was responsible for developing a great number of talented men.

I will have more to say about Mr. Tachikawa, but I'd like to   19
start with an incident that took place when I was still behind the others of my age in my intellectual development and very timid about it. Mr. Tachikawa came to my aid and for the first time in my life enabled me to feel what is called confidence. It happened during art class.

In the old days—in my day, that is—art education was ter-   20
ribly haphazard. Some tasteless picture would be the model, and it was simply a matter of copying it. The student drawings that most closely resembled the original would always get the highest marks.

But Mr. Tachikawa did nothing so foolish. He just said,   21
"Draw whatever you like." Everyone took out drawing paper and colored pencils and began. I too started to draw—I don't remember what it was I attempted to draw, but I drew with all my might. I pressed so hard the pencils broke, and then I put saliva on my fingertips and smeared the colors around, eventually ending up with my hands a variety of hues.

When we finished, Mr. Tachikawa took each student's pic-   22
ture and put it up on the blackboard. He asked the class to express opinions freely on each in turn, and when it came to mine, the only response was raucous laughter. But Mr. Tachikawa

turned a stern gaze on the laughing multitude and proceeded to praise my picture to the skies. I don't remember exactly what he said. But I do seem to recall that he called special attention to the places where I had rubbed my spit-covered fingers on the colors. Then he took my picture and put three big concentric circles on it in bright red ink: the highest mark. That I remember perfectly.

From that time on, even though I still hated school, I some- 23 how found myself hurrying to school in anticipation on the days when we had art classes. That grade of three circles had led me to enjoy drawing pictures. I drew everything. And I became really good at drawing. At the same time my marks in other subjects suddenly began to improve. By the time Mr. Tachikawa left Kuroda, I was the president of my class, wearing a little gold badge with a purple ribbon on my chest.

I have another unforgettable memory of Mr. Tachikawa 24 during my time at Kuroda Primary School. One day—I think it was during handicrafts class—he came into the classroom carrying a huge roll of thick paper. When he opened it up and showed it to us, laid out flat, it was a map, with streets drawn on it. He then instructed us to build our own houses on these streets and make our own town. Everyone started in with great enthusiasm. Many ideas came forth, and we ended with not only each student's own dream house, but with landscaping for tree-lined streets, ancient trees that had always been on the site and living fences of flowering vines. It was a lovely city, and it had been created by cleverly drawing out the individual personality of each child in the class. Upon completion of our project, our eyes shone, our faces glowed and we gazed proudly at our handiwork. I remember the feeling of that moment as if it were yesterday.

In the early Taishō era (1912–1926), when I started school, 25 the word "teacher" was synonymous with "scary person." The fact that at such a time I encountered such free and innovative education with such creative impulse behind it—that I encountered a teacher like Mr. Tachikawa at such a time—I cherish among the rarest of blessings.

There was a third hidden force that helped me grow. In my 26 class at Kuroda there was another crybaby, a child who was worse than I. The very existence of this child was like having a

mirror thrust in front of my face. I was forced to see myself ob-
jectively. I recognized that he was like me, and watching him and
realizing how unacceptable his behavior was made me feel uneasy about myself. The child who resembled me and who afforded me the opportunity of seeing my own reflection, this perfect specimen of a crybaby, was named Uekusa Keinosuke,
much later co-scriptwriter with me on several films. (Now, don't
get angry, Kei-chan. We're both crybabies, aren't we? Only now
you've become a romantic crybaby and I'm a humanist crybaby.)

Through some kind of strange fate, Uekusa and I were 27
joined together from childhood to adolescence. We grew like two
wisteria vines, clinging and twining around each other. The details of our life in this era can be found in a novel Uekusa wrote.
But Uekusa has his viewpoint and I have mine. And because
people want themselves to have been a certain way, they have a
disturbing tendency to convince themselves they really were that
way. Perhaps if I wrote an account of my childhood with Uekusa
to be compared with the account in his novel, we would come
very close to the truth. Be that as it may, Uekusa was unable to
describe his own childhood without writing about me, just as I
can't write about myself without talking about him.

When I try to write about Uekusa and me when we were 28
students at Kuroda Primary School, all I can remember is the
two of us like tiny dots of human figures in an Oriental landscape
painting. I see us standing beneath the wisteria arbor on the
school grounds, the clusters of flowers waving in the wind. I see
us walking up the slope of Hattorizaka, or up Kagurazaka hill. I
see us under a huge Zelkova tree busily nailing up straw dolls to
exorcise evil spirits during a shrine visit at the Hour of the Ox,
between two and four a.m. In every instance the landscape
comes to mind with glistening clarity, but the two boys remain
nothing more than silhouettes.

Whether this lack of distinctness is due to the passage of so 29
much time, or whether it has something to do with my personality, I can't tell. Whatever the cause, it requires a special effort
for me to recall the detailed characteristics of these two boys. I
have to do something equivalent to removing the wide-angle lens
from the camera and replacing it with a telephoto lens, then look-

ing once again through the viewfinder. And even this isn't enough. I need to concentrate all my lights on these two boys and stop down the lens so as to record them clearly.

Well, then, looking at Uekusa Keinosuke through my tele- 30 photo lens, I now see that, like me, he was someone who differed from the rest of the students at Kuroda Primary School. Even his clothes were different: he wore some kind of silk-like flowing material, and his hakama trousers weren't the usual duck cloth, but a soft fabric. The overall impression was that of a stage actor's child. He was like a miniature player of lover-boy roles, the kind you can knock over with one punch.

Speaking of knocking him over with one punch, Uekusa the 31 primary-school student was always falling down and crying. I remember him falling once on a stretch of bad road and ruining his fancy clothes. I accompanied him as he cried all the way home. Another time, at a track meet, he fell in a mud puddle and turned his sparkling white athletic outfit pitch black; I had to try to comfort him while he blubbered.

The saying goes that birds of a feather flock together. Cry- 32 baby Uekusa and I felt something in common; we were drawn to each other, and soon we were playing together continually. Gradually I came to treat Uekusa the way my older brother had treated me.

Our relations are very frankly described in the passage 33 about the track meet in Uekusa's novel. Once Uekusa, who always came in last in any race, for some inexplicable reason was running in second place. I rushed up behind and shouted, "Good! Good! Come on, come on!" Together we ran the last stretch and leaped across the finish line into the open arms of the beaming Mr. Tachikawa.

When the meet was over, we took our prizes—colored pen- 34 cils or paints or whatever—and went to see Uekusa's mother on her sickbed. She cried tears of joy and kept thanking me on her son's behalf. But, looking back on it all now, I am the one who should have been saying "Thank you," because while this weakling Uekusa made me feel protective toward him, I somehow at the same time became someone the school bully could no longer push around.

Mr. Tachikawa seems to have looked favorably on our 35
friendship. He once called me in for consultation as the class
president and asked me what I thought of appointing a vice president. Thinking this meant I had been doing a poor job as president, I fell into a dark silence. Mr. Tachikawa studied my expression and asked whom I would recommend. I named one of the
best students in the class. Mr. Tachikawa said that he would prefer to try putting a less impressive student in that position. I
stared at him in surprise. He went on to say with a big smile that
if we put someone who was not very good in the job now, that
person would be sure to shape up and prove worthy. Then, addressing me as my classmates did, he said, "So, Kuro-chan,
what do you say to making Uekusa vice president?" At this point
I became painfully aware of the warmth of Mr. Tachikawa's feeling toward us.

Deeply moved, I stood staring at him. "Fine," he an- 36
nounced, "it's all settled, then." He slapped me on the shoulder
and with a grin told me to go and tell Uekusa's mother straightaway; he knew she'd be happy. As he walked away, there
seemed to be a kind of halo around his head.

From this time on, Uekusa wore a silver badge with a red 37
ribbon on his chest, and in both the classroom and the schoolyard he was always at my side. Recognition of him as vice president of the class was instantaneous. It was as if he had been
planted in the flower pot of the class vice presidency and placed
in full sun. He began to bloom. Mr. Tachikawa had referred to
him as "not very good" in a way that may sound disparaging,
but in reality I think he had observed the talent that lay dormant
within Uekusa.

1982

The Transaction
William Zinsser

Five or six years ago a school in Connecticut held "a day   1
devoted to the arts," and I was asked if I would come and talk
about writing as a vocation. When I arrived I found that a second
speaker had been invited—Dr. Brock (as I'll call him), a surgeon
who had recently begun to write and had sold some stories to national magazines. He was going to talk about writing as an avo-
cation. That made us a panel, and we sat down to face a crowd of
student newspaper editors and reporters, English teachers and
parents, all eager to learn the secrets of our glamorous work.

Dr. Brock was dressed in a bright red jacket, looking   2
vaguely Bohemian, as authors are supposed to look, and the first
question went to him. What was it like to be a writer?

He said it was tremendous fun. Coming home from an ar-   3
duous day at the hospital, he would go straight to his yellow pad
and write his tensions away. The words just flowed. It was easy.

I then said that writing wasn't easy and it wasn't fun. It was   4
hard and lonely, and the words seldom just flowed.

Next Dr. Brock was asked if it was important to rewrite.   5
Absolutely not, he said. "Let it all hang out," and whatever form
the sentences take will reflect the writer at his most natural.

I then said that rewriting is the essence of writing. I pointed   6
out that professional writers rewrite their sentences repeatedly
and then rewrite what they have rewritten. I mentioned that
E. B. White and James Thurber were known to rewrite their
pieces eight or nine times.

"What do you do on days when it isn't going well?" Dr.   7
Brock was asked. He said he just stopped writing and put the
work aside for a day when it would go better.

I then said that the professional writer must establish a   8
daily schedule and stick to it. I said that writing is a craft, not an
art, and that the man who runs away from his craft because he
lacks inspiration is fooling himself. He is also going broke.

"What if you're feeling depressed or unhappy?" a student   9
asked. "Won't that affect your writing?"

Probably it will, Dr. Brock replied. Go fishing. Take a   10
walk.

Probably it won't, I said. If your job is to write every day,   11
you learn to do it like any other job.

A student asked if we found it useful to circulate in the lit-   12
erary world. Dr. Brock said that he was greatly enjoying his new
life as a man of letters, and he told several lavish stories of being
taken to lunch by his publisher and his agent at Manhattan res-
taurants where writers and editors gather. I said that professional
writers are solitary drudges who seldom see other writers.

"Do you put symbolism in your writing?" a student asked   13
me.

"Not if I can help it," I replied. I have an unbroken record   14
of missing the deeper meaning in any story, play or movie, and
as for dance and mime, I have never had even a remote notion of
what is being conveyed.

"I *love* symbols!" Dr. Brock exclaimed, and he described   15
with gusto the joys of weaving them through his work.

So the morning went, and it was a revelation to all of us. At   16
the end Dr. Brock told me he was enormously interested in my
answers—it had never occurred to him that writing could be
hard. I told him I was just as interested in *his* answers—it had
never occurred to me that writing could be easy. (Maybe I should
take up surgery on the side.)

As for the students, anyone might think that we left them   17
bewildered. But in fact we probably gave them a broader glimpse
of the writing process than if only one of us had talked. For of
course there isn't any "right" way to do such intensely personal
work. There are all kinds of writers and all kinds of methods, and
any method that helps somebody to say what he wants to say is
the right method for him.

Some people write by day, others by night. Some people   18
need silence, others turn on the radio. Some write by hand, some
by typewriter, some by talking into a tape recorder. Some people
write their first draft in one long burst and then revise; others
can't write the second paragraph until they have fiddled endlessly with the first.

But all of them are vulnerable and all of them are tense. 19
They are driven by a compulsion to put some part of themselves
on paper, and yet they don't just write what comes naturally.
They sit down to commit an act of literature, and the self who
emerges on paper is a far stiffer person than the one who sat
down. The problem is to find the real man or woman behind all
the tension.

For ultimately the product that any writer has to sell is not 20
his subject, but who he is. I often find myself reading with interest about a topic that I never thought would interest me—some
unusual scientific quest, for instance. What holds me is the enthusiasm of the writer for his field. How was he drawn into it?
What emotional baggage did he bring along? How did it change
his life? It is not necessary to want to spend a year alone at Wal-
den Pond to become deeply involved with a man who did.

This is the personal transaction that is at the heart of good 21
nonfiction writing. Out of it come two of the most important
qualities that this book will go in search of: humanity and
warmth. Good writing has an aliveness that keeps the reader
reading from one paragraph to the next, and it's not a question of
gimmicks to "personalize" the author. It's a question of using
the English language in a way that will achieve the greatest
strength and the least clutter.

Can such principles be taught? Maybe not. But most of 22
them can be learned.

1976

Testimonies of Guatemalan Women*
Luz Alicia Herrera
Translated by Maria Alice Jacob

INTRODUCTION

As a contribution to the knowledge of Guatemalan social   1
reality, I offer the following statements as they were told to me
by the women themselves. Each is selected for a reason.
Through the statement of the first woman, we discover thousands of Guatemalan women: poor peasants, agricultural workers, maids, industrial workers, unmarried mothers, and the
women who are active in the struggle of popular organizations.
Through the statement of the second woman, we see an example
of a person from a wealthy background who opts for the interests
of the great oppressed majority of Guatemalans. We present this
second interview, knowing full well that it may generate the common psychological interpretation that this serious process of
transformation is actually a manifestation of "social resentment." With such an explanation the bourgeoisie tries to dismiss
the choice of those who side with the majority of the people.

FIRST WOMAN'S TESTIMONY

I was born in a little village on the southeast coast. I was   2
fifteen when we moved to a parcel of land far away, still on the
same south coast. My mother was a widow. There were four
children, three girls and a boy. In the new place where we went
to live, my mother established a little restaurant. We cooked for
thirty people. We also picked cotton. My mother, my thirteen-
year-old sister, and I would get up at one in the morning to do the
household chores: cook corn, make tortillas, prepare food and
clean the house. At 6 o'clock all was ready, and at 7 a.m. we
would take the bus to the cotton fields. I used to go with my sis-

*Excerpted and abridged from *Latin American Perspectives,* Issues 25 and 26,
Spring and Summer 1980, Vol. VII, Nos. 2 and 3.

ter to a plantation that employed between 150 and 200 cotton pickers, men and women.

On the plantation, an active picker would pick 100 to 150 pounds of cotton. My sister and I would pick 100 pounds between us and be paid one cent per pound. We would take our own food with us. When it rained, we would work from 8 a.m. in the morning to 3 p.m. in the afternoon. If the weather was very humid, we would work from 12 noon to 3 p.m. in the afternoon. 3

It is hard work under the hot sun on a cotton plantation. The women wore hats to protect their heads from the sun. There would be many of us women with the sack of cotton tied to our waists. The foreman and the labor contractors made sure that the workers kept their attention on the picking and tried to keep them from establishing contact with their fellow workers. 4

Sometimes, when we were picking cotton, the airplane would fly over us, spraying insecticide, and the majority of the workers would get poisoned. We had to hide the water and food so that the poison wouldn't get to them. 5

The foremen were rough and would make the women use the plough by themselves if they left some cotton behind. They treated us badly and humiliated us. The indigenous workers were treated even worse than other workers. They were given only tortillas and beans to eat. Indigenous workers were forced to weigh their cotton on a different scale, undoubtedly to pay them less. The indigenous workers came with their whole families to work—wives and children. The children were only five years old when they began to pick cotton. 6

Working on the plantation, I was angry about earning so little. Working under the hot sun all day and for so little pay! The foreman and the labor contractors who took advantage of us thought they were kings. A man from the village—a contractor—hired the rest of the workers from the village to do the picking. The foremen were also exploited people but they chose to be on the side of the bosses. We would get home from work at 6 or 7 p.m. and after that feed the other workers—about thirty people outside of our family. Then we would do the dishes and start to cook corn all over again. We would cook 25 pounds of corn a day. 7

"Serious work. Get up, get up, it's time." That's how my 8

mother would wake us up. So short was the night! We would go
to bed at 10 p.m. the evening before and get up at 1 a.m. in the
morning. At that time, I was fifteen years old and my sister was
thirteen; since we were the eldest, we were made to do the hard-
est work. We also worked on the little plot of land that was given
to my mother. On it, we would plant corn, *maicillo* (millet), and
chile for everyday use. Sometimes we would sell the little bit that
was left. For us, there were no Sundays, no good times. Only
weeks of work.

In 1963, through a friend, I got a job working as a babysitter   9
and maid in Escuintla. I worked there for five years. The first six
months they paid me seven *quetzales* a month[1] to take care of a
little girl from 7 a.m. in the morning to noon when the woman of
the house, who was a secretary in an office, would get home.

After this job I returned to my mother's place in the village.   10
The three of us sisters separated from my mother because she
was with a man who didn't like us. We rented a tiny house. With
a little money that my mother gave us we started a store, and,
there in the house, my sister (since she is a dressmaker) had her
sewing machine, and we continued with the little restaurant, just
we three. There we had thirty mobile military police and the people who passed by on their way to the *fincas* (ranches) for customers. The three of us lived happily. We earned very little, just
enough to eat, more or less dress, and shoe ourselves.

After that, I came once again to work in Escuintla, in a soft-   11
drink stand. There I worked only for room and board. During
this time I had the stupidity to run off with a boyfriend. He studied in the capital and his parents paid for him to stay in a board-
ing house. From the soft-drink stand, I went with him to the capital. I lived a year and a half with him. We lived on what his
parents sent us in a small room that didn't have a place to cook
so we bought our meals. I put up with this difficult situation for a
year and a half. I went to work in a clothing factory. I was a
seam-gatherer. It was my job to gather and trim. I earned four
quetzales and twelve cents weekly. I didn't know how to sew on
the electric machines. There were times when I worked extra

---

[1]One quetzal is the equivalent of U.S. $1.

hours and then I would earn twenty quetzales a month. But I didn't continue in this factory because he didn't like me to work. At the same time, what we had didn't cover anything. I became so desperate that I went home to my mother in the village, once again.

My boyfriend fought with me a lot because I didn't get 12 pregnant. "You'll never have a child; heaven knows what things you do" [he would say]. Well, it was just my bad luck that the month I left him I was already pregnant, but neither of us knew it then. Once when I was with my mother, I noticed how I was, and I told my sister and she told my mother. And my mother caused a big uproar. My mother did not like the boy and she was angry at me. My mother threw me out of the house on my own. I went to a friend's, the one with the soft-drink stand and told her my problem, and I worked with her for room and board.

After two months, my mother arrived to look for me and 13 took me back to the house. I returned to the house and in the state I was in, no one would give me work. An uncle told me, "You can't work in a bar anymore." I told the problem to a neighbor who had a *nixtamal* (the dough used for tortillas) mill. She let me go there and grind for one quetzal a day. I felt very tired and worn-out working there. Everyday my belly grew larger. My friend found some women who would buy tortillas from me each day and she ground my corn without charging me a cent. Daily, I ground twenty pounds of corn, made and sold the corn. After that, I washed clothes for people, did embroidery and needlework, and bought small clothing to sell with the earnings of the needlework. My stepfather would say: "I will not maintain someone else's children," and my mother would get angry with me.

I sent a message to my boyfriend about my pregnancy, and 14 the response he gave was that the child I was about to have was no child of his, and he wouldn't pass me one cent—at least until the child was born. My son was three months old when my boyfriend came to see him with his mother. They came with the idea of taking him away from me but, like the majority of mothers who struggle to keep their children, I wouldn't give him up.

My ex-boyfriend had married another girl and he wanted to 15

keep me as his lover. He only arrived to see his child when he
was drunk and never even brought him candy. One time he even
arrived with a revolver, threatening us from the window. My sister and I threw him out and punched him. Not until my son was
three years old did I manage to convince his father to recognize
him. I did it because children need to carry their father's name.

My son didn't like his father. Because he is not with us, he 16
would say. He would notice that other fathers would bring their
little children home from school. I've told him everything, and he
doesn't like his father. "Because he was bad with us, because of
that, I only love you," the child would say to me.

I began working for the revolution some time ago. My step- 17
father was from a peasant organization. Aside from the fact that
he was bad with us, sometimes, when he was in good humor, he
gave us advice and we began to collaborate with the organization
in the countryside. I, working as a babysitter, already collabo-
rated.

He did not think like me.[2] He is a teacher but he doesn't 18
understand the necessity of organizing the workers. He didn't
know that I had those ideas and when he realized it, he told me
not to get involved in anything, that this was bad for me. I told
him that as long as I lived, I would continue struggling for an organization wherever I was and that there were no limits on where
my commitment might take me. "You believe in a struggle that
will never triumph, one that won't ever even end," he would
say. I went to work in a factory again, and there, convinced that
I should stay, joined a union. I have girlfriends who say I am
crazy, that I shouldn't get involved in these things, that all I am
going to get in return is unemployment or death. But I feel even
braver when they tell me that I am going to end up dead. Also, it
makes me want to know things I haven't known before.

I have had a lot of serious problems, but I have never been 19
afraid. They have taken away my job....I think about my son.
But he tells me: "If my mother dies, I will stay with the *compañeros* (comrades)...." The compañeros are from the *sindicato*
(union). Therefore, thinking about the welfare of my child has

---

[2]Here she seems to be referring back to her ex-boyfriend (rather than her stepfather).

not kept me from organizing. Sooner or later we all have to die. It might be in some accident. My little boy already is aware of everything and I have taught him how one survives here. He already pays attention to the movements of the police...and advises us of them.

SECOND WOMAN'S TESTIMONY

What motivated you to join the struggle to transform Guatemalan society?

I am going to answer you with what may seem to be a contradiction but it was, precisely, because of my nonproletarian class background. I come from what could be called the agro-export bourgeoisie. As a child, I customarily spent my end-of-the-year vacation at the *finca*. This vacation coincided with cutting and harvesting. It was there where the answers that were given to my innumerable questions didn't satisfy my childhood curiosity about the conditions I confronted daily. 20

My father considered the Indian a species half-way between human and animal. I noticed this in a number of incidents. For example, one day, seeing hundreds of men, women, and children descend from the mountains bathed in sweat, carrying enormous loads, I had an enormous feeling of pain and anguish. My father must have noticed it because he explained that Indians were born to do such work, that they were incapable of doing any other, that they were dumb, lazy, drunken, that they had no desire to better themselves, and that they lacked our intelligence—those of us who were descendants of Spaniards. (He never referred to us as *ladinos;* he considered us to be located at the top of the social stratification among whites, and the term *ladino* was applied to the *mestizo* or white who did not possess a powerful name). 21

At harvest time, the labor of *mozos colonos* (resident tenants) or *rancheros* (ranch hands) who live on the finca is not sufficient, and day laborers are contracted from more arid regions where from necessity they migrate to the fincas to supplement their precarious family income. They would arrive in trucks, 22 piled up like animals, dragging along with them their misery and disease. They were put up in enormous *galeras* (sheds) which only had a few posts, a roof, and no walls. There, each family gathered around a fireplace previously placed, was given a *comal* (a piece of clay on which corn tortillas are cooked), an empty tin can of milk or whatever other product in which the corn could be cooked, a grinding stone, and naturally, tools. There wouldn't even be a cloth dividing one family from another.

I was strictly prohibited from entering these sheds because 23 the Indians were said to have fleas, were dirty, and some were sick. One night, I remember, a child in one of the sheds began to cough. The next day, there were about five children coughing; the next week, all of the children had whooping cough. The sheds were almost in front of the house of the finca, and during the night you could hear the coughing of the little children as though it were part of a bad dream. A certain fear overcame me and I ran to my father's room to tell my father that these children were going to die, that they were suffocating, and that we had to do something. My father took my hand and walked me back to my room, put me to bed, covered me up and said sweetly, "Don't worry, they're not children, they're Indians."

Thus, I later saw, lined up in front of the house, some little 24 caskets, painted white, accompanied only by the fathers, mothers, and others who were most likely relatives. The rest of their fellow workers were missing because the harvest had to continue. At night, much larger groups of people climbed up to the cemetery; many Indians, lighting the way with candles, lanterns of wood and paper, moving in silence or with low voices, speaking in low voices in dialect, carrying out their rituals. My father pointed out to me "these pagans who worship idols and get drunk and weep and wail in the cemetery."

"You see?" he would say, "they don't even care that their 25 children have died; the only thing that interests them is the *guaro* (liquor); they are not like us."

My questions were endless. Innocently, I asked why shoes 26 weren't bought for them, why they weren't given food, why the children had inflated stomachs, why they never laughed, why they spoke differently, why doctors weren't called for them.

Why? Why? Until one day, my father, tired of so much questioning, said, "Because they are Indians, understand? I don't want
to hear another word about the matter again."

I began to ask questions again and I received a beating. I   27
learned, then, "not to stick your nose in matters that don't concern you," and I opted for silence. For several years I lived
these experiences, always painful.

I remember that in order to reach the finca, two jeeps were   28
necessary, one for us and one for the baggage and food. One
would suppose that these were marvelous vacations; our friends
and my father's friends would arrive at the ranch, I would entertain myself and almost grow accustomed to the situation. But as
I grew to adolescence, I began to judge my parents and their
friends; now it was no longer necessary to ask questions. I knew
by then there was injustice and exploitation; but not at the level
of reason. I just felt it.

One of the last times I was there at the *finca,* there was a   29
storm, rains that wouldn't stop. The rivers grew and we had to
return to the capital. The jeeps couldn't pass to the other side.
Up on their shoulders, I saw my mother and brothers and sisters
who went ahead. All on the shoulders of Indians, dirty and
sweaty. I swore I would never return, and so I never did.

I had a turbulent adolescence. I lived in a world of total fri-   30
volity. Sex presented itself in a very natural manner. I had a
group of friends who often got together to have fun. There were
parties with everything—food, alcohol, even drugs. Accustomed
as I was to not asking questions, I only observed. Inside me I had
a lot of doubts: why was it necessary for us to have stimulants in
order to be happy? I saw this decadence, this rottenness, this
promiscuity as natural, but I didn't stop thinking. I was always
looking for another path, another way out, another life.

My parents didn't stop worrying about me. They thought it   31
wasn't normal for me to be worried about such things. To them,
it was irrational for me to be sad at seeing a beggar or kids who
sleep on the streets covered with newspapers or drunkards lying
on the streets. I was crazy! They sent me to a psychologist. La-
ziness was my problem. They registered me at the university so
I would "do something." It wasn't the national university, of

course, but the Catholic one (Universidad de Rafael Landiver). I
wasn't enthusiastic about it at first, but to my surprise, I met
young men and women from the same background as my own,
with the same concerns. We started to look together for solu-
tions, read books, make hypotheses, and try to change the
world. We were a group of seven people. Five of them have died,
victims of repression.

How was your political education after that?

This group of seven who shared the same ideas, not yet   32
clearly defined, fell apart. I returned to being alone. I took a trip
to Europe where I met an old militant who lived in political exile.
He started telling me his personal experiences, answering my
many doubts, lecturing to me, showing me the way. Back in Guatemala, I immediately tried to get involved in practice. That's
when I acquired my real education. A new conception of the
world and of life. A well-defined objective: contribute to the con-
tinuation of the revolution that was stopped in Guatemala in
1954, a revolution that Guatemala still needs.

Studying and practicing Marxism resolved the doubts of my   33
childhood and adolescence. Now I know what the Indian is,
what my father and other landlords like him are, what we—myself included—the salaried middle sectors are, what the urban
and agricultural proletariat is.

*In what way have you been affected by political repression in
Guatemala?*

Before responding to this question, I'd like to relate what I   34
know of the repression: in the houses of the bourgeoisie, particularly in that of my parents, there is economic aid to repressive
groups. Fortunately, at the time when these right-wing parami-
tary groups appeared, I already had a political formation, and I
knew how to take advantage of all occasions. I knew many people in "La Mano" (National Organized Anti-Communist Movement), made up of groups of assassins who massacred thousands
of peasants in the eastern part of the country under the orders of
ex-President Arana Osorio. Many times I have had to bite my

tongue. I would hear these men speak of us, vainglorious about their exploits, telling how they personally fight against the guerrillas, mentioning forms of tortures that Cuban exiles in Guatemala would provide them. I knew of their assaults and their links. All of this we studied and interpreted with the compañeros; they never said more in my house than what they wanted me to hear, but they always revealed more than they thought they did.

I remember, for example, that in an assault on the Bank of 35 Guatemala, they dressed up as priests. I knew, likewise, that it was the priest of a certain Church who gave them the cassocks. I saw them dressed up as women on one occasion (for purposes of disguise, they said). I saw my mother dye the hair of one of them. In short, I had them very close and what I most remember about them was the death outlined in their eyes. Such hard looks behind friendly smiles. Since they were dealing with paid groups, little by little they began to degenerate into common delinquents, and in doing so entered into conflict with their "papa" Arana who took responsibility for eliminating them one by one after the supposed "pacification" of the eastern part of the country.

These events were clear manifestations of the union be- 36 tween the Church and the dominant classes. "The faithful, above all the poor and the miserable, should be humble and accept the Christian dogma along with exploitation because God knows what he does. Some were born to be poor and some to be rich. It is the law of God."

I, personally, have not been a victim of repression. Never- 37 theless, many compañeros in the struggle, which is much broader than the popular organization to which I belong, have been its victims. With so many of these Guatemalans (men and women) who have been captured or have died I feel solidarity!

What has been your relation with your compañeros?

I had to pass several difficult tests and demonstrate my loy- 38 alty to the revolutionary struggle. Revolutionary discipline demands of us a behavior worthy of someone who struggles with the oppressed of Guatemala, our brothers and sisters. In this struggle, men and women have equal rights and obligations such that I can say that my relationship with both is very good.

What has been the historic participation of Guatemalan women in social change?

Definitely the participation of women throughout the long 39 history of Guatemala is undeniable. At the moment, I can think of the example of Maria Chinchilla who died struggling for changes in the schools and the working conditions of teachers. Women within the dominant classes play a role too; remember, for example, the participation of women in the 1954 campaign to overthrow President Arbenz.

In your opinion, what do women need to do to achieve their liberation?

In this case, let me speak concretely of the revolutionary 40 woman. The fundamental tasks that are necessary to achieve her liberation cannot be separated from the political emancipation of the population. To speak of personal liberation doesn't make sense for us. Men and women linked to the revolutionary strug-gle work together for the liberation from dependency, underde-velopment, and the ignorance that typifies us as a backward country, by means of a permanent struggle that will allow us to construct a society free of exploitation of man by man. It is only possible to speak of liberation in a society not divided in classes.

Within all of the groups that struggle for the interests of the 41 great majority of oppressed people, there are remnants of typical bourgeois *machismo,* and there, fundamentally, the revolution-ary woman has a well-defined task. These particular cases have to be eliminated through study, dialogue, criticism and self-criticism.

Is there some particular experience you would like to share?

Yes, there is one. After several years in this struggle—ones 42 dedicated exclusively to the study of Marxism, education of

young people and theoretical work—I became anxious to go out
to the countryside. One nice day in the month of July, two compañeros and I went out destined for a place in one of the departments (provinces). During the day, we rested a little but at night
we walked all the time in order to finally arrive at different little
towns, intersections, and fincas where we would meet with
agrarian workers to talk about their struggle. There for the first
time since I had first seen Indians in the service of my father, we
talked together as equals, as comrades.

1983

The Discus Thrower
Richard Selzer

I spy on my patients. Ought not a doctor to observe his   1
patients by any means and from any stance, that he might the
more fully assemble evidence? So I stand in the doorways of
hospital rooms and gaze. Oh, it is not all that furtive an act.
Those in bed need only look up to discover me. But they never
do.

From the doorway of Room 542 the man in the bed seems   2
deeply tanned. Blue eyes and close-cropped white hair give him
the appearance of vigor and good health. But I know that his skin
is not brown from the sun. It is rusted, rather, in the last stage of
containing the vile repose within. And the blue eyes are frosted,
looking inward like the windows of a snowbound cottage. This
man is blind. This man is also legless—the right leg missing from
midthigh down, the left from just below the knee. It gives him the
look of a bonsai, roots and branches pruned into the dwarfed fac-
simile of a great tree.

Propped on pillows, he cups his right thigh in both hands.   3

Now and then he shakes his head as though acknowledging the intensity of his suffering. In all of this he makes no sound. Is he mute as well as blind?

The room in which he dwells is empty of all possessions—   **4** no get-well cards, small, private caches of food, day-old flowers, slippers, all the usual kickshaws of the sickroom. There is only the bed, a chair, a nightstand, and a tray on wheels that can be swung across his lap for meals.

                                                     5

"What time is it?" he asks.

"Three o'clock."   **6**

"Morning or afternoon?"   **7**

"Afternoon."   **8**

He is silent. There is nothing else he wants to know.   **9**

"How are you?" I say.   **10**

"Who is it?" he asks.   **11**

"It's the doctor. How do you feel?"   **12**

He does not answer right away.   **13**

"Feel?" he says.   **14**

"I hope you feel better," I say.   **15**

I press the button at the side of the bed.   **16**

"Down you go," I say.   **17**

"Yes, down," he says.   **18**

He falls back upon the bed awkwardly. His stumps, un- **19** weighted by legs and feet, rise in the air, presenting themselves. I unwrap the bandages from the stumps, and begin to cut away the black scabs and the dead, glazed fat with scissors and forceps. A shard of white bone comes loose. I pick it away. I wash the wounds with disinfectant and redress the stumps. All this while, he does not speak. What is he thinking behind those lids that do not blink? Is he remembering a time when he was whole? Does he dream of feet? Of when his body was not a rotting log?

He lies solid and inert. In spite of everything, he remains **20** impressive, as though he were a sailor standing athwart a slanting deck.

"Anything more I can do for you?" I ask.   **21**

For a long moment he is silent.   **22**

"Yes," he says at last and without the least irony. "You 23
can bring me a pair of shoes."

In the corridor, the head nurse is waiting for me. 24

"We have to do something about him," she says. "Every 25
morning he orders scrambled eggs for breakfast, and, instead of
eating them, he picks up the plate and throws it against the
wall."

"Throws his plate?" 26

"Nasty. That's what he is. No wonder his family doesn't 27
come to visit. They probably can't stand him any more than we
can."

She is waiting for me to do something. 28

"Well?" 29

"We'll see," I say. 30

The next morning I am waiting in the corridor when the 31
kitchen delivers his breakfast. I watch the aide place the tray on
the stand and swing it across his lap. She presses the button to
raise the head of the bed. Then she leaves.

In time the man reaches to find the rim of the tray, then on 32
to find the dome of the covered dish. He lifts off the cover and
places it on the stand. He fingers across the plate until he probes
the eggs. He lifts the plate in both hands, sets it on the palm of
his right hand, centers it, balances it. He hefts it up and down
slightly, getting the feel of it. Abruptly, he draws back his right
arm as far as he can.

There is the crack of the plate breaking against the wall at 33
the foot of his bed and the small wet sound of the scrambled eggs
dropping to the floor.

And then he laughs. It is a sound you have never heard. It 34
is something new under the sun. It could cure cancer.

Out in the corridor, the eyes of the head nurse narrow. 35

"Laughed, did he?" 36

She writes something down on her clipboard. 37

A second aide arrives, brings a second breakfast tray, puts 38
it on the nightstand, out of his reach. She looks over at me shaking her head and making her mouth go. I see that we are to be
accomplices.

"I've got to feed you," she says to the man.   39

"Oh, no you don't," the man says.   40

"Oh, yes I do," the aide says, "after the way you just did. 41
Nurse says so."

"Get me my shoes," the man says.   42

"Here's oatmeal," the aide says. "Open." And she 43
touches the spoon to his lower lip.

"I ordered scrambled eggs," says the man.   44

"That's right," the aide says.   45

I step forward.   46

"Is there anything I can do?" I say.   47

"Who are you?" the man asks.   48

In the evening I go once more to that ward to make my 49
rounds. The head nurse reports to me that Room 542 is deceased. She has discovered this quite by accident, she says.
No, there had been no sound. Nothing. It's a blessing, she
says.

I go into his room, a spy looking for secrets. He is still there 50
in his bed. His face is relaxed, grave, dignified. After a while, I
turn to leave. My gaze sweeps the wall at the foot of the bed, and
I see the place where it has been repeatedly washed, where the
wall looks very clean and very white.

1979

Somewhere, Some Time, Some Place
Olive Schreiner

When a child, not yet nine years old, I walked out one 1
morning along the mountain tops on which my home stood. The
sun had not yet risen, and the mountain grass was heavy with
dew; as I looked back I could see the marks my feet had made on

the long, grassy slope behind me. I walked till I came to a place where a little stream ran, which farther on passed over the precipices into the deep valley below. Here it passed between soft, earthy banks; at one place a large slice of earth had fallen away from the bank on the other side, and it had made a little island a few feet wide with water flowing all round it. It was covered with wild mint and a weed with yellow flowers and long waving grasses. I sat down on the bank at the foot of a dwarfed olive tree, the only tree near. All the plants on the island were dark with the heavy night's dew, and the sun had not yet risen.

I had got up so early because I had been awake much in the night and could not sleep longer. My heart was heavy; my physical heart seemed to have a pain in it, as if small, sharp crystals were cutting into it. All the world seemed wrong to me. It was not only that sense of the small misunderstandings and tiny injustices of daily life, which perhaps all sensitive children feel at some time pressing down on them; but the whole Universe seemed to be weighing on me. 2

I had grown up in a land where wars were common. From my earliest years I had heard of bloodshed and battles and hairbreadth escapes; I had heard them told of by those who had seen and taken part in them. In my native country dark men were killed and their lands taken from them by white men armed with superior weapons; even near to me such things had happened. I knew also how white men fought white men; the stronger even hanging the weaker on gallows when they did not submit; and I had seen how white men used the dark as beasts of labour, often without any thought for their good or happiness. Three times I had seen an ox striving to pull a heavily loaded wagon up a hill, the blood and foam streaming from its mouth and nostrils as it struggled, and I had seen it fall dead, under the lash. In the bush in the kloof below I had seen bush-bucks and little long-tailed monkeys that I loved so shot dead, not from any necessity but for the pleasure of killing, and the cock-o-veets and the honeysuckers and the wood-doves that made the bush so beautiful to me. And sometimes I had seen bands of convicts going past to work on the roads, and had heard the chains clanking which went round their waists and passed between their legs to the irons on 3 their feet; I had seen the terrible look in their eyes of a wild creature, when every man's hand is against it, and no one loves it, and it only hates and fears. I had got up early in the morning to drop small bits of tobacco at the roadside, hoping they would find them and pick them up. I had wanted to say to them, 'Someone loves you'; but the man with the gun was always there. Once I had seen a pack of dogs set on by men to attack a strange dog, which had come among them and had done no harm to anyone. I had watched it torn to pieces, though I had done all I could to save it. Why did everyone press on everyone and try to make them do what they wanted? Why did the strong always crush the weak? Why did we hate and kill and torture? Why was it all as it was? Why had the world ever been made? Why, oh why, had I ever been born?

The little sharp crystals seemed to cut deeper into my heart. 4

And then, as I sat looking at that little, damp, dark island, 5 the sun began to rise. It shot its lights across the long, grassy slopes of the mountains and struck the little mound of earth in the water. All the leaves and flowers and grasses on it turned bright gold, and the dewdrops hanging from them were like diamonds; and the water in the stream glinted as it ran. And, as I looked at that almost intolerable beauty, a curious feeling came over me. It was not what I *thought* put into exact words, but I seemed to *see* a world in which creatures no more hated and crushed, in which the strong helped the weak, and men understood each other, and forgave each other, and did not try to crush others, but to help. I did not think of it, as something to be in a distant picture; it was there, about me, and I was in it, and a part of it. And there came to me, as I sat there, a joy such as never besides have I experienced, except perhaps once, a joy without limit.

And then, as I sat on there, the sun rose higher and higher, 6 and shone hot on my back, and the morning light was everywhere. And slowly and slowly the vision vanished, and I began to think and question myself.

How could that glory ever really be? In a world where crea- 7 ture preys on creature, and man, the strongest of all, preys more than all, how could this be? And my mind went back to the dark thoughts I had in the night. In a world where the little ant-lion digs his hole in the sand and lies hidden at the bottom for the small ant to fall in and be eaten, and the leopard's eyes gleam yellow through bushes as it watches the little bush-buck coming down to the fountain to drink, and millions and millions of human beings use all they know, and their wonderful hands, to kill and press down others, what hope could there ever be? The world was as it was! And what was I? A tiny, miserable worm, a speck within a speck, an imperceptible atom, a less than a nothing! What did it matter what *I* did, how *I* lifted my hands, and how *I* cried out? The great world would roll on, and on, just as it had! What if nowhere, at no time, in no place, was there anything else?

The band about my heart seemed to grow tighter and tighter. A helpless, tiny, miserable worm! Could I prevent one man from torturing an animal that was in his power; stop one armed man from going out to kill? In my own heart, was there not bitterness, the anger against those who injured me or others, till my heart was like a burning coal? If the world had been made so, so it was! But, why, oh why, had I ever been born? Why did the Universe exist?   **8**

And then, as I sat on there, another thought came to me; and in some form or other it has remained with me ever since, all my life. It was like this: You cannot by willing it alter the vast world outside of you; you cannot, perhaps, cut the lash from one whip; you cannot stop the march of even one armed man going out to kill; you cannot, perhaps, strike the handcuff from one chained hand; you cannot even remake your own soul so that there shall be no tendency to evil in it; the great world rolls on, and *you* cannot reshape it; but this one thing only you can do—in that one, small, minute, almost infinitesimal spot in the Universe, where your will rules, there where alone you are as God, *strive* to make that you hunger for real! No man can prevent you there. In your own heart strive to kill out all hate, all desire to see evil come even to those who have injured you or another; what is weaker than yourself try to help; whatever is in pain or unjustly treated and cries out, say, 'I am here! I, little, weak, feeble, but I will do what I can for you.' This is all you can do; but do it; it is not nothing! And then this feeling came to me, a feeling it is not easy to put into words, but it was like this: You also are   **9** a part of the great Universe; what you strive for something strives for; *and nothing in the Universe is quite alone;* you are moving on towards something.

And as I walked back that morning over the grass slopes, I 10 was not sorry I was going back to the old life. I did not wish I was dead and that the Universe had never existed. I, also, had something to live for—and even if I failed to reach it utterly— somewhere, some time, some place, it was! I was not alone.

More than a generation has passed since that day, but it re- 11 mains to me the most important and unforgettable of my life. In the darkest hour its light has never quite died out.

In the long years which have passed, the adult has seen 12 much of which the young child knew nothing.

In my native land I have seen the horror of a great war. 13 Smoke has risen from burning homesteads; women and children by thousands have been thrown into great camps to perish there; men whom I have known have been tied in chairs and executed for fighting against strangers in the land of their own birth. In the world's great cities I have seen how everywhere the upper stone grinds hard on the nether, and men and women feed upon the toil of their fellow men without any increase of spiritual beauty or joy for themselves, only a heavy congestion; while those who are fed upon grow bitter and narrow from the loss of the life that is sucked from them. Within my own soul I have perceived ele- ments militating against all I hungered for, of which the young child knew nothing; I have watched closely the great, terrible world of public life, of politics, diplomacy, and international re- lations, where, as under a terrible magnifying glass, the greed, the ambition, the cruelty and falsehood of the individual soul are seen, in so hideously enlarged and wholly unrestrained a form that it might be forgiven to one who cried out to the powers that lie behind life: 'Is it not possible to put out a sponge and wipe up humanity from the earth? It is stain!' I have realised that the strug- gle against the primitive, self-seeking instincts in human nature, whether in the individual or in the larger social organism, is a life- and-death struggle, to be renewed by the individual till death, by the race through the ages. I have tried to wear no blinkers. I have not held a veil before my eyes, that I might profess that cruelty, injustice, and mental and physical anguish were not. I have tried to look nakedly in the face those facts which make most against all hope—and yet, in the darkest hour, the consciousness which I carried back with me that morning has never wholly deserted me; even as a man who clings with one hand to a rock, though the waves pass over his head, yet knows what his hand touches.

But, in the course of the long years which have passed, something else has happened. That which was for the young child only a vision, a flash of almost blinding light, which it could hardly even to itself translate, has, in the course of a long life's experience, become a hope, which I think the cool reason can find grounds to justify, and which a growing knowledge of human nature and human life does endorse.   14

Somewhere, some time, some place—even on earth!   15

1920

2

Description

Where the World Began

Margaret Laurence

A strange place it was, that place where the world began. A place of incredible happenings, splendors and revelations, despairs like multitudinous pits of isolated hells. A place of shadow-spookiness, inhabited by the unknowable dead. A place of jubilation and of mourning, horrible and beautiful.

It was, in fact, a small prairie town.

Because that settlement and that land were my first and for many years my only real knowledge of this planet, in some profound way they remain my world, my way of viewing. My eyes were formed there. Towns like ours, set in a sea of land, have been described thousands of times as dull, bleak, flat, uninteresting. I have had it said to me that the railway trip across Canada is spectacular, except for the prairies, when it would be desirable to go to sleep for several days, until the ordeal is over. I am always unable to argue this point effectively. All I can say is— well, you really have to live there to know that country. The town of my childhood could be called bizarre, agonizingly repressive or cruel at times, and the land in which it grew could be called harsh in the violence of its seasonal changes. But never merely flat or uninteresting. Never dull.

In winter, we used to hitch rides on the back of the milk 4
sleigh, our moccasins squeaking and slithering on the hard rutted
snow of the roads, our hands in ice-bubbled mitts hanging onto
the box edge of the sleigh for dear life, while Bert grinned at us
through his great frosted mustache and shouted the horse into
speed, daring us to stay put. Those mornings, rising, there would
be the perpetual fascination of the frost feathers on windows, the
ferns and flowers and eerie faces traced there during the night by
unseen artists of the wind. Evenings, coming back from skating,
the sky would be black but not dark, for you could see a cold
glitter of stars from one side of the earth's rim to the other. And
then the sometime astonishment when you saw the Northern
Lights flaring across the sky, like the scrawled signature of God.
After a blizzard, when the snowplow hadn't yet got through,
school would be closed for the day, the assumption being that the
town's young could not possibly flounder through five feet of
snow in the pursuit of education. We would then gaily don snow-
shoes and flounder for miles out into the white dazzling deserts,
in pursuit of a different kind of knowing. If you came back too
close to night, through the woods at the foot of the town hill, the
thin black branches of poplar and chokecherry now meringued
with frost, sometimes you heard coyotes. Or maybe the banshee
wolf-voices were really only inside your head.

Summers were scorching, and when no rain came and the 5
wheat became bleached and dried before it headed, the faces of
farmers and townsfolk would not smile much, and you took for
granted, because it never seemed to have been any different, the
frequent knocking at the back door and the young men standing
there, mumbling or thrusting defiantly their requests for a drink
of water and a sandwich if you could spare it. They were riding
the freights, and you never knew where they had come from, or
where they might end up, if anywhere. The Drought and Depression were like evil deities which had been there always. You understood and did not understand.

Yet the outside world had its continuing marvels. The pop- 6
lar bluffs and the small river were filled and surrounded with a
zillion different grasses, stones, and weed flowers. The meadow-
larks sang undaunted from the twanging telephone wires along

the gravel highway. Once we found an old flat-bottomed scow, and launched her, poling along the shallow brown waters, mending her with wodges of hastily chewed Spearmint, grounding her among the tangles of yellow marsh marigolds that grew succulently along the banks of the shrunken river, while the sun made our skins smell dusty-warm.

My best friend lived in an apartment above some stores on   7
Main Street (its real name was Mountain Avenue, goodness knows why), an elegant apartment with royal-blue velvet curtains. The back roof, scarcely sloping at all, was corrugated tin, of a furnace-like warmth on a July afternoon, and we would sit there drinking lemonade and looking across the back lane at the Fire Hall. Sometimes our vigil would be rewarded. Oh joy! Somebody's house burning down! We had an almost-perfect callousness in some ways. Then the wooden tower's bronze bell would clonk and toll like a thousand speeded funerals in a time of plague, and in a few minutes the team of giant black horses would cannon forth, pulling the fire wagon like some scarlet chariot of the Goths, while the firemen clung with one hand, adjusting their helmets as they went.

The oddities of the place were endless. An elderly lady   8
used to serve, as her afternoon tea offering to other ladies, soda biscuits spread with peanut butter and topped with a whole marshmallow. Some considered this slightly eccentric, when compared with chopped egg sandwiches, and admittedly talked about her behind her back, but no one ever refused these delicacies or indicated to her that they thought she had slipped a cog. Another lady dyed her hair a bright and cherry orange, by strangers often mistaken at twenty paces for a feather hat. My own beloved stepmother wore a silver fox neckpiece, a whole pelt, *with the embalmed* (?) *head still on*. My Ontario Irish grandfather said, "sparrow grass," a more interesting term than asparagus. The town dump was known as "the nuisance grounds," phrase fraught with weird connotations, as though the effluvia of our lives was beneath contempt but at the same time was subtly threatening to the determined and sometimes hysterical propriety of our ways.

Some oddities were, as idiom had it, "funny ha ha"; others   9
were "funny peculiar." Some were not so very funny at all. An

old man lived, deranged, in a shack in the valley. Perhaps he wasn't even all that old, but to us he seemed a wild Methuselah figure, shambling among the underbrush and the tall couchgrass, muttering indecipherable curses or blessings, a prophet who had forgotten his prophecies. Everyone in town knew him, but no one knew him. He lived among us as though only occasionally and momentarily visible. The kids called him Andy Gump, and feared him. Some sought to prove their bravery by tormenting him. They were the medieval bear baiters, and he the lumbering bewildered bear, half blind, only rarely turning to snarl. Everything is to be found in a town like mine. Belsen, writ small but with the same ink.

All of us cast stones in one shape or another. In grade 10 school, among the vulnerable and violet girls we were, the feared and despised were those few older girls from what was charmingly termed "the wrong side of the tracks." Tough in talk and tougher in muscle, they were said to be whores already. And may have been, that being about the only profession readily available to them.

The dead lived in that place, too. Not only the grandparents 11 who had, in local parlance, "passed on" and who gloomed, bearded or bonneted, from the sepia photographs in old albums, but also the uncles, forever eighteen or nineteen, whose names were carved on the granite family stones in the cemetery, but whose bones lay in France. My own young mother lay in that graveyard, beside other dead of our kin, and when I was ten, my father, too, only forty, left the living town for the dead dwelling on the hill.

When I was eighteen, I couldn't wait to get out of that 12 town, away from the prairies. I did not know then that I would carry the land and town all my life within my skull, that they would form the mainspring and source of the writing I was to do, wherever and however far away I might live.

This was my territory in the time of my youth, and in a 13 sense my life since then has been an attempt to look at it, to come to terms with it. Stultifying to the mind it certainly could be, and sometimes was, but not to the imagination. It was many things, but it was never dull.

The same, I now see, could be said for Canada in general. 14
Why on earth did generations of Canadians pretend to believe
this country dull? We knew perfectly well it wasn't. Yet for so
long we did not proclaim what we knew. If our upsurge of so-
called nationalism seems odd or irrelevant to outsiders, and even
to some of our own people (*what's all the fuss about?*), they
might try to understand that for many years we valued ourselves
insufficiently, living as we did under the huge shadows of those two
dominating figures, Uncle Sam and Britannia. We have only just
begun to value ourselves, our land, our abilities. We have only just
begun to recognize our legends and to give shape to our myths.

There are, God knows, enough aspects to deplore about 15
this country. When I see the killing of our lakes and rivers with
industrial wastes, I feel rage and despair. When I see our industries and natural resources increasingly taken over by America, I
feel an overwhelming discouragement, especially as I cannot
simply say "damn Yankees." It should never be forgotten that it
is we ourselves who have sold such a large amount of our birth-
right for a mess of plastic Progress. When I saw the War Measures Act being invoked in 1970, I lost forever the vestigial remains of the naïve wish-belief that repression could not happen
here, or would not. And yet, of course, I had known all along in
the deepest and often hidden caves of the heart that anything can
happen anywhere, for the seeds of both man's freedom and his
captivity are found everywhere, even in the microcosm of a prairie town. But in raging against our injustices, our stupidities, I do
so *as family,* as I did, and still do in writing, about those aspects
of my town which I hated and which are always in some ways
aspects of myself.

The land still draws me more than other lands. I have lived 16
in Africa and in England, but splendid as both can be, they do
not have the power to move me in the same way as, for example,
that part of southern Ontario where I spent four months last summer in a cedar cabin beside a river. "Scratch a Canadian, and
you find a phony pioneer," I used to say to myself in warning.
But all the same it is true, I think, that we are not yet totally
alienated from physical earth, and let us only pray we do not become so. I once thought that my lifelong fear and mistrust of cit-

ies made me a kind of old-fashioned freak; now I see it differently.

    The cabin has a long window across its front western wall,   17
and sitting at the oak table there in the mornings, I used to look
out at the river and at the tall trees beyond, green-gold in the
early light. The river was bronze; the sun caught it strangely, reflecting upon its surface the near-shore sand ripples underneath.
Suddenly, the crescenting of a fish, gone before the eye could
clearly give image to it. The old man next door said these leaping
fish were carp. Himself, he preferred muskie, for he was a real
fisherman and the muskie gave him a fight. The wind most often
blew from the south, and the river flowed toward the south, so
when the water was wind-riffled, and the current was strong, the
river seemed to be flowing both ways. I liked this, and interpreted it as an omen, a natural symbol.

    A few years ago, when I was back in Winnipeg, I gave a   18
talk at my old college. It was open to the public, and afterward a
very old man came up to me and asked me if my maiden name
had been Wemyss. I said yes, thinking he might have known my
father or my grandfather. But no. "When I was a young lad," he
said, "I once worked for your great-grandfather, Robert Wemyss, when he had the sheep ranch at Raeburn." I think that
was a moment when I realized all over again something of great
importance to me. My long-ago families came from Scotland and
Ireland, but in a sense that no longer mattered so much. My true
roots were here.

    I am not very patriotic, in the usual meaning of that word. I   19
cannot say "My country right or wrong" in any political, social
or literary context. But one thing is inalterable, for better or
worse, for life.

    This is where my world began. A world which includes the   20
ancestors—both my own and other people's ancestors who become mine. A world which formed me, and continues to do so,
even while I found it in some of its aspects, and continue to do
so. A world which gave me my own lifework to do, because it
was here that I learned the sight of my own particular eyes.

1976

The Metropolitan Cathedral
in San Salvador

Joan Didion

During the week before I flew down to El Salvador a Sal- 1
vadoran woman who works for my husband and me in Los Angeles gave me repeated instructions about what we must and
must not do. We must not go out at night. We must stay off the
street whenever possible. We must never ride in buses or taxis,
never leave the capital, never imagine that our passports would
protect us. We must not even consider the hotel a safe place:
people were killed in hotels. She spoke with considerable vehe-
mence, because two of her brothers had been killed in Salvador
in August of 1981, in their beds. The throats of both brothers had
been slashed. Her father had been cut but stayed alive. Her
mother had been beaten. Twelve of her other relatives, aunts and
uncles and cousins, had been taken from their houses one night
the same August, and their bodies had been found some time
later, in a ditch. I assured her that we would remember, we
would be careful, we would in fact be so careful that we would
probably (trying for a light touch) spend all our time in church.

She became still more agitated, and I realized that I had   2
spoken as a *norteamericana:* churches had not been to this
woman the neutral ground they had been to me. I must remember: Archbishop Romero killed saying mass in the chapel of the
Divine Providence Hospital in San Salvador. I must remember:
more than thirty people killed at Archbishop Romero's funeral in
the Metropolitan Cathedral in San Salvador. I must remember:
more than twenty people killed before that on the steps of the
Metropolitan Cathedral. CBS had filmed it. It had been on television, the bodies jerking, those still alive crawling over the dead
as they tried to get out of range. I must understand: the Church
was dangerous.

I told her that I understood, that I knew all that, and I did,   3
abstractly, but the specific meaning of the Church she knew
eluded me until I was actually there, at the Metropolitan Cathe-

dral in San Salvador, one afternoon when rain sluiced down its
corrugated plastic windows and puddled around the supports of
the Sony and Phillips billboards near the steps. The effect of the
Metropolitan Cathedral is immediate, and entirely literary. This
is the cathedral that the late Archbishop Oscar Arnulfo Romero
refused to finish, on the premise that the work of the Church
took precedence over its display, and the high walls of raw concrete bristle with structural rods, rusting now, staining the concrete, sticking out at wrenched and violent angles. The wiring is
exposed. Fluorescent tubes hang askew. The great high altar is
backed by warped plyboard. The cross on the altar is of bare in-
candescent bulbs, but the bulbs, that afternoon, were unlit: there
was in fact no light at all on the main altar, no light on the cross,
no light on the globe of the world that showed the northern
American continent in gray and the southern in white; no light on
the dove above the globe, *Salvador del Mundo*. In this vast bru-
talist space that was the cathedral, the unlit altar seemed to offer
a single ineluctable message: at this time and in this place the
light of the world could be construed as out, off, extinguished.

In many ways the Metropolitan Cathedral is an authentic 4
piece of political art, a statement for El Salvador as *Guernica*
was for Spain. It is quite devoid of sentimental relief. There are
no decorative or architectural references to familiar parables, in
fact no stories at all, not even the Stations of the Cross. On the
afternoon I was there the flowers laid on the altar were dead.
There were no traces of normal parish activity. The doors were
open to the barricaded main steps, and down the steps there was
a spill of red paint, lest anyone forget the blood shed there. Here
and there on the cheap linoleum inside the cathedral there was
what seemed to be actual blood, dried in spots, the kind of spots
dropped by a slow hemorrhage, or by a woman who does not
know or does not care that she is menstruating.

There were several women in the cathedral during the hour 5
or so I spent there, a young woman with a baby, an older woman
in house slippers, a few others, all in black. One of the women
walked the aisles as if by compulsion, up and down, across and
back, crooning loudly as she walked. Another knelt without
moving at the tomb of Archbishop Romero in the right transept.

"LOOR A MONSENOR ROMERO," the crude needlepoint tapestry by
the tomb read, "Praise to Monsignor Romero from the Mothers
of the Imprisoned, the Disappeared, and the Murdered," the *Co-
mité de Madres y Familiares de Presos, Desaparecidos, y Asesi-
nados Politicos de El Salvador.*

The tomb itself was covered with offerings and petitions,   6
notes decorated with motifs cut from greeting cards and car-
toons. I recall one with figures cut from a Bugs Bunny strip, and
another with a pencil drawing of a baby in a crib. The baby in
this drawing seemed to be receiving medication or fluid or blood
intravenously, through the IV line shown on its wrist. I studied
the notes for a while and then went back and looked again at the
unlit altar, and at the red paint on the main steps, from which it
was possible to see the guardsmen on the balcony of the National
Palace hunching back to avoid the rain. Many Salvadorans are
offended by the Metropolitan Cathedral, which is as it should be,
because the place remains perhaps the only unambiguous political statement in El Salvador, a metaphorical bomb in the ultimate power station.

1983

Tuesday Morning
William Least Heat Moon

Tuesday morning: the country east of Heber was a desert of   1
sagebrush and globe-shaped junipers and shallow washes with
signs warning of flash floods. I turned north at Snowflake,
founded by Erastus Snow and Bill Flake, and headed toward the
twenty-five thousand square miles of Navajo reservation (nearly
equal to West Virginia) which occupies most of the northeastern
corner of Arizona. The scrub growth disappeared entirely and

only the distant outlines of red rock mesas interrupted the emptiness. But for the highway, the land was featureless.

Holbrook used to be a tough town where boys from the   2
Hash Knife cattle outfit cut loose. Now, astride I-44 (once route 66), Holbrook was a tourist stop for women with Instamatics and men with metal detectors; no longer was the big business cattle, but rather rocks and gems.

North of the interstate, I entered the reserve. Although the   3
area has been part of the Navajo homeland for five hundred years, settlers of a century before, led by Kit Carson, drove the Navajo out of Arizona in retribution for their raids against whites and other Indians alike. A few years later, survivors of the infamous "Long Walk" returned to take up their land again. Now the Navajo possess the largest reservation in the United States and the one hundred fifty thousand descendants of the seven thousand survivors comprise far and away the largest tribe. Their reservation is the only one in the country to get bigger—five times bigger—after it was first set aside; their holdings increased largely because white men had believed Navajo land worthless. But in fact, the reservation contains coal, oil, gas, uranium, helium, and timber; those resources may explain why Navajos did not win total control over their land until 1972.

Liquor bottles, beercans, an occasional stripped car littered   4
the unfenced roadside. Far off the highway, against the mesa bottoms, stood small concrete-block or frame houses, each with a television antenna, pickup, privy, and ceremonial hogan of stone, adobe, and cedar. Always the hogan doors faced east.

In a classic scene, a boy on a pinto pony herded a flock of   5
sheep and goats—descendants of the Spanish breed—across the highway. A few miles later, a man wearing a straw Stetson and pegleg Levi's guided up a draw a pair of horses tied together at the neck in the Indian manner. With the white man giving up on the economics of cowpunching, it looked as if the old categories of cowboys and Indians had merged; whoever the last true cowboy in America turns out to be, he's likely to be an Indian.

At the center of the reservation lay Hopi territory, a large   6
rectangle with boundaries the tribes cannot agree on because

part of the increase of Navajo land has come at the expense of the Hopis. A forbidding sign in Latinate English:

YOU ARE ENTERING THE EXCLUSIVE
HOPI RESERVATION AREA. YOUR
ENTRANCE CONSTITUTES CONSENT
TO THE JURISDICTION OF THE HOPI
TRIBE AND ITS COURTS.

Although the Hopi have lived here far longer than any other 7 surviving people and consider their mile-high spread of rock and sand, wind and sun, the center of the universe, they are now, by Anglo decree, surrounded by their old enemies, the Navajo, a people they see as latecomers. In 1880, Hopis held two and one half million acres; today it has decreased to about a half million.

Holding on to their land has been a long struggle for the 8 Hopi. Yet for a tribe whose name means "well behaved," for Indians without war dances, for a group whose first defense against the conquistadors was sprinkled lines of sacred cornmeal, for a people who protested priestly corruption (consorting with Hopi women and whipping men) by quietly pitching a few padres over the cliffs, Hopis have done well. But recently they have fought Navajo expansion in federal courts, and a strange case it is: those who settled first seeking judgment from those who came later through laws of those who arrived last.

Because the Navajo prefer widely dispersed clusters of 9 clans to village life, I'd seen nothing resembling a hamlet for seventy-five miles. But Hopi Polacca almost looked like a Western town in spite of Indian ways here and there: next to a floral-print bedsheet on a clothesline hung a coyote skin, and beside box houses were adobe bread ovens shaped like skep beehives. The Navajo held to his hogan, the Hopi his oven. Those things persisted.

Like bony fingers, three mesas reached down from larger 10 Black Mesa into the middle of Hopi land; not long ago, the only way onto these mesas was by handholds in the steep rock heights. From the tops, the Hopi look out upon a thousand square miles. At the heart of the reservation, topographically and culturally, was Second Mesa. Traditionally, Hopis, as do the eagles they hold sacred, prefer to live on precipices; so it was not far from the edge of Second Mesa that they built the Hopi Cultural Center. In the gallery were drawings of mythic figures by Hopi children who fused centuries and cultures with grotesque Mudhead Kachinas wearing large terra-cotta masks and jacko-lantern smiles, dancing atop spaceships with Darth Vader and Artoo Deetoo.

At the Center, I ate *nokquivi,* a good hominy stew with baked chile peppers, but I had no luck in striking up a conversation. I drove on toward the western edge of the mesa. Not far from the tribal garage (TRIBAL VEHICLES ONLY) stood small sandstone houses, their slabs precisely cut and fitted as if by ancient Aztecs, a people related to the Hopi. The solid houses blended with the tawny land so well they appeared part of the living rock. All were empty. The residents had moved to prefabs and double-wides. 11

I couldn't see how anyone could survive a year in this severe land, yet Hopis, like other desert life, are patient and clever and not at all desperate; they have lasted here for ten centuries by using tiny terraced plots that catch spring rain and produce a desert-hardy species of blue corn, as well as squash, onions, beans, peppers, melons, apricots, peaches. The bristlecone pine of American Indians, Hopis live where almost nothing else will, thriving long in adverse conditions: poor soil, drought, temperature extremes, high winds. Those give life to the bristlecone and the Hopi. 12

Clinging to the southern lip of Third Mesa was ancient Oraibi, most probably the oldest continuously occupied village in the United States. Somehow the stone and adobe have been able to hang on to the precipitous edge since the twelfth century. More than eight hundred Hopis lived at Oraibi in 1901—now only a few. All across the reservation I'd seen no more than a dozen people, and on the dusty streets of the old town I saw just one bent woman struggling against the wind. But somewhere there must have been more. 13

To this strangest of American villages the Franciscan father, Tomás Garces, came in 1776 from Tucson with gifts and "true religion." Hopis permitted him to stay at Oraibi, looking then as now if you excluded an occasional television antenna, 14 but they refused his gifts and god, and, on the fourth day of July, sent him off disheartened. To this time, no other North American tribe has held closer to its own religion and culture. Although the isolated Hopi had no knowledge of the importance of religious freedom to the new nation surrounding them, several generations successfully ignored "the code of religious offenses"—laws designed by the Bureau of Indian Affairs to destroy the old rituals and way of life—until greater bureaucratic tolerance came when Herbert Hoover appointed two Quakers to direct the BIA.

A tribal squadcar checked my speed at Hotevilla, where the 15 highway started a long descent off the mesa. The wind was getting up, and tumbleweed bounded across the road, and sand hummed against the Ghost. West, east, north, south—to each a different weather: sandstorm, sun, rain, and bluish snow on the San Francisco Peaks, that home of the Kachinas who are the spiritual forces of Hopi life.

Tuba City, founded by Mormon missionaries as an agency 16 and named after a Hopi chieftain although now mostly a Navajo town, caught the sandstorm full face. As I filled the gas tank, I tried to stay behind the van, but gritty gusts whipped around the corners and stung me and forced my eyes shut. School was just out, and children, shirts pulled over their heads, ran for the trading post, where old Navajo men who had been sitting outside took cover as the sand changed the air to matter. I ducked in too. The place was like an A&P, TG&Y, and craft center.

In viridescent velveteen blouses and violescent nineteenth- 17 century skirts, Navajo women of ample body, each laden with silver and turquoise bracelets, necklaces, and rings—not the trading post variety but heavy bands gleaming under the patina of long wear—reeled off yards of fabric. The children, like schoolkids anywhere, milled around the candy; they spoke only English. But the old men, now standing at the plate glass windows and looking into the brown wind, popped and puffed out the ancient words. I've read that Navajo, a language related to that of the Indians of Alaska and northwest Canada, has no curse words unless you consider "coyote" cursing. By comparison with other native tongues, it's remarkably free of English and Spanish; a Navajo mechanic, for example, has more than two hundred purely Navajo terms to describe automobile parts. And it might be Navajo that will greet the first extraterrestrial ears to hear from planet Earth: on board each *Voyager* spacecraft traveling toward the edge of the solar system and beyond is a gold-plated, long-playing record; following an aria from Mozart's *Magic Flute* and Chuck Berry's "Johnny B. Goode," is a Navajo night chant, music the conquistadors heard.

Intimidated by my ignorance of Navajo and by fear of the contempt that full-bloods often show lesser bloods, I again failed to stir a conversation. After the storm blew on east, I followed the old men back outside, where they squatted to watch the day take up the weather of an hour earlier. To one with a great round head like an earthen pot, I said, "Is the storm finished now?" He looked at me, then slowly turned his head, while the others examined before them things in the air invisible to me. 18

I took a highway down the mesa into a valley of the Painted Desert, where wind had textured big drifts of orange sand into rills. U.S. 89 ran north along the Echo Cliffs. Goats grazed in stubble by the roadsides, and to the west a horseman moved his sheep. Hogans here stood alone; they were not ceremonial lodges but homes. For miles at the highway edges sat little cardboard and scrapwood ramadas, each with a windblasted sign advertising jewelry and cedar beads. In another era, white men came in wagons to trade beads to Indians; now they came in stationwagons and bought beads. History may repeat, but sometimes things get turned around in the process. 19

1982

Cyclone! Rising to the Fall
Peter Schjeldahl

The Cyclone is art, sex, God, the greatest. It is the most fun you can have without risking bad ethics. I rode the Cyclone seven times one afternoon last summer, and I am here to tell everybody that it is fun for fun's sake, the pure abstract heart of the 1 human capacity for getting a kick out of anything. Yes, it may be anguishing initially. (I promise to tell the truth.) Terrifying, even, the first time or two the train is hauled upward with groans and creaks and with you in it. At the top then—where there is sudden strange quiet but for the fluttering of two tattered flags, and you have a poignantly brief view of Brooklyn, and of ships far out on the Atlantic—you may feel very lonely and that you have made a serious mistake, cursing yourself in the last gleam of the reflective consciousness you are about, abruptly, to leave up there between the flags like an abandoned thought-balloon. To keep yourself company by screaming may help, and no one is noticing: try it. After a couple of rides, panic abates, and after four or five you aren't even frightened, exactly, but *stimulated,* blissed, sent. The squirt of adrenaline you will never cease to have at the top as the train lumbers, wobbling slightly, into the plunge, finally fuels just happy wonderment because you can't, and never will, *believe* what is going to happen.

Every roller coaster has that first, immense drop. In practical terms, it provides the oomph for the entire ride, which is of course impelled by nothing but ecologically sound gravity, momentum, and the odd slingshot of centrifugal force. The coaster is basically an ornate means of falling and a poem about physics in parts or stanzas, with jokes. The special quality of the Cyclone is how different, how *articulated,* all the components of its poem are, the whole of which lasts a minute and thirty-some seconds— exactly the right length, composed of distinct and perfect moments. By my fifth ride, my heart was leaping at the onset of each segment as at the approach of a dear old friend, and melting with instantaneous nostalgia for each at its finish.

I think every part of the Cyclone should have a name, the better to be recalled and accurately esteemed. In my mind, the big drop is Kismet—fate, destiny. I can't think of what to call the second, a mystery drop commenced in a jiffy after we have been whipped around, but good, coming out of Kismet. (Someday soon I will devote particular attention to the huge and violent but elusive second drop.) I do know that the third drop's name can only be Pasha. It is so round and generous, rich and powerful, looking like a killer going in but then actually like a crash landing in feathers that allows, for the first time in the ride, an instant for luxuriating in one's endorphin rush.

This brings me to another important function of the first   4
drop, which (I firmly contend) is to trigger the release of endorphins, natural morphine, into the bloodstream by persuading the
organism that it is going to die. I know all about endorphins from
reading the *New York Times* science section, and from an accident a few years ago. I broke my elbow, which is something not
to do. It hurts. Or let me put it this way: in relation to what I had
previously understood of pain, the sensation of breaking an elbow was *a whole new idea,* a new continent suddenly—whole
unknown worlds of pain out there over the horizon. I was aghast,
when I broke my elbow, at the extent of my naïveté about pain—
but only for a second. Then I was somewhere else, pain-free, I
think it was a cocktail party, but confusing, I didn't recognize
anybody. On some level I knew the party wasn't real, that I was
in another, real place which had something unpleasant about it
that made me not want to be there, but then I began to be afraid
that if I stayed at the party I would be unable ever to be real
again, so with an effort of will I returned to my body, which was
sitting up with family members leaning over. The pain returned,
but muffled and dull, drastically lessened. Endorphins.

Other things than breaking an elbow can give you an endor-   5
phin high, and one of them is suddenly falling ninety-some feet,
seeing the ground charge directly at you. I think the forebrain,
loaded with all sorts of chemical gimmicks we don't suspect, just
there for special occasions, registers the situation, and, quick,
pours a last-minute, bon voyage endorphin highball: "Hey, [*your
name here*], this one's for you!" That's why it's important to ride
the Cyclone many times, to comb out the distraction of terror—
which gradually yields to the accumulating evidence that you are
not dead—in order to savor the elixir for its own sake and for the
sake of loving God or whatever—Nature—for cunningly secreted
kindnesses. But Kismet is such a zonk, and the anonymous second drop is so perplexing and a zonk, too, that it isn't until mid-
Pasha, in great fleshy Pasha's lap, that consciousness catches up
with physiologic ravishment. Some part of my soul, because of
the Cyclone, is still and will remain forever in that state, which I

think is a zone of overlap among the heavens of all the world's mystic religions, where transcendent swamis bump around with freaked Spanish women saints. Blitzed in Pasha permanently, I have this lasting glimpse into the beyond that is not beyond, and you know what I'm talking about, or you don't.

Rolling up out of Pasha, we enter the part of the Cyclone **6** that won't quit laughing. First there's the whoop of a whipping hairpin curve, which, if someone is sitting with you, Siamese-twins you. (Having tried different cars in different company, I prefer being alone at the very front—call me a classicist.) The ensuing dips, humps, dives, and shimmies that roar, chortle, cackle, and snort continue just long enough to suggest that they may go on forever—as worrisome as the thought, when you're laughing hard, that maybe you can never stop—and then it's hello, Irene. Why do I think Irene is the name of the very sharp drop, not deep but savage, that wipes the grin off the laughing part of the Cyclone? (Special about it is a crosspiece, low over the track at the bottom, that you swear is going to fetch you square in the eyebrows.) Irene is always the name—or kind of name, slightly unusual but banal—of the ordinary-seeming girl whom a young man may pursue idly, in a bored time, and then *wham!* fall horribly in love with, blasted in love with this person he never bothered to even particularly look at and now it's too late, she's his universe, Waterloo, *personal* Kismet. This is one good reason I can think of for growing older: learning an aversion reflex for girls named something like Irene. In this smallish but vicious, sobering drop, abstract shapes of my own youthful romantic sorrows do not fail to flash before my inner eye...but then, with a jarring zoom up and around, I am once more grown-up, wised-up me, and the rest of the ride is rejoicing.

The Cyclone differs from other roller coasters in being (a) a **7** work of art and (b) old, and not only old but old-looking, decrepit, rusting in its metal parts and peeling in its more numerous wooden parts, filthy throughout and jammed into a wire (Cyclone!) fence abutting cracked sidewalks of the Third World sinkhole that Coney Island is, intoxicatingly. Nor is it to be denied or concealed that the Cyclone, unlike newer coasters, tends to run *rough,* though each ride is unique and some are inexplicably velvety. One time the vibration, with the wheels shrieking and the cars threatening to explode with strain, made me think, "This is *no fun at all!*" It was an awful moment, with a sickening sense of betrayal and icy-fingered doubt: was my love malign?

That was my worst ride, which left me with a painfully **8** yanked muscle in my shoulder, but I am glad to say it wasn't my last. I got back on like a thrown cowboy and discovered that the secret of handling the rough rides is indeed like riding a horse, at trot or gallop—not tensing against it, as I had, but posting and rolling. It's all in the thighs and rear end, as I especially realized when—what the hell—I joined pimpled teenagers in the arms-raised *no hands!* trick. I should mention that a heavy, cushioned restraining bar locks down snugly into your lap and is very reassuring, although, like everything upholstered in the cars, it may be cracked or slashed and leaking tufts of stuffing from under swatches of gray gaffer's tape. One thing consistently disquieting is how, under stress, a car's wooden sides may *give* a bit. I wish they wouldn't do that, or that my imagination were less vivid. If a side did happen to fail on a curve, one would depart like toothpaste from a stomped-on tube.

I was proud of braving the *no hands!* posture—as trusting **9** in the restraining bar as a devout child in his heavenly Father—particularly the first time I did it, while emerging from the slinging turn that succeeds Irene into the long, long careen that bottoms out at absolute ground level a few feet from the fence where pedestrians invariably gather to watch, transfixed. I call this swift, showy glide Celebrity: the ride's almost over, and afflatus swells the chest. But going *no hands!* soon feels as cheap and callow as it looks, blocking with vulgar self-centeredness the wahoo-glimmering-away-of-personality-in-convulsive-Nirvana that is the Cyclone's essence. A righteous ride is hands on, though lightly, like grace. The payoff is intimacy in the sweet diminuendo, the jiggling and chuckling smart little bumps and dandling dips that bring us to a quick, pillowy deceleration in the shed, smelling of dirty machine oil, where we began and will begin again. It is a warm debriefing, this last part: "Wasn't that *great?*" it says. "Want to go again?"

Of course I do, but first there is the final stage of absorp- 10 tion, when you squeeze out (it's easy to bang a knee then, so watch it) to stand wobbly but weightless, euphoric, and then to enjoy the sensation of walking as if it were a neat thing you had just invented. Out on the sidewalk, the object of curious gazes, you see that they see that you see them, earthlings, in a diminishing perspective, through the wrong end of the telescope of your pleasure, and your heart is pitying. You nod, smiling, to convey that yes, they should ride, and no, they won't regret it.

1988

Main Street
Mordecai Richler

Two streets below our own came the Main. Rich in de- 1 lights, but also squalid, filthy, and hollering with stores whose wares, whether furniture or fruit, were ugly or damaged. The signs still say FANTASTIC DISCOUNTS or FORCED TO SELL PRICES HERE, but the bargains so bitterly sought after are illusory—and perhaps they always were.

The Main, with something for all our appetites, was dedi- 2 cated to pinching pennies from the poor, but it was there to entertain, educate and comfort us too. Across the street from the synagogue you could see THE PICTURE THEY CLAIMED COULD NEVER BE MADE. A little further down the street there was the Workman's Circle and, if you liked, a strip show. Peaches, Margo, Lili St. Cyr. Around the corner there was the ritual baths, the *shvitz* or *mikva,* where my grandfather and his cronies went before the

High Holidays, emerging boiling red from the highest reaches of the steam rooms to happily flog each other with brushes fashioned of pine tree branches. Where supremely orthodox women went once a month to purify themselves.

It was to the Main, once a year before the High Holidays,   3 that I was taken for a new suit (the itch of the cheap tweed was excruciating) and shoes (with a built-in squeak). We also shopped for fruit on the Main, meat and fish, and here the important thing was to watch the man at the scales. On the Main, too, was the Chinese laundry—"Have you ever seen such hard workers?"—the Italian hat-blocker—"Tony's a good goy, you know. Against Mussolini from the very first."—and strolling French Canadian priests—"Some of them speak Hebrew now." "Well, if you ask me, it's none of their business. Enough's enough, you know." Kids like myself were dragged along on shopping expeditions to carry parcels. Old men gave us snuff, at the delicatessens we were allowed salami butts, card players pushed candies on us for luck, and everywhere we were poked and pinched by the mothers. Absolutely the best that could be said of us was, "He eats well, knock wood," and later, as we went off to school, "He's a rank-one boy."

After the shopping, once our errands had been done, we re- 4 turned to the Main once more, either for part-time jobs or to study with our *melamud*. Jobs going on the Main included spotting pins in a bowling alley, collecting butcher bills and, best of all, working at a newsstand, where you could devour the *Police Gazette* free and pick up a little extra short-changing strangers during the rush hour. Work was supposed to be good for our character development and the fact that we were paid was incidental. To qualify for a job we were supposed to be "bright, ambitious, and willing to learn." An ad I once saw in a shoe store window read:

PART-TIME BOY WANTED FOR EXPANDING BUSINESS. EXPERIENCE ABSOLUTELY NECESSARY, BUT NOT ESSENTIAL

Our jobs and lessons finished, we would wander the street   5 in small groups smoking Turret cigarettes and telling jokes.

"Hey, *shmo-hawk,* what's the difference between a mail 6
box and an elephant's ass?"

"I dunno." 7

"Well, I wouldn't send *you* to mail my letters." 8

As the French Canadian factory girls passed arm-in-arm we 9
would call out, "I've got the time, if you've got the place."

Shabus it was back to the Main again and the original 10
Young Israel synagogue. While our grandfathers and fathers
prayed and gossiped and speculated about the war in Europe in
the musty room below, we played chin the bar in the upstairs attic and told jokes that began, "Confucius say..." or, "Once
there was an Englishman, an Irishman, and a Hebe...."

We would return to the Main once more when we wanted a 11
fight with the pea-soups. Winter, as I recall it, was best for this
type of sport. We could throw snowballs packed with ice or frozen horse buns, and with darkness falling early, it was easier to
elude pursuers. Soon, however, we developed a technique of
battle that served us well even in the spring. Three of us would
hide under an outside staircase while the fourth member of our
group, a kid named Eddy, would idle provocatively on the sidewalk. Eddy was a good head-and-a-half shorter than the rest of
us. (For this, it was rumoured, his mother was to blame. She
wouldn't let Eddy have his tonsils removed and that's why he
was such a runt. It was not that Eddy's mother feared surgery,
but Eddy sang in the choir of a rich synagogue, bringing in some
thirty dollars a month, and if his tonsils were removed it was
feared that his voice would go too.) Anyway, Eddy would stand
out there alone and when the first solitary pea-soup passed he
would kick him in the shins. "Your mother fucks," he'd say.

The pea-soup, looking down on little Eddy, would naturally 12
knock him one on the head. Then, and only then, would we
emerge from under the staircase.

"Hey, that's my kid brother you just slugged." 13

And before the bewildered pea-soup could protest, we were 14
scrambling all over him.

These and other fights, however, sprang more out of bore- 15
dom than from racial hatred, not that there were no racial problems on the Main.

If the Main was a poor man's street, it was also a dividing 16
line. Below, the French Canadians. Above, some distance
above, the dreaded WASPS. On the Main itself there were some
Italians, Yugoslavs and Ukrainians, but they did not count as
true Gentiles. Even the French Canadians, who were our enemies, were not entirely unloved. Like us, they were poor and
coarse with large families and spoke English badly.

Looking back, it's easy to see that the real trouble was 17
there was no dialogue between us and the French Canadians,
each elbowing the other, striving for WASP acceptance. We
fought the French Canadians stereotype for stereotype. If many
of them believed that the St. Urbain Street Jews were secretly
rich, manipulating the black market, then my typical French Canadian was a moronic gum-chewer. He wore his greasy black
hair parted down the middle and also affected an eyebrow moustache. His zoot trousers were belted just under the breastbone
and ended in a peg hugging his ankles. He was the dolt who held
up your uncle endlessly at the liquor commission while he tried
unsuccessfully to add three figures or, if he was employed at the
customs office, never knew which form to give you. Furthermore, he only held his liquor commission or customs or any
other government job because he was the second cousin of a
backwoods notary who had delivered the village vote to the
Union Nationale for a generation. Other French Canadians were
speed cops, and if any of these ever stopped you on the highway
you made sure to hand him a folded two dollar bill with your li-
cence.

Wartime shortages, the admirable Protestant spirit of 18
making-do, benefited both Jews and French Canadians. Jews
with clean fingernails were allowed to teach within the Protestant
School system and French Canadians off the Atwater League
and provincial sandlots broke into the International Baseball
League. Jean-Pierre Roy won twenty-five games for the Montreal Royals one year and a young man named Stan Breard enjoyed a season as a stylish but no-hit shortstop. Come to think of
it, the only French Canadians I heard of were athletes. Of course
there was Maurice Richard, the superb hockey player, but there
was also Dave Castiloux, a cunning welterweight, and, above all,

the wrestler-hero, Yvon Robert, who week after week gave the
blond Anglo-Saxon wrestlers what for at the Forum.

Aside from boyhood street fights and what I read on the 19
sports pages, all I knew of French Canadians was that they were
clearly hilarious. Our Scots schoolmaster would always raise a
laugh in class by reading us the atrocious Uncle Tom-like dialect
verse of William Henry Drummond: *Little Baptiste & Co.*

On wan dark night on Lac St. Pierre,
De win' she blow, blow, blow,
An' de crew of de wood scow "Julie Plante"
Got scar't and run below—
Bimeby she blow some more,
An' de scow bus' up on Lac St. Pierre
Wan arpent from de shore.

Actually, it was only the WASPS who were truly hated and 20
feared. "Among them," I heard it said, "with those porridge
faces, who can tell what they're thinking?" It was, we felt, their
country, and given sufficient liquor who knew when they would
make trouble?

We were a rude, aggressive bunch round the Main. Cocky 21
too. But bring down the most insignificant, pinched WASP fire
insurance inspector and even the most arrogant merchant on the
street would dip into the drawer for a ten spot or a bottle and
bow and say, "Sir."

After school we used to race down to the Main to play 22
snooker at the Rachel or the Mount Royal. Other days, when we
chose to avoid school altogether, we would take the No. 55
streetcar as far as St. Catherine Street, where there was a variety
of amusements offered. We could play the pinball machines and
watch archaic strip-tease movies for a nickel at the Silver Game-
land. At the Midway or the Crystal Palace we could see a double
feature and a girlie show for as little as thirty-five cents. The
Main, at this juncture, was thick with drifters, panhandlers and
whores. Available on both sides of the street were "Tourist
Rooms by Day and Night," and everywhere there was the smell
of french fried potatoes cooking in stale oil. Tough, unshaven
men in checked shirts stood in knots outside the taverns and
cheap cafés. There was the promise of violence.

As I recall it, we were always being warned about the 23
Main. Our grandparents and parents had come there by steerage
from Rumania or by cattleboat from Poland by way of Liverpool.
No sooner had they unpacked their bundles and cardboard suit-
cases than they were planning a better, brighter life for us, the
Canadian-born children. The Main, good enough for them, was
not to be for us, and that they told us again and again was what
the struggle was for. The Main was for *bummers,* drinkers, and
(heaven forbid) failures.

During the years leading up to the war, the ideal of the 24
ghetto, no different from any other in America, was the doctor.
This, mistakenly, was taken to be the very apogee of learning
and refinement. In those days there also began the familiar and
agonizing process of alienation between immigrant parents and
Canadian-born children. Our older brothers and cousins, off to
university, came home to realize that our parents spoke with
embarrassing accents. Even the younger boys, like myself,
were going to "their" schools. According to them, the priests
had made a tremendous contribution to the exploration and
development of this country. Some were heroes. But our parents had other memories, different ideas, about the priest-
hood. At school we were taught about the glory of the Cru-
sades and at home we were instructed in the bloodier side of
the story. Though we wished Lord Tweedsmuir, the
Governor-General, a long life each Saturday morning in the
synagogue, there were those among us who knew him as John
Buchan. From the very beginning there was their history, and
ours. Our heroes, and theirs.

Our parents used to apply a special standard to all men and 25
events. "Is it good for the Jews?" By this test they interpreted
the policies of Mackenzie King and the Stanley Cup play-offs
and earthquakes in Japan. To take one example—if the Montreal
Canadiens won the Stanley Cup it would infuriate the WASPS in
Toronto, and as long as the English and French were going at
each other they left us alone: *ergo,* it was good for the Jews if the
Canadiens won the Stanley Cup.

We were convinced that we gained from dissension be- 26
tween Canada's two cultures, the English and the French, and

we looked neither to England nor France for guidance. We turned to the United States. The real America.

America was Roosevelt, the Yeshiva College, Max Baer, 27 Mickey Katz records, Danny Kaye, a Jew in the Supreme Court, the *Jewish Daily Forward,* Dubinsky, Mrs. Nussbaum of Allen's Alley, and Gregory Peck looking so cute in *Gentleman's Agreement.* Why, in the United States a Jew even wrote speeches for the president. Returning cousins swore they had heard a cop speak Yiddish in Brooklyn. There were the Catskill hotels, Jewish soap operas on the radio and, above all earthly pleasure grounds, Florida. Miami. No manufacturer had quite made it in Montreal until he was able to spend a month each winter in Miami.

We were governed by Ottawa, we were also British sub- 28 jects, but our true capital was certainly New York. Success was (and still is) acceptance by the United States. For a boxer this meant a main bout at Madison Square Garden, for a writer or an artist, praise from New York critics, for a businessman, a Miami tan and, today, for comics, an appearance on the Ed Sullivan Show or for actors, not an important part at the Stratford Festival, but Broadway, or the lead in a Hollywood TV series (Lorne Green in *Bonanza*). The outside world, "their" Canada, only concerned us insofar as it affected our living conditions. All the same, we liked to impress the *goyim.* A knock on the knuckles from time to time wouldn't hurt them. So, while we secretly believed that the baseball field or the prize-fighting ring was no place for a Jewish boy, we took enormous pleasure in the accomplishments of, say, Kermit Kitman, the Montreal Royals outfielder, and Maxie Berger, the welterweight.

Streets such as ours and Outremont, where the emergent 29 middle-class and the rich lived, comprised an almost self-contained world. Outside of business there was a minimal contact with the Gentiles. This was hardly petulant clannishness or naive fear. In the years leading up to the war neo-fascist groups were extremely active in Canada. In the United States there was Father Coughlin, Lindbergh, and others. We had Adrian Arcand. The upshot was almost the same. So I can recall seeing swastikas and *"A bas les Juifs"* painted on the Laurentian highway. There

were suburbs and hotels in the mountains and country clubs
where we were not wanted, beaches with signs that read GEN-
TILES ONLY, quotas at the universities, and occasional racial alter-
cations on Park Avenue. The democracy we were being invited
to defend was flawed and hostile to us. Without question it was
better for us in Canada than in Europe, but this was still their
country, not ours.

I was only a boy during the war. I can remember signs in 30
cigar stores that warned us THE WALLS HAVE EARS and THE ENEMY
IS EVERYWHERE. I can also recall my parents, uncles and aunts,
cracking peanuts on a Friday night and waiting for those two un-
equalled friends of the Jews, Roosevelt and Walter Winchell, to
come off it and get into the war. We admired the British, they
were gutsy, but we had more confidence in the United States
Marines. Educated by Hollywood, we could see the likes of John
Wayne, Gable, and Robert Taylor making minced meat out of
the Panzers, while Noel Coward, Laurence Olivier, and others,
seen in a spate of British war films, looked all too humanly vulnerable to us. Briefly, then, Pearl Harbour was a day of jubilation, but the war itself made for some confusions. In another
country, relatives recalled by my grandparents were being murdered. But on the street in our air cadet uniforms, we F.F.H.S.
boys were more interested in seeking out the fabulously wicked
V-girls ("They go the limit with guys in uniform, see.") we had
read about in the *Herald*. True, we made some sacrifices. American comic books were banned for the duration due, I think, to a
shortage of U.S. funds. So we had to put up a quarter on the black
market for copies of the *Batman* and *Tip-Top Comics*. But at the
same newsstand we bought a page on which four pigs had been
printed. When we folded the paper together, as directed, the four
pigs' behinds made up Hitler's hateful face. Outside Cooperman's
Superior Provisions, where if you were a regular customer you
could get sugar without ration coupons, we would chant "Black-
market Cooperman! Black-market Cooperman!" until the old man
came out, wielding his broom, and sent us flying down the street.

The war in Europe brought about considerable changes 31
within the Jewish community in Montreal. To begin with, there

was the coming of the refugees. These men, interned in England as enemy aliens and sent to Canada where they were eventually released, were to make a profound impact on us. I think we had conjured up a picture of the refugees as penurious *hassidim* with packs on their backs. We were eager to be helpful, our gestures were large, but in return we expected more than a little gratitude. As it turned out, the refugees, mostly German and Austrian Jews, were far more sophisticated and better educated than we were. They had not, like our immigrant grandparents, come from *shtetls* in Galicia or Russia. Neither did they despise Europe. On the contrary, they found our culture thin, the city provincial, and the Jews narrow. This bewildered and stung us. But what cut deepest, I suppose, was that the refugees spoke English better than many of us did and, among themselves, had the effrontery to talk in the abhorred German language. Many of them also made it clear that Canada was no more than a frozen place to stop over until a u.s. visa was forthcoming. So for a while we real Canadians were hostile.

For our grandparents who remembered those left behind in **32** Rumania and Poland the war was a time of unspeakable grief. Parents watched their sons grow up too quickly and stood by helplessly as the boys went off to the fighting one by one. They didn't have to go, either, for until the last days of the war Canadians could only be drafted for service within Canada. A boy had to volunteer before he could be sent overseas.

For those of my age the war was something else. I cannot **33** remember it as a black time, and I think it must be so for most boys of my generation. The truth is that for many of us to look back on the war is to recall the first time our fathers earned a good living. Even as the bombs fell and the ships went down, always elsewhere, our country was bursting out of a depression into a period of hitherto unknown prosperity. For my generation the war was hearing of death and sacrifice but seeing with our own eyes the departure from cold-water flats to apartments in Outremont, duplexes and split-levels in the suburbs. It was when we read of the uprising in the Warsaw ghetto and saw, in Montreal, the changeover from poky little *shuls* to big synagogue-cum-parochial schools with stained glass windows and mosaics outside. During the war some of us lost brothers and cousins but in

Canada we had never had it so good, and we began the run from rented summer shacks with outhouses in Shawbridge to Colonial-style summer houses of our own and speedboats on the lake in Ste. Agathe.

1969

The Death of the Moth
Virginia Woolf

Moths that fly by day are not properly to be called moths; they do not excite that pleasant sense of dark autumn nights and ivy-blossom which the commonest yellow-underwing asleep in the shadow of the curtain never fails to rouse in us. They are hybrid creatures, neither gay like butterflies nor sombre like their own species. Nevertheless the present specimen, with his narrow hay-coloured wings, fringed with a tassel of the same colour, seemed to be content with life. It was a pleasant morning, mid-September, mild, benignant, yet with a keener breath than that of the summer months. The plough was already scoring the field opposite the window, and where the share had been, the earth was pressed flat and gleamed with moisture. Such vigour came rolling in from the fields and the down beyond that it was difficult to keep the eyes strictly turned upon the book. The rooks too were keeping one of their annual festivities; soaring round the tree tops until it looked as if a vast net with thousands of black knots in it had been cast up into the air; which, after a few moments sank slowly down upon the trees until every twig seemed to have a knot at the end of it. Then, suddenly, the net would be thrown into the air again in a wider circle this time, with the utmost clamour and vociferation, as though to be thrown into the air and settle slowly down upon the tree tops were a tremendously exciting experience.

The same energy which inspired the rooks, the ploughmen,   2
the horses, and even, it seemed, the lean bare-backed downs,
sent the moth fluttering from side to side of his square of the
window-pane. One could not help watching him. One was, indeed, conscious of a queer feeling of pity for him. The possibilities of pleasure seemed that morning so enormous and so various that to have only a moth's part in life, and a day moth's at
that, appeared a hard fate, and his zest in enjoying his meagre
opportunities to the full, pathetic. He flew vigorously to one corner of his compartment, and, after waiting there a second, flew
across to the other. What remained for him but to fly to a third
corner and then to a fourth? That was all he could do, in spite of
the size of the downs, the width of the sky, the far-off smoke of
houses, and the romantic voice, now and then, of a steamer out
at sea. What he could do he did. Watching him, it seemed as if a
fibre, very thin but pure, of the enormous energy of the world
had been thrust into his frail and diminutive body. As often as he
crossed the pane, I could fancy that a thread of vital light became
visible. He was little or nothing but life.

Yet, because he was so small, and so simple a form of the   3
energy that was rolling in at the open window and driving its way
through so many narrow and intricate corridors in my own brain
and in those of other human beings, there was something mar-
vellous as well as pathetic about him. It was as if someone had
taken a tiny bead of pure life and decking it as lightly as possible
with down and feathers, had set it dancing and zig-zagging to
show us the true nature of life. Thus displayed one could not get
over the strangeness of it. One is apt to forget all about life, seeing it humped and bossed and garnished and cumbered so that it
has to move with the greatest circumspection and dignity. Again,
the thought of all that life might have been had he been born in
any other shape caused one to view his simple activities with a
kind of pity.

After a time, tired by his dancing apparently, he settled on   4
the window ledge in the sun, and, the queer spectacle being at an
end, I forgot about him. Then, looking up, my eye was caught by
him. He was trying to resume his dancing, but seemed either so
stiff or so awkward that he could only flutter to the bottom of the

windowpane; and when he tried to fly across it he failed. Being intent on other matters I watched these futile attempts for a time without thinking, unconsciously waiting for him to resume his flight, as one waits for a machine, that has stopped momentarily, to start again without considering the reason of its failure. After perhaps a seventh attempt he slipped from the wooden ledge and fell, fluttering his wings, on to his back on the window sill. The helplessness of his attitude roused me. It flashed upon me that he was in difficulties; he could no longer raise himself; his legs struggled vainly. But, as I stretched out a pencil, meaning to help him to right himself, it came over me that the failure and awkwardness were the approach of death. I laid the pencil down again.

The legs agitated themselves once more. I looked as if for the enemy against which he struggled. I looked out of doors. What had happened there? Presumably it was midday, and work in the fields had stopped. Stillness and quiet had replaced the previous animation. The birds had taken themselves off to feed in the brooks. The horses stood still. Yet the power was there all the same, massed outside, indifferent, impersonal, not attending to anything in particular. Somehow it was opposed to the little hay-coloured moth. It was useless to try to do anything. One could only watch the extraordinary efforts made by those tiny legs against an oncoming doom which could, had it chosen, have submerged an entire city, not merely a city, but masses of human beings; nothing, I knew, had any chance against death. Nevertheless after a pause of exhaustion the legs fluttered again. It was superb this last protest, and so frantic that he succeeded at last in righting himself. One's sympathies, of course, were all on the side of life. Also, when there was nobody to care or to know, this gigantic effort on the part of an insignificant little moth, against a power of such magnitude, to retain what no one else valued or desired to keep, moved one strangely. Again, somehow, one saw life, a pure bead. I lifted the pencil again, useless though I knew it to be. But even as I did so, the unmistakable tokens of death showed themselves. The body relaxed, and instantly grew stiff. The struggle was over. The insignificant little creature now knew death. As I looked at the dead moth, this minute wayside tri-

umph of so great a force over so mean an antagonist filled me
with wonder. Just as life had been strange a few minutes before,
so death was now as strange. The moth having righted himself
now lay most decently and uncomplainingly composed. O yes,
he seemed to say, death is stronger than I am.

1942

The Crime of the Tooth:
Dentistry in the Chair
Peter Freundlich

If you are anything like me (and you must pray, of course,   1
that you are not, and behave yourself besides, or your prayers
will be denied), you will have experienced this. Just before eye-
crack on a sunny day, warm light on the eyelids only, and already a trickle of pleasure, a soft worm in the ear, an electric tin-
gle to which—still asleep—your muscles react, tightening in
preparation for the flinging back of the covers and the springing
up from the bed.

And then, awesome quick change of weather, there is a   2
blackness across the sun and a dampness in the soul. You recol-
lect, at the very moment of the leap from bed, with feet high and
arms wide, that this is the day you go to the dentist.

How well, as Auden wrote, the Old Masters understood   3
suffering. How the calamity happens on a mild golden day, and
goes unseen by the happy and the hard at work. Auden was talking about the fall of Icarus, and so am I, for what else is the sudden recollection of an appointment with the dentist than a terrible chuteless fall from hopeful, sleepy midair, a melting—no, a
vaporizing—of the wax wings of dream and a blind drop to the
killing ground.

The truth on such a morning is that in half an hour you will   4 be laid out on a morgue slab rigged to look like a reclining chair, with Dr. Kaliper's masked face filling your entire sky, and all eight of his hands at play in your mouth.

The knowledge that you are going to the dentist changes everything. Where a minute ago the sunlight seemed marmalade, richly spread across your window, now it is a mockery. It does not beckon, it jeers.

You would have jumped into your clothes before, all eager cinchings and zippings and knottings. Now you drag your leggings on, shrug mournfully into your shirt, fuss thick-fingered with every button. Your face in the mirror is smudged with worry.

It is not the local pain that causes dread, but the *greater* pain: the loss of speech, the pinioning, the drool tides coming in and washing out, the marooning of the brain. For two hours, the brain is Robinson Crusoe alone in the bone cup of the skull, peering out at faraway chrome implements and rubber-sheathed fingers and cotton cylinders red with blood, peering out but forbidden to signal for help.

Pushing open the lobby door, you descend three marble steps into the anteroom of the underworld. In place of Charon, there is only a buzzer to conduct you across this Styx; you are vacuumed into the starched white smile of the receptionist and, behind her, the starched white smile of the hygienist and, behind her, the green-tunic smile of Kaliper himself.

There is perfunctory talk. How are you today? You are fine. (Or would be, if not here.) And how is the practitioner this morning? He too is fine.

Meanwhile you have been settling yourself into Kaliper's astronaut's couch, in preparation for the launching.

Of course, he would not have you go uninformed into that good night. He explains at length his objectives and methods while showing you what looks to be the seating plan of a Greek amphitheater, two opposed semicircles with many Xs along the perimeters. These do not mark reserved seats but the sites of work to be done.

Kaliper continues to hold forth on such matters as roots and canals and crowns and tiaras and diadems. You pretend to follow it all, but in fact have already turned your attention in-

ward, into your mouth, which is independently alive: All the little underskin creatures—the stalks and cones and antlered antennae—are nervously atwit, snuffling, shuffling, pawing, like forest
animals before a storm.

You have had the X-rays already. The lead blanket was laid 13
on your chest and you were told to be still while that timid
funnel-beaked behemoth with its triple-jointed metal neck poked
its snout against your face. Though eyeless, the creature still
managed an audible wink wherever it stopped tenderly to nuzzle.
All that by which you are everywhere known to be you and not
someone else—your entire exterior, your features, hair color,
eye color, skin color, marks commemorating your birth and
childhood diseases—the funnel-beaked thing sees not at all. It is
blind except to your insides.

Now Dr. Kaliper stands by the X-ray lightbox and points to 14
the snapshots: a valley to be filled, a ridge to be rounded off, a
cave in which something rotten lurks. Kaliper will turn spe-
lunker, go into the cave and yank out the rot. You continue to
nod sagely; the underskin animals are braying wildly now.

He asks, rhetorically, if you are ready. Then, pressing a 15
button that makes the machinery of the chair moan, he causes
your head to be lowered. You turn pink as blood sloshes down
from your feet and legs.

They must be taught in school not to let their patients see 16
the needles and the instruments coming. Kaliper manages the
sleight of hand nicely. His forearm grazing your nose, he takes
the novocaine-filled syringe from the hygienist. Then he brings
the thing down along your jawline, too low for your radar to pick
up. Finally, he has it under your chin, then up, aimed, and ready.
It is now too close for you to focus on; you have only an impression—an orange cylinder and a glint.

Hold on just a bit, he says, *you're going to feel this.*   17

There is a small intrusion into your gum, a cold, sharp 18
pinch, as if a steel no-see-um had landed there. Then the midge
grows suddenly much heavier, sinking in. It is Kaliper, of
course, his arm behind the work now.

Okay, we'll give that a minute or two to numb you up.   19

It seems that your upper lip is growing not numb but fat and 20 thick, as if swollen with liquid. It is now out beyond the tip of your nose, billowing in a spinnaker curve until finally it is so big and heavy that it hangs down even over your lower lip.

Starting to work?   21

You mutter as much of a *yeah* as you can with your lower 22 lip alone, the upper answering to no authority now.

Kaliper is ready to begin.   23

And your brain, crazy Crusoe, settles in a hunker on a bone 24 ridge.

This, unless you ask for fumes, is one of the few things in 25 life from which you cannot turn away. It is an event that happens *on* you, *in* you: a subcutaneous circus, a riot under your nose.

And only your brain, that ball bearing in its bone cup, only 26 your brain is free. Under any other circumstances, you would flee before these chrome threats. All your greater muscles would clench and work—legs wildly pumping, arms wildly swinging— and you'd be gone in a flash from a masked mugger like Kaliper. But now all your retreats must be microscopic, tics and twitches and tremors only. All you can do, on a large scale, is think.

And you do. What *don't* you think?   27

This is what a road would feel, if it were sentient, when the 28 yellow trucks of early spring bring burly armed men and pots of tar to repair frost heaves. Just so, you are being worked on: jack-hammered, steam-chiseled, bulldozed.

You yourself, having become a structure, are sentient in a 29 different way now. You feel a pounding in your joists, as if the dentist were a carpenter working in your attic. The thudding he causes with his little mallets and mauls is conducted down through your studs, raising a pulse to rival the heart's.

Why was Shakespeare silent on this subject? Hath not a 30 Jew teeth? Does he not cry out to high heaven when, molar-pierced, he feels the iron worm in the velvet hand, and hears the keening of his own resisting bone?

There are no dentists in nature. Animals doctor themselves 31 and each other, probing and licking and tamping on wounds mud- and spittle-bound grass. But no animal puts on rubber gloves and...

Wider. Open wider.   32

Wider? The corners of your mouth have already met at the   33
back of your head, and Dr. Kaliper blandly asks for easier access. To what?

How fine to feel your bronchioles warmed by his lamp, and   34
the fresh breeze from his nostrils rippling your intestines.

Turn toward me.   35

Only lovemaking happens at this range: Arm's length is   36
otherwise the closest we come, but this is finger's length, and finger's width, and less.

What confidence these men must have, to work so very   37
close to hostile observers, offering themselves for microscopic
inspection, aware as they must be that their every pore looks like
a dreadful hole from this vantage point. Look: the tapioca surface of the skin, the thick upstanding face-hair bristles grown out
from that cheesy plain like cacti, like the legs of half-buried scorpions struggling to right themselves.

But then this is the scale at which they work (and tit for tat):   38
they, nose up against your breath, digging with microshovels in the
topsoil of your tooth-rot, and you, threatened by their follicles.

Our mouths should be full of horn, sharp wedges of antler   39
or tortoise shell, grinders that grow like fingernails trimmed
weekly to a new, fresh edge.

There is music playing, yes. *Music:* old tunes made tooth-   40
less by accordions and violas and clarinets. Soothing music, Kaliper must think it is. But it is not music enough to catch the ear,
or really to engage the brain. It is just a mask for the drill sounds,
and ineffective even at that. The drill plays an octave higher than
any instrument on the radio.

The body rejects foreign objects and Kaliper is most for-   41
eign. You gag and guff and hack, your throat-flap lashed by drill-
storm, a minuscule typhoon of spray.

You have down your gullet already air-jets and water-jets   42
and a teeny goddamn bilge pump on a metal hook. Now comes a
vacuum cleaner on a stick put in your mouth to slurp up more of
your juices.

Hold on now. Be still a moment.   43

You would laugh sardonically, if you could. Snake-fingered   44
Gorgon Kaliper, who has long since turned you to stone, now
commands stillness.

Through your mouth he is drilling holes in your wallet. 45

Last night, you remember now, you had a dream. You were 46
eating money. Your own money, green and fibrous, vegetal.
Next to you was an insurance-looking man. He threw coins into
your mouth, a nickel for every dollar of your own. Looking up
beyond him, you saw a vast herd of big-eyed dentists, all of them
placidly grazing in a field of rippling sawbucks.

What is the prayer for surcease from dentistry? 47

You remember your daughter's first tooth, and the joy: she 48
in that scootling thing she had, a sling seat hung in a wheeled
metal frame with a foremounted tray, and one day in the wide
smile, a glint of white in the upper pink ridge. A toof! A toof!
Lookit, lookit, clap clap clap. The sight made you break into ecstatic Eddie Cantorish dumbshow, palms pushed repeatedly flat
together, fingers straight up, just below the chin. A toof, a toof,
welcome to toddler's estate.

And welcome to all this. 49

Dentists are our alchemists, transmuting rot into gold. 50

There was an Ancient Dentist, and he drilleth one of three. 51
Then he drilleth the other two. Then he billeth.

There is no fetish involving teeth. Men secretly adore feet 52
and buttocks and thighs and axillae. But Krafft-Ebing never
lapsed into Latin over teeth. Some aborigines wear teeth around
their necks: they ought to wear dentists—little shriveled sun-
dried dentists.

It is high tide in your mouth now. Your nose is Cape Horn, 53
and, God help you, Kaliper means to round it, to point his
chrome prow toward the rocky promontories of your teeth, to
find safe passage between them. He means to land somewhere
under your uvula.

Peace, peace. You are here for a reason and you must hug 54
close the promise, which is that you will have a smile of tourist-
attraction quality, a smile of such perfection and brilliance that
omnibuses bursting with camera-strewn pilgrims will pull up at
your door, Japanese, Germans, Italians, all with their heads
cocked attentively toward their bull-horned tour-guides who, in
their respective languages, will tell the tale of your teeth, will put
your teeth in their proper dento-historical contexts, who will
make plain to the milling bell-shaped women and the big-nosed

men that, in your mouth, they will be seeing the dental Sistine
ceiling, the periodontal Pietà, the bridgework winged Victory of
Samothrace.

You will feel the long lenses and the moist eyes trained 55
upon you, and you will favor the pilgrims with a glimpse of the
fabled teeth. But slowly, gradually, so as not literally to knock
them arse over teakettle with the splendor of the sight. You will
be impoverished, yes, but with God's own smile.

The Brits will not come, of course, they of the gnarled yel- 56
low choppers, overlapped, jagged. A people of deplorable dental
cavalierness, the Brits would rather invest their money in Savile
Row tailoring and Harley Street doctoring and Bentley motor
cars and manor houses. A fine thing. The thirtieth Duke approaches, tall, fair-skinned, as richly veined about the nose and
cheeks as Stilton cheese, in balmoral and balmacaan, walking
stick at the ready; says hello and, beneath the grenadier's mustache, shows chiaroscuro smile, some teeth long and tending toward the spiral, some squat and striated, as rune-covered as river
rocks. Of course he has money, having forsworn dentistry.

Why exactly does Kaliper wear a mask? Is it to hide his 57
own teeth? Do they become, when he's working, black and
pointed or blood-red and outward-curled, like the tips of Turkish
slippers?

Kaliper is hot with enthusiasm now. His hands fly about the 58
tray held by his mechanical butler, selecting picks and spears. Inside your mouth, your pulse must be visible again, a growing and
shrinking of the veins. Kaliper construes this, you suppose, as a
readiness to reach a dental climax, in tandem with him.

Nearly there, he says, *nearly there.*   59

How do they endure this, the famous? They must endure it 60
with great regularity, for, as is well known, the teeth of the famous are not teeth at all. They are wonderful facsimiles, made by
master technicians and implanted by master dentists. If Mich-
elangelo were alive today, he'd be carving teeth in Hollywood.

The drill sounds like a winch now, makes the sound the 61
winch makes when, the mourners having turned to go, the coffin
begins to be lowered. You feel pain, not in your teeth, but every-

where else—the small of your back, your legs, your neck, your shoulders, and especially your face because you've been holding your mouth scream-wide for so long.

Or you *were* holding your mouth open. Now it is stuffed, 62 overstuffed, filled to cracking, with egg-beaters and chrome tricycles and socket wrenches and antique wristwatches, small prams, suits of armor, coffee-makers.

You think you feel the lower end of a ramp being placed on 63 your tongue, and you think you hear, from a distance, the sound of a motor being cranked. Kaliper must be mounting an expedition into your interior, with fresh supplies loaded aboard a Land-Rover.

You gurgle. 64

You alright? Kaliper asks. 65

You gurgle again. 66

Good, he says. 67

Kaliper is maneuvering into position, for a trial fitting, the 68 crown he has had made. It is a bit of porcelain-covered metal, very like a tooth. But it is not a tooth, and your flesh knows it.

You are given a mirror to see what Kaliper has wrought. 69 And of course your eyes, stupid gelatinous organs, are fooled.

Looks good, you mumble. 70

And you mean it: the simulacrum *does* look good. But your 71 tongue worries the thing, frets and pushes at it as would an animal at something dead. Your gum, the flesh most directly intruded upon, pulses, is offended. And there is an undulation in your cheek, a threadwide, millimeters-long surf—your cheek is offended on behalf of your gum.

Kaliper has emptied your mouth of his gear. His work now, 72 a tightly controlled scratching, has an air of finality. You think he may be etching his name on the permanently installed crown. You will have *Kaliper fecit* inscribed on the dark side of the not-tooth, a joke to be appreciated someday by the coroner.

All done, he says. 73

And his assistant swings away an arm of the chair on which 74 you have been marooned, so that you may stand.

Which you do, crowned now, and dizzy. 75

1987

My Father
Doris Lessing

We use our parents like recurring dreams, to be entered   1
into when needed; they are always there for love or for hate; but
it occurs to me that I was not always there for my father. I've
written about him before, but novels, stories, don't have to be
"true." Writing this article is difficult because it has to be
"true." I knew him when his best years were over.

There are photographs of him. The largest is of an officer in   2
the 1914–18 war. A new uniform—buttoned, badged, strapped,
tabbed—confines a handsome, dark young man who holds himself stiffly to confront what he certainly thought of as his duty.
His eyes are steady, serious, and responsible, and show no signs
of what he became later. A photograph at sixteen is of a dark,
introspective youth with the same intent eyes. But it is his mouth
you notice—a heavily-jutting upper lip contradicts the rest of a
regular face. His moustache was to hide it: "Had to do something—a damned fleshy mouth. Always made me uncomfortable,
that mouth of mine."

Earlier a baby (eyes already alert) appears in a lace water-   3
fall that cascades from the pillowy bosom of a fat, plain woman
to her feet. It is the face of a head cook. "Lord, but my mother
was a practical female—almost as bad as you!" as he used to
say, or throw at my mother in moments of exasperation. Beside
her stands, or droops, arms dangling, his father, the source of the
dark, arresting eyes, but otherwise masked by a long beard.

The birth certificate says: Born 3rd August, 1886, Walton   4
Villa, Creffield Road, S. Mary at the Wall, R.S.D. Name, Alfred
Cook. Name and surname of Father: Alfred Cook Tayler. Name
and maiden name of Mother: Caroline May Batley. Rank or Profession: Bank Clerk. Colchester, Essex.

They were very poor. Clothes and boots were a problem.   5
They "made their own amusements." Books were mostly the Bible and *The Pilgrim's Progress*. Every Saturday night they
bathed in a hipbath in front of the kitchen fire. No servants.

Church three times on Sundays. "Lord, when I think of those Sundays! I dreaded them all week, like a nightmare coming at you full tilt and no escape." But he rabbited with ferrets along the lanes and fields, bird-nested, stole fruit, picked nuts and mushrooms, paid visits to the blacksmith and the mill and rode a farmer's carthorse.

They ate economically, but when he got diabetes in his for- 6
ties and subsisted on lean meat and lettuce leaves, he remembered suet puddings, treacle puddings, raisin and currant puddings, steak and kidney puddings, bread and butter pudding,
"batter cooked in the gravy with the meat," potato cake, plum
cake, butter cake, porridge with treacle, fruit tarts and pies,
brawn, pig's trotters and pig's cheek and home-smoked ham and
sausages. And "lashings of fresh butter and cream and eggs."
He wondered if this diet had produced the diabetes, but said it
was worth it.

There was an elder brother described by my father as: 7
"Too damned clever by half. One of those quick, clever brains.
Now I've always had a slow brain, but I get there in the end,
damn it!"

The brothers went to a local school and the elder did well, 8
but my father was beaten for being slow. They both became bank
clerks in, I think, the Westminster Bank, and one must have
found it congenial, for he became a manager, the "rich brother,"
who had cars and even a yacht. But my father did not like it,
though he was conscientious. For instance, he changed his writing, letter by letter, because a senior criticised it. I never saw his
unregenerate hand, but the one he created was elegant, spiky,
careful. Did this mean he created a new personality for himself,
hiding one he did not like, as he hid his "damned fleshy mouth"?
I don't know.

Nor do I know when he left home to live in Luton, or why. 9
He found family life too narrow? A safe guess—he found everything too narrow. His mother was too down-to-earth? He had to
get away from his clever elder brother?

Being a young man in Luton was the best part of his life. It 10
ended in 1914, so he had a decade of happiness. His reminis-
cences of it were all of pleasure, the delight of physical move-

ment, of dancing in particular. All his girls were "a beautiful dancer, light as a feather." He played billiards and ping-pong (both for his country); he swam, boated, played cricket and football, went to picnics and horse races, sang at musical evenings. One family of a mother and two daughters treated him "like a son only better. I didn't know whether I was in love with the mother or the daughters, but oh I did love going there; we had such good times." He was engaged to one daughter, then, for a time, to the other. An engagement was broken off because she was rude to a waiter. "I could not marry a woman who allowed herself to insult someone who was defenceless." He used to say to my wryly smiling mother: "Just as well I didn't marry either of *them;* they would never have stuck it out the way you have, old girl."

Just before he died he told me he had dreamed he was 11 standing in a kitchen on a very high mountain holding X in his arms. "Ah, yes, that's what I've missed in my life. Now don't you let yourself be cheated out of life by the old dears. They take all the colour out of everything if you let them."

But in that decade—"I'd walk 10, 15 miles to a dance two 12 or three times a week and think nothing of it. Then I'd dance every dance and walk home again over the fields. Sometimes it was moonlight, but I liked the snow best all crisp and fresh. I loved walking back and getting into my digs just as the sun was rising. My little dog was so happy to see me, and I'd feed her, and make myself porridge and tea, then I'd wash and shave and go off to work."

The boy who was beaten at school, who went too much to 13 church, who carried the fear of poverty all his life, but who nevertheless was filled with the memories of country pleasures; the young bank clerk who worked such long hours for so little money, but who danced, sang, played, flirted—this naturally vigorous, sensuous being was killed in 1914, 1915, 1916. I think the best of my father died in that war, that his spirit was crippled by it. The people I've met, particularly the women, who knew him young, speak of his high spirits, his energy, his enjoyment of life. Also of his kindness, his compassion and—a word that keeps recurring—his wisdom. "Even when he was just a boy he understood things that you'd think even an old man would find it easy to condemn." I do not think these people would have easily recognised the ill, irritable, abstracted, hypochondriac man I knew.

He "joined up" as an ordinary soldier out of a characteristically quirky scruple: it wasn't right to enjoy officers' privileges when the Tommies had such a bad time. But he could not stick the communal latrines, the obligatory drinking, the collective visits to brothels, the jokes about girls. So next time he was offered a commission he took it.   **14**

His childhood and young man's memories, kept fluid, were added to, grew, as living memories do. But his war memories were congealed in stories that he told again and again, with the same words and gestures, in stereotyped phrases. They were anonymous, general, as if they had come out of a communal war memoir. He met a German in no-man's-land, but both slowly lowered their rifles and smiled and walked away. The Tommies were the salt of the earth, the British fighting men the best in the world. He had never known such comradeship. A certain brutal officer was shot in a sortie by his men, but the other officers, recognising rough justice, said nothing. He had known men intimately who saw the Angels at Mons. He wished he could force all the generals on both sides into the trenches for just one day, to see what the common soldiers endured—*that* would have ended the war at once.   **15**

There was an undercurrent of memories, dreams, and emotions much deeper, more personal. This dark region in him, fate-ruled, where nothing was true but horror, was expressed inarticulately, in brief, bitter exclamations or phrases of rage, incredulity, betrayal. The men who went to fight in that war believed it when they said it was to end war. My father believed it. And he was never able to reconcile his belief in his country with his anger at the cynicism of its leaders. And the anger, the sense of betrayal, strengthened as he grew old and ill.   **16**

But in 1914 he was naïve, the German atrocities in Belgium inflamed him, and he enlisted out of idealism, although he knew he would have a hard time. He knew because a fortuneteller told him. (He could be described as uncritically superstitious or as psychically gifted.) He would be in great danger twice, yet not   **17**

die—he was being protected by a famous soldier who was his ancestor. "And sure enough, later I heard from the Little Aunties
that the church records showed we were descended the back-
stairs way from the Duke of Wellington, or was it Marlborough?
Damn it, I forget. But one of them would be beside me all
through the war, she said." (He was romantic, not only about
this solicitous ghost, but also about being a descendant of the
Huguenots, on the strength of the "e" in Tayler; and about "the
wild blood" in his veins from a great uncle who, sent unjustly to
prison for smuggling, came out of a ten-year sentence and earned
it, very efficiently, along the coasts of Cornwall until he died.)

The luckiest thing that ever happened to my father, he said,   18
was getting his leg shattered by shrapnel ten days before Passchendaele. His whole company was killed. He knew he was going to be wounded because of the fortuneteller, who had said he
would know. "I did not understand what she meant, but both
times in the trenches, first when my appendix burst and I nearly
died, and then just before Passchendaele, I felt for some days as
if a thick, black velvet pall was settled over me. I can't tell you
what it was like. Oh, it was awful, awful, and the second time it
was so bad I wrote to the old people and told them I was going to
be killed."

His leg was cut off at mid-thigh, he was shell-shocked, he   19
was very ill for many months, with a prolonged depression afterwards. "You should always remember that sometimes people
are all seething underneath. You don't know what terrible things
people have to fight against. You should look at a person's eyes,
that's how you tell.... When I was like that, after I lost my leg, I
went to a nice doctor man and said I was going mad, but he said,
don't worry, everyone locks up things like that. You don't
know—horrible, horrible, awful things. I was afraid of myself, of
what I used to dream. I wasn't myself at all."

In the Royal Free Hospital was my mother, Sister   20
McVeagh. He married his nurse which, as they both said often
enough (though in different tones of voice), was just as well. That
was 1919. He could not face being a bank clerk in England, he
said, not after the trenches. Besides, England was too narrow
and conventional. Besides, the civilians did not know what the

soldiers had suffered, they didn't want to know, and now it wasn't done even to remember "The Great Unmentionable." He went off to the Imperial Bank of Persia, in which country I was born.

The house was beautiful, with great stone-floored high- 21 ceilinged rooms whose windows showed ranges of snow-streaked mountains. The gardens were full of roses, jasmine, pomegranates, walnuts. Kermanshah he spoke of with liking, but soon they went to Teheran, populous with "Embassy people," and my gregarious mother created a lively social life about which he was irritable even in recollection.

Irritableness—that note was first struck here, about Persia. 22 He did not like, he said, "the graft and the corruption." But here it is time to try and describe something difficult—how a man's good qualities can also be his bad ones, or if not bad, a danger to him.

My father was honourable—he always knew exactly what 23 that word meant. He had integrity. His "one does not do that sort of thing," his "no, it is *not* right," sounded throughout my childhood and were final for all of us. I am sure it was true he wanted to leave Persia because of "the corruption." But it was also because he was already unconsciously longing for something freer, because as a bank official he could not let go into the dream-logged personality that was waiting for him. And later in Rhodesia, too, what was best in him was also what prevented him from shaking away the shadows: it was always in the name of honesty or decency that he refused to take this step or that out of the slow decay of the family's fortunes.

In 1925 there was leave from Persia. That year in London 24 there was an Empire Exhibition, and on the Southern Rhodesian stand some very fine maize cobs and a poster saying that for-tunes could be made on maize at 25/- a bag. So on an impulse, turning his back forever on England, washing his hands of the corruption of the East, my father collected all his capital, £800, I think, while my mother packed curtains from Liberty's, clothes from Harrods, visiting cards, a piano, Persian rugs, a governess and two small children.

Soon, there was my father in a cigar-shaped house of thatch 25 and mud on the top of a kopje that overlooked in all directions a great system of mountains, rivers, valleys, while overhead the sky arched from horizon to empty horizon. This was a couple of hundred miles south from the Zambesi, a hundred or so west from Mozambique, in the district of Banket, so called because certain of its reefs were of the same formation as those called *banket* on the Rand. Lomagundi—gold country, tobacco country, maize country—wild, almost empty. (The Africans had been turned off it into reserves.) Our neighbours were four, five, seven miles off. In front of the house...no neighbours, nothing; no farms, just wild bush with two rivers but no fences to the mountains seven miles away. And beyond these mountains and bush again to the Portuguese border, over which "our boys" used to escape when wanted by the police for pass or other offences.

And then? There was bad luck. For instance, the price of   26 maize dropped from 25/- to 9/- a bag. The seasons were bad, prices bad, crops failed. This was the sort of thing that made it impossible for him ever to "get off the farm," which, he agreed with my mother, was what he most wanted to do.

It was an absurd country, he said. A man could "own" a   27 farm for years that was totally mortgaged to the Government and run from the Land Bank, meanwhile employing half-a-hundred Africans at 12/- a month and none of them knew how to do a day's work. Why, two farm labourers from Europe could do in a day what twenty of these ignorant black savages would take a week to do. (Yet he was proud that he had a name as a just employer, that he gave "a square deal.") Things got worse. A fortuneteller had told him that her heart ached when she saw the misery ahead for my father: this was the misery.

But it was my mother who suffered. After a period of neu-   28 rotic illness, which was a protest against her situation, she became brave and resourceful. But she never saw that her husband was not living in a real world, that he had made a captive of her common sense. We were always about to "get off the farm." A miracle would do it—a sweepstake, a goldmine, a legacy. And then? What a question! We would go to England where life would be normal with people coming in for musical evenings and nice supper parties at the Trocadero after a show. Poor woman, for the twenty years we were on the farm, she waited for when life would begin for her and for her children, for she never understood that what was a calamity for her was for them a blessing.

Meanwhile my father sank towards his death (at 61). Every- 29 thing changed in him. He had been a dandy and fastidious, now he hated to change out of shabby khaki. He had been sociable, now he was misanthropic. His body's disorders—soon diabetes and all kinds of stomach ailments—dominated him. He was brave about his wooden leg, and even went down mine shafts and climbed trees with it, but he walked clumsily and it irked him badly. He greyed fast, and slept more in the day, but would be awake half the night pondering about....

It could be gold divining. For ten years he experimented on 30 private theories to do with the attractions and repulsions of met- als. His whole soul went into it but his theories were wrong or he was *unlucky*—after all, if he had found a mine he would have had to leave the farm. It could be the relation between the minerals of the earth and of the moon; his decision to make infusions of all the plants on the farm and drink them himself in the interests of science; the criminal folly of the British Government in not re- alising that the Germans and the Russians were conspiring as Anti-Christ to...the inevitability of war because no one would listen to Churchill, but it would be all right because God (by then he was a British Israelite) had destined Britain to rule the world; a prophecy said 10 million dead would surround Jerusalem—how would the corpses be cleared away?; people who wished to abol- ish flogging should be flogged; the natives understood nothing but a good beating; hanging must not be abolished because the Old Testament said "an eye for an eye and a tooth for a tooth...."

Yet, as this side of him darkened, so that it seemed all his 31 thoughts were of violence, illness, war, still no one dared to make an unkind comment in his presence or to gossip. Criticism of people, particularly of women, made him more and more un- comfortable till at last he burst out with: "It's all very well, but no one has the right to say that about another person."

In Africa, when the sun goes down, the stars spring up, all 32 of them in their expected places, glittering and moving. In the rainy season, the sky flashed and thundered. In the dry season, the great dark hollow of night was lit by veld fires: the mountains burned through September and October in chains of red fire. Every night my father took out his chair to watch the sky and the mountains, smoking, silent, a thin shabby fly-away figure under the stars. "Makes you think—there are so many worlds up there, wouldn't really matter if we did blow ourselves up—plenty more where we came from."

The Second World War, so long foreseen by him, was a bad 33 time. His son was in the Navy and in danger, and his daughter a sorrow to him. He became very ill. More and more often it was necessary to drive him into Salisbury with him in a coma, or in danger of one, on the back seat. My mother moved him into a pretty little suburban house in town near the hospitals, where he took to his bed and a couple of years later died. For the most part he was unconscious under drugs. When awake he talked obsessively (a tongue licking a nagging sore place) about "the old war." Or he remembered his youth. "I've been dreaming— Lord, to see those horses come lickety-split down the course with their necks stretched out and the sun on their coats and everyone shouting....I've been dreaming how I walked along the river in the mist as the sun was rising....Lord, lord, lord, what a time that was, what good times we all had then, before the old war."

1956

3

Process

Attaining Moral Virtue
Benjamin Franklin

It was about this time I conceived the bold and arduous 1
project of arriving at moral perfection. I wished to live without
committing any fault any time; I would conquer all that either
natural inclination, custom, or company might lead me into. As I
knew, or thought I knew, what was right and wrong, I did not see
why I might not always do the one and avoid the other. But I
soon found I had undertaken a task of more difficulty than I had
imagined. While my care was employed in guarding against one
fault, I was often surprised by another; habit took the advantage
of inattention; inclination was sometimes too strong for reason. I
concluded at length, that the mere speculative conviction that it
was our interest to be completely virtuous was not sufficient to
prevent our slipping; and that the contrary habits must be broken, and good ones acquired and established, before we can have
any dependence on a steady, uniform rectitude of conduct. For
this purpose I therefore contrived the following method.

In the various enumerations of the moral virtues I had met 2
with in my reading, I found the catalogue more or less numerous,
as different writers included more or fewer ideas under the same
name. Temperance, for example, was by some confined to eating

and drinking, while by others it was extended to mean the moderating every other pleasure, appetite, inclination, or passion, bodily or mental, even to our avarice and ambition. I proposed to myself, for the sake of clearness, to use rather more names, with fewer ideas annexed to each, than a few names with more ideas; and I included under thirteen names of virtues all that at that time occurred to me as necessary or desirable, and annexed to each a short precept, which fully expressed the extent I gave to its meaning.

These names of virtues, with their precepts, were: 3

1. TEMPERANCE. Eat not to dullness; drink not to elevation.
2. SILENCE. Speak not but what may benefit others or yourself; avoid trifling conversation.
3. ORDER. Let all your things have their places; let each part of your business have its time.
4. RESOLUTION. Resolve to perform what you ought; perform without fail what you resolve.
5. FRUGALITY. Make no expense but to do good to others or yourself; *i.e.*, waste nothing.
6. INDUSTRY. Lose no time; be always employed in something useful; cut off all unnecessary actions.
7. SINCERITY. Use no hurtful deceit; think innocently and justly, and, if you speak, speak accordingly.
8. JUSTICE. Wrong none by doing injuries, or omitting the benefits that are your duty.
9. MODERATION. Avoid extremes; forbear resenting injuries so much as you think they deserve.
10. CLEANLINESS. Tolerate no uncleanliness in body, clothes, or habitation.
11. TRANQUILITY. Be not disturbed at trifles, or at accidents common or unavoidable.
12. CHASTITY. Rarely use venery but for health or offspring, never to dullness, weakness, or the injury of your own or another's peace or reputation.
13. HUMILITY. Imitate Jesus and Socrates.

My intention being to acquire the *habitude* of all these virtues, I judged it would be well not to distract my attention by attempting the whole at once, but to fix it on one of them at a time; and, when I should be master of that, then to proceed to another, and so on, till I should have gone through the thirteen;   4 and, as the previous acquisition of some might facilitate the acquisition of certain others, I arranged them with that view, as they stand above. *Temperance* first, as it tends to procure that coolness and clearness of head, which is so necessary where constant vigilance was to be kept up, and guard maintained against the unremitting attraction of ancient habits, and the force of perpetual temptations. This being acquired and established, *Silence* would be more easy; and my desire being to gain knowledge at the same time that I improved in virtue, and considering that in conversation it was obtained rather by the use of the ears than of the tongue, and therefore wishing to break a habit I was getting into of prattling, punning, and joking, which only made me acceptable to trifling company, I gave *Silence* the second place. This and the next, *Order,* I expected would allow me more time for attending to my project and my studies. *Resolution,* once become habitual, would keep me firm in my endeavors to obtain all the subsequent virtues; *Frugality* and *Industry* freeing me from my remaining debt, and producing affluence and independence, would make more easy the practice of *Sincerity and Justice,* etc., etc. Conceiving then, that, agreeably to the advice of Pythagoras in his Golden Verses, daily examination would be necessary, I contrived the following method for conducting that examination.

The precept of *Order* requiring that *every part of my business should have its allotted time,* one page in my little book contained the following scheme of employment for the twenty-four hours of a natural day.

THE MORNING
Question. What good shall
I do this day?

| 5 | Rise, wash and address *Powerful Goodness!* Contrive day's business, and take the resolution of the day; prosecute the present study, and breakfast. |
| 6 |
| 7 |

| 8 | Work. |
| 9 |
| 10 |
| 11 |

NOON	12	Read, or overlook my accounts, and dine.
	1	
	2	
	3	Work.
	4	
	5	
	6	Put things in their places.
Question. What good have I done to-day?	7	Supper. Music or diversion,
	8	or conversation. Examination of the day.
	9	
	10	
	11	
	12	
NIGHT	1	Sleep.
	2	
	3	
	4	

My list of virtues contained at first but twelve; but a 6 Quaker friend having kindly informed me that I was generally thought proud; that my pride showed itself frequently in conversation; that I was not content with being in the right when discussing any point, but was overbearing, and rather insolent, of which he convinced me by mentioning several instances; I determined endeavoring to cure myself, if I could, of this vice or folly among the rest, and I added *Humility* to my list, giving an extensive meaning to the word.

I cannot boast of much success in acquiring the *reality* of 7 this virtue, but I had a good deal with regard to the *appearance* of it.

1784

The Spider and the Wasp
Alexander Petrunkevitch

To hold its own in the struggle for existence, every species 1
of animal must have a regular source of food, and if it happens to
live on other animals, its survival may be very delicately balanced. The hunter cannot exist without the hunted; if the latter
should perish from the earth, the former would, too. When the
hunted also prey on some of the hunters, the matter may become
complicated.

This is nowhere better illustrated than in the insect world. 2
Think of the complexity of a situation such as the following:
There is a certain wasp, *Pimpla inquisitor,* whose larvae feed on
several years in succession. In a Paris museum is a tropical specimen which is said to have been living in captivity for 25 years.

A fertilized female tarantula lays from 200 to 400 eggs at a 3
time; thus it is possible for a single tarantula to produce several
thousand young. She takes no care of them beyond weaving a
cocoon of silk to enclose the eggs. After they hatch, the young
walk away, find convenient places in which to dig their burrows
and spend the rest of their lives in solitude. Tarantulas feed
mostly on insects and millipedes. Once their appetite is ap-
peased, they digest the food for several days before eating again.
Their sight is poor, being limited to sensing a change in the intensity of light and to the perception of moving objects. They apparently have little or no sense of hearing, for a hungry tarantula
will pay no attention to a loudly chirping cricket placed in its
cage unless the insect happens to touch one of its legs.

But all spiders, and especially hairy ones, have an ex- 4
tremely delicate sense of touch. Laboratory experiments prove
that tarantulas can distinguish three types of touch: pressure
against the body wall, stroking of the body hair, and riffling of
certain very fine hairs on the legs called trichobothria. Pressure
against the body, by a finger or the end of a pencil, causes the
tarantula to move off slowly for a short distance. The touch ex-
cites no defensive response unless the approach is from above,
where the spider can see the motion, in which case it rises on its

hind legs, lifts its front legs, opens its fangs and holds this threatening posture as long as the object continues to move. When the
motion stops, the spider drops back to the ground, remains quiet
for a few seconds, and then moves slowly away.

The entire body of a tarantula, especially its legs, is thickly   5
clothed with hair. Some of it is short and woolly, some long and
stiff. Touching this body hair produces one of two distinct reactions. When the spider is hungry, it responds with an immediate
and swift attack. At the touch of a cricket's antennae the tarantula seizes the insect so swiftly that a motion picture taken at the
rate of 64 frames per second shows only the result not the process of capture. But when the spider is not hungry, the stimulation of its hair merely causes it to shake the touched limb. An
insect can walk under its hairy belly unharmed.

The trichobothria, very fine hairs growing from disklike   6
membranes of the legs, were once thought to be the spider's
hearing organs, but we now know that they have nothing to do
with sound. They are sensitive only to air movement. A light
breeze makes them vibrate slowly without disturbing the common hair. When one blows gently on the trichobothria, the tarantula reacts with a quick jerk of its four front legs. If the front and
hind legs are stimulated at the same time, the spider makes a sudden jump. This reaction is quite independent of the state of its
appetite.

These three tactile responses—to pressure on the body   7
wall, to moving of the common hair, and to flexing of the trichobothria—are so different from one another that there is no possibility of confusing them. They serve the tarantula adequately
for most of its needs and enable it to avoid most annoyances and
dangers. But they fail the spider completely when it meets its
deadly enemy, the digger wasp *Pepsis*.

These solitary wasps are beautiful and formidable crea-   8
tures. Most species are either a deep shiny blue all over, or deep
blue with rusty wings. The largest have a wing span of about four
inches. They live on nectar. When excited, they give off a pun-
gent odor—a warning that they are ready to attack. The sting is
much worse than that of a bee or common wasp, and the pain
and swelling last longer. In the adult stage the wasp lives only a

few months. The female produces but a few eggs, one at a time at intervals of two or three days. For each egg the mother must provide one adult tarantula, alive but paralyzed. The tarantula must be of the correct species to nourish the larva. The mother wasp attaches the egg to the paralyzed spider's abdomen. Upon hatching from the egg, the larva is many hundreds of times smaller than its living but helpless victim. It eats no other food and drinks no water. By the time it has finished its single gargantuan meal and becomes ready for wasphood, nothing remains of the tarantula but its indigestible chitinous skeleton.

The mother wasp goes tarantula-hunting when the egg in 9 her ovary is almost ready to be laid. Flying low over the ground late on a sunny afternoon, the wasp looks for its victim or for the mouth of a tarantula burrow, a round hole edged by a bit of silk. The sex of the spider makes no difference, but the mother is highly discriminating as to species. Each species of *Pepsis* requires a certain species of tarantula, and the wasp will not attack the wrong species. In a cage with a tarantula which is not its normal prey the wasp avoids the spider, and is usually killed by it in the night.

Yet when a wasp finds the correct species, it is the other 10 way about. To identify the species the wasp apparently must explore the spider with her antennae. The tarantula shows an amazing tolerance to this exploration. The wasp crawls under it and walks over it without evoking any hostile response. The molestation is so great and so persistent that the tarantula often rises on all eight legs, as if it were on stilts. It may stand this way for several minutes. Meanwhile the wasp, having satisfied itself that the victim is of the right species, moves off a few inches to dig the spider's grave. Working vigorously with legs and jaws, it excavates a hole 8 to 10 inches deep with a diameter slightly larger than the spider's girth. Now and again the wasp pops out of the hole to make sure that the spider is still there.

When the grave is finished, the wasp returns to the taran- 11 tula to complete her ghastly enterprise. First she feels it all over once more with her antennae. Then her behavior becomes more aggressive. She bends her abdomen, protruding her sting, and searches for the soft membrane at the point where the spider's leg joins its body—the only spot where she can penetrate the horny skeleton. From time to time, as the exasperated spider slowly shifts ground, the wasp turns on her back and slides along with the aid of her wings, trying to get under the tarantula for a shot at the vital spot. During all this maneuvering, which can last for several minutes, the tarantula makes no move to save itself. Finally the wasp corners it against some obstruction and grasps one of its legs in her powerful jaws. Now at last the harassed spider tries a desperate but vain defense. The two contestants roll over and over on the ground. It is a terrifying sight and the outcome is always the same. The wasp finally manages to thrust her sting into the soft spot and holds it there for a few seconds while she pumps in the poison. Almost immediately the tarantula falls paralyzed on its back. Its legs stop twitching; its heart stops beating. Yet it is not dead, as is shown by the fact that if taken from the wasp it can be restored to some sensitivity by being kept in a moist chamber for several months.

After paralyzing the tarantula, the wasp cleans herself by **12** dragging her body along the ground and rubbing her feet, sucks the drop of blood oozing from the wound in the spider's abdomen, then grabs a leg of the flabby, helpless animal in her jaws and drags it down to the bottom of the grave. She stays there for many minutes, sometimes for several hours, and what she does all that time in the dark we do not know. Eventually she lays her egg and attaches it to the side of the spider's abdomen with a sticky secretion. Then she emerges, fills the grave with soil carried bit by bit in her jaws, and finally tramples the ground all around to hide any trace of the grave from prowlers. Then she flies away, leaving her descendant safely started in life.

In all this the behavior of the wasp evidently is qualitatively **13** different from that of the spider. The wasp acts like an intelligent animal. This is not to say that instinct plays no part or that she reasons as man does. But her actions are to the point; they are not automatic and can be modified to fit the situation. We do not know for certain how she identifies the tarantula—probably it is by some olfactory or chemotactile sense—but she does it purposefully and does not blindly tackle a wrong species.

On the other hand, the tarantula's behavior shows only **14** confusion. Evidently the wasp's pawing gives it no pleasure, for it tries to move away. That the wasp is not simulating sexual stimulation is certain, because male and female tarantulas react in the same way to its advances. That the spider is not anesthetized by some odorless secretion is easily shown by blowing lightly at the tarantula and making it jump suddenly. What, then, makes the tarantula behave as stupidly as it does?

No clear, simple answer is available. Possibly the stimulation by the wasp's antennae is masked by a heavier pressure on the spider's body, so that it reacts as when prodded by a pencil. But the explanation may be much more complex. Initiative in attack is not in the nature of tarantulas; most species fight only when cornered so that escape is impossible. Their inherited patterns of behavior apparently prompt them to avoid problems rather than attack them. For example, spiders always weave their webs in three dimensions, and when a spider finds that there is insufficient space to attach certain threads in the third dimension, it leaves the place and seeks another, instead of finishing the web in a single plane. This urge to escape seems to arise under all circumstances, in all phases of life, and to take the place of reasoning. For a spider to change the pattern of its web is as impossible as for an inexperienced man to build a bridge across a chasm obstructing his way. 15

In a way the instinctive urge to escape is not only easier but more efficient than reasoning. The tarantula does exactly what is most efficient in all cases except in an encounter with a ruthless and determined attacker dependent for the existence of her own species on killing as many tarantulas as she can lay eggs. Perhaps in this case the spider follows its usual pattern of trying to escape, instead of seizing and killing the wasp, because it is not aware of its danger. In any case, the survival of the tarantula species as a whole is protected by the fact that the spider is much more fertile than the wasp. 16

1952

The Grey Beginnings
Rachel Carson

And the earth was without form, and void; and darkness was upon the face of the deep.

                                                             Genesis

Beginnings are apt to be shadowy, and so it is with the be- 1
ginnings of that great mother of life the sea. Many people have
debated how and when the earth got its ocean, and it is not surprising that their explanations do not always agree. For the plain
and inescapable truth is that no one was there to see, and in the
absence of eyewitness accounts there is bound to be a certain
amount of disagreement. So if I tell here the story of how the
young planet Earth acquired an ocean, it must be a story pieced
together from many sources and containing whole chapters the
details of which we can only imagine. The story is founded on
the testimony of the earth's most ancient rocks, which were
young when the earth was young; on other evidence written on
the face of the earth's satellite, the moon; and on hints contained
in the history of the sun and the whole universe of star-filled
space. For although no man was there to witness this cosmic
birth, the stars and the moon and the rocks were there, and, indeed, had much to do with the fact that there is an ocean.

The events of which I write must have occurred somewhat 2
more than 2 billion years ago. As nearly as science can tell that is
the approximate age of the earth, and the ocean must be very
nearly as old. It is possible now to discover the age of the rocks
that compose the crust of the earth by measuring the rate of decay of the radioactive materials they contain. The oldest rocks
found anywhere on earth—in Manitoba—are about 2.3 billion
years old. Allowing 100 million years or so for the cooling of the
earth's materials to form a rocky crust, we arrive at the suppo-
sition that the tempestuous and violent events connected with
our planet's birth occurred nearly 2½ billion years ago. But this

is only a minimum estimate, for rocks indicating an even greater age may be found at any time.

The new earth, freshly torn from its parent sun, was a ball 3 of whirling gases, intensely hot, rushing through the black spaces of the universe on a path and at a speed controlled by immense forces. Gradually the ball of flaming gases cooled. The gases began to liquefy, and Earth became a molten mass. The materials of this mass eventually became sorted out in a definite pattern: the heaviest in the center, the less heavy surrounding them, and the least heavy forming the outer rim. This is the pattern which persists today—a central sphere of molten iron, very nearly as hot as it was 2 billion years ago, an intermediate sphere of semi-plastic basalt, and a hard outer shell, relatively quite thin and composed of solid basalt and granite.

The outer shell of the young earth must have been a good 4 many millions of years changing from the liquid to the solid state, and it is believed that, before this change was completed, an event of the greatest importance took place—the formation of the moon. The next time you stand on a beach at night, watching the moon's bright path across the water, and conscious of the moon-drawn tides, remember that the moon itself may have been born of a great tidal wave of earthly substance, torn off into space. And remember that if the moon was formed in this fashion, the event may have had much to do with shaping the ocean basins and the continents as we know them.

There were tides in the new earth, long before there was an 5 ocean. In response to the pull of the sun the molten liquids of the earth's whole surface rose in tides that rolled unhindered around the globe and only gradually slackened and diminished as the earthly shell cooled, congealed, and hardened. Those who believe that the moon is a child of earth say that during an early stage of the earth's development something happened that caused this rolling, viscid tide to gather speed and momentum and to rise to unimaginable heights. Apparently the force that created these greatest tides the earth has ever known was the force of resonance, for at this time the period of the solar tides had come to approach, then equal, the period of the free oscillation of the liquid earth. And so every sun tide was given increased momentum by the push of the earth's oscillation, and each of the twice-daily tides was larger than the one before it. Physicists have calculated that, after 500 years of such monstrous, steadily increasing tides, those on the side toward the sun became too high for stability, and a great wave was torn away and hurled into space. But immediately, of course, the newly created satellite became subject to physical laws that sent it spinning in an orbit of its own about the earth. This is what we call the moon.

There are reasons for believing that this event took place   6
after the earth's crust had become slightly hardened, instead of during its partly liquid state. There is to this day a great scar on the surface of the globe. This scar or depression holds the Pacific Ocean. According to some geophysicists, the floor of the Pacific is composed of basalt, the substance of the earth's middle layer, while all other oceans are floored with a thin layer of granite, which makes up most of the earth's outer layer. We immediately wonder what became of the Pacific's granite covering and the most convenient assumption is that it was torn away when the moon was formed. There is supporting evidence. The mean density of the moon is much less than that of the earth (3.3 compared with 5.5), suggesting that the moon took away none of the earth's heavy iron core, but that it is composed only of the granite and some of the basalt of the outer layers.

The birth of the moon probably helped shape other regions   7
of the world ocean besides the Pacific. When part of the crust was torn away, strains must have been set up in the remaining granite envelope. Perhaps the granite mass cracked open on the side opposite the moon scar. Perhaps, as the earth spun on its axis and rushed on its orbit through space, the cracks widened and the masses of granite began to drift apart, moving over a tarry, slowly hardening layer of basalt. Gradually the outer portions of the basalt layer became solid and the wandering continents came to rest, frozen into place with oceans between them. In spite of theories to the contrary, the weight of geologic evidence seems to be that the locations of the major ocean basins

and the major continental land masses are today much the same as they have been since a very early period of the earth's history.

But this is to anticipate the story, for when the moon was born there was no ocean. The gradually cooling earth was enveloped in heavy layers of cloud, which contained much of the water of the new planet. For a long time its surface was so hot that no moisture could fall without immediately being reconverted to steam. This dense, perpetually renewed cloud covering must have been thick enough that no rays of sunlight could penetrate it. And so the rough outlines of the continents and the empty ocean basins were sculptured out of the surface of the earth in darkness, in a Stygian world of heated rock and swirling clouds and gloom.

As soon as the earth's crust cooled enough, the rains began ⁹ to fall. Never have there been such rains since that time. They fell continuously, day and night, days passing into months, into years, into centuries. They poured into the waiting ocean basins, or, falling upon the continental masses, drained away to become sea.

That primeval ocean, growing in bulk as the rains slowly ¹⁰ filled its basins, must have been only faintly salt. But the falling rains were the symbol of the dissolution of the continents. From the moment the rains began to fall, the lands began to be worn away and carried to the sea. It is an endless, inexorable process that has never stopped—the dissolving of the rocks, the leaching out of their contained minerals, the carrying of the rock fragments and dissolved minerals to the ocean. And over the eons of time, the sea has grown ever more bitter with the salt of the continents.

In what manner the sea produced the mysterious and won- ¹¹ derful stuff called protoplasm we cannot say. In its warm, dimly lit waters the unknown conditions of temperature and pressure and saltiness must have been the critical ones for the creation of life from nonlife. At any rate they produced the result that neither the alchemists with their crucibles nor modern scientists in their laboratories have been able to achieve.

Before the first living cell was created, there may have been ¹² many trials and failures. It seems probable that, within the warm saltiness of the primeval sea, certain organic substances were fashioned from carbon dioxide, sulphur, nitrogen, phosphorus, potassium, and calcium. Perhaps these were transition steps from which the complex molecules of protoplasm arose—molecules that somehow acquired the ability to reproduce themselves and begin the endless stream of life. But at present no one is wise enough to be sure.

Those first living things may have been simple microorgan- 13 isms rather like some of the bacteria we know today—mysterious borderline forms that were not quite plants, not quite animals, barely over the intangible line that separates the non-living from the living. It is doubtful that this first life possessed the substance chlorophyll, with which plants in sunlight transform lifeless chemicals into the living stuff of their tissues. Little sunshine could enter their dim world, penetrating the cloud banks from which fell the endless rains. Probably the sea's first children lived on the organic substances then present in the ocean waters, or, like the iron and sulphur bacteria that exist today, lived directly on inorganic food.

All the while the cloud cover was thinning, the darkness of 14 the nights alternated with palely illumined days, and finally the sun for the first time shone through upon the sea. By this time some of the living things that floated in the sea must have developed the magic of chlorophyll. Now they were able to take the carbon dioxide of the air and the water of the sea and of these elements, in sunlight, build the organic substances they needed. So the first true plants came into being.

Another group of organisms, lacking the chlorophyll but 15 needing organic food, found they could make a way of life for themselves by devouring the plants. So the first animals arose, and from that day to this, every animal in the world has followed the habit it learned in the ancient seas and depends, directly or through complex food chains, on the plants for food and life.

As the years passed, and the centuries, and the millions of 16 years, the stream of life grew more and more complex. From simple, one-celled creatures, others that were aggregations of specialized cells arose, and then creatures with organs for feeding, digesting, breathing, reproducing. Sponges grew on the rocky bottom of the sea's edge and coral animals built their habitations in warm, clear waters. Jellyfish swam and drifted in the sea. Worms evolved, and starfish, and hard-shelled creatures with many-jointed legs, the arthropods. The plants, too, progressed, from the microscopic algae to branched and curiously fruiting seaweeds that swayed with the tides and were plucked from the coastal rocks by the surf and cast adrift.

During all this time the continents had no life. There was 17 little to induce living things to come ashore, forsaking their all-providing, all-embracing mother sea. The lands must have been bleak and hostile beyond the power of words to describe. Imagine a whole continent of naked rock, across which no covering mantle of green had been drawn—a continent without soil, for there were no land plants to aid in its formation and bind it to the rocks with their roots. Imagine a land of stone, a silent land, except for the sound of the rains and winds that swept across it. For there was no living voice, and no living thing moved over the surface of the rocks.

Meanwhile, the gradual cooling of the planet, which had 18 first given the earth its hard granite crust, was progressing into its deeper layers; and as the interior slowly cooled and contracted, it drew away from the outer shell. This shell, accommodating itself to the shrinking sphere within it, fell into folds and wrinkles—the earth's first mountain ranges.

Geologists tell us that there must have been at least two periods of mountain building (often called "revolutions") in that dim period, so long ago that the rocks have no record of it, so long ago that the mountains themselves have long since been worn away. Then there came a third great period of upheaval and readjustment of the earth's crust, about a billion years ago, but of all its majestic mountains the only reminders today are the Laurentian hills of eastern Canada, and a great shield of granite over the flat country around Hudson Bay.

The epochs of mountain building only served to speed up 20 the processes of erosion by which the continents were worn down and their crumbling rock and contained minerals returned to the sea. The uplifted masses of the mountains were prey to the bitter cold of the upper atmosphere and under the attacks of frost and snow and ice the rocks cracked and crumbled away. The rains beat with greater violence upon the slopes of the hills and carried away the substance of the mountains in torrential streams. There was still no plant covering to modify and resist the power of the rains.

And in the sea, life continued to evolve. The earliest forms 21 have left no fossils by which we can identify them. Probably they were soft-bodied, with no hard parts that could be preserved. Then, too, the rock layers formed in those early days have since been so altered by enormous heat and pressure, under the foldings of the earth's crust, that any fossils they might have contained would have been destroyed.

For the past 500 million years, however, the rocks have 22 preserved the fossil record. By the dawn of the Cambrian period, when the history of living things was first inscribed on rock pages, life in the sea had progressed so far that all the main groups of backboneless or invertebrate animals had been developed. But there were no animals with backbones, no insects or spiders, and still no plant or animal had been evolved that was capable of venturing on to the forbidding land. So for more than three-fourths of geologic time the continents were desolate and uninhabited, while the sea prepared the life that was later to invade them and make them habitable. Meanwhile, with violent tremblings of the earth and with the fire and smoke of roaring volcanoes, mountains rose and wore away, glaciers moved to and fro over the earth, and the sea crept over the continents and again receded.

It was not until Silurian time, some 350 million years ago, 23 that the first pioneer of land life crept out on the shore. It was an arthropod, one of the great tribe that later produced crabs and lobsters and insects. It must have been something like a modern scorpion, but, unlike some of its descendants, it never wholly severed the ties that united it to the sea. It lived a strange life, half-terrestrial, half-aquatic, something like that of the ghost crabs that speed along the beaches today, now and then dashing into the surf to moisten their gills.

Fish, tapered of body and stream-molded by the press of 24 running waters, were evolving in Silurian rivers. In times of drought, in the drying pools and lagoons, the shortage of oxygen forced them to develop swim bladders for the storage of air. One form that possessed an air-breathing lung was able to survive the dry period by burying itself in mud, leaving a passage to the surface through which it breathed.

It is very doubtful that the animals alone would have succeeded in colonizing the land, for only the plants had the power to bring about the first amelioration of its harsh conditions. They helped make soil of the crumbling rocks, they held back the soil from the rains that would have swept it away, and little by little they softened and subdued the bare rock, the lifeless desert. We know very little about the first land plants, but they must have been closely related to some of the larger seaweeds that had learned to live in the coastal shallows, developing strengthened stems and grasping, rootlike holdfasts to resist the drag and pull of the waves. Perhaps it was in some coastal lowlands, periodically drained and flooded, that some such plants found it possible to survive, though separated from the sea. This also seems to have taken place in the Silurian period.   25

The mountains that had been thrown up by the Laurentian revolution gradually wore away, and as the sediments were washed from their summits and deposited on the lowlands, great areas of the continents sank under the load. The seas crept out of their basins and spread over the lands. Life fared well and was exceedingly abundant in those shallow, sunlit seas. But with the later retreat of the ocean water into the deeper basins, many creatures must have been left stranded in shallow, landlocked bays. Some of these animals found means to survive on land. The lakes, the shores of the rivers, and the coastal swamps of those days were the testing grounds in which plants and animals either became adapted to the new conditions or perished.   26

As the lands rose and the seas receded, a strange fishlike creature emerged on the land, and over the thousands of years its fins became legs, and instead of gills it developed lungs. In the Devonian sandstone this first amphibian left its footprint.   27

On land and sea the stream of life poured on. New forms evolved; some old ones declined and disappeared. On land the mosses and the ferns and the seed plants developed. The reptiles   28 for a time dominated the earth, gigantic, grotesque, and terrifying. Birds learned to live and move in the ocean of air. The first small mammals lurked inconspicuously in hidden crannies of the earth as though in fear of the reptiles.

When they went ashore the animals that took up a land life 29 carried with them part of the sea in their bodies, a heritage which they passed on to their children and which even today links each land animal with its origin in the ancient sea. Fish, amphibian, and reptile, warm-blooded bird and mammal—each of us carries in our veins a salty stream in which the elements sodium, potassium, and calcium are combined in almost the same proportions as in sea water. This is our inheritance from the day untold millions of years ago, when a remote ancestor, having progressed from the one-celled to the many-celled stage, first developed a circulatory system in which the fluid was merely the water of the sea. In the same way, our lime-hardened skeletons are a heritage from the calcium-rich ocean of Cambrian time. Even the protoplasm that streams within each cell of our bodies has the chemical structure impressed upon all living matter when the first simple creatures were brought forth in the ancient sea. And as life itself began in the sea, so each of us begins his individual life in a miniature ocean within his mother's womb, and in the stages of his embryonic development repeats the steps by which his race evolved, from gill-breathing inhabitants of a water world to creatures able to live on land.

Some of the land animals later returned to the ocean. After 30 perhaps 50 million years of land life, a number of reptiles entered the sea about 170 million years ago, in the Triassic period. They were huge and formidable creatures. Some had oarlike limbs by which they rowed through the water; some were web-footed, with long, serpentine necks. These grotesque monsters disappeared millions of years ago, but we remember them when we come upon a large sea turtle swimming many miles at sea, its barnacle-encrusted shell eloquent of its marine life. Much later, perhaps no more than 50 million years ago, some of the mammals, too, abandoned a land life for the ocean. Their descendants are the sea lions, seals, sea elephants, and whales of today.

Among the land mammals there was a race of creatures that 31 took to an arboreal existence. Their hands underwent remark-able development, becoming skilled in manipulating and examin-ing objects, and along with this skill came a superior brain power that compensated for what these comparatively small mammals lacked in strength. At last, perhaps somewhere in the vast inte-rior of Asia, they descended from the trees and became again ter-restrial. The past million years have seen their transformation into beings with the body and brain of man.

Eventually man, too, found his way back to the sea. Stand- 32 ing on its shores, he must have looked out upon it with wonder and curiosity, compounded with an unconscious recognition of his lineage. He could not physically re-enter the ocean as the seals and whales had done. But over the centuries, with all the skill and ingenuity and reasoning powers of his mind, he has sought to explore and investigate even its most remote parts, so that he might re-enter it mentally and imaginatively.

He built boats to venture out on its surface. Later he found 33 ways to descend to the shallow parts of its floor, carrying with him the air that, as a land mammal long unaccustomed to aquatic life, he needed to breathe. Moving in fascination over the deep sea he could not enter, he found ways to probe its depths, he let down nets to capture its life, he invented mechanical eyes and ears that could re-create for his senses a world long lost, but a world that, in the deepest part of his subconscious mind, he had never wholly forgotten.

And yet he has returned to his mother sea only on her own 34 terms. He cannot control or change the ocean as, in his brief ten-ancy of earth, he has subdued and plundered the continents. In the artificial world of his cities and towns, he often forgets the true nature of his planet and the long vistas of its history, in which the existence of the race of men has occupied a mere mo-ment of time. The sense of all these things comes to him most clearly in the course of a long ocean voyage, when he watches day after day the receding rim of the horizon, ridged and fur-rowed by waves; when at night he becomes aware of the earth's rotation as the stars pass overhead; or when, alone in this world of water and sky, he feels the loneliness of his earth in space. And then, as never on land, he knows the truth that his world is a water world, a planet dominated by its covering mantle of ocean, in which the continents are but transient intrusions of land above the surface of the all-encircling sea.

1950

How to Cook a Carp
Euell Gibbons

When I was a lad of about eighteen, my brother and I were 1
working on a cattle ranch in New Mexico that bordered on the Rio Grande. Most Americans think of the Rio Grande as a warm southern stream, but it rises among the high mountains of Colorado, and in the spring it is fed by melting snows. At this time of the year, the water that rushed by the ranch was turbulent, icy-cold and so silt-laden as to be semisolid. "A little too thick to drink, and a little too thin to plow" was a common description of the waters of the Rio Grande.

A few species of fish inhabited this muddy water. Unfortu- 2
nately, the most common was great eight- to ten-pound carp, a fish that is considered very poor eating in this country, although the Germans and Asiatics have domesticated this fish, and have developed some varieties that are highly esteemed for the table.

On the ranch where we worked, there was a drainage ditch 3
that ran through the lower pasture and emptied its clear waters into the muddy Rio Grande. The carp swimming up the river would strike this clear warmer water and decide they preferred it to the cold mud they had been inhabiting. One spring day, a cow-hand who had been riding that way reported that Clear Ditch was becoming crowded with huge carp.

On Sunday we decided to go fishing. Four of us armed our- 4
selves with pitchforks, saddled our horses and set out. Near the mouth of the ditch, the water was running about two feet deep

and twelve to sixteen feet wide. There is a saying in that part of the country that you can't get a cowboy to do anything unless it can be done from the back of a horse, so we forced our mounts into the ditch and started wading them upstream, four abreast, herding the carp before us.

By the time we had ridden a mile upstream, the water was   5
less than a foot deep and so crystal clear that we could see our herd of several hundred carp still fleeing from the splashing, wading horses. As the water continued to shallow, our fish began to get panicky. A few of the boldest ones attempted to dart back past us and were impaled on pitchforks. We could see that the whole herd was getting restless and was about to stampede back downstream, so we piled off our horses into the shallow water to meet the charge. The water boiled about us as the huge fish swirled past us and we speared madly in every direction with our pitchforks, throwing each fish we managed to hit over the ditch bank. This was real fishing—cowhand style. The last of the fish herd was by us in a few minutes and it was all over, but we had caught a tremendous quantity of fish.

Back at the ranch house, after we had displayed our tro-   6
phies, we began wondering what we were going to do with so many fish. This started a series of typical cowboy tall tales on "how to cook a carp." The best of these yarns was told by a grizzled old *vaquero,* who claimed he had made his great discovery when he ran out of food while camping on a tributary of the Rio Grande. He said that he had found the finest way to cook a carp was to plaster the whole fish with a thick coating of fresh cow manure and bury it in the hot ashes of a campfire. In an hour or two, he said, the casing of cow manure had become black and very hard. He then related how he had removed the fish from the fire, broken the hard shell with the butt of his Winchester and peeled it off. He said that as the manure came off the scales and skin adhered to it, leaving the baked fish, white and clean. He then ended by saying, "Of course, the carp still wasn't fit to eat, but manure in which it was cooked tasted pretty good."

There were also some serious suggestions and experiments.   7
The chief objection to the carp is that its flesh is full of many forked bones. One man said that he had enjoyed carp sliced very

thin and fried so crisp that one could eat it, bones and all. He demonstrated, and you really could eat it without the bones bothering you, but it was still far from being an epicurean dish. One cowboy described the flavor as "a perfect blend of Rio Grande mud and rancid hog lard."

Another man said that he had eaten carp that had been 8 cooked in a pressure cooker until the bones softened and became indistinguishable from the flesh. A pressure cooker is almost a necessity at that altitude, so we had one at the ranch house. We tried this method, and the result was barely edible. It tasted like the poorest possible grade of canned salmon flavored with a bit of mud. It was, however, highly appreciated by the dogs and cats on the ranch, and solved the problem of what to do with the bulk of the fish we had caught.

It was my brother who finally devised a method of cooking 9 carp that not only made it fit for human consumption, but actually delicious. First, instead of merely scaling the fish, he skinned them. Then, taking a large pinch, where the meat was thickest, he worked his fingers and thumb into the flesh until he struck the median bones, then he worked his thumb and fingers together and tore off a handful of meat. Using this tearing method, he could get two or three goodsized chunks of flesh from each side of the fish. He then heated a pot of bland vegetable shortening, rubbed the pieces of fish with salt and dropped them into the hot fat. He used no flour, meal, crumbs or seasoning other than salt. They cooked to a golden brown in a few minutes, and everyone pronounced them "mighty fine eating." The muddy flavor seemed to have been eliminated by removing the skin and the large bones. The forked bones were still there, but they had not been multiplied by cutting across them, and one only had to remove several bones still intact with the fork from each piece of fish.

For the remainder of that spring, every few days one or an- 10 other of the cowboys would take a pitchfork and ride over to Clear Ditch and spear a mess of carp. On these evenings, my brother replaced the regular *cocinero* and we enjoyed some delicious fried carp.

The flavor of carp varies with the water from which it is 11 caught. Many years after the above incidents I attended a fish fry at my brother's house. The main course was all of his own catching, and consisted of bass, catfish and carp, all from Elephant Butte Lake farther down the Rio Grande. All the fish were prepared exactly alike, except that the carp was pulled apart as described above, while the bass and catfish, being all twelve inches or less in length, were merely cleaned and fried whole. None of his guests knew one fish from another, yet all of them preferred the carp to the other kinds. These experiences have convinced me that the carp is really a fine food fish when properly prepared.

Carp can, of course, be caught in many ways besides spearing them with pitchforks from the back of a horse. In my adopted home state, Pennsylvania, they are classed as "trash fish" and one is allowed to take them almost any way. They will sometimes bite on worms, but they are vegetarians by preference and are more easily taken on dough balls. Some states allow the use of gill nets, and other states, because they would like to reduce the population of this unpopular fish, will issue special permits for the use of nets to catch carp.   12

A good forager will take advantage of the lax regulations on carp fishing while they last. When all fishermen realize that the carp is really a good food fish when prepared in the right way, maybe this outsized denizen of our rivers and lakes will no longer be considered a pest and will take his rightful place among our valued food and game fishes.   13

1962

Behind the Formaldehyde Curtain
Jessica Mitford

The drama begins to unfold with the arrival of the corpse at the mortuary.   1

Alas, poor Yorick! How surprised he would be to see how his counterpart of today is whisked off to a funeral parlor and is   2 in short order sprayed, sliced, pierced, pickled, trussed, trimmed, creamed, waxed, painted, rouged and neatly dressed— transformed from a common corpse into a Beautiful Memory Picture. This process is known in the trade as embalming and restorative art, and is so universally employed in the United States and Canada that the funeral director does it routinely, without consulting corpse or kin. He regards as eccentric those few who are hardy enough to suggest that it might be dispensed with. Yet no law requires embalming, no religious doctrine commends it, nor is it dictated by considerations of health, sanitation, or even of personal daintiness. In no part of the world but in Northern America is it widely used. The purpose of embalming is to make the corpse presentable for viewing in a suitably costly container; and here too the funeral director routinely, without first consulting the family, prepares the body for public display.

Is all this legal? The processes to which a dead body may   3
be subjected are after all to some extent circumscribed by law. In most states, for instance, the signature of next of kin must be obtained before an autopsy may be performed, before the deceased may be cremated, before the body may be turned over to a medical school for research purposes; or such provision must be made in the decedent's will. In the case of embalming, no such permission is required nor is it ever sought. A textbook, *The Principles and Practices of Embalming,* comments on this: "There is some question regarding the legality of much that is done within the preparation room." The author points out that it would be most unusual for a responsible member of a bereaved family to instruct the mortician, in so many words, to *"embalm"* the body of a deceased relative. The very term "embalming" is so seldom used that the mortician must rely upon custom in the matter. The author concludes that unless the family specifies otherwise, the act of entrusting the body to the care of a funeral establishment carries with it an implied permission to go ahead and embalm.

Embalming is indeed a most extraordinary procedure, and   4
one must wonder at the docility of Americans who each year pay hundreds of millions of dollars for its perpetuation, blissfully ignorant of what it is all about, what is done, how it is done. Not

one in ten thousand has any idea of what actually takes place. Books on the subject are extremely hard to come by. They are not to be found in most libraries or bookshops.

In an era when huge television audiences watch surgical op- 5 erations in the comfort of their living rooms, when, thanks to the animated cartoon, the geography of the digestive system has become familiar territory even to the nursery school set, in a land where the satisfaction of curiosity about almost all matters is a national pastime, the secrecy surrounding embalming can, surely, hardly be attributed to the inherent gruesomeness of the subject. Custom in this regard has within this century suffered a complete reversal. In the early days of American embalming, when it was performed in the home of the deceased, it was almost mandatory for some relative to stay by the embalmer's side and witness the procedure. Today, family members who might wish to be in attendance would certainly be dissuaded by the funeral director. All others, except apprentices, are excluded by law from the preparation room.

A close look at what does actually take place may explain 6 in large measure the undertaker's intractable reticence concerning a procedure that has become his major *raison d'être*. It is possible he fears that public information about embalming might lead patrons to wonder if they really want this service? If the funeral men are loath to discuss the subject outside the trade, the reader may, understandably, be equally loath to go on reading at this point. For those who have the stomach for it, let us part the formaldehyde curtain....

The body is first laid out in the undertaker's morgue—or 7 rather, Mr. Jones is reposing in the preparation room—to be readied to bid the world farewell.

The preparation room in any of the better funeral establish- 8 ments has the tiled and sterile look of a surgery, and indeed the embalmer-restorative artist who does his chores there is beginning to adopt the term "dermasurgeon" (appropriately corrupted by some mortician-writers as "demi-surgeon") to describe his calling. His equipment, consisting of scalpels, scissors, augers, forceps, clamps, needles, pumps, tubes, bowls and basins, is crudely imitative of the surgeon's, as is his technique, acquired in a nine- or twelve-month post-high-school course in an embalming school. He is supplied by an advanced chemical industry with a bewildering array of fluids, sprays, pastes, oils, powders, creams, to fix or soften tissue, shrink or distend it as needed, dry it here, restore the moisture there. There are cosmetics, waxes and paints to fill and cover features, even plaster of Paris to replace entire limbs. There are ingenious aids to prop and stabilize the cadaver: a Vari-Pose Head Rest, the Edwards Arm and Hand Positioner, the Repose Block (to support the shoulders during the embalming), and the Throop Foot Positioner, which resembles an old-fashioned stocks.

Mr. John H. Eckels, president of the Eckels College of **9** Mortuary Science, thus describes the first part of the embalming procedure: "In the hands of a skilled practitioner, this work may be done in a comparatively short time and without mutilating the body other than by slight incision—so slight that it scarcely would cause serious inconvenience if made upon a living person. It is necessary to remove the blood, and doing this not only helps in the disinfecting, but removes the principal cause of disfigurements due to discoloration."

Another textbook discusses the all-important time element: **10** "The earlier this is done, the better, for every hour that elapses between death and embalming will add to the problems and complications encountered...." Just how soon should one get going on the embalming? The author tells us, "On the basis of such scanty information made available to this profession through its rudimentary and haphazard system of technical research, we must conclude that the best results are to be obtained if the subject is embalmed before life is completely extinct—that is, before cellular death has occurred. In the average case, this would mean within an hour after somatic death." For those who feel that there is something a little rudimentary, not to say haphazard, about this advice, a comforting thought is offered by another writer. Speaking of fears entertained in early days of premature burial, he points out, "One of the effects of embalming by chemical injection, however, has been to dispel fears of live burial." How true; once the blood is removed, chances of live burial are indeed remote.

To return to Mr. Jones, the blood is drained out through the 11
veins and replaced by embalming fluid pumped in through the arteries. As noted in *The Principles and Practices of Embalming,*
"every operator has a favorite injection and drainage point—a
fact which becomes a handicap only if he fails or refuses to for-
sake his favorites when conditions demand it." Typical favorites
are the carotid artery, femoral artery, jugular vein, subclavian
vein. There are various choices of embalming fluid. If Flextone is
used, it will produce a "mild, flexible rigidity. The skin retains a
velvety softness, the tissues are rubbery and pliable. Ideal for
women and children." It may be blended with B. and G. Products Company's Lyf-Lyk tint, which is guaranteed to reproduce
"nature's own skin texture...the velvety appearance of living
tissue." Suntone comes in three separate tints: Suntan; Special
Cosmetic Tint, a pink shade "especially indicated for female subjects"; and Regular Cosmetic Tint, moderately pink.

About three to six gallons of a dyed and perfumed solution 12
of formaldehyde, glycerin, borax, phenol, alcohol and water is
soon circulating through Mr. Jones, whose mouth has been sewn
together with a "needle directed upward between the upper lip
and gum and brought out through the left nostril," with the corners raised slightly "for a more pleasant expression." If he
should be bucktoothed, his teeth are cleaned with Bon Ami and
coated with colorless nail polish. His eyes, meanwhile, are
closed with flesh-tinted eye caps and eye cement.

The next step is to have at Mr. Jones with a thing called a 13
trocar. This is a long, hollow needle attached to a tube. It is
jabbed into the abdomen, poked around the entrails and chest
cavity, the contents of which are pumped out and replaced with
"cavity fluid." This done, and the hole in the abdomen sewn up,
Mr. Jones's face is heavily creamed (to protect the skin from
burns which may be caused by leakage of the chemicals), and he
is covered with a sheet and left unmolested for a while. But not
for long—there is more, much more, in store for him. He has
been embalmed, but not yet restored, and the best time to start
the restorative work is eight to ten hours after embalming, when
the tissues have become firm and dry.

The object of all this attention to the corpse, it must be re- 14

membered, is to make it presentable for viewing in an attitude of
healthy repose. "Our customs require the presentation of our
dead in the semblance of normality...unmarred by the ravages
of illness, disease or mutilation," says Mr. J. Sheridan Mayer in
his *Restorative Art*. This is rather a large order since few people
die in the full bloom of health, unravaged by illness and un-
marked by some disfigurement. The funeral industry is equal to
the challenge: "In some cases the gruesome appearance of a mu-
tilated or disease-ridden subject may be quite discouraging. The
task of restoration may seem impossible and shake the confidence of the embalmer. This is the time for intestinal fortitude
and determination. Once the formative work is begun and affected tissues are cleaned or removed, all doubts of success vanish. It is surprising and gratifying to discover the results which
may be obtained."

The embalmer, having allowed an appropriate interval to   15
elapse, returns to the attack, but now he brings into play the skill
and equipment of sculptor and cosmetician. Is a hand missing?
Casting one in plaster of Paris is a simple matter. "For replace-
ment purposes, only a cast of the back of the hand is necessary;
this is within the ability of the average operator and is quite adequate." If a lip or two, a nose or an ear should be missing, the
embalmer has at hand a variety of restorative waxes with which
to model replacements. Pores and skin texture are simulated by
stippling with a little brush, and over this cosmetics are laid on.
Head off? Decapitation cases are rather routinely handled.
Ragged edges are trimmed, and head joined to torso with a series
of splints, wires and sutures. It is a good idea to have a little
something at the neck—a scarf or a high collar—when time for
viewing comes. Swollen mouth? Cut out tissue as needed from
inside the lips. If too much is removed, the surface contour can
easily be restored by padding with cotton. Swollen necks and
cheeks are reduced by removing tissue through vertical incisions
made down each side of the neck. "When the deceased is cas-
keted, the pillow will hide the suture incisions...as an extra pre-
caution against leakage, the suture may be painted with liquid
sealer."

The opposite condition is more likely to present itself—that   16 of emaciation. His hypodermic syringe now loaded with massage cream, the embalmer seeks out and fills the hollowed and sunken areas by injection. In this procedure the backs of the hands and fingers and the under-chin area should not be neglected.

Positioning the lips is a problem that recurrently challenges 17 the ingenuity of the embalmer. Closed too tightly, they tend to give a stern, even disapproving expression. Ideally, embalmers feel, the lips should give the impression of being ever so slightly parted, the upper lip protruding slightly for a more youthful appearance. This takes some engineering, however, as the lips tend to drift apart. Lip drift can sometimes be remedied by pushing one or two straight pins through the inner margin of the lower lip and then inserting them between the two front upper teeth. If Mr. Jones happens to have no teeth, the pins can just as easily be anchored in his Armstrong Face Former and Denture Replacer. Another method to maintain lip closure is to dislocate the lower jaw, which is then held in its new position by a wire run through holes which have been drilled through the upper and lower jaws at the midline. As the French are fond of saying, *il faut souffrir pour être belle*.

If Mr. Jones has died of jaundice, the embalming fluid will 18 very likely turn him green. Does this deter the embalmer? Not if he has intestinal fortitude. Masking pastes and cosmetics are heavily laid on, burial garments and casket interiors are color-correlated with particular care, and Jones is displayed beneath rose-colored lights. Friends will say "How *well* he looks." Death by carbon monoxide, on the other hand, can be rather a good thing from the embalmer's viewpoint: "One advantage is the fact that this type of discoloration is an exaggerated form of a natural pink coloration." This is nice because the healthy glow is already present and needs but little attention.

The patching and filling completed, Mr. Jones is now 19 shaved, washed and dressed. Cream-based cosmetic, available in pink, flesh, suntan, brunette and blond, is applied to his hands and face, his hair is shampooed and combed (and, in the case of Mrs. Jones, set), his hands manicured. For the horny-handed son of toil special care must be taken; cream should be applied to remove ingrained grime, and the nails cleaned. "If he were not in the habit of having them manicured in life, trimming and shaping is advised for better appearance—never questioned by kin.''

Jones is now ready for casketing (this is the present parti- 20 ciple of the verb "to casket"). In this operation his right shoulder should be depressed slightly "to turn the body a bit to the right and soften the appearance of lying flat on the back." Positioning the hands is a matter of importance, and special rubber positioning blocks may be used. The hands should be cupped slightly for a more lifelike, relaxed appearance. Proper placement of the body requires a delicate sense of balance. It should lie as high as possible in the casket, yet not so high that the lid, when lowered, will hit the nose. On the other hand, we are cautioned, placing the body too low "creates the impression that the body is in a box."

Jones is next wheeled into the appointed slumber room 21 where a few last touches may be added—his favorite pipe placed in his hand or, if he was a great reader, a book propped into position. (In the case of little Master Jones a Teddy bear may be clutched.) Here he will hold open house for a few days, visiting hours 10 A.M. to 9 P.M.

All now being in readiness, the funeral director calls a staff 22 conference to make sure that each assistant knows his precise duties. Mr. Wilber Kriege writes: "This makes your staff feel that they are a part of the team, with a definite assignment that must be properly carried out if the whole plan is to succeed. You never heard of a football coach who failed to talk to his entire team before they go on the field. They have drilled on the plays they are to execute for hours and days, and yet the successful coach knows the importance of making even the bench-warming third-string substitute feel that he is important if the game is to be won." The winning of *this* game is predicated upon glass-smooth handling of the logistics. The funeral director has notified the pallbearers whose names were furnished by the family, has arranged for the presence of clergyman, organist, and soloist, has provided transportation for everybody, has organized and listed the flowers sent by friends. In *Psychology of Funeral Service* Mr. Edward A. Martin points out: "He may not always do as much as the family thinks he is doing, but it is his helpful guidance that they appreciate in knowing they are proceeding as they should....The important thing is how well his services can be used to make the family believe they are giving unlimited expression to their own sentiment."

The religious service may be held in a church or in the 23 chapel of the funeral home; the funeral director vastly prefers the latter arrangement, for not only is it more convenient for him but it affords him the opportunity to show off his beautiful facilities to the gathered mourners. After the clergyman has had his say, the mourners queue up to file past the casket for a last look at the deceased. The family is *never* asked whether they want an open-casket ceremony; in the absence of their instruction to the contrary, this is taken for granted. Consequently well over 90 percent of all American funerals feature the open casket—a custom unknown in other parts of the world. Foreigners are astonished by it. An English woman living in San Francisco described her reaction in a letter to the writer:

> I myself have attended only one funeral here—that of an elderly fellow worker of mine. After the service I could not understand why everyone was walking towards the coffin (sorry, I mean casket), but thought I had better follow the crowd. It shook me rigid to get there and find the casket open and poor old Oscar lying there in his brown tweed suit, wearing a suntan makeup and just the wrong shade of lipstick. If I had not been extremely fond of the old boy, I have a horrible feeling that I might have giggled. Then and there I decided that I could never face another American funeral—even dead.

The casket (which has been resting throughout the service 24 on a Classic Beauty Ultra Metal Casket Bier) is now transferred by a hydraulically operated device called Porto-Lift to a balloon-tired, Glide Easy casket carriage which will wheel it to yet another conveyance, the Cadillac Funeral Coach. This may be lavender, cream, light green—anything but black. Interiors, of course, are color-correlated, "for the man who cannot stop short of perfection."

At graveside, the casket is lowered into the earth. This of- 25 fice, once the prerogative of friends of the deceased, is now performed by a patented mechanical lowering device. A "Lifetime

Green" artificial grass mat is at the ready to conceal the sere earth, and overhead, to conceal the sky, is a portable Steril Chapel Tent ("resists the intense heat and humidity of summer and the terrific storms of winter...available in Silver Grey, Rose or Evergreen"). Now is the time for the ritual scattering of earth over the coffin, as the solemn words "earth to earth, ashes to ashes, dust to dust" are pronounced by the officiating cleric. This can today be accomplished "with a mere flick of the wrist with the Gordon Leak-Proof Earth Dispenser. No grasping of a handful of dirt, no soiled fingers. Simple, dignified, beautiful, reverent! The modern way!" The Gordon Earth Dispenser (at $5) is of nickel-plated brass construction. It is not only "attractive to the eye and long wearing"; it is also "one of the 'tools' for building better public relations" if presented as "an appropriate noncommercial gift" to the clergyman. It is shaped something like a saltshaker.

Untouched by human hand, the coffin and the earth are now united. 26

It is in the function of directing the participants through this maze of gadgetry that the funeral director has assigned to himself his relatively new role of "grief therapist." He has relieved the family of every detail, he has revamped the corpse to look like a living doll, he has arranged for it to nap for a few days in a slumber room, he has put on a well-oiled performance in which the concept of *death* has played no part whatsoever—unless it was inconsiderately mentioned by the clergyman who conducted the religious service. He has done everything in his power to make the funeral a real pleasure for everybody concerned. He and his team have given their all to score an upset victory over death. 27

1963

Introduction to *Frankenstein*
Mary Wollstonecraft Shelley

The publishers of the standard novels, in selecting *Franken-* 1
stein for one of their series, expressed a wish that I should furnish them with some account of the origin of the story. I am the
more willing to comply because I shall thus give a general answer
to the question so very frequently asked me—how I, then a
young girl, came to think of and to dilate upon so very hideous an
idea. It is true that I am very averse to bringing myself forward in
print, but as my account will only appear as an appendage to a
former production, and as it will be confined to such topics as
have connection with my authorship alone, I can scarcely accuse
myself of a personal intrusion.

It is not singular that, as the daughter of two persons of dis- 2
tinguished literary celebrity, I should very early in life have
thought of writing. As a child I scribbled, and my favourite pastime during the hours given me for recreation was to "write stories." Still, I had a dearer pleasure than this, which was the formation of castles in the air—the indulging in waking dreams—the
following up trains of thought, which had for their subject the
formation of a succession of imaginary incidents. My dreams
were at once more fantastic and agreeable than my writings. In
the latter I was a close imitator—rather doing as others had done
than putting down the suggestions of my own mind. What I wrote
was intended at least for one other eye—my childhood's companion and friend; but my dreams were all my own; I accounted
for them to nobody; they were my refuge when annoyed—my
dearest pleasure when free.

I lived principally in the country as a girl and passed a con- 3
siderable time in Scotland. I made occasional visits to the more
picturesque parts, but my habitual residence was on the blank
and dreary northern shores of the Tay, near Dundee. Blank and
dreary on retrospection I call them; they were not so to me then.
They were the aerie of freedom and the pleasant region where
unheeded I could commune with the creatures of my fancy. I

wrote then, but in a most commonplace style. It was beneath the trees of the grounds belonging to our house, or on the bleak sides of the woodless mountains near, that my true compositions, the airy flights of my imagination, were born and fostered. I did not make myself the heroine of my tales. Life appeared to me too commonplace an affair as regarded myself. I could not figure to myself that romantic woes or wonderful events would ever be my lot; but I was not confined to my own identity, and I could people the hours with creations far more interesting to me at that age than my own sensations.

After this my life became busier, and reality stood in place 4 of fiction. My husband, however, was from the first very anxious that I should prove myself worthy of my parentage and enrol myself on the page of fame. He was forever inciting me to obtain literary reputation, which even on my own part I cared for then, though since I have become infinitely indifferent to it. At this time he desired that I should write, not so much with the idea that I could produce anything worthy of notice, but that he might himself judge how far I possessed the promise of better things hereafter. Still I did nothing. Travelling, and the cares of a family, occupied my time; and study, in the way of reading or improving my ideas in communication with his far more cultivated mind was all of literary employment that engaged my attention.

In the summer of 1816 we visited Switzerland and became 5 the neighbours of Lord Byron. At first we spent our pleasant hours on the lake or wandering on its shores; and Lord Byron, who was writing the third canto of *Childe Harold,* was the only one among us who put his thoughts upon paper. These, as he brought them successively to us, clothed in all the light and harmony of poetry, seemed to stamp as divine the glories of heaven and earth, whose influences we partook with him.

But it proved a wet, ungenial summer, and incessant rain 6 often confined us for days to the house. Some volumes of ghost stories translated from the German into French fell into our hands. There was the *History of the Inconstant Lover,* who, when he thought to clasp the bride to whom he had pledged his vows, found himself in the arms of the pale ghost of her whom he had deserted. There was the tale of the sinful founder of his race whose miserable doom it was to bestow the kiss of death on all the younger sons of his fated house, just when they reached the age of promise. His gigantic, shadowy form, clothed like the ghost in *Hamlet,* in complete armour, but with the beaver up, was seen at midnight, by the moon's fitful beams, to advance slowly along the gloomy avenue. The shape was lost beneath the shadow of the castle walls; but soon a gate swung back, a step was heard, the door of the chamber opened, and he advanced to the couch of the blooming youths, cradled in healthy sleep. Eternal sorrow sat upon his face as he bent down and kissed the forehead of the boys, who from that hour withered like flowers snapped upon the stalk. I have not seen these stories since then, but their incidents are as fresh in my mind as if I had read them yesterday.

"We will each write a ghost story," said Lord Byron, and 7 his proposition was acceded to. There were four of us. The noble author began a tale, a fragment of which he printed at the end of his poem of Mazeppa. Shelley, more apt to embody ideas and sentiments in the radiance of brilliant imagery and in the music of the most melodious verse that adorns our language than to invent the machinery of a story, commenced one founded on the experiences of his early life. Poor Polidori had some terrible idea about a skull-headed lady who was so punished for peeping through a key-hole—what to see I forget: something very shocking and wrong of course; but when she was reduced to a worse condition than the renowned Tom of Coventry, he did not know what to do with her and was obliged to dispatch her to the tomb of the Capulets, the only place for which she was fitted. The illustrious poets also, annoyed by the platitude of prose, speedily relinquished their uncongenial task.

I busied myself *to think of a story*—a story to rival those 8 which had excited us to this task. One which would speak to the mysterious fears of our nature and awaken thrilling horror—one to make the reader dread to look round, to curdle the blood, and quicken the beatings of the heart. If I did not accomplish these things, my ghost story would be unworthy of its name. I thought and pondered—vainly. I felt that blank incapability of invention which is the greatest misery of authorship, when dull Nothing re-

plies to our anxious invocations. "Have you thought of a story?"
I was asked each morning, and each morning I was forced to reply with a mortifying negative.

Everything must have a beginning, to speak in Sanchean   9
phrase; and that beginning must be linked to something that went
before. The Hindus give the world an elephant to support it, but
they make the elephant stand upon a tortoise. Invention, it must
be humbly admitted, does not consist in creating out of void, but
out of chaos; the materials must, in the first place, be afforded: it
can give form to dark, shapeless substances but cannot bring into
being the substance itself. In all matters of discovery and invention, even of those that appertain to the imagination, we are continually reminded of the story of Columbus and his egg. Invention consists in the capacity of seizing on the capabilities of a
subject and in the power of moulding and fashioning ideas suggested by it.

Many and long were the conversations between Lord By-   10
ron and Shelley to which I was a devout but nearly silent listener. During one of these, various philosophical doctrines were
discussed, and among others the nature of the principle of life,
and whether there was any probability of its ever being discovered and communicated. They talked of the experiments of Dr.
Darwin (I speak not of what the doctor really did or said that he
did, but, as more to my purpose, of what was then spoken of as
having been done by him), who preserved a piece of vermicelli in
a glass case till by some extraordinary means it began to move with
voluntary motion. Not thus, after all, would life be given. Perhaps
a corpse would be reanimated; galvanism had given token of such
things: perhaps the component parts of a creature might be manufactured, brought together, and endued with vital warmth.

Night waned upon this talk, and even the witching hour had   11
gone by before we retired to rest. When I placed my head on my
pillow I did not sleep, nor could I be said to think. My imagination, unbidden, possessed and guided me, gifting the successive
images that arose in my mind with a vividness far beyond the
usual bounds of reverie. I saw—with shut eyes, but acute mental
vision—I saw the pale student of unhallowed arts kneeling beside
the thing he had put together. I saw the hideous phantasm of a

man stretched out, and then, on the working of some powerful engine, show signs of life and stir with an uneasy, half-vital motion. Frightful must it be, for supremely frightful would be the effect of any human endeavour to mock the stupendous mechanism of the Creator of the world. His success would terrify the artist; he would rush away from his odious handiwork, horror-stricken. He would hope that, left to itself, the slight spark of life which he had communicated would fade, that this thing which had received such imperfect animation would subside into dead matter, and he might sleep in the belief that the silence of the grave would quench forever the transient existence of the hideous corpse which he had looked upon as the cradle of life. He sleeps; but he is awakened; he opens his eyes; behold, the horrid thing stands at his bedside, opening his curtains and looking on him with yellow, watery, but speculative eyes.

I opened mine in terror. The idea so possessed my mind that 12 a thrill of fear ran through me, and I wished to exchange the ghastly image of my fancy for the realities around. I see them still: the very room, the dark parquet, the closed shutters with the moonlight struggling through, and the sense I had that the glassy lake and white high Alps were beyond. I could not so easily get rid of my hideous phantom; still it haunted me. I must try to think of something else. I recurred to my ghost story—my tiresome, unlucky ghost story! Oh! If I could only contrive one which would frighten my reader as I myself had been frightened that night!

Swift as light and as cheering was the idea that broke in upon 13 me. "I have found it! What terrified me will terrify others; and I need only describe the spectre which had haunted my midnight pillow." On the morrow I announced that I had *thought of a story*....

1819

How to Write a Rotten Poem with Almost No Effort

Richard Howey

So you want to write a poem. You've had a rotten day or an 1
astounding thought or a car accident or a squalid love affair and
you want to record it for all time. You want to organize those emotions that are pounding through your veins. You have something to
communicate via a poem but you don't know where to start.

This, of course, is the problem with poetry. Most people 2
find it difficult to write a poem so they don't even try. What's
worse, they don't bother reading any poems either. Poetry has
become an almost totally foreign art form to many of us. As a
result, serious poets either starve or work as account executives.
There is no middle ground. Good poets and poems are lost forever simply because there is no market for them, no people who
write their own verse and seek out further inspiration from other
bards.

Fortunately, there is a solution for this problem, as there 3
are for all imponderables. The answer is to make it easy for everyone to write at least one poem in his life. Once a person has
written a poem, of whatever quality, he will feel comradeship
with fellow poets and, hopefully, read their works. Ideally, there
would evolve a veritable society of poet-citizens, which would
elevate the quality of life worldwide. Not only that, good poets
could make a living for a change.

So, to begin. Have your paper ready. You must first under- 4
stand that the poem you write here will not be brilliant. It won't
even be mediocre. But it will be better than 50% of all song lyrics
and at least equal to one of Rod McKuen's best efforts. You will
be instructed how to write a four-line poem but the basic structure can be repeated at will to create works of epic length.

The first line of your poem should start and end with these 5
words: "In the———of my mind." The middle word of this line
is optional. Any word will do. It would be best not to use a word
that has been overdone, such as "windmills" or "gardens" or

"playground." Just think of as many nouns as you can and see what fits best. The rule of thumb is to pick a noun that seems totally out of context, such as "filing cabinet" or "radiator" or "parking lot." Just remember, the more unusual the noun, the more profound the image.

The second line should use two or more of the human 6 senses in a conflicting manner, as per the famous, "listen to the warm." This is a sure way to conjure up "poetic" feeling and atmosphere. Since there are five different senses, the possibilities are endless. A couple that come to mind are "see the noise" and "touch the sound." If more complexity is desired other senses can be added, as in "taste the color of my hearing," or "I cuddled your sight in the aroma of the night." Rhyming, of course, is optional.

The third line should be just a simple statement. This is 7 used to break up the insightful images that have been presented in the first two lines. This line should be as prosaic as possible to give a "down-to-earth" mood to the poem. An example would be "she gave me juice and toast that morning," or perhaps "I left for work next day on the 8:30 bus." The content of this line may or may not relate to what has gone before.

The last line of your poem should deal with the future in 8 some way. This gives the poem a forward thrust that is always helpful. A possibility might be, "tomorrow will be a better day," or "I'll find someone sometime," or "maybe we'll meet again in July." This future-oriented ending lends an aura of hope and yet need not be grossly optimistic.

By following the above structure, anyone can write a poem. 9 For example, if I select one each of my sample lines, I come up with:

In the parking lot of my mind,
   I cuddled your sight in the aroma of the night.
I left for work next day on the 8:30 bus.
   Maybe we'll meet again in July.

Now that poem (like yours, when you're finished) is rotten. 10 But at least it's a poem and you've written it, which is an accomplishment that relatively few people can claim.

Now that you're a poet, feel free to read poetry by some of 11
your more accomplished brothers and sisters in verse. Chances
are, you'll find their offerings stimulating and refreshing. You
might even try writing some more of your own poems, now that
you've broken the ice. Observe others' emotions and experience
your own—that's what poetry is all about.

Incidentally, if you find it impossible to sell the poem you 12
write to Bobby Goldsboro or John Denver, burn it. It will look
terrible as the first page of your anthology when it's published.

1978

4

Definition

The Holocaust
Bruno Bettelheim

To begin with, it was not the hapless victims of the Nazis 1
who named their incomprehensible and totally unmasterable fate
the "holocaust." It was the Americans who applied this artificial
and highly technical term to the Nazi extermination of the European Jews. But while the event when named as mass murder
most foul evokes the most immediate, most powerful revulsion,
when it is designated by a rare technical term, we must first in
our minds translate it back into emotionally meaningful language.
Using technical or specially created terms instead of words from
our common vocabulary is one of the best-known and most
widely used distancing devices, separating the intellectual from
the emotional experience. Talking about "the holocaust" permits us to manage it intellectually where the raw facts, when
given their ordinary names, would overwhelm us emotionally—
because it was catastrophe beyond comprehension, beyond the
limits of our imagination, unless we force ourselves against our
desire to extend it to encompass these terrible events.

This linguistic circumlocution began while it all was only in 2
the planning stage. Even the Nazis—usually given to grossness
in language and action—shied away from facing openly what

they were up to and called this vile mass murder "the final solution of the Jewish problem." After all, solving a problem can be made to appear like an honorable enterprise, as long as we are not forced to recognize that the solution we are about to embark on consists of the completely unprovoked, vicious murder of millions of helpless men, women, and children. The Nuremberg judges of these Nazi criminals followed their example of circumlocution by coining a neologism out of one Greek and one Latin root: genocide. These artificially created technical terms fail to connect with our strongest feelings. The horror of murder is part of our most common human heritage. From earliest infancy on, it arouses violent abhorrence in us. Therefore in whatever form it appears we should give such an act its true designation and not hide it behind polite, erudite terms created out of classical words.

To call this vile mass murder "the holocaust" is not to give 3 it a special name emphasizing its uniqueness which would permit, over time, the word becoming invested with feelings germane to the event it refers to. The correct definition of "holocaust" is "burnt offering." As such, it is part of the language of the psalmist, a meaningful word to all who have some acquaintance with the Bible, full of the richest emotional connotations. By using the term "holocaust," entirely false associations are established through conscious and unconscious connotations between the most vicious of mass murders and ancient rituals of a deeply religious nature.

Using a word with such strong unconscious religious con- 4 notations when speaking of the murder of millions of Jews robs the victims of this abominable mass murder of the only thing left to them: their uniqueness. Calling the most callous, most brutal, most horrid, most heinous mass murder a burnt offering is a sacrilege, a profanation of God and man.

Martyrdom is part of our religious heritage. A martyr, 5 burned at the stake, is a burnt offering to his god. And it is true that after the Jews were asphyxiated, the victims' corpses were burned. But I believe we fool ourselves if we think we are honoring the victims of systematic murder by using this term, which has the highest moral connotations. By doing so, we connect for our own psychological reasons what happened in the extermination camps with historical events we deeply regret, but also greatly admire. We do so because this makes it easier for us to cope; only in doing so we cope with our distorted image of what happened, not with the events the way they did happen.

By calling the victims of the Nazis "martyrs," we falsify their fate. The true meaning of "martyr" is: "one who voluntarily undergoes the penalty of death for refusing to renounce his faith" (*Oxford English Dictionary*). The Nazis made sure that nobody could mistakenly think that their victims were murdered for their religious beliefs. Renouncing their faith would have saved none of them. Those who had converted to Christianity were gassed, as were those who were atheists, and those who were deeply religious Jews. They did not die for any conviction, and certainly not out of choice. 6

Millions of Jews were systematically slaughtered, as were untold other "undesirables," not for any convictions of theirs, but only because they stood in the way of the realization of an illusion. They neither died for their convictions, nor were they slaughtered because of their convictions, but only in consequence of the Nazis' delusional belief about what was required to protect the purity of their assumed superior racial endowment, and what they thought necessary to guarantee them the living space they believed they needed and were entitled to. Thus while these millions were slaughtered for an idea, they did not die for one. 7

Millions—men, women, and children—were processed after they had been utterly brutalized, their humanity destroyed, their clothes torn from their bodies. Naked, they were sorted into those who were destined to be murdered immediately, and those others who had a short-term usefulness as slave labor. But after a brief interval they, too, were to be herded into the same gas chambers into which the others were immediately piled, there to be asphyxiated so that, in their last moments, they could not prevent themselves from fighting each other in vain for a last breath of air. 8

To call these most wretched victims of a murderous delusion, of destructive drives run rampant, martyrs or a burnt offer- 9

ing is a distortion invented for our comfort, small as it may be. It
pretends that this most vicious of mass murders had some deeper
meaning; that in some fashion the victims either offered themselves or at least became sacrifices to a higher cause. It robs
them of the last recognition which could be theirs, denies them
the last dignity we could accord them: to face and accept what
their death was all about, not embellishing it for the small psychological relief this may give us.

   We could feel so much better if the victims had acted out of   10
choice. For our emotional relief, therefore, we dwell on the tiny
minority who did exercise some choice: the resistance fighters of
the Warsaw ghetto, for example, and others like them. We are
ready to overlook the fact that these people fought back only at a
time when everything was lost, when the overwhelming majority
of those who had been forced into the ghettos had already been
exterminated without resisting. Certainly those few who finally
fought for their survival and their convictions, risking and losing
their lives in doing so, deserve our admiration; their deeds give
us a moral lift. But the more we dwell on these few, the more
unfair are we to the memory of the millions who were slaughtered—who gave in, did not fight back—because we deny them
the only thing which up to the very end remained uniquely their
own: their fate.

                                                                1979

Beauty
Susan Sontag

   For the Greeks, beauty was a virtue: a kind of excellence.   1
Persons then were assumed to be what we now have to call—
lamely, enviously—*whole* persons. If it did occur to the Greeks
to distinguish between a person's "inside" and "outside," they

still expected that inner beauty would be matched by beauty of the other kind. The well-born young Athenians who gathered around Socrates found it quite paradoxical that their hero was so intelligent, so brave, so honorable, so seductive—and so ugly. One of Socrates' main pedagogical acts was to be ugly—and teach those innocent, no doubt splendid-looking disciples of his how full of paradoxes life really was.

They may have resisted Socrates' lesson. We do not. Several thousand years later, we are more wary of the enchantments of beauty. We not only split off—with the greatest facility—the "inside" (character, intellect) from the "outside" (looks); but we are actually surprised when someone who is beautiful is also intelligent, talented, good. 2

It was principally the influence of Christianity that deprived beauty of the central place it had in classical ideals of human excellence. By limiting excellence (*virtus* in Latin) to *moral* virtue only, Christianity set beauty adrift—as an alienated, arbitrary, superficial enchantment. And beauty has continued to lose prestige. For close to two centuries it has become a convention to attribute beauty to only one of the two sexes: the sex which, however Fair, is always Second. Associating beauty with women has put beauty even further on the defensive, morally. 3

A beautiful woman, we say in English. But a handsome man. "Handsome" is the masculine equivalent of—and refusal of—a compliment which has accumulated certain demeaning overtones, by being reserved for women only. That one can call a man "beautiful" in French and in Italian suggests that Catholic countries—unlike those countries shaped by the Protestant version of Christianity—still retain some vestiges of the pagan admiration for beauty. But the difference, if one exists, is of degree only. In every modern country that is Christian or post-Christian, women *are* the beautiful sex—to the detriment of the notion of beauty as well as of women. 4

To be called beautiful is thought to name something essential to women's character and concerns. (In contrast to men—whose essence is to be strong, or effective, or competent.) It does not take someone in the throes of advanced feminist awareness to perceive that the way women are taught to be involved 5 with beauty encourages narcissism, reinforces dependence and immaturity. Everybody (women and men) knows that. For it is "everybody," a whole society, that has identified being feminine with caring about how one *looks*. (In contrast to being masculine—which is identified with caring about what one *is* and *does* and only secondarily, if at all, about how one looks.) Given these stereotypes, it is no wonder that beauty enjoys, at best, a rather mixed reputation.

It is not, of course, the desire to be beautiful that is wrong   6 but the obligation to be—or to try. What is accepted by most women as a flattering idealization of their sex is a way of making women feel inferior to what they actually are—or normally grow to be. For the ideal of beauty is administered as a form of self-oppression. Women are taught to see their bodies in *parts,* and to evaluate each part separately. Breasts, feet, hips, waistline, neck, eyes, nose, complexion, hair, and so on—each in turn is submitted to an anxious, fretful, often despairing scrutiny. Even if some pass muster, some will always be found wanting. Nothing less than perfection will do.

In men, good looks is a whole, something taken in at a   7 glance. It does not need to be confirmed by giving measurements of different regions of the body, nobody encourages a man to dissect his appearance, feature by feature. As for perfection, that is considered trivial—almost unmanly. Indeed, in the ideally good-looking man a small imperfection or blemish is considered positively desirable. According to one movie critic (a woman) who is a declared Robert Redford fan, it is having that cluster of skin-colored moles on one cheek that saves Redford from being merely a "pretty face." Think of the depreciation of women—as well as of beauty—that is implied in that judgment.

"The privileges of beauty are immense," said Cocteau. To   8 be sure, beauty is a form of power. And deservedly so. What is lamentable is that it is the only form of power that most women are encouraged to seek. This power is always conceived in relation to men; it is not the power to do but the power to attract. It is a power that negates itself. For this power is not one that can be chosen freely—at least, not by women—or renounced without social censure.

To preen, for a woman, can never be just a pleasure. It is   9
also a duty. It is her work. If a woman does real work—and even
if she has clambered up to a leading position in politics, law,
medicine, business, or whatever—she is always under pressure
to confess that she still works at being attractive. But in so far as
she is keeping up as one of the Fair Sex, she brings under suspi-
cion her very capacity to be objective, professional, authorita-
tive, thoughtful. Damned if they do—women are. And damned if
they don't.

One could hardly ask for more important evidence of the   10
dangers of considering persons as split between what is "inside"
and what is "outside" than that interminable half-comic half-
tragic tale, the oppression of women. How easy it is to start off
by defining women as caretakers of their surfaces, and then to
disparage them (or find them adorable) for being "superficial." It
is a crude trap, and it has worked for too long. But to get out of
the trap requires that women get some critical distance from that
excellence and privilege which is beauty, enough distance to see
how much beauty itself has been abridged in order to prop up the
mythology of the "feminine." There should be a way of saving
beauty *from* women—and *for* them.

1975

The Virtues of Ambition
Joseph Epstein

Ambition is one of those Rorschach words: define it and   1
you instantly reveal a great deal about yourself. Even that most
neutral of works, *Webster's,* in its Seventh New Collegiate Edition, gives itself away, defining ambition first and foremost as
"an ardent desire for rank, fame, or power." Ardent immediately assumes a heat incommensurate with good sense and sta-

bility, and rank, fame, and power have come under fairly heavy
attack for at least a century. One can, after all, be ambitious for
the public good, for the alleviation of suffering, for the enlightenment of mankind, though there are some who say that these
are precisely the ambitious people most to be distrusted.

Surely ambition is behind dreams of glory, of wealth, of   2
love, of distinction, of accomplishment, of pleasure, of goodness. What life does with our dreams and expectations cannot, of
course, be predicted. Some dreams, begun in selflessness, end in
rancor; other dreams, begun in selfishness, end in large-
heartedness. The unpredictability of the outcome of dreams is no
reason to cease dreaming.

To be sure, ambition, the sheer thing unalloyed by some   3
larger purpose than merely clambering up, is never a pretty prospect to ponder. As drunks have done to alcohol, the single-
minded have done to ambition—given it a bad name. Like a taste
for alcohol, too, ambition does not always allow for easy satia-
tion. Some people cannot handle it; it has brought grief to others,
and not merely the ambitious alone. Still, none of this seems sufficient cause for driving ambition under the counter.

What is the worst that can be said—that has been said—   4
about ambition? Here is a (surely) partial list:

To begin with, it, ambition, is often antisocial, and indeed is   5
now outmoded, belonging to an age when individualism was
more valued and useful than it is today. The person strongly im-
bued with ambition ignores the collectivity; socially detached, he
is on his own and out for his own. Individuality and ambition are
firmly linked. The ambitious individual, far from identifying himself and his fortunes with the group, wishes to rise above it. The
ambitious man or woman sees the world as a battle; rivalrous-
ness is his or her principal emotion: the world has limited prizes
to offer, and he or she is determined to get his or hers. Ambition
is, moreover, jesuitical; it can argue those possessed by it into
believing that what they want for themselves is good for everyone—that the satisfaction of their own desires is best for the
commonweal. The truly ambitious believe that it is a dog-eat-dog
world, and they are distinguished by wanting to be the dogs that
do the eating.

From here it is but a short hop to believe that those who 6
have achieved the common goals of ambition—money, fame,
power—have achieved them through corruption of a greater or
lesser degree, mostly a greater. Thus all politicians in high
places, thought to be ambitious, are understood to be, ipso facto,
without moral scruples. How could they have such scruples—a
weighty burden in a high climb—and still have risen as they
have?

If ambition is to be well regarded, the rewards of ambi- 7
tion—wealth, distinction, control over one's destiny—must be
deemed worthy of the sacrifices made on ambition's behalf. If
the tradition of ambition is to have vitality, it must be widely
shared; and it especially must be esteemed by people who are
themselves admired, the educated not least among them. The educated not least because, nowadays more than ever before, it is
they who have usurped the platforms of public discussion and
wield the power of the spoken and written word in newspapers,
in magazines, on television. In an odd way, it is the educated
who have claimed to have given up on ambition as an ideal. What
is odd is that they have perhaps most benefited from ambition—if
not always their own then that of their parents and grandparents.
There is a heavy note of hypocrisy in this; a case of closing the
barn door after the horses have escaped—with the educated
themselves astride them.

Certainly people do not seem less interested in success and 8
its accoutrements now than formerly. Summer homes, European
travel, BMWs—the locations, place names and name brands may
change, but such items do not seem less in demand today than a
decade or two years ago. What has happened is that people cannot own up to their dreams, as easily and openly as once they
could, lest they be thought pushing, acquisitive, vulgar. Instead
we are treated to fine pharisaical spectacles, which now more
than ever seem in ample supply: the revolutionary lawyer quar-
tered in the $250,000 Manhattan condominium; the critic of
American materialism with a Southampton summer home; the
publisher of radical books who takes his meals in three-star res-
taurants; the journalist advocating participatory democracy in all
phases of life, whose own children are enrolled in private

schools. For such people and many more perhaps not so egregious, the proper formulation is, "Succeed at all costs but refrain from *appearing* ambitious."

The attacks on ambition are many and come from various 9 angles; its public defenders are few and unimpressive, where they are not extremely unattractive. As a result, the support for ambition as a healthy impulse, a quality to be admired and inculcated in the young, is probably lower than it has ever been in the United States. This does not mean that ambition is at an end, that people no longer feel its stirrings and promptings, but only that, no longer openly honored, it is less often openly professed. Consequences follow from this, of course, some of which are that ambition is driven underground, or made sly, or perverse. It can also be forced into vulgarity, as witness the blatant pratings of its contemporary promoters. Such, then, is the way things stand: on the left angry critics, on the right obtuse supporters, and in the middle, as usual, the majority of earnest people trying to get on in life.

Many people are naturally distrustful of ambition, feeling 10 that it represents something intractable in human nature. Thus John Dean entitled his book about his involvement in the Watergate affair during the Nixon administration *Blind Ambition,* as if ambition were to blame for his ignoble actions, and not the constellation of qualities that make up his rather shabby character. Ambition, it must once again be underscored, is morally a two-sided street. Place next to John Dean Andrew Carnegie, who, among other philanthropic acts, bought the library of Lord Acton, at a time when Acton was in financial distress, and assigned its custodianship to Acton, who never was told who his benefactor was. Need much more be said on the subject than that, important though ambition is, there are some things that one must not sacrifice to it?

But going at things the other way, sacrificing ambition so as 11 to guard against its potential excesses, is to go at things wrongly. To discourage ambition is to discourage dreams of grandeur and greatness. All men and women are born, live, suffer, and die; what distinguishes us one from another is our dreams, whether they be dreams about worldly or unworldly things, and what we do to make them come about.

It may seem an exaggeration to say that ambition is the 12 linchpin of society, holding many of its disparate elements together, but it is not an exaggeration by much. Remove ambition and the essential elements of society seem to fly apart. Ambition, as opposed to mere fantasizing about desires, implies work and discipline to achieve goals, personal and social, of a kind society cannot survive without. Ambition is intimately connected with family, for men and women not only work partly for their families; husbands and wives are often ambitious for each other, but harbor some of their most ardent ambitions for their children. Yet to have a family nowadays—with birth control readily available, and inflation a good economic argument against having children—is nearly an expression of ambition in itself. Finally, though ambition was once the domain chiefly of monarchs and aristocrats, it has, in more recent times, increasingly become the domain of the middle classes. Ambition and futurity—a sense of building for tomorrow—are inextricable. Working, saving, planning—these, the daily aspects of ambition—have always been the distinguishing marks of a rising middle class. The attack against ambition is not incidentally an attack on the middle class and what it stands for. Like it or not, the middle class has done much of society's work in America; and it, the middle class, has from the beginning run on ambition.

It is not difficult to imagine a world shorn of ambition. It 13 would probably be a kinder world: without demands, without abrasions, without disappointments. People would have time for reflection. Such work as they did would not be for themselves but for the collectivity. Competition would never enter in. Conflict would be eliminated, tension become a thing of the past. The stress of creation would be at an end. Art would no longer be troubling, but purely celebratory in its functions. The family would become superfluous as a social unit, with all its former power for bringing about neurosis drained away. Longevity would be increased, for fewer people would die of heart attack or stroke caused by tumultuous endeavor. Anxiety would be extinct. Time would stretch on and on, with ambition long departed from the human heart.

Ah, how unrelievedly boring life would be!   14

There is a strong view that holds that success is a myth, and 15 ambition therefore a sham. Does this mean that success does not really exist? That achievement is at bottom empty? That the efforts of men and women are of no significance alongside the force of movements and events? Now not all success, obviously, is worth esteeming, nor all ambition worth cultivating. Which are and which are not is something one soon enough learns on one's own. But even the most cynical secretly admit that success exists; that achievement counts for a great deal; and that the true myth is that the actions of men and women are useless. To believe otherwise is to take on a point of view that is likely to be deranging. It is, in its implications, to remove all motive for competence, interest in attainment, and regard for posterity.

We do not choose to be born. We do not choose our parents. 16 ents. We do not choose our historical epoch, the country of our birth or the immediate circumstances of our upbringing. We do not, most of us, choose to die; nor do we choose the time or conditions of our death. But within all this realm of choicelessness, we do choose how we shall live: courageously or in cowardice, honorably or dishonorably, with purpose or in drift. We decide what is important and what is trivial in life. We decide that what makes us significant is either what we do or what we refuse to do. But no matter how indifferent the universe may be to our choices and decisions, these choices and decisions are ours to make. We decide. We choose. And as we decide and choose, so are our lives formed. In the end, forming our own destiny is what ambition is about.

1980

Moral Ambiguity
Barbara Grizzuti Harrison

The main thrust of the feminist movement, in all its histor- 1
ical manifestations, has been to recognize the value and to enhance the dignity of human life. At its best—its most noble and
most useful—it has always said *no* to that which degrades and
diminishes the quality of life; *no* to the sexual and economic exploitation of women and children in factories, mills, homes, offices; *no* to the slaughter of women, children, sons, lovers, husbands, and fathers in senseless wars; and *yes* to that which
enlarges the possibilities of goodness. The main thrust of femi-
nism has always been pro-life.

What an irony that feminists now find themselves locked in 2
battle with people who describe themselves as "pro-life"; that
we who have so passionately proclaimed, with all the authentic-
ity of suffering, that our minds and bodies are inviolate find ourselves in bitter opposition to those whose rallying cry is the
"sanctity of human life."

Feminists may protest that the highly organized, well- 3
financed "pro-life" forces have been known to use violence to
achieve their "pious" ends. We may say that—inasmuch as
"pro-lifers" were remarkably silent when lives were being lost in
Indochina and were silent on the issue of capital punishment—
they are not pro-life, but merely antiabortion. But to say that is
not to address ourselves to a real, heartbreaking question: have
we become so brutalized by our struggles that we see abortion
only in terms of expediency?

Now that our right to legal abortion stands in jeopardy, one 4
is frequently given to understand that it is not expedient to explore moral and emotional ambiguities. Of course that is wrong.
Now that we are at the barricades, precisely *because* we are at
the barricades, when moral sensitivity tends to crumble in the
face of action, I think we need to ask ourselves many questions.
The consequence of not discussing the moral ambiguities of abor-

tion is that we allow "pro-lifers" to catch the moral ball and run with it. We are afraid to say that abortion is terrible—for the woman whose body undergoes the trauma, and (I think) for the other life involved. Afraid to give our "enemies" ammunition, we whisper these things to one another; we are afraid to say them out loud.

Is it really so awful to admit to confusion and unhappiness   5
over the issue of abortion?

That is what Linda Bird Francke did. In 1973 Francke, the   6
mother of three children, had an abortion. Three years later, under a pseudonym, she published an account of her experience in
the *The New York Times,* and she was roundly denounced, both
by Right-to-Lifers and by women she describes as "pro-abortion
zealots." Neither group liked her "line."

The truth is that Francke didn't have a "line." Her brief   7
piece was a masterpiece of ambivalence: it spoke implicitly of
her relief—and explicitly of her remorse. Like most pieces written for catharsis (Francke had originally no intention to publish),
it had more of sensibility than of sense. In spite of its shortcomings, however—perhaps because of them—Francke's piece
struck a nerve. The *Times* received hundreds of letters in response. *The Ambivalence of Abortion* grew out of those responses.

Like Francke, women spoke of relief; they also spoke of   8
anger (sometimes turned inward, sometimes directed toward
doctors, clergymen, husbands, lovers, men in general, mothers,
fathers, and the women's movement, and the fetus); they spoke
of anguish, grieving, remorse, physical and emotional estrange-
ment from loved ones. Not a few of the women interviewed felt
betrayed by feminists who'd led them to believe that abortion
was "as easy as pulling a tooth."

Francke allows the hundreds of women interviewed—   9
young, old, single, and married women—to speak for themselves. The interviews are revelatory, painful, vivid. But I would
wish for more editorial comment. Francke addresses herself only
to the emotional ambivalence surrounding abortion. She doesn't
deal with moral ambiguity (or she chooses to regard morality and
emotion as synonymous). I think I understand her difficulty. It is

this: when one considers abortion as a moral issue, one is confronted with two absolute positions. *One,* the fetus is a human life, and abortion is, therefore, immoral. *Two,* women have the absolute right to control their bodies, and the placing of any limits on that control is, therefore, immoral. Unhappily, it is perfectly possible to have one's emotions *and* one's morality colored by both those positions—and the collision of absolutes throws one into the realm of relative morality, a realm from which it is next to impossible to write with any degree of clarity.

Francke chose not to wade into this messy territory, though 10 she would undoubtedly describe herself as "pro-choice":

> Regardless of whether [a woman] chooses to continue her pregnancy or to terminate it...it is her decision alone. So it falls to all of us to support that decision with grace, safety, and understanding—and to live with it, and each other, as best we can.

Francke takes an "I'm okay/You're okay" approach: she 11 hopes that, as a result of her book, "women who are suffering from guilt will feel comforted that others have suffered like them, and that women who feel guilty because they *don't* feel guilty will also find comfort in the stories of others who have no regrets."

Francke says that many abortions were a "life-style 12 choice." What she means, by that deplorable jargon, is that some women chose to abort because—as they unhesitatingly tell us—they didn't want to be cursed with morning sickness while on a Caribbean vacation; they didn't want their graduate degrees deferred; or, chillingly, because the fetus was the "wrong" sex. I think such "life-style" choices are wasteful, frivolous—immoral.

I was also appalled by the number of women who became 13 pregnant because neither they nor their insensitive lovers took the trouble to use contraceptive devices; I was even more appalled by the women who routinely use abortion as a contraceptive device—and astounded that these same women could righteously mouth clichés about "control of their bodies," when the idea of exercising "control" never seemed to occur to them before having intercourse. (I want to say that the notion that we have, or ought to have, *absolute* control of our bodies is a sloppy one. I have no "right," for example, to place my body in front of a moving car; I have no "right" to perform private bodily functions in public. Civilization—as well as good sense—implies a measure of restraint.)

If all of this sounds like fodder for "pro-lifers," one has 14 only to read the testimony of women who were too young, too old, or simply too worn out by life to bear children without devastating physical and emotional consequences. Most of all, one has to read the testimonies of women who had abortions before abortion was legal. Their experiences were so savage, so degrading, that—at the bottom line—one can only say that this kind of brutality, this carnage, can never be allowed to occur again.

The trouble is that to say this is also to say that one life— 15 the life of the unborn child—must be sacrificed to preserve the life of another. This is a very great trouble: unless one does a moral/intellectual tap dance (such as likening the right to abortion to the concept of the "just" war), there seems to be no morally tenable position one can take, no "pure" position.

As feminists, we tend now to focus our moral indignation 16 on the fact that poor women will not be able to receive Medicaid funds for legal abortions. Here we seem to be standing on morally unambiguous ground: why should poor women be so unjustly penalized? We care about the quality of life; and giving birth to a baby that may be ill-fed, ill-educated, or physically abused does nothing to enhance the quality of anybody's life. But the other side of the moral coin, as amply demonstrated by Francke's interviewees, is that many poor women abort *because* they are poor; many women wanted babies but believed they couldn't afford them. Where should one direct one's anger? Toward the life-isn't-fair people who would *deny* women the right to abort, or toward the economic system (perpetuated, of course, by the same life-isn't-fair people) that allows poverty and affluence to coexist and *forces* women to abort? (One thing I didn't need to be convinced of before I read this book was that abortion does not cure poverty.)

I can imagine no circumstances under which I would have 17
an abortion; I consider the fetus a human life. But I would also
consider it immoral to bend my efforts to stop any other human
being from having an abortion she deemed necessary. I hate the
idea of abortion, but I hate even more the death of a woman by
coat hangers or lye. I hate, that is to say, the idea of murder
twice done.

We live in a secular, pluralistic society. I believe that 18
Heaven is an actual place—as real as the physical headquarters
of Planned Parenthood. But the promise of a Heavenly Reward is
cold comfort to those who do not so believe—and, even if I
wished to, I could not impose my belief on others.

Young Bolshevist revolutionaries once said that murder 19
was sometimes necessary, but never justifiable. That thinking in-
forms my thinking about abortion—and makes it no easier to
come to a comfortably unambiguous conclusion about it.

I have a teenage daughter. If she were to become pregnant, 20
I would consider it a violation of her integrity to tell her that she
could not have an abortion if she chose to have one; I would take
her to a doctor—and I would thank God that we had legal access
to a doctor who would not maim or butcher her. But if she were,
of her own free will and without coercion, to choose to give birth
to a child, I would consider it sinful not to support her in that
decision.

To read *The Ambivalence of Abortion* is to be convinced 21
that the problems raised by abortion cannot be satisfied by right-
on slogans. What, for example, are the consequences, for the
mother, of bearing a child to term and offering it up for adoption?
Is this truly a humane solution, or does that mother also grieve
and mourn the loss of her child forever? I think the real message
of Francke's book is something philosophers and moral logicians
have always known: the most painful moral struggles are not
those between good and evil, but between the good and the
lesser good.

1978

What Is Poverty?

Jo Goodwin Parker

You ask me what is poverty? Listen to me. Here I am,   1
dirty, smelly, and with no "proper" underwear on and with the
stench of my rotting teeth near you. I will tell you. Listen to me.
Listen without pity. I cannot use your pity. Listen with understanding. Put yourself in my dirty, worn out, ill-fitting shoes, and
hear me.

Poverty is getting up every morning from a dirt- and illness-   2
stained mattress. The sheets have long since been used for diapers. Poverty is living in a smell that never leaves. This is a smell
of urine, sour milk, and spoiling food sometimes joined with the
strong smell of long-cooked onions. Onions are cheap. If you
have smelled this smell, you did not know how it came. It is the
smell of the outdoor privy. It is the smell of young children who
cannot walk the long dark way in the night. It is the smell of the
mattresses where years of "accidents" have happened. It is the
smell of the milk which has gone sour because the refrigerator
long has not worked, and it costs money to get it fixed. It is the
smell of rotting garbage. I could bury it, but where is the shovel?
Shovels cost money.

Poverty is being tired. I have always been tired. They told   3
me at the hospital when the last baby came that I had chronic
anemia caused from poor diet, a bad case of worms, and that I
needed a corrective operation. I listened politely—the poor are
always polite. The poor always listen. They don't say that there
is no money for iron pills, or better food, or worm medicine. The
idea of an operation is frightening and costs so much that, if I had
dared, I would have laughed. Who takes care of my children?
Recovery from an operation takes a long time. I have three children. When I left them with "Granny" the last time I had a job,
I came home to find the baby covered with fly specks, and a diaper that had not been changed since I left. When the dried diaper came off, bits of my baby's flesh came with it. My other child
was playing with a sharp bit of broken glass, and my oldest was

playing alone at the edge of a lake. I made twenty-two dollars a week, and a good nursery school costs twenty dollars a week for three children. I quit my job.

Poverty is dirt. You can say in your clean clothes coming **4** from your clean house, "Anybody can be clean." Let me explain about housekeeping with no money. For breakfast I give my children grits with no oleo or cornbread without eggs and oleo. This does not use up many dishes. What dishes there are, I wash in cold water and with no soap. Even the cheapest soap has to be saved for the baby's diapers. Look at my hands, so cracked and red. Once I saved for two months to buy a jar of Vaseline for my hands and the baby's diaper rash. When I had saved enough, I went to buy it and the price had gone up two cents. The baby and I suffered on. I have to decide every day if I can bear to put my cracked sore hands into the cold water and strong soap. But you ask, why not hot water? Fuel costs money. If you have a wood fire it costs money. If you burn electricity, it costs money. Hot water is a luxury. I do not have luxuries. I know you will be surprised when I tell you how young I am. I look so much older. My back has been bent over the wash tubs every day for so long, I cannot remember when I ever did anything else. Every night I wash every stitch my school age child has on and just hope her clothes will be dry by morning.

Poverty is staying up all night on cold nights to watch the **5** fire knowing one spark on the newspaper covering the walls means your sleeping child dies in flames. In summer poverty is watching gnats and flies devour your baby's tears when he cries. The screens are torn and you pay so little rent you know they will never be fixed. Poverty means insects in your food, in your nose, in your eyes, and crawling over you when you sleep. Poverty is hoping it never rains because diapers won't dry when it rains and soon you are using newspapers. Poverty is seeing your children forever with runny noses. Paper handkerchiefs cost money and all your rags you need for other things. Even more costly are antihistamines. Poverty is cooking without food and cleaning without soap.

Poverty is asking for help. Have you ever had to ask for **6** help, knowing your children will suffer unless you get it? Think about asking for a loan from a relative, if this is the only way you can imagine asking for help. I will tell you how it feels. You find out where the office is that you are supposed to visit. You circle that block four or five times. Thinking of your children, you go in. Everyone is very busy. Finally, someone comes out and you tell her that you need help. That never is the person you need to see. You go see another person, and after spilling the whole shame of your poverty all over the desk between you, you find that this isn't the right office after all—you must repeat the whole process, and it never is any easier at the next place.

You have asked for help, and after all it has a cost. You are again told to wait. You are told why, but you don't really hear because of the red cloud of shame and the rising cloud of despair. 7

Poverty is remembering. It is remembering quitting school in junior high because "nice" children had been so cruel about my clothes and my smell. The attendance officer came. My mother told him I was pregnant. I wasn't, but she thought that I could get a job and help out. I had jobs off and on, but never long enough to learn anything. Mostly I remember being married. I was so young then. I am still young. For a time, we had all the things you have. There was a little house in another town, with hot water and everything. Then my husband lost his job. There was unemployment insurance for a while and what few jobs I could get. Soon, all our nice things were repossessed and we moved back here. I was pregnant then. This house didn't look so bad when we first moved in. Every week it gets worse. Nothing is ever fixed. We now had no money. There were a few odd jobs for my husband, but everything went for food then, as it does now. I don't know how we lived through three years and three babies, but we did. I'll tell you something, after the last baby I destroyed my marriage. It had been a good one, but could you keep on bringing children in this dirt? Did you ever think how much it costs for any kind of birth control? I knew my husband was leaving the day he left, but there were no goodbys between us. I hope he has been able to climb out of this mess somewhere. He never could hope with us to drag him down. 8

That's when I asked for help. When I got it, you know how much it was? It was, and is, seventy-eight dollars a month for the 9

four of us; that is all I ever can get. Now you know why there is
no soap, no needles and thread, no hot water, no aspirin, no
worm medicine, no hand cream, no shampoo. None of these
things forever and ever and ever. So that you can see clearly, I
pay twenty dollars a month rent, and most of the rest goes for
food. For grits and cornmeal, and rice and milk and beans. I try
my best to use only the minimum electricity. If I use more, there
is that much less for food.

Poverty is looking into a black future. Your children won't 10
play with my boys. They will turn to other boys who steal to get
what they want. I can already see them behind the bars of their
prison instead of behind the bars of my poverty. Or they will turn
to the freedom of alcohol or drugs, and find themselves enslaved.
And my daughter? At best, there is for her a life like mine.

But you say to me, there are schools. Yes, there are 11
schools. My children have no extra books, no magazines, no extra pencils, or crayons, or paper and most important of all, they
do not have health. They have worms, they have infections, they
have pink-eye all summer. They do not sleep well on the floor, or
with me in my one bed. They do not suffer from hunger, my
seventy-eight dollars keeps us alive, but they do suffer from malnutrition. Oh yes, I do remember what I was taught about health
in school. It doesn't do much good. In some places there is a surplus commodities program. Not here. The country said it cost
too much. There is a school lunch program. But I have two children who will already be damaged by the time they get to school.

But, you say to me, there are health clinics. Yes, there are 12
health clinics and they are in the towns. I live out here eight
miles from town. I can walk that far (even if it is sixteen miles
both ways), but can my little children? My neighbor will take me
when he goes; but he expects to get paid, *one way or another*. I
bet you know my neighbor. He is that large man who spends his
time at the gas station, the barbershop, and the corner store complaining about the government spending money on the immoral
mothers of illegitimate children.

Poverty is an acid that drips on pride until all pride is worn 13
away. Poverty is a chisel that chips on honor until honor is worn
away. Some of you say that you would do *something* in my sit-

uation, and maybe you would, for the first week or the first
month, but for year after year after year?

Even the poor can dream. A dream of a time when there is 14
money. Money for the right kinds of food, for worm medicine,
for iron pills, for toothbrushes, for hand cream, for a hammer
and nails and a bit of screening, for a shovel, for a bit of paint, for
some sheeting, for needles and thread. Money to pay *in money*
for a trip to town. And, oh, money for hot water and money for
soap. A dream of when asking for help does not eat away the last
bit of pride. When the office you visit is as nice as the offices of
other governmental agencies, when there are enough workers to
help you quickly, when workers do not quit in defeat and despair. When you have to tell your story to only one person, and
that person can send you for other help and you don't have to
prove your poverty over and over and over again.

I have come out of my despair to tell you this. Remember I 15
did not come from another place or another time. Others like me
are all around you. Look at us with an angry heart, anger that
will help you help me. Anger that will let you tell of me. The poor
are always silent. Can you be silent too?

1971

Pornoviolence

Tom Wolfe

"*Keeps His Mom-in-law in Chains*, meet *Kills Son and* 1
Feeds Corpse to Pigs."

"Pleased to meet you."   2

"*Teenager Twists Off Corpse's Head...to Get Gold Teeth*, 3
meet *Strangles Girl Friend, Then Chops Her to Pieces*."

"How you doing?"   4

"Nurse's Aide Sees Fingers Chopped Off in Meat Grinder, 5
meet *I Left My Babies in the Deep Freeze."*

"It's a pleasure." 6

It's a pleasure! No doubt about that! In all these years of 7
journalism I have covered more conventions than I care to remember. Podiatrists, theosophists, Professional Budget Finance
dentists, oyster farmers, mathematicians, truckers, dry cleaners,
stamp collectors, Esperantists, nudists, and newspaper editors—
I have seen them all, together, in vast assemblies, sloughing
through the wall-to-wall of a thousand hotel lobbies (the nudists
excepted) in their shimmering gray-metal suits and pajama-stripe
shirts with white Plasti-Coat name cards on their chests, and I
have sat through their speeches and seminars (the nudists included) and attentively endured ear baths such as you wouldn't
believe. And yet none has ever been quite like the convention of
the stringers for *The National Enquirer.*

The Enquirer is a weekly newspaper that is probably known 8
by sight to millions more than know it by name. No one who ever
came face-to-face with *The Enquirer* on a newsstand in its wild-
est days is likely to have forgotten the sight: a tabloid with great
inky shocks of type all over the front page saying something on
the order of *Gouges Out Wife's Eyes to Make Her Ugly, Dad
Hurls Hot Grease in Daughter's Face, Wife Commits Suicide after 2 Years of Poisoning Fails to Kill Husband*...

The stories themselves were supplied largely by stringers, 9
i.e., correspondents, from all over the country, the world, for
that matter, mostly copy editors and reporters on local newspapers. Every so often they would come upon a story, usually via
the police beat, that was so grotesque the local sheet would dis-
card it or run it in a highly glossed form rather than offend or
perplex its readers. The stringers would preserve them for *The
Enquirer,* which always rewarded them well and respectfully.

One year *The Enquirer* convened and feted them at a hotel 10
in Manhattan. This convention was a success in every way. The
only awkward moment was at the outset when the stringers all
pulled in. None of them knew each other. Their hosts got around
the problem by introducing them by the stories they had supplied. The introductions went like this:

"Harry, I want you to meet Frank here. Frank did that 11
story, you remember that story, *Midget Murderer Throws Girl
Off Cliff after She Refuses to Dance with Him.*"

"Pleased to meet you. That was some story." 12

"And Harry did the one about *I Spent Three Days Trapped* 13
*at Bottom of Forty-Foot-Deep Mine Shaft and Was Saved by a
Swarm of Flies.*"

"Likewise, I'm sure." 14

And *Midget Murderer Throws Girl Off Cliff* shakes hands 15
with *I Spent Three Days Trapped at Bottom of Forty-Foot-Deep
Mine Shaft,* and *Buries Her Baby Alive* shakes hands with *Boy,
Twelve, Strangles Two-Year-Old Girl,* and *Kills Son and Feeds
Corpse to Pigs* shakes hands with *He Strangles Old Woman and
Smears Corpse with Syrup, Ketchup, and Oatmeal*...and...

...There was a great deal of esprit about the whole thing. 16
These men were, in fact, the avant-garde of a new genre that
since then has become institutionalized throughout the nation
without anyone knowing its proper name. I speak of the new pornography, the pornography of violence.

Pornography comes from the Greek word "*porne,*" mean- 17
ing harlot, and pornography is literally the depiction of the acts
of harlots. In the new pornography, the theme is not sex. The
new pornography depicts practitioners acting out another, murk-
ier drive: people staving teeth in, ripping guts open, blowing
brains out, and getting even with all those bastards...

The success of *The Enquirer* prompted many imitators to 18
enter the field, *Midnight, The Star Chronicle, The National Insider, Inside News, The National Close-up, The National Tat-
tler, The National Examiner.* A truly competitive free press
evolved, and soon a reader could go to the newspaper of his
choice for *Kill the Retarded! (Won't You Join My Movement?)*
and *Unfaithful Wife? Burn Her Bed!, Harem Master's Mistress
Chops Him with Machete, Babe Bites Off Boy's Tongue,* and
*Cuts Buddy's Face to Pieces for Stealing His Business and Fi-
ancée.*

And yet the last time I surveyed the Violence press, I no- 19
ticed a curious thing. These pioneering journals seem to have
pulled back. They seem to be regressing to what is by now the

Redi-Mix staple of literate Americans, mere sex. *Ecstasy and Me (by Hedy Lamarr)*, says *The National Enquirer. I Run a Sex Art Gallery*, says *The National Insider*. What has happened, I think, is something that has happened to avant-gardes in many fields, from William Morris and the Craftsmen to the Bauhaus group. Namely, their discoveries have been preempted by the Establishment and so thoroughly dissolved into the mainstream they no longer look original.

Robert Harrison, the former publisher of *Confidential*, and 20 later publisher of the aforementioned *Inside News*, was perhaps the first person to see it coming. I was interviewing Harrison early in January 1964 for a story in *Esquire* about six weeks after the assassination of President Kennedy, and we were in a cab in the West Fifties in Manhattan, at a stoplight, by a newsstand, and Harrison suddenly pointed at the newsstand and said, "Look at that. They're doing the same thing *The Enquirer* does."

There on the stand was a row of slick-paper, magazine-size 21 publications, known in the trade as one-shots, with titles like *Four Days That Shook the World, Death of a President, An American Tragedy*, or just *John Fitzgerald Kennedy (1921–1963)*. "You want to know why people buy those things?" said Harrison. "People buy those things to see a man get his head blown off."

And, of course, he was right. Only now the publishers were 22 in many cases the pillars of the American press. Invariably, these "special coverages" of the assassination bore introductions piously commemorating the fallen President, exhorting the American people to strength and unity in a time of crisis, urging greater vigilance and safeguards for the new President, and even raising the nice metaphysical question of collective guilt in "an age of violence."

In the years since then, of course, there has been an inces- 23 sant replay, with every recoverable clinical detail, of those less than five seconds in which a man got his head blown off. And throughout this deluge of words, pictures, and film frames, I have been intrigued with one thing: The point of view, the vantage point, is almost never that of the victim, riding in the Presidential Lincoln Continental. What you get is...the view from

Oswald's rifle. You can step right up here and look point-blank right through the very hairline cross in Lee Harvey Oswald's Optics Ordnance in weaponry four-power Japanese telescope sight and watch, frame by frame by frame by frame, as that man there's head comes apart. Just a little History there before your very eyes.

The television networks have schooled us in the view from 24 Oswald's rifle and made it seem a normal pastime. The TV viewpoint is nearly always that of the man who is going to strike. The last time I watched *Gunsmoke,* which was not known as a very violent Western in TV terms, the action went like this: The Wellington agents and the stagecoach driver pull guns on the badlands gang leader's daughter and Kitty, the heart-of-gold saloon-keeper, and kidnap them. Then the badlands gang shoots two Wellington agents. Then they tie up five more and talk about shooting them. Then they desist because they might not be able to get a hotel room in the next town if the word got around. Then one badlands gang gunslinger attempts to rape Kitty while the gang leader's younger daughter looks on. Then Kitty resists, so he slugs her one in the jaw. Then the gang leader slugs him. Then the gang leader slugs Kitty. Then Kitty throws hot stew in a gang member's face and hits him over the back of the head with a revolver. Then he knocks her down with a rock. Then the gang sticks up a bank. Here comes the marshal, Matt Dillon. He shoots a gang member and breaks it up. Then the gang leader shoots the guy who was guarding his daughter and the woman. Then the marshal shoots the gang leader. The final exploding bullet signals The End.

It is not the accumulated slayings and bone crushings that 25 make this pornoviolence, however. What makes it pornoviolence is that in almost every case the camera angle, therefore the viewer, is with the gun, the fist, the rock. The pornography of violence has no point of view in the old sense that novels do. You do not live the action through the hero's eyes. You live with the aggressor, whoever he may be. One moment you are the hero. The next you are the villain. No matter whose side you may be on consciously, you are in fact with the muscle, and it is you who disintegrate all comers, villains, lawmen, women, anybody. On the rare occasions in which the gun is emptied into the camera—i.e., into your face—the effect is so startling that the pornography of violence all but loses its fantasy charm. There are not nearly so many masochists as sadists among those little devils whispering into one's ears.

In fact, sex—"sadomasochism"—is only a part of the pornography of violence. Violence is much more wrapped up, simply, with status. Violence is the simple, ultimate solution for problems of status competition, just as gambling is the simple, ultimate solution for economic competition. The old pornography was the fantasy of easy sexual delights in a world where sex was kept unavailable. The new pornography is the fantasy of easy triumph in a world where status competition has become so complicated and frustrating. 26

Already the old pornography is losing its kick because of over-exposure. In the late thirties, Nathanael West published his last and best-regarded novel, *The Day of the Locust,* and it was a terrible flop commercially, and his publisher said if he ever published another book about Hollywood it would "have to be *My Thirty-nine Ways of Making Love by Hedy Lamarr.*" He thought he was saying something that was funny because it was beyond the realm of possibility. Less than thirty years later, however, Hedy Lamarr's *Ecstasy and Me* was published. Whether she mentions thirty-nine ways, I'm not sure, but she gets off to a flying start: "The men in my life have ranged from a classic case history of impotence, to a whip-brandishing sadist who enjoyed sex only after he tied my arms behind me with the sash of his robe. There was another man who took his pleasure with a girl in my own bed, while he thought I was asleep in it." 27

Yet she was too late. The book very nearly sank without a trace. The sin itself is wearing out. Pornography cannot exist without certified taboo to violate. And today Lust, like the rest of the Seven Deadly Sins—Pride, Sloth, Envy, Greed, Anger, and Gluttony—is becoming a rather minor vice. The Seven Deadly Sins, after all, are only sins against the self. Theologically, the idea of Lust—well, the idea is that if you seduce some poor girl from Akron, it is not a sin because you are ruining her, but because you are wasting your time and your energies and 28 damaging your own spirit. This goes back to the old work ethic, when the idea was to keep every able-bodied man's shoulder to the wheel. In an age of riches for all, the ethic becomes more nearly: Let him do anything he pleases, as long as he doesn't get in my way. And if he does get in my way, or even if he doesn't...well...we have *new* fantasies for that. *Put hair on the walls*.

"Hair on the walls" is the invisible subtitle of Truman Capote's book *In Cold Blood*. The book is neither a who-done-it nor a will-they-be-caught, since the answers to both questions are known from the outset. It does ask why-did-they-do-it, but the answer is soon as clear as it is going to be. Instead, the book's suspense is based largely on a totally new idea in detective stories: the promise of gory details, and the withholding of them until the end. Early in the game one of the two murderers, Dick, starts promising to put "plenty of hair on them-those walls" with a shotgun. So read on, gentle readers, and on and on; you are led up to the moment before the crime on page 60—yet the specifics, what happened, the gory details, are kept out of sight, in grisly dangle, until page 244.

But Dick and Perry, Capote's killers, are only a couple of Low Rent bums. With James Bond the new pornography reached a dead center, the bureaucratic middle class. The appeal of Bond has been explained as the appeal of the lone man who can solve enormously complicated, even world problems through his own bravery and initiative. But Bond is not a lone man at all, of course. He is not the Lone Ranger. He is much easier to identify than that. He is a salaried functionary in a bureaucracy. He is a sport, but a believable one; not a millionaire, but a bureaucrat on an expense account. He is not even a high-level bureaucrat. He is an operative. This point is carefully and repeatedly made by having his superiors dress him down for violations of standard operating procedure. Bond, like the Lone Ranger, solves problems with guns and fists. When it is over, however, the Lone Ranger leaves a silver bullet. Bond, like the rest of us, fills out a report in triplicate.

Marshall McLuhan says we are in a period in which it will become harder and harder to stimulate lust through words and pictures—i.e., the old pornography. In the latest round of pornographic movies the producers have found it necessary to introduce violence, bondage, torture, and aggressive physical destruction to an extraordinary degree. The same sort of bloody escalation may very well happen in the pure pornography of violence. Even such able craftsmen as Truman Capote, Ian Fleming, NBC, and CBS may not suffice. Fortunately, there are historical models to rescue us from this frustration. In the latter days of the Roman Empire, the Emperor Commodus became jealous of the celebrity of the great gladiators. He took to the arena himself, with his sword, and began dispatching suitably screened cripples and hobbled fighters. Audience participation became so popular that soon various *illuminati* of the Commodus set, various boys and girls of the year, were out there, suited up, gaily cutting a sequence of dwarfs and feebles down to short ribs. Ah, swinging generations, what new delights await?

1967

Good Souls

Dorothy Parker

All about us, living in our very families, it may be, there   1
exists a race of curious creatures. Outwardly, they possess no marked peculiarities; in fact, at a hasty glance, they may be readily mistaken for regular human beings. They are built after the popular design; they have the usual number of features, arranged in the conventional manner; they offer no variations on the general run of things in their habits of dressing, eating, and carrying on their business.

Yet, between them and the rest of the civilized world, there   2
stretches an impassable barrier. Though they live in the very thick of the human race, they are forever isolated from it. They are fated to go through life, congenital pariahs. They live out their little lives, mingling with the world, yet never a part of it.

They are, in short, Good Souls.   3

And the piteous thing about them is that they are wholly   4
unconscious of their condition. A Good Soul thinks he is just like
anyone else. Nothing could convince him otherwise. It is
heartrending to see him, going cheerfully about, even whistling
or humming as he goes, all unconscious of his terrible plight. The
utmost he can receive from the world is an attitude of good-
humored patience, a perfunctory word of approbation, a praising
with faint damns, so to speak—yet he firmly believes that everything is all right with him.

There is no accounting for Good Souls.   5

They spring up anywhere. They will suddenly appear in   6
families which, for generations, have had no slightest stigma attached to them. Possibly they are throw-backs. There is scarcely
a family without at least one Good Soul somewhere in it at the
present moment—maybe in the form of an elderly aunt, an unmarried sister, an unsuccessful brother, an indigent cousin. No
household is complete without one.

The Good Soul begins early; he will show signs of his con-   7
dition in extreme youth. Go now to the nearest window, and look
out on the little children playing so happily below. Any group of
youngsters that you may happen to see will do perfectly. Do you
observe the child whom all the other little dears make "it" in
their merry games? Do you follow the child from whom the other
little ones snatch the cherished candy, to consume it before his
streaming eyes? Can you get a good look at the child whose precious toys are borrowed for indefinite periods by the other playful youngsters, and are returned to him in fragments? Do you see
the child upon whom all the other kiddies play their complete
repertory of childhood's winsome pranks—throwing bags of water on him, running away and hiding from him, shouting his name
in quaint rhymes, chalking coarse legends on his unsuspecting
back?

Mark that child well. He is going to be a Good Soul when   8
he grows up.

Thus does the doomed child go through early youth and ad-   9
olescence. So does he progress towards the fulfillment of his destiny. And then, some day, when he is under discussion, someone

will say of him, "Well, he means well, anyway." That settles it.
For him, that is the end. Those words have branded him with the
indelible mark of his pariahdom. He has come into his majority;
he is a full-fledged Good Soul.

The activities of the adult of the species are familiar to us 10
all. When you are ill, who is it that hastens to your bedside bearing molds of blancmange, which, from infancy, you have hated
with unspeakable loathing? As usual, you are way ahead of me,
gentle reader—it is indeed the Good Soul. It is the Good Souls
who efficiently smooth out your pillow when you have just
worked it into the comfortable shape, who creak about the room
on noisy tiptoe, who tenderly lay on your fevered brow damp
cloths which drip ceaselessly down your neck. It is they who
ask, every other minute, if there isn't something that they can do
for you. It is they who, at great personal sacrifice, spend long
hours sitting beside your bed, reading aloud the continued stories
in the *Woman's Home Companion,* or chatting cozily on the increase in the city's death rate.

In health, as in illness, they are always right there, ready to 11
befriend you. No sooner do you sit down, than they exclaim that
they can see you aren't comfortable in that chair, and insist on
your changing places with them. It is the Good Souls who just
know that you don't like your tea that way, and who bear it mas-
terfully away from you to alter it with cream and sugar until it is
a complete stranger to you. At the table, it is they who always
feel that their grapefruit is better than yours and who have to be
restrained almost forcibly from exchanging with you. In a restaurant the waiter invariably makes a mistake and brings them
something which they did not order—and which they refuse to
have changed, choking it down with a wistful smile. It is they
who cause traffic blocks, by standing in subway entrances arguing altruistically as to who is to pay the fare.

At the theater, should they be members of a box-party, it is 12
the Good Souls who insist on occupying the rear chairs; if the
seats are in the orchestra, they worry audibly, all through the
performance, about their being able to see better than you, until
finally in desperation you grant their plea and change seats with
them. If, by so doing, they can bring a little discomfort on them-

selves—sit in a draught, say, or behind a pillar—then their happiness is complete. To feel the genial glow of martyrdom—that is all they ask of life....

The lives of Good Souls are crowded with Occasions, each 13 with its own ritual which must be solemnly followed. On Mother's Day, Good Souls conscientiously wear carnations; on St. Patrick's Day, they faithfully don boutonnieres of shamrocks; on Columbus Day, they carefully pin on miniature Italian flags. Every feast must be celebrated by the sending out of cards—Valentine's Day, Arbor [Day], Groundhog Day, and all the other important festivals, each is duly observed. They have a perfect genius for discovering appropriate cards of greeting for the event. It must take hours of research.

If it's too long a time between holidays, then the Good Soul 14 will send little cards or little mementoes, just by way of surprises. He is strong on surprises, anyway. It delights him to drop in unexpectedly on his friends. Who has not known the joy of those evenings when some Good Soul just runs in, as a surprise? It is particularly effective when a chosen company of other guests happens to be present—enough for two tables of bridge, say. This means that the Good Soul must sit wistfully by, patiently watching the progress of the rubber, or else must cut in at intervals, volubly voicing his desolation at causing so much inconvenience, and apologizing constantly during the evening.

His conversation, admirable though it is, never receives its 15 just due of attention and appreciation. He is one of those who believe and frequently quote the exemplary precept that there is good in everybody; hanging in his bedchamber is the whimsically phrased, yet vital, statement, done in burned leather—"There is so much good in the worst of us and so much bad in the best of us that it hardly behooves any of us to talk about the rest of us." This, too, he archly quotes on appropriate occasions. Two or three may be gathered together, intimately discussing some mutual acquaintance. It is just getting really absorbing, when comes the Good Soul, to utter his dutiful, "We mustn't judge harshly—after all, we must always remember that many times our own actions may be misconstrued." Somehow, after several of these little reminders, there seems to be a general waning of interest; the

little gathering breaks up, inventing quaint excuses to get away
and discuss the thing more fully, adding a few really good details,
some place where the Good Soul will not follow. While the Good
Soul pitifully ignorant of their evil purpose glows with the
warmth of conscious virtue, and settles himself to read the Con-
tributors' Club, in the *Atlantic Monthly*, with a sense of duty well
done....

    Good Souls are no mean humorists. They have a time- 16
honored formula of fun-making, which must be faithfully followed. Certain words or phrases must be whimsically distorted
every time they are used. "Over the river," they dutifully say,
whenever they take their leave. "Don't you cast any asparagus
on me," they warn, archly; and they never fail to speak of "three
times in concussion." According to their ritual, these screaming
phrases must be repeated several times, for the most telling effect, and are invariably followed by hearty laughter from the
speaker, to whom they seem eternally new.

    Perhaps the most congenial role of the Good Soul is that of 17
advice-giver. He loves to take people aside and have serious little personal talks, all for their own good. He thinks it only right
to point out faults or bad habits which are, perhaps unconsciously, growing on them. He goes home and laboriously writes
long, intricate letters, invariably beginning, "Although you may
feel that this is no affair of mine, I think that you really ought to
know," and so on, indefinitely. In his desire to help, he reminds
one irresistibly of Marcelline, who used to try so pathetically and
so fruitlessly to be of some assistance in arranging the circus
arena, and who brought such misfortunes on his own innocent
person thereby.

    The Good Souls will, doubtless, gain their reward in 18
Heaven; on this earth, certainly, theirs is what is technically
known as a rough deal. The most hideous outrages are perpetrated on them. "Oh, he won't mind," people say. "He's a Good
Soul." And then they proceed to heap the rankest impositions
upon him. When Good Souls give a party, people who have accepted weeks in advance call up at the last second and refuse,
without the shadow of an excuse save that of a subsequent engagement. Other people are invited to all sorts of entertaining af-

fairs; the Good Soul, unasked, waves them a cheery good-bye and hopes wistfully that they will have a good time. His is the uncomfortable seat in the motor; he is the one to ride backwards in the train; he is the one who is always chosen to solicit subscriptions and make up deficits. People borrow his money, steal his servants, lose his golf balls, use him as a sort of errand boy, leave him flat whenever something more attractive offers—and carry it all off with their cheerful slogan, "Oh, he won't mind—he's a Good Soul."

And that's just it—Good Souls never do mind. After each 19 fresh atrocity they are more cheerful, forgiving and virtuous, if possible, than they were before. There is simply no keeping them down—back they come, with their little gifts, and their little words of advice, and their little endeavors to be of service, always anxious for more.

Yes, there can be no doubt about it—their reward will come 20 to them in the next world.

Would that they were even now enjoying it!   21

1919

5

Division and Classification

Thinking as a Hobby

William Golding

While I was still a boy, I came to the conclusion that there 1
were three grades of thinking; and since I was later to claim
thinking as my hobby, I came to an even stranger conclusion—
namely, that I myself could not think at all.

I must have been an unsatisfactory child for grownups to 2
deal with. I remember how incomprehensible they appeared to
me at first, but not, of course, how I appeared to them. It was the
headmaster of my grammar school who first brought the subject
of thinking before me—though neither in the way, nor with the
result he intended. He had some statuettes in his study. They
stood on a high cupboard behind his desk. One was a lady wearing nothing but a bath towel. She seemed frozen in an eternal
panic lest the bath towel slip down any farther; and since she had
no arms, she was in an unfortunate position to pull the towel up
again. Next to her, crouched the statuette of a leopard, ready to
spring down at the top drawer of a filing cabinet labeled A–AH.
My innocence interpreted this as the victim's last, despairing
cry. Beyond the leopard was a naked, muscular gentleman, who

167

sat, looking down, with his chin on his fist and his elbow on his knee. He seemed utterly miserable.

Some time later, I learned about these statuettes. The head- 3 master had placed them where they would face delinquent children, because they symbolized to him the whole of life. The naked lady was the Venus of Milo. She was Love. She was not worried about the towel. She was just busy being beautiful. The leopard was Nature, and he was being natural. The naked, muscular gentleman was not miserable. He was Rodin's Thinker, an image of pure thought. It is easy to buy small plaster models of what you think life is like.

I had better explain that I was a frequent visitor to the 4 headmaster's study, because of the latest thing I had done or left undone. As we now say, I was not integrated. I was, if anything, disintegrated; and I was puzzled. Grownups never made sense. Whenever I found myself in a penal position before the headmaster's desk, with the statuettes glimmering whitely above him, I would sink my head, clasp my hands behind my back and writhe one shoe over the other.

The headmaster would look opaquely at me through flash- 5 ing spectacles.

"What are we going to do with you?"   6

Well, what *were* they going to do with me? I would writhe 7 my shoe some more and stare down at the worn rug.

"Look up, boy! Can't you look up?"   8

Then I would look up at the cupboard, where the naked 9 lady was frozen in her panic and the muscular gentleman contemplated the hindquarters of the leopard in endless gloom. I had nothing to say to the headmaster. His spectacles caught the light so that you could see nothing human behind them. There was no possibility of communication.

"Don't you ever think at all?"   10

No, I didn't think, wasn't thinking, couldn't think—I was 11 simply waiting in anguish for the interview to stop.

"Then you'd better learn—hadn't you?"   12

On one occasion the headmaster leaped to his feet, reached 13 up and plonked Rodin's masterpiece on the desk before me.

"That's what a man looks like when he's really thinking." 14

I surveyed the gentleman without interest or comprehension.   15
"Go back to your class."   16

Clearly there was something missing in me. Nature had en-   17
dowed the rest of the human race with a sixth sense and left me
out. This must be so, I mused, on my way back to the class,
since whether I had broken a window, or failed to remember
Boyle's Law, or been late for school, my teachers produced me
one, adult answer: "Why can't you think?"

As I saw the case, I had broken the window because I had   18
tried to hit Jack Arney with a cricket ball and missed him; I could
not remember Boyle's Law because I had never bothered to
learn it; and I was late for school because I preferred looking
over the bridge into the river. In fact, I was wicked. Were my
teachers, perhaps, so good that they could not understand the
depths of my depravity? Were they clear, untormented people
who could direct their every action by this mysterious business
of thinking? The whole thing was incomprehensible. In my earlier years, I found even the statuette of the Thinker confusing. I
did not believe any of my teachers were naked, ever. Like someone born deaf, but bitterly determined to find out about sound, I
watched my teachers to find out about thought.

There was Mr. Houghton. He was always telling me to   19
think. With a modest satisfaction, he would tell me that he had
thought a bit himself. Then why did he spend so much time
drinking? Or was there more sense in drinking than there appeared to be? But if not, and if drinking were in fact ruinous to
health—and Mr. Houghton was ruined, there was no doubt about
that—why was he always talking about the clean life and the virtues of fresh air? He would spread his arms wide with the action
of a man who habitually spent his time striding along mountain
ridges.

"Open air does me good, boys—I know it!"   20

Sometimes, exalted by his own oratory, he would leap from   21
his desk and hustle us outside into a hideous wind.

"Now, boys! Deep breaths! Feel it right down inside you—   22
huge draughts of God's good air!"

He would stand before us, rejoicing in his perfect health, an   23
open-air man. He would put his hands on his waist and take a

tremendous breath. You could hear the wind, trapped in the cavern of his chest and struggling with all the unnatural impediments. His body would reel with shock and his ruined face go white at the unaccustomed visitation. He would stagger back to his desk and collapse there, useless for the rest of the morning.

Mr. Houghton was given to high-minded monologues about   24
the good life, sexless and full of duty. Yet in the middle of one of these monologues, if a girl passed the window, tapping along on her neat little feet, he would interrupt his discourse, his neck would turn of itself and he would watch her out of sight. In this instance, he seemed to me ruled not by thought but by an invisible and irresistible spring in his nape.

His neck was an object of great interest to me. Normally it   25
bulged a bit over his collar. But Mr. Houghton had fought in the First World War alongside both Americans and French, and had come—by who knows what illogic?—to a settled detestation of both countries. If either happened to be prominent in current affairs, no argument could make Mr. Houghton think well of it. He would bang the desk, his neck would bulge still further and go red. "You can say what you like," he would cry, "but I've thought about this—and I know what I think!"

Mr. Houghton thought with his neck.   26

There was Miss Parsons. She assured us that her dearest   27
wish was our welfare, but I knew even then, with the mysterious clairvoyance of childhood, that what she wanted most was the husband she never got. There was Mr. Hands—and so on.

I have dealt at length with my teachers because this was my   28
introduction to the nature of what is commonly called thought. Through them I discovered that thought is often full of unconscious prejudice, ignorance and hypocrisy. It will lecture on disinterested purity while its neck is being remorselessly twisted toward a skirt. Technically, it is about as proficient as most businessmen's golf, as honest as most politicians' intentions, or—to come near my own preoccupation—as coherent as most books that get written. It is what I came to call grade-three thinking, though more properly, it is feeling, rather than thought.

True, often there is a kind of innocence in prejudices, but in   29
those days I viewed grade-three thinking with an intolerant con-

tempt and an incautious mockery. I delighted to confront a pious lady who hated the Germans with the proposition that we should love our enemies. She taught me a great truth in dealing with grade-three thinkers; because of her, I no longer dismiss lightly a mental process which for nine-tenths of the population is the nearest they will ever get to thought. They have immense solidarity. We had better respect them, for we are outnumbered and surrounded. A crowd of grade-three thinkers, all shouting the same thing, all warming their hands at the fire of their own prejudices, will not thank you for pointing out the contradictions in their beliefs. Man is a gregarious animal, and enjoys agreement as cows will graze all the same way on the side of a hill.

Grade-two thinking is the detection of contradictions. I 30 reached grade two when I trapped the poor, pious lady. Grade-two thinkers do not stampede easily, though often they fall into the other fault and lag behind. Grade-two thinking is a withdrawal, with eyes and ears open. It became my hobby and brought satisfaction and loneliness in either hand. For grade-two thinking destroys without having the power to create. It set me watching the crowds cheering His Majesty and King and asking myself what all the fuss was about, without giving me anything positive to put in the place of that heady patriotism. But there were compensations. To hear people justify their habit of hunting foxes and tearing them to pieces by claiming that the foxes liked it. To hear our Prime Minister talk about the great benefit we conferred on India by jailing people like Pandit Nehru and Gandhi. To hear American politicians talk about peace in one sentence and refuse to join the League of Nations in the next. Yes, there were moments of delight.

But I was growing toward adolescence and had to admit 31 that Mr. Houghton was not the only one with an irresistible spring in his neck. I, too, felt the compulsive hand of nature and began to find that pointing out contradiction could be costly as well as fun. There was Ruth, for example, a serious and attractive girl. I was an atheist at the time. Grade-two thinking is a menace to religion and knocks down sects like skittles. I put myself in a position to be converted by her with an hypocrisy worthy of grade three. She was a Methodist—or at least, her parents were, and Ruth had to follow suit. But, alas, instead of relying on the Holy Spirit to convert me, Ruth was foolish enough to open her pretty mouth in argument. She claimed that the Bible (King James Version) was literally inspired. I countered by saying that the Catholics believed in the literal inspiration of Saint Jerome's *Vulgate,* and the two books were different. Argument flagged.

At last she remarked that there were an awful lot of Meth- 32 odists, and they couldn't be wrong, could they—not all those millions? That was too easy, said I restively (for the nearer you were to Ruth, the nicer she was to be near to) since there were more Roman Catholics than Methodists anyway; and they couldn't be wrong, could they—not all those hundreds of millions? An awful flicker of doubt appeared in her eyes. I slid my arm around her waist and murmured breathlessly that if we were counting heads, the Buddhists were the boys for my money. But Ruth had *really* wanted to do me good, because I was so nice. She fled. The combination of my arm and those countless Buddhists was too much for her.

That night her father visited my father and left, red-cheeked 33 and indignant. I was given the third degree to find out what had happened. It was lucky we were both of us only fourteen. I lost Ruth and gained an undeserved reputation as a potential libertine.

So grade-two thinking could be dangerous. It was in this 34 knowledge, at the age of fifteen, that I remember making a comment from the heights of grade two, on the limitations of grade three. One evening I found myself alone in the school hall, preparing it for a party. The door of the headmaster's study was open. I went in. The headmaster had ceased to thump Rodin's Thinker down on the desk as an example to the young. Perhaps he had not found any more candidates, but the statuettes were still there, glimmering and gathering dust on top of the cupboard. I stood on a chair and rearranged them. I stood Venus in her bath towel on the filing cabinet, so that now the top drawer caught its breath in a gasp of sexy excitement. "A-ah!" The portentous Thinker I placed on the edge of the cupboard so that he looked down at the bath towel and waited for it to slip.

Grade-two thinking, though it filled life with fun and excite- 35 ment, did not make for content. To find out the deficiencies of our elders bolsters the young ego but does not make for personal security. I found that grade two was not only the power to point out contradictions. It took the swimmer some distance from the shore and left him there, out of his depth. I decided that Pontius Pilate was a typical grade-two thinker. "What is truth?" he said, a very common grade-two thought, but one that is used always as the end of an argument instead of the beginning. There is still a higher grade of thought which says, "What is truth?" and sets out to find it.

But these grade-one thinkers were few and far between. **36** They did not visit my grammar school in the flesh though they were there in books. I aspired to them, partly because I was ambitious and partly because I now saw my hobby as an unsatisfactory thing if it went no further. If you set out to climb a mountain, however high you climb, you have failed if you cannot reach the top.

I *did* meet an undeniably grade-one thinker in my first year **37** at Oxford. I was looking over a small bridge in Magdalen Deer Park, and a tiny mustached and hatted figure came and stood by my side. He was a German who had just fled from the Nazis to Oxford as a temporary refuge. His name was Einstein.

But Professor Einstein knew no English at that time and I **38** knew only two words of German. I beamed at him, trying wordlessly to convey by my bearing all the affection and respect that the English felt for him. It is possible—and I have to make the admission—that I felt here were two grade-one thinkers standing side by side; yet I doubt if my face conveyed more than a formless awe. I would have given my Greek and Latin and French and a good slice of my English for enough German to communicate. But we were divided; he was as inscrutable as my headmaster. For perhaps five minutes we stood together on the bridge, undeniable grade-one thinker and breathless aspirant. With true greatness, Professor Einstein realized that my contact was better than none. He pointed to a trout wavering in midstream.

He spoke: "*Fisch.*"   **39**

My brain reeled. Here I was, mingling with the great, and **40** yet helpless as the veriest grade-three thinker. Desperately I sought for some sign by which I might convey that I, too, re-

vered pure reason. I nodded vehemently. In a brilliant flash I
used up half of my German vocabulary.

"Fisch. Ja Ja."   41

For perhaps another five minutes we stood side by side.   42
Then Professor Einstein, his whole figure still conveying good
will and amiability, drifted away out of sight.

I, too, would be a grade-one thinker. I was irreverent at the   43
best of times. Political and religious systems, social customs,
loyalties and traditions, they all came tumbling down like so
many rotten apples off a tree. This was a fine hobby and a sensible substitute for cricket, since you could play it all the year
round. I came up in the end with what must always remain the
justification for grade-one thinking, its sign, seal and charter. I
devised a coherent system for living. It was a moral system,
which was wholly logical. Of course, as I readily admitted, conversion of the world to my way of thinking might be difficult,
since my system did away with a number of trifles, such as big
business, centralized government, armies, marriage....

It was Ruth all over again. I had some very good friends   44
who stood by me, and still do. But my acquaintances vanished,
taking the girls with them. Young women seemed oddly contented with the world as it was. They valued the meaningless ceremony with a ring. Young men, while willing to concede the
chaining sordidness of marriage, were hesitant about abandoning
the organizations which they hoped would give them a career. A
young man on the first rung of the Royal Navy, while perfectly
agreeable to doing away with big business and marriage, got as
rednecked as Mr. Houghton when I proposed a world without
any battleships in it.

Had the game gone too far? Was it a game any longer? In   45
those prewar days, I stood to lose a great deal, for the sake of a
hobby.

Now you are expecting me to describe how I saw the folly   46
of my ways and came back to the warm nest, where prejudices
are so often called loyalties, where pointless actions are hallowed
into custom by repetition, where we are content to say we think
when all we do is feel.

But you would be wrong. I dropped my hobby and turned   47
professional.

If I were to go back to the headmaster's study and find the 48
dusty statuettes still there, I would arrange them differently. I
would dust Venus and put her aside, for I have come to love her
and know her for the fair thing she is. But I would put the
Thinker, sunk in his desperate thought, where there were shadows before him—and at his back, I would put the leopard,
crouched and ready to spring.

1961

Bicycles
Erika Ritter

It wasn't always like this. There was a time in the life of the 1
world when adults were adults, having firmly put away childish
things and thrown away the key.

Not any more. The change must have come about inno- 2
cently enough, I imagine. Modern Man learning to play nicely in
the sandbox with the other grown-ups. Very low-tension stuff.

Now, in every direction you look, your gaze is met by the 3
risible spectacle of adults postponing adolescence well into senil-
ity by means of adult toys: running shoes, baseball bats, roller
skates, and—bicycles!

But the attitude is no longer the fun-loving approach of a 4
bunch of superannuated kids, and I'm sure you can envision how
the evolution occurred. Jogging progressed from a casual encounter with the fresh air to an intensive relationship, attended
by sixty-dollar jogging shoes and a designer sweatband. Playing
baseball stopped being fun unless you had a Lacoste (as opposed
to low-cost) tee-shirt in which to impress your teammates. And
where was the thrill in running around a squash court unless it
was with a potentially important client?

As for bicycles—well, let's not even talk about bicycles. 5
On the other hand, maybe we *should* talk about them, because

there's something particularly poignant about how it all went wrong for the bicycle, by what declension this once proud and carefree vehicle sank into the role of beast of burden, to bear the weight of sobersided grown-ups at their supposed sport.

First, there was the earliest domestication of the North 6 American bicycle (*cyclus pedalis americanus*) in the late Hippie Scene Era of the 1960s. This was the age of the no-nuke whole-grain cyclist, who saw in the bicycle the possibility of Making a Statement while he rode. A statement about pollution, about materialism, about imperialism, about militarism, about—enough already. You get the picture: two wheels good, four wheels bad.

Thus it was that the basic bicycle gradually evolved into a 7 chunky three-speed number from China, bowed down under a plastic kiddie carrier, army surplus knapsacks, and a faded fender-sticker advising Make Tofu, Not War. And a rider clad in a red plaid lumber-jacket, Birkenstock sandals, and an expression of urgent concern for all living things.

Once the very act of bicycle riding had become an act of 8 high moral purpose, it was an easy step to the next phase of the bicycle's journey along the path of post-Meanderthal seriousness.

I'm speaking of the era of the high-strung thoroughbred bi- 9 cycle, whose rider had also made advances, from pedalling peacenik to a hunched and humorless habitué of the velodrome, clad in leather-seated shorts, white crash helmet, and fingerless gloves, whizzing soundlessly, and with no hint of joy, down city streets and along the shoulders of super-highways, aboard a vehicle sculpted in wisps of silver chrome. A vehicle so overbred, in its final evolutionary stages, that it began to resemble the mere exoskeleton of a conventional cycle, its flesh picked away by birds of carrion.

Having been stripped of any connection with its innocent 10 and leisurely origins, the bicycle now no longer bore the slightest resemblance to the happy creature it once had been. And in the mid-Plastic Scene Era, another crippling blow was struck by the upscale name-brand cyclist, who came along to finish what the fanatical velodromist had refined. Namely, the complete transformation of an ambling and unhurried mode of transit into a fast, nerve-wracking, expensive, and utterly competitive display of high speed, high technology, and high status.

The Upscale Cyclist was looking for a twelve-speed Bottec- 11 chia that matches his eyes, something that he'd look trendy upon the seat of, when riding to the office (the office!), and he was ready to pay in four figures for it.

Not only that, he was also prepared to shell out some heavy 12 bread for those status accessories to complete the picture: the backpack designed by the engineers at NASA, the insulated water-bottle to keep his Perrier chilled just right, the sixteen-track Walkman that would virtually assure him the envy of all his friends.

So much for the cyclist. What of his poor debased mount? 13

Not surprisingly, amongst the breed of bicycle, morale is 14 currently low, and personal pride all but a thing of the past. And yet...and yet, there are those who say that *cyclus pedalis americanus* is an indomitable creature, and that it is the bicycle, not its rider, who will make the last evolution of the wheel.

In fact, some theorize that the present high incidence of bi- 15 cycle thievery, far from being evidence of crime, is actually an indication that the modern bicycle has had enough of oppressive exploitation and man's joyless ways, and is in the process of reverting to the wild in greater and greater numbers.

There have always remained a few aboriginal undomesti- 16 cated bicycles—or so the theory goes—and now it is these free-spirited mavericks, down from the hills at night, who visit urban bikeracks, garages, and back porches to lure tame bicycles away with them.

Costly Kryptonite locks are wrenched asunder, expensive 17 accoutrements are shrugged off, intricate gear systems are torn away, and lo—look what is revealed! Unadorned, undefiled *cyclus* in all his pristine glory, unfettered and unencumbered once more, and free to roam.

A wistful fantasy, you might say? The maundering illusions 18 of someone who's been riding her bicycle too long without a crash helmet? I wonder.

Just the other day, there was that piece in the paper about a 19 bicycle that went berserk in a shopping centre, smashing two display windows before it was subdued. And did you hear about the recent sighting of a whole herd of riderless bicycles, all rolling soundlessly across a park in the night?

It all kind of gets you to thinking. I mean, do *you* know   20 where your ten-speed is tonight?

1984

Struggle for Justice
American Friends Service Committee

A criminal justice system reflects the values of those who   1 hold power in society. In colonial Massachusetts, for example, the most serious crimes were blasphemy, not attending church, and other activities that would appear harmless to us but were heinous to the ruling theocracy. As we examine the contemporary criminal justice system we can expect to find reflected the values and fears of those who hold power in our society. By their control of the legislative, policing, and criminal labeling processes they define what acts are criminal and set the penalties. Thus criminal law, in both content and administration, often becomes a political instrument, formulated and enforced by those with status and power against those who, predominantly, are status-poor and powerless.

The Founding Fathers were aware of these problems. With   2 the Constitution, the Bill of Rights, and the Fourteenth Amendment they constructed a legal system to protect the exercise of political freedoms unmatched anywhere in the history of representative government. These procedural safeguards include prohibition of ex post facto laws, guarantees of due process and equal protection under the law, and the outlawing of cruel and unusual punishment. They attempted to create an independent judiciary, protecting judges from political reprisals and temptations by means of high salaries and long (or lifelong) terms. Our federal system, a "government of laws not men," was developed to act as a brake on transitory majority opinion and the growth of governmental power.

Yet we see gross inequities in American criminal justice.   3

. . .

By and large our prisons are reserved for those with dark   4 skins, little money, or unconventional life-styles. In our view crimes committed by all those now in prison are far less damaging to our society than acts against life and health perpetrated by the powerful. We refer to those who develop and manufacture genocidal weapons, those who perpetuate the arms race or prolong the Indochina war for their own commercial advantage, those who pollute or destroy this country's natural resources for financial profit, those who manufacture unsafe automobiles and other dangerous products, price fixers, slum landlords, and others.

Not only do the powerful manage, by and large, to escape   5 the sanctions of the criminal justice system, they also manipulate the system for their own political ends. These are the functions of the criminal justice system we will examine here.

ECONOMIC DOMINANCE

Manipulation of the criminal justice system by the powerful   6 is perhaps most evident in the economic sphere. The struggle by labor for the right to organize is one of the bloodiest chapters in American history. Throughout the nineteenth century and into the twentieth, the courts and police repeatedly took the side of industrialists in blocking attempts to form labor unions and in preventing workers from striking. Violence marked many labor struggles, including the 1877 railroad strike, the 1910 Chicago clothing-industry strike, the 1919 strike against U.S. Steel, and the CIO's attempt to organize Little Steel in 1937, when eighteen were killed.

Judicial intervention was also used in labor disputes. When   7

owners were unable to find excuses for court action in the law
itself, they obtained court injunctions against strikers. As late as
1921, the United States Supreme Court upheld the position that
peaceful picketing could be enjoined on the grounds that it was
inherently intimidating and coercive in a strike controversy.
Court injunctions against picketing in labor disputes are not uncommon even today.

The prosecution of labor leaders under the Sherman Anti-   8
trust Act, originally intended to curb business monopolies, indicates the extent to which the Justice Department and the courts
identified themselves with business interests. Although the act is
a criminal law, the government is given the option of administrative or criminal proceedings. In the 438 actions initiated by the
government between 1890 and 1929 with decisions favorable to
the government prosecution, 27 percent of the actions against
businesses and business associations were criminal, compared
with 71 percent of the actions against labor unions.

The use of the courts and police to hamper the organization   9
of labor continues today. The United Farm Workers are a prime
example. Their struggle to gain collective strength has been a bitter one, hampered by court injunctions granted the owners of
large grape and lettuce farms. Cesar Chavez and other organizers
have been jailed for defying such injunctions. Their organizing
successes probably would have been impossible without the support of nationwide consumer boycotts.

In New Jersey and other states where migrant laborers   10
have not yet been able to initiate collective efforts, the local institutions of justice are still used to protect the exploitative economic relationship, subordinating the well-being of the pickers to
the profits of the growers. Predictable abuses occur within the
courts and local jails, especially for Spanish-speaking people.
Migrants are arrested without real cause or are given a phony
reason. A man arrested on a minor charge who does not have a
driver's license or other acceptable identification can be held in
jail until the court in that municipality meets—and in some places
the court meets only once a month! Bail is set beyond the capacity to pay. Loosely worded trespass laws are enforced in an intimidating manner. As one migrant worker complained to a re-
porter, "It's very bad. If you don't do what the farmer says, if

you cause any trouble, he call the police and get you arrested. Don't tell me about justice here. There is no justice for Puerto Ricans here."[1] Legal Services lawyers attempting to remedy this situation have won a series of legal victories. If these decisions are implemented, the migrant worker will have a little more freedom in Cumberland County, New Jersey.

Tax laws are another means whereby the powerful increase 11 their economic dominance. Efforts to plug scandalous tax loopholes have been unsuccessful for years. Today there are dozens of millionaires who pay no income tax at all. Taxes are extracted from salaried workers every payday by means of withholding; those in the upper brackets have considerably more opportunity to avoid taxes, legally, semilegally, or illegally. When violations are detected, the government rarely invokes the criminal process. The tax cheater can usually get off by paying a fine.

War tax resisters are particularly aware of the selective en- 12 forcement of tax laws. These citizens are convinced of the illegality and the immorality of the war in Vietnam and of the genocidal weapons being developed and manufactured. On grounds of conscience they refuse to pay taxes for these activities. They find that they are sometimes hounded by IRS agents for insignificant sums. Refusers have had automobiles seized and auctioned for tax liabilities of less than $5. Refusers acting publicly have been convicted of income-tax fraud. Rather than securing compliance with the tax laws, government efforts to penalize principaled tax refusers may serve, rather, to build a resistance movement.

The government has been extremely reluctant to prosecute 13 business leaders for such widespread and socially harmful crimes as deceptive advertising, pollution, selling dangerous merchandise, and violating antitrust laws. Real-estate agents are almost never prosecuted for blockbusting or for practicing racial discrimination in renting and selling, even though these practices are illegal. Election laws limiting political campaign contributions are violated every two and four years but enforcement policies are lax to the point of not existing. The campaign chests of politicians are regularly enriched by contributions from unions and

[1]*The New York Times,* August 17, 1970.

corporations, even though the Corrupt Practices Act prohibits such institutions from giving money to federal candidates. In its massive *Federal Civil Rights Enforcement Efforts,* the United States Civil Rights Commission recently documented widespread governmental refusal to enforce civil-rights statutes, particularly in the fields of employment, housing, education, agricultural services, labor programs, public accommodations, and public facilities.

14   When the government acts at all in such cases, it again usually prefers administrative rather than criminal proceedings. Enforcement statutes for economic regulations regularly provide for a variety of mechanisms for enforcement, with criminal procedure clearly regarded as a last resort. Dealing with violations by written warnings was the course the government took in the vast majority of the 980 white-collar crimes E. H. Sutherland found the top seventy corporations to have committed.[2] Only in 159 of the cases was an adverse decision reached in criminal court; the other 821 adverse decisions were all reached either by an administrative commission or by courts under civil or equity jurisdiction. In those rare instances when criminal procedures are used, penalties are relatively mild, usually including a fine and a short term in a minimum-security prison farm. We do not mean to imply that civil procedures are in themselves unjustified; what must be faulted is the class nature of the law enforcement process. Price-fixing General Electric executives receive a penalty of one month, while a thief who may steal only one item receives a penalty of several years.

15   Studies indicate that white-collar criminals such as the General Electric executives are far from rare. A 1947 study,[3] for example, revealed that 91 percent of a group of almost seventeen hundred New York City residents, chosen for their resemblance to the general population's socioeconomic characteristics but weighted accidentally toward upper income brackets, had committed at least one felony or serious misdemeanor. Among the forty-nine offenses listed on the questionnaire were robbery,

---

[2]*White Collar Crime* (New York: Holt, Rinehart and Winston, 1949).
[3]James Wallerstein and C. J. Wyle, "Our Law-abiding Law-breakers," *Probation,* 1947, pp. 107–112.

bribery, disorderly conduct, malicious mischief, criminal libel, falsification and fraud, perjury, indecency, and health code violations. Thirteen percent of the males had committed grand larcency, 26 percent auto theft, 17 percent burglary. The mean number of offenses per person was eighteen. Roughly half had committed at least one felony for which he had not been caught. Other studies have also documented the universality of undetected or unreported crime.

These results are confirmed by everyday experience. Many 16 Americans at some time have removed items from a motel room, failed to report income tax accurately, smoked pot, or cashed a check without sufficient funds. Most of these offenses are trivial and injure no one, which explains why we can commit them occasionally or even frequently without regarding ourselves as criminals. But then again, people have been sentenced to long prison terms for offenses equally trivial. The boundary line between harmless middle-class offenses and someone else's harmful violations of the law is a fuzzy one. This prejudice in favor of "our own kind" can be seen at its most blatant in the suggestion made in standard reference works on criminal procedure that prosecutors wisely refrain from prosecuting in cases of law violation where the offender comes from a "respectable" background. It never occurs to those who write lawbooks, apparently, that people other than professors and white businessmen might be hurt by a trial or a conviction.

SLAVERY AND RACISM

The justice system functions to maintain a racist relation- 17 ship between the white majority and the black, brown, red and yellow minorities in America. The command-obedience structure of racism has existed in the criminal justice system since the settlement of the country. Possessing the status of real estate or livestock under the cruel system of chattel slavery, black slaves were legal nullities in the eyes of the courts. They were systematically excluded from jury service, holding judgeships, acting in their own defense, and every other provision of criminal law procedure that protected white propertied males. Rendered "three-fifths of a man" by the Constitution, the slave came to know the legal system only as an extension of the rule of the slave system.

Before the Civil War the legal status of the freed Negro par-   18
alleled the slave's utter legal powerlessness. Criminal sentences often included the provision that freedmen could be sold into slavery as punishment for a criminal offense or in lieu of payment of taxes, fines, or civil judgments. Vaguely worded vagrancy statutes were ideal weapons for intimidating supposedly free black people. Vagrancy and other laws commonly provided for immediate punishment—usually whipping—without trial, enpoweringslave patrols and private citizens to be at one time complainant, judge, jury, and enforcement officer.

States outside the South also passed freed Negro laws   19
which, though often less severe than the South's, served the same purpose. The testimony of persons with "one-eighth Negro blood" was declared incompetent by Illinois and Delaware statutes. In Iowa free black persons could not be witnesses in cases involving whites. In Ohio blacks had to post bond as a condition of good behavior to secure residence. In 1853 Illinois made it a misdemeanor for a black to enter the state with the intention of residing. Throughout the country, by law and tradition, blacks were nonpersons in the eyes of the justice system, a status that mirrored their lack of rights of any political, economic, or social consequence in any other area of life.

After the Civil War emancipated black people saw the   20
master-slave relationship replaced by a master-servant relationship. Many of the restrictive provisions originally applied to freed Negroes were included in the infamous Black Codes. Several states created separate systems of criminal courts for blacks, who could not testify in white courts, nor could they serve as judges or jurors in either court system. Although such punishments had been abolished for whites, blacks could be confined in public stocks or whipped.

As blatantly discriminatory laws were repealed during the   21
era of Radical Reconstruction, more subtly restrictive statutes replaced them. Blacks were allowed to serve as witnesses, but a widely enacted statute provided that "whenever a person of color shall be examined as a witness, the court shall warn the

witness to declare the truth." Whites were not similarly warned. Although the Black Code of Texas provided that "there shall be no discrimination against such persons [blacks] in the administration of the criminal laws of this state," it included the qualifications that the law did not permit blacks to intermarry with whites, serve on juries, vote, or testify in cases involving whites.

The socially subordinate position of blacks within the criminal justice system has remained practically unchanged. Police brutality and summary violence still characterize the police presence in the black community. Jury service remains a restricted white privilege, making a mockery of the concept of investigation and judgment by one's peers. With token exceptions, the personnel of the justice system are white, forcing members of minority groups to face police, district attorneys, wardens, judges, and parole-board members who represent historically the oppressor's caste. Other forms of racism are more hidden. A judge or jury may weigh the credibility of a black witness's testimony differently from a white's. Cultural differences in dress, hairstyle, and speech may work to the disadvantage of minority men and women. Residual racial practices surviving from the era of slavery show that discrimination is not simply a matter of intentional policy; it also emerges from deeply ingrained attitudes and institutional prejudices that still survive.

In prisons racism is manifested in unequal job assignments, with blacks assigned to the most menial tasks. Black nationalist and Black Muslim literature is often banned. Individual guards who are racists or sadists or both have ample opportunity to abuse prisoners. Blacks who are affirming their cultural and racial identity are particularly likely targets. Those who show signs of becoming inmate leaders or who challenge institutional practices through lawsuits commonly suffer administrative punishments (the hole, strip cells, restricted diet, loss of privileges), or are transferred punitively, often to prisons with notorious reputations for brutal racist environments.

Racism is often consciously encouraged by prison officials who hope to keep black, brown, and white inmates occupied with fighting each other and hence more easily managed. Their strategy is to divide the races and control the convicts. A letter smuggled out by a black prisoner in Soledad Prison gives a picture of the depths of racial oppression and degradation that can occur behind walls:

> Never more than 6 blacks were allowed on max. row,
> which houses 24 inmates. Thus the remaining 18 cells were
> occupied by anti-black Caucasian and Mexican inmates
> who race talk us in shifts so that it's done 24 hours a day.
> On their exercise periods they spit, throw urine and feces
> in our cells while the officials stand by in indifference and
> approval. They, the officials call us HAMMERS and
> NIGGERS too. (Both expressions mean the same thing.)
> The prison officials here stopped serving the meals and
> deliberately selected the Caucasian and Mexican inmates
> (described throughout this letter) to serve the meals and
> they immediately proceeded to poison our meals by filling
> food to be issued to us with cleanser powder, crushed up
> glass, spit, urine and feces while the officials stood by and
> laughed.[4]

Another example of officially inspired racism is given by a 25 prisoner at the Federal Youth Center in Ashland, Kentucky, who described an incident in which a black inmate beat up a white guard.

> Notice that this "race trouble" was initiated by a fight
> between an inmate and a guard, and that the inmate got
> the better of the guard. Recognizing that the event could
> readily inspire similar attacks on them, the dormitory
> guards played up their racist solidarity with white
> southerners by interpreting the fray as a conflict between
> black and white instead of as a conflict between guard and
> prisoner. If they could sell their interpretation, they would
> at least gain a few white inmate protectors and possibly
> create enough tension between black and white inmates
> that the threat to themselves would be removed. The crew
> bosses' lectures the next day performed the same function
> of convincing prisoners to fight each other rather than the
> staff. The racial attack that was successfully instigated in

[4]"Black Caucus Report: Treatment of Prisoners at California Training Facility at Soledad Central," Black Caucus in the California State Legislature, July 1970.

this way set the whole compound on edge and effectively took the heat off the Man.[5]

The experiences of other oppressed minorities within the justice system parallel the treatment of blacks. An an instrument of Anglo domination, the justice apparatus serves to oppress Mexican-Americans in the Southwest. The United States Civil Rights Commission has reported widespread patterns of excessive police violence, discriminatory treatment of Chicano juveniles, biased enforcement of motor vehicle regulations, discourtesies to local Chicano citizens, and excessive use of stop-and-frisk laws to harass and intimidate local communities.[6] The commission found an almost total absence of Mexican-Americans on juries and noted that the "wide disparities" between jury service and population proportion could not be accounted for by language difficulties, educational levels, or other commonly offered excuses. Officials "abused their discretion" in setting excessive bail. In noting an almost total absence of Mexican-Americans among justice system employees, the commission found an almost systematic avoidance of the Spanish language by law enforcement personnel, which meant that routine contacts with police could easily escalate into major conflicts and that Chicanos in criminal courts "cannot plead intelligently, advise their lawyers with respect to the facts, fully understand the testimony of witnesses against them, or otherwise adequately prepare or assist in their own defense." The same pattern extends to probation and parole boards.

The brutality of racism and the indignities of second-class citizenship still characterize much of the administration of criminal justice. The racist ideologies of chattel slavery and of "separate but equal" have been declared legally dead, but the funeral continues and the ugly corpse has not yet been buried. The justice system remains an instrument of white Anglo domination and a barrier to the development of full power within communities of oppressed peoples.

[5]Jim Wessner, "Racism in Federal Prison," *The Peacemaker,* May 2, 1970, pp. 1–2.

[6]"Mexican-Americans and the Administration of Justice in the Southwest," March 1970.

JUVENILES

Blacks and Chicanos are not the only groups in our society 28
upon whom cultural assimilation has been forced. The American
majority has found all minority races and cultures threatening
and has treated many of them ruthlessly. Consider the wholesale
slaughter of the American Indian.

In the nineteenth century the waves of European immi- 29
grants came in for their share of forced assimilation. Being less
different from the majority than Indians and blacks, they were
treated less barbarically, but they were still treated as second-
class citizens. The criminal justice apparatus was part of the social structure used to repress them. One method of accomplishing this was through the creation of a new category of criminals:
juvenile delinquents.

Under the guise of saving children from a debauching envi- 30
ronment, juvenile delinquency laws made into crimes types of
youthful behavior that in the past had been handled informally—
sexual promiscuity, staying out late at night, drinking, smoking,
reading comic books, truancy, running away, and disobedience
to parents and teachers.

Of course the child-saving movement was bathed in a sea of 31
self-righteousness.[7] Heavy emphasis was placed on "rescuing"
victims of unhealthy environments—usually city slums—and
"elevating" them to a middle-class style of life. An 1855 report
from a New York City agency makes reference to

> large numbers of poor Italian children engaged in street
> occupations, following the heart and the hand-organ,
> selling newspapers, blackening boots, and the like, who
> were growing up utterly without education or moral
> discipline...The greatest difficulties were the greed of the
> parents to get all possible earnings from their children
> without regard to their education, the bigotry of some of
> their advisers and the existence amongst them of a species
> of serfdom.

This kind of theme runs with monotonous regularity 32

[7]We have drawn on Anthony Platt, *The Child-Savers: The Invention of Delinquency* (Chicago: University of Chicago Press, 1969).

through report after report: Get the Italian children (in Boston it would have been the Irish) away from their "bigoted" advisers (who else but the Catholic priest?) so that they can receive moral and religious treatment from instructors whose denominational neutrality, so the report tells us, runs the gamut from Episcopalian to Unitarian. Save these children from greedy parents and the labor of blackening boots by placing them in child-labor manufacturing establishments or, if female, in domestic service in respectable homes.

To accomplish these ends, new judicial and correctional institutions were created. Since criminal court procedures were thought to be unsuitable to cases involving juveniles—who were, after all, being "helped," not "punished"—procedural guarantees were abolished in favor of an informal approach. Almost every conceivable abuse occurs—the use of unsubstantiated rumor as evidence, coercive imposition of psychiatric or social welfare treatment on the basis of presumed need, confusing procedures that leave parents and child unable to present evidence without the assistance of a lawyer, confusion of child-neglect cases with delinquency, arbitrary sentences, and unnecessary stigmatization through failure to keep records confidential. 33

Although the juvenile may expect to be rewarded in return for the waiver of so many rights, the rewards are often scanty. The juvenile court system of "Metropolitan City," studied by Abraham Blumberg,[8] convicted juveniles more frequently than adults. Sentences are indeterminate and may be longer than for adults. Perhaps the worst feature of the juvenile court system is that no specific law-violating act has to be committed by a juvenile for him or her to be brought under the "parental" care of the courts. Thus, "growing up in idleness," exhibiting "vicious or immoral behavior," "incorrigibility," or "living with any vicious or disreputable person" can justify judicial intervention. 34

In addition, the shortcomings of the criminal justice system already described are inflicted upon juvenile offenders as well. Often, because of their youth, the consequences are worse. In reformatories there is probably more brutality, intimidation, and homosexual coercion than in adult prisons. Educational and vo- 35

[8]*Criminal Justice* (Chicago): Quadrangle, 1967.

cational programs are probably more outmoded. The juvenile offender probably has less chance than his adult counterpart of
breaking away from a life of repeated return to imprisonment.

WOMEN

The law is both the mirror of a biased society and the 36
source of prejudice. Just as the black man was described originally in the Constitution as three-fifths of a man, so under common law "a woman has no legal existence separate from her husband, who was regarded as her head and representative in the
social state," according to a United States Supreme Court decision in 1872. Some years later, in 1898, a Virginia court decided
that under law a "woman" is not a "person." In 1966 the Supreme Court upheld a Texas law providing that a married woman
does not have the capacity to enter into a binding contract. Justice Hugo Black dissented, deploring the fact that the Court
"should exalt this archaic remnant of a primitive caste
system...This rule has worked out in reality to mean that though
the husband and wife are one, the one is the husband."[9]

A woman under the common-law tradition loses her legal 37
personality when she marries. Issues are raised of "right to a
separate domicile; capacity to sue and be sued; change in citizenship upon marriage to an alien."[10] One contemporary example of
hardship resulting from a denial of the right to separate domicile
is the case of a young woman who tried to enter law school in a
Pennsylvania state-supported university. Because her husband,
from whom she was separated but not divorced, had his legal residence in another state, the fee would have been doubled and,
consequently, she was unable to enroll. In another instance, the
woman on welfare has been subjected in recent years to the
searching of her home to see if she is having a sexual relationship
and if so, cutting off her welfare. Known as the "man in the

[9]Quoted by Diane B. Schulder, "Does the Law Oppress Women?" in *Sisterhood Is Powerful*, Robin Morgan, ed. (New York: Vintage, 1970), p. 149. This excellent article also contains complete citations of the court decisions mentioned.
[10]Ibid.

house" rule, it was not balanced by a "woman in the house" rule.

Gunnar Myrdal, in his classic *An American Dilemma,* com- 38 ments that the myth of the "contented woman," who does not want suffrage or other civil rights and equal opportunities, has the same social function as the myth of the "contented Negro." Women, black and white, remained unenfranchised until 1920— sixty-five years after the vote had technically at least been granted to males of any race.

Almost one-fourth of the complaints received since passage 39 of Title VII of the 1964 Civil Rights Act, which forbids discrimination, including discrimination on the basis of sex, in employment, have been from women.[11] Approximately half of the women surveyed in a recent study covering all women law-school graduates of the years 1956–1965 stated that they have been discriminated against by employers and that their average income differed sharply, based on sex.[12]

In 1968 the United States Supreme Court considered the 40 case of a girl who was imprisoned for "lascivious carriage" under a Connecticut law authorizing imprisonment of young women if they are "in manifest danger of falling into habits of vice." Laws may provide for different lengths of jail sentences for the same crime, depending on whether the perpetrator is male or female (1968). In many states, dispensing birth-control information is a crime and the struggle of women for legalized and safe abortion is far from won. Thus in the areas of sex and reproduction the law has more direct control over women than men.

One of the most discriminatory areas of criminal law relates 41 to prostitution. "In New York City policemen actively entrap women and then charge them with prostitution...This despite the fact that New York law states that prostitutes and their customers are guilty of equal violations...The New York District Attorney's office has also chosen not to prosecute the men customers [lest] big business conventions...cancel out of New York

[11]"Report of the U.S. Commission on Civil Rights," 1970.
[12]Schulder, op. cit., p. 146.

City and go elsewhere."[13] This practice is not confined to New York City.

Little has been written about women in prison. The defini- 42 tive report of the President's Commission on Law Enforcement and the Administration of Justice devotes not even a paragraph to the female "offender." Although only a very small percentage of the crimes committed by women involve violence, alternatives to incarceration are almost nonexistent. "The only advantage women have over men [in America's] penal system is that fewer of them are in it.... But those who are handcuffed and ushered into cells [throughout the nation] face some of the worst conditions available."[14] A special torment for women is separation from their children and the fear that the state may take them away. Often women who are arrested and prohibited from making a phone call have left young children at home and become frantic about their safety. One of the grievances of the inmates of the Tombs was the lack of respect shown by the guards to their wives, mothers, and sisters who came to visit. The wives of prisoners must shoulder responsibility for both parents, often face the scorn and hostility of the community, and are often subjected to insulting treatment from the administrators of prisons.

Jails for women include one federal reformatory, at Alder- 43 son, Virginia, which also has the only woman superintendent in the Federal Bureau of Prisons. Some inmates feel that because a woman is its chief officer it is perhaps the "best of the worst" of all the places that incarcerate women. The superintendent has said:

> I don't like jails and I'm not going to defend them. There's no jail in the world that's any good. They're bad places and you're in them against your will. If you're black, poor or a woman in twentieth-century America the dice have been loaded against you.[15]

[13]Ibid., pp. 155–156.
[14]Kitsi Burkhart in a prizewinning series on prisons in the Philadelphia *Evening Bulletin,* January 1971.
[15]Kitsi Burkhart, "Women in Prison," *Ramparts,* June 1971.

CULTURAL ASSIMILATION TODAY

As part of treatment and rehabilitation, cultural assimila- 44 tion is forced upon wayward, threatening, or unconventional groups. Every day criminal justice personnel make hundreds of low-level discretionary decisions that glorify their middle-class life-style. This can be seen in a batch of probation and parole reports involving neglect proceedings against mothers of very young children.

The reports constantly reiterate such factors as the "sub- 45 ject's" "slovenly housekeeping," "sexual promiscuity," "failure to keep her appointments," "frequenting taverns," "allowing older children to loiter on street corners," and "her apparent willingness to let welfare continue supporting her." We will look at the implications of some of these phrases.

The designation of the mother-defendant as a "subject" de- 46 means her, emphasizing her inequality. It also reflects the cold impersonality of a bureaucracy too dehumanized to call her by name.

References to "slovenly housekeeping" reveal a Puritani- 47 cal dust phobia. References to "promiscuity," "taverns," and "loitering" reflect the pervasive middle-class inability to understand why the poor do not unwind in the privacy and quiet of their living rooms instead of in public establishments of dubious propriety. Why don't they take the air on golf courses instead of loitering on street corners? Why don't they conduct their love affairs secretly? Why do they shoot craps in back alleys instead of playing bingo at a neighborhood church? Or why don't they fly to Las Vegas for more elaborate entertainment? References to "welfare" reveal the increasingly outmoded Protestant work ethic.

Complaints about not keeping appointments are frequent in 48 welfare and correctional literature. Woe betide the parolee who misses an appointment! Here we have in microcosm the clash between a life-style where time is relatively unimportant and an establishment whose agencies have long waiting lists, whose courts are smothered by their dockets, whose social workers are bowed down by their case loads, and whose officials exaggerate their own importance. One can imagine Thoreau, who believed in

wide margins and had little use for those who voluntarily spent
their lives under the crushing weight of a barn and forty acres,
siding with the "subjects" and joining in an amused contempla-
tion of the uptight caseworker.

For the prisoner time has a different perspective. It is 49
something to be marked off, endured. He has already learned all
too painfully in most contacts with officials that what he really
wants or feels or thinks will be ignored. By the time the case
worker gets to him, the "subject" will already have experienced
an appointed counsel or public defender who gave him the once
over lightly; a judge who disposed of his life alternatives in a moment or two of judicial time as part of an assembly-line process,
and a whole series of unthinking, unfeeling functionaries within
institutions. No wonder the "subjects" keep failing to keep their
appointments with those who are trying to "help" them.

One could search the criminal code in vain to find laws pro- 50
hibiting lateness to appointments or unconventionality of dress
and social habits. Yet these are the standards being enforced.
Many prison treatment programs carry this degradation to an extreme. Heavy emphasis is placed on unquestioned obedience to
authority, the sanctity of the employer-employee relationship,
acquiescence to perform drudgery work or service occupations,
and the centrality of money and materialistic goals.

POLITICAL REPRESSION

A fundamental though unacknowledged function of the 51
criminal justice system is political repression. This was the motive for passage of the federal Antiriot and Conspiracy Act of
1968 and for its use in the Chicago and Seattle trials. These trials
are in every substantial respect today's counterpart of the prosecution of Communists during the Smith Act trials of the 1950s,
the aim in each case being to discredit political opponents. In
both instances there were already ample statutes on the books to
punish violent disruption and to safeguard society.

The prosecutions of H. Rap Brown, Lee Otis Johnson, 52
John Sinclair, and the Harrisburg 6 are similarly political in mo-

tivation. Likewise, a strong element of vindictiveness and persecution for political reasons pervades the treatment of those whose conscience has led them to break the law. We refer, for example, to the Catonsville 9 and the Washington May Day demonstrators. Whatever one may think about the necessity of pressing criminal charges in such cases, the government has responded with overkill tactics in the press and in the courtroom.

The same response to "political" crimes may also be observed on the local level. The authorities find some offenses more offensive than others. The Philadelphia Police Department swiftly removes and arrests peace demonstrators blocking the Induction Center but has yet to arrest housewives conducting sit-ins in busy intersections to protest the absence of a traffic light. 53

At times the police have acted as political executioners, as seems to be the case in the alleged murder of Black Panther leaders Mark Clark and Fred Hampton by sheriff's deputies while they slept. 54

The use of the courts and police against radicals is nothing new in American history. Abolitionists and labor organizers came up against these sorts of repression time and time again. In the first decades of this century the Wobblies—Industrial Workers of the World—were persecuted from coast to coast. They were convicted of such crimes as "criminal syndicalism" and their movement was eventually smashed. During the 1960s the full range of repression was used against civil-rights workers in the South. 55

This country now appears to be entering a new phase of repression against activist forces struggling for change. In addition to the overt political repression already mentioned, there is an ominous expansion of police power that has scarcely been noticed. Police forces, built up after the civil and campus disorders of the late 1960s, have become paramilitary. They have received training from the Department of Defense and are adapting to domestic use weapons developed for Vietnam. 56

This trend within police departments has led to the emergence of a police/industrial/educational complex spawned by the Pentagon. The Law Enforcement Assistance Administration 57

(LEAA), a federal agency created in 1968, is budgeted for $1,750,000,000 in 1973 and is slated to continue to expand.[16] LEAA funds police training programs in 880 colleges and universities. It also includes work on counterinsurgency techniques and the development of new weapons and equipment.

Secret police have sprung up like mushrooms in recent 58 years. Not only the FBI, the CIA, and the Intelligence branches of the various armed forces, but dozens of other agencies, national and local, are spying on hundreds of thousands of us. They have at their disposal sophisticated electronic surveillance equipment and computerized storage and retrieval of information. Spying has snowballed and is now out of control. Implications for the future are frightening.

In the face of this strong thrust toward highly centralized, 59 strongly armed, computerized, and professionalized police departments, plus secret police, the traditional concept of the police function in a free society is breaking down. The police are no longer peacekeepers under the control of civilian governments and responsive to the needs and wishes of the people. What can be done to bring the police back under the control of the communities they are supposed to serve? The prospect is not bright.

In a totalitarian society the repressive functions we have 60 enumerated...dominate the criminal justice system. In a free society such functions should be minimized or eliminated. We hope that an awareness of the pervasiveness of these functions in the American system can lead to change. We will not be able to do away with these repressive functions until social prejudice and inequality are uprooted and eradicated from society as a whole.

1971

[16]Lee Webb, "Back Home: Campus Beat," in *Police on the Homefront* (Philadelphia: National Action/Research on the Military-Industrial Complex, 1971), p. 8.

Presidential Character and How to Foresee It

James David Barber

When a citizen votes for a Presidential candidate he makes,   1
in effect, a prediction. He chooses from among the contenders
the one he thinks (or feels, or guesses) would be the best President. He operates in a situation of immense uncertainty. If he has
a long voting history, he can recall time and time again when he
guessed wrong. He listens to the commentators, the politicians,
and his friends, then adds it all up in some rough way to produce
his prediction and his vote. Earlier in the game, his anticipations
have been taken into account, either directly in the polls and pri-
maries or indirectly in the minds of politicians who want to nom-
inate someone he will like. But he must choose in the midst of a
cloud of confusion, a rain of phony advertising, a storm of ser-
mons, a hail of complex issues, a fog of charisma and boredom,
and a thunder of accusation and defense. In the face of this
chaos, a great many citizens fall back on the past, vote their old
allegiances, and let it go at that. Nevertheless, the citizen's vote
says that on balance he expects Mr. X would outshine Mr. Y in
the Presidency....

The burden of this book is that the crucial differences can   2
be anticipated by an understanding of a potential President's
character, his world view, and his style. This kind of prediction
is not easy; well-informed observers often have guessed wrong
as they watched a man step toward the White House. One thinks
of Woodrow Wilson, the scholar who would bring reason to politics; of Herbert Hoover, the Great Engineer who would organize
chaos into progress; of Franklin D. Roosevelt, that champion of
the balanced budget; of Harry Truman, whom the office would
surely overwhelm; of Dwight D. Eisenhower, militant crusader;
of John F. Kennedy, who would lead beyond moralisms to
achievements; of Lyndon B. Johnson, the Southern conservative; and of Richard M. Nixon, conciliator. Spotting the errors is
easy. Predicting with even approximate accuracy is going to re-

quire some sharp tools and close attention in their use. But the experiment is worth it because the question is critical and because it lends itself to correction by evidence.

My argument comes in layers.   3

First, a President's personality is an important shaper of his   4
Presidential behavior on nontrivial matters.

Second, Presidential personality is patterned. His charac-   5
ter, world view, and style fit together in a dynamic package understandable in psychological terms.

Third, a President's personality interacts with the power   6
situation he faces and the national "climate of expectations" dominant at the time he serves. The tuning, the resonance—or lack of it—between these external factors and his personality sets in motion the dynamic of his Presidency.

Fourth, the best way to predict a President's character,   7
world view, and style is to see how they were put together in the first place. That happened in his early life, culminating in his first independent political success.

But the core of the argument (which organizes the structure   8
of the book) is that Presidential character—the basic stance a man takes toward his Presidential experience—comes in four varieties. The most important thing to know about a President or candidate is where he fits among these types, defined according to (a) how active he is and (b) whether or not he gives the impression he enjoys his political life.

Let me spell out these concepts briefly before getting down   9
to cases....

FOUR TYPES OF PRESIDENTIAL CHARACTER

The five concepts—character, world view, style, power sit-   10
uation, and climate of expectations—run through the accounts of Presidents in the chapters to follow, which cluster the Presidents since Theodore Roosevelt into four types. This is the fundamental scheme of the study. It offers a way to move past the complexities to the main contrasts and comparisons.

The first baseline in defining Presidential types is *activity-* 11
passivity. How much energy does the man invest in his Presidency? Lyndon Johnson went at his day like a human cyclone, coming to rest long after the sun went down. Calvin Coolidge often slept eleven hours a night and still needed a nap in the middle of the day. In between the Presidents array themselves on the high or low side of the activity line.

The second baseline is *positive-negative affect* toward 12
one's activity—that is, how he feels about what he does. Relatively speaking, does he seem to experience his political life as happy or sad, enjoyable or discouraging, positive or negative in its main effect. The feeling I am after here is not grim satisfaction in a job well done, not some philosophical conclusion. The idea is this: is he someone who, on the surfaces we can see, gives forth the feeling that he has *fun* in political life? Franklin Roosevelt's Secretary of War, Henry L. Stimson wrote that the Roosevelts "not only understood the *use* of power, they knew the *enjoyment* of power, too.... Whether a man is burdened by power or enjoys power; whether he is trapped by responsibility or made free by it; whether he is moved by other people and outer forces or moves them—that is the essence of leadership."

The positive-negative baseline then, is a general symptom 13
of the fit between the man and his experience, a kind of register of *felt* satisfaction.

Why might we expect these two simple dimensions to outline 14
the main character types? Because they stand for two central features of anyone's orientation toward life. In nearly every study of personality, some form of the active-passive contrast is critical; the general tendency to act or be acted upon is evident in such concepts as dominance-submission, extraversion-introversion, aggression-timidity, attack-defense, fight-flight, engagement-withdrawal, approach-avoidance. In everyday life we sense quickly the general energy output of the people we deal with. Similarly we catch on fairly quickly to the affect dimension—whether the person seems to be optimistic or pessimistic, hopeful or skeptical, happy or sad. The two baselines are clear and they are also independent of one another: all of us know people who are very active but seem discour-

aged, others who are quite passive but seem happy, and so forth. The activity baseline refers to what one does, the affect baseline to how one feels about what he does.

Both are crude clues to character. They are leads into four **15** basic character patterns long familiar in psychological research. In summary form, these are the main configurations:

Active-positive: There is a congruence, a consistency, be- **16** tween much activity and the enjoyment of it, indicating relatively high self-esteem and relative success in relating to the environment. The man shows an orientation toward productiveness as a value and an ability to use his styles flexibly, adaptively, suiting the dance to the music. He sees himself as developing over time toward relatively well defined personal goals—growing toward his image of himself as he might yet be. There is an emphasis on rational mastery, on using the brain to move the feet. This may get him into trouble; he may fail to take account of the irrational in politics. Not everyone he deals with sees things his way and he may find it hard to understand why.

Active-negative: The contradiction here is between rela- **17** tively intense effort and low emotional reward for that effort. The activity has a compulsive quality, as if the man were trying to make up for something or to escape from anxiety into hard work. He seems ambitious, striving upward, power-seeking. His stance toward the environment is aggressive and he has a persistent problem in managing his aggressive feelings. His self-image is vague and discontinuous. Life is a hard struggle to achieve and hold power, hampered by the condemnations of a perfectionistic conscience. Active-negative types pour energy into the political system, but it is an energy distorted from within.

Passive-positive: This is the receptive, compliant, other- **18** directed character whose life is a search for affection as a reward for being agreeable and cooperative rather than personally assertive. The contradiction is between low self-esteem (on grounds of being unlovable, unattractive) and a superficial optimism. A hopeful attitude helps dispel doubt and elicits encouragement from others. Passive-positive types help soften the harsh edges of politics. But their dependence and the fragility of their hopes and enjoyments make disappointment in politics likely.

Passive-negative: The factors are consistent—but how are we 19 to account for the man's *political* role-taking? Why is someone who does little in politics and enjoys it less there at all? The answer lies in the passive-negative's character-rooted orientation toward doing dutiful service; this compensates for low self-esteem based on a sense of uselessness. Passive-negative types are in politics because they think they ought to be. They may be well adapted to certain nonpolitical roles, but they lack the experience and flexibility to perform effectively as political leaders. Their tendency is to withdraw, to escape from the conflict and uncertainty of politics by emphasizing vague principles (especially prohibitions) and procedural arrangements. They become guardians of the right and proper way, above the sordid politicking of lesser men.

Active-positive Presidents want most to achieve results. 20 Active-negatives aim to get and keep power. Passive-positives are after love. Passive-negatives emphasize their civic virtue. The relation of activity to enjoyment in a President thus tends to outline a cluster of characteristics, to set apart the adapted from the compulsive, compliant, and withdrawn types.

The first four Presidents of the United States, conveniently, 21 ran through this gamut of character types. (Remember, we are talking about tendencies, broad directions; no individual man exactly fits a category.) George Washington—clearly the most important President in the pantheon—established the fundamental legitimacy of an American government at a time when this was a matter in considerable question. Washington's dignity, judiciousness, his aloof air of reserve and dedication to duty fit the passive-negative or withdrawing type best. Washington did not seek innovation, he sought stability. He longed to retire to Mount Vernon, but fortunately was persuaded to stay on through a second term, in which, by rising above the political conflict between Hamilton and Jefferson and inspiring confidence in his own integrity, he gave the nation time to develop the organized means for peaceful change.

John Adams followed, a dour New England Puritan, much **22** given to work and worry, an impatient and irascible man—an active-negative President, a compulsive type. Adams was far more partisan than Washington; the survival of the system through his Presidency demonstrated that the nation could tolerate, for a time, domination by one of its nascent political parties. As President, an angry Adams brought the United States to the brink of war with France, and presided over the new nation's first experiment in political repression: the Alien and Sedition Acts, forbidding, among other things, unlawful combinations "with intent to oppose any measure or measures of the government of the United States," or "any false, scandalous, and malicious writing or writings against the United States, or the President of the United States, with intent to defame...or to bring them or either of them, into contempt or disrepute."

Then came Jefferson. He too had his troubles and fail- **23** ures—in the design of national defense, for example. As for his Presidential character (only one element in success or failure), Jefferson was clearly active-positive. A child of the Enlightenment, he applied his reason to organizing connections with Congress aimed at strengthening the more popular forces. A man of catholic interests and delightful humor, Jefferson combined a clear and open vision of what the country could be with a profound political sense, expressed in his famous phrase, "Every difference of opinion is not a difference of principle."

The fourth President was James Madison, "Little Jemmy," **24** the constitutional philosopher thrown into the White House at a time of great international turmoil. Madison comes closest to the passive-positive, or compliant, type; he suffered from irresolution, tried to compromise his way out, and gave in too readily to the "warhawks" urging combat with Britain. The nation drifted into war, and Madison wound up ineptly commanding his collection of amateur generals in the streets of Washington. General Jackson's victory at New Orleans saved the Madison administration's historical reputation; but he left the Presidency with the United States close to bankruptcy and secession.

These four Presidents—like all Presidents—were persons 25 trying to cope with the roles they had won by using the equipment they had built over a lifetime. The President is not some shapeless organism in a flood of novelties, but a man with a memory in a system with a history. Like all of us, he draws on his past to shape his future. The pathetic hope that the White House will turn a Caligula into a Marcus Aurelius is as naive as the fear that ultimate power inevitably corrupts. The problem is to understand—and to state understandably—what in the personal past foreshadows the Presidential future.

1972

The Climythology of America
David M. Ludlum

History is full of myths, and so is climatology. Every gen- 1 eration of historians gives rise to a revisionist school that reinterprets the past in light of new material and facts. Sometimes the revisions join the body of history; other times they are revised by the next generation. Overall, the process leads to a richer and more truthful history.

The settlement of America produced a series of myths 2 about the climate of different regions of our country. Even before the first British settlements in North America, Europeans held certain concepts concerning the supposed climate of the New World, and those concepts greatly influenced their efforts to establish colonies from Newfoundland to the Carolinas.

Once the seaboard was occupied, new myths arose about 3 the lands west of the Allegheny Mountains. Other unfounded beliefs appeared to influence the occupation of the Mississippi Valley and Great Plains until, in the last decade of the nineteenth century, the land office in Washington officially declared the frontier closed, though much territory remained unsettled. Most of this, however, was thought to be wasteland unsuitable for cultivation. This belief would be dispelled in the next century by the introduction of scientific methods of agriculture and the construction of huge irrigation projects.

THE EQUAL-LATITUDE MYTH

The intellectual content of climatology had made little **4** progress from the time of Ptolemy, the Greek astronomer and geographer of the second century A.D., to the year 1601, which marked the beginning of the century of colonization of North America by the English and the French. The concept of *clima,* or parallel bands around the world which shared comparable temperatures and hence weather conditions, was the generally accepted view of global arrangements. So much so, in fact, that the word clima was used by English writers interchangeably with "latitude." This gave rise to what I shall call the equal-latitude myth.

The planners and backers of the new colonies held to the **5** classical view of the distribution of global temperatures and thus were greatly surprised and chagrined when their environmental expectations were not met by the realities of the New World. The French were perplexed by the harsh winter conditions they met in Nova Scotia and the St. Lawrence Valley because both lay at the same latitudes as northern and central France. The British ultimately gave up constant efforts to settle Newfoundland in the early years of the seventeenth century because of the severe winters, despite the fact that it lay at the same latitude as southernmost England, where winters were usually moderate in temperature.

The history of all the British colonies from Maine to the **6** Carolinas ran much the same. The commercial backers of each colony expressed surprise and dismay that these settlements, though at the latitudes of France and Spain, could not produce the exotic agricultural products of those countries.

Believing Virginia to have a Mediterranean climate, the 7 proprietors tried silk culture until the realities of the winter killed all hopes of producing such a tropical product.

Almost a century passed before the backers of the colonies 8 realized that the American climate differed from the European at the same latitudes. By the beginning of the eighteenth century, a more realistic viewpoint prevailed about the climate of the New World. Facts replaced the equal-latitude myth.

THE CLIMATE CHANGE MYTH

During the first two centuries of settlement of the American 9 seaboard, a popular misconception arose about the observed climate. Where were the record snows of yesteryear? Why did we not have the harsh winters so often mentioned by grandfather and great-grandfather? Many homespun philosophers pondered these questions and suggested answers. Though no actual facts were brought forth, most colonists believed that conditions had grown milder and that the seasons had changed, with spring coming later and autumn lasting longer.

These ideas were expressed in an article by Dr. Hugh 10 Williamson of North Carolina in the first issue of the *Transactions of the American Philosophical Society* in 1771: "An attempt to account for the change observed in the Middle Colonies in North America."

Williamson's thesis was that the cutting down of the forests 11 for farms and settlements had produced a warming of the soil for two reasons. First, the felling of the trees allowed easterly winds to penetrate more deeply into the country, bringing temperate marine influences inland. Second, the bare soil received and stored more solar heat than did forested lands, and snow melted more quickly when exposed to direct sunlight.

In addition, some colonials suggested that the rise of urban 12 communities with heated buildings and smokepots was leading to a milder climate, as they claimed had occurred in Europe. These ideas were the first of many about climate change that were to arise and claim a body of believers among Americans.

THE OHIO COUNTRY MYTH

After almost 200 years of English settlement along the At- 13 lantic seaboard, the vast interior of the North American continent remained a *terra incognita* as far as an exact knowledge of its geography and climate was concerned. The French had sent voyageurs, couriers de bois and missionaries deep into the interior, but their first-hand knowledge of the conditions encountered did not reach the seaboard-bound British. Though the barrier of the Appalachian Mountains was breached during the war years that marked the closing decades of the eighteenth century, few scientific men went westward to observe and report on the physical and atmospheric geography of the interior.

A vigorous controversy as to the nature of the climate of 14 the Ohio Country beyond the Allegheny Mountains arose as the century drew to a close and continued to spark lively arguments well into the next century. The controversy became known as the Ohio Country myth.

Between October 1795 and June 1796, Constantin Francois 15 de Chaseboeuf, Comte de Volney, traveled from Washington, D.C., to Vincennes on the Wabash River in Indiana. He was familiar with Jefferson's view, expressed in his *Notes on the State of Virginia,* that the annual temperature west of the mountains was several degrees warmer than at the same latitude east of the mountains along the Atlantic seaboard. Jefferson based his opinion on the different types of plants thriving on opposite sides of the mountains. Volney's seeming confirmation of Jefferson's opinion received wide dissemination in the *View of the Climate and Soil of the United States,* published in London and Paris in 1804.

The first refutation of the ideas promulgated by Volney 16 came from Dr. Daniel Drake in *Notices concerning Cincinnati,* published in 1810, which produced actual comparative temperature readings. Others soon took up their scientific cudgels. In an address before the Albany Institute in 1823, Dr. Lewis Beck took each of Volney's statements and demolished them with facts from more recent material.

William Darby, in his *View of the United States: Historical,* 17 *Geographical and Statistical* (1828), referred to Volney's "by no means innoxious vulgar error." As late as 1842, Dr. Samuel Forry, in the first climatological survey to employ meteorological observations, felt constrained to criticize Volney's opinions as being "barren of precise data."

In 1857, Lorin Blodget put the Ohio Country myth to final 18 rest in his comprehensive *Climatology of the United States:* "The early distinction between the Atlantic States and the Mississippi has been quite dropped, as the progress of observation has shown them to be essentially the same, or to differ only in unimportant particulars."

THE GREAT AMERICAN DESERT MYTH

"When I was a schoolboy my map of the United States showed 19 between the Missouri River and the Rocky Mountains a long, broad white blotch, upon which was printed in small capitals 'THE GREAT AMERICAN DESERT—UNEXPLORED.' " So wrote Colonel Richard Irving Dodge in 1877 when commencing his revealing survey, *The Great Plains of the Great West.* He concluded: "What was then 'unexplored' is now almost thoroughly known. What was regarded as a desert supports, in some portions, thriving populations. The blotch of thirty years ago is now known as 'The Plains'."

Sergeant John Ordway, who had accompanied Lewis and 20 Clark in 1804, had stated "...this country may with propriety be called the Deserts of North America." Captain Zebulon Pike in exploring the headwaters of the Arkansas River had declared that "...these vast plains of the western hemisphere may become in time as celebrated as the sandy deserts of Africa." And Major Stephen H. Long had written, "...the Great Desert at the

Base of the Rocky Mountains...is almost wholly unfit for cultivation, and of course uninhabitable...."

When Lorin Blodget published his comprehensive *Clima-* 21
tology of the United States in 1857, he marked a zone running
east of the 100°W meridian on his precipitation chart "the eastern limit of the dry plains," and labeled the area of western Kansas and Nebraska "the Desert Plains."

Following the Civil War, a counterattack was launched on 22
the pessimistic opinion about the future of the plains. The pressure for new lands to settle caused a change of view regarding
the farming possibilities of the plains west of the Missouri River.
Optimistic projections were penned by enthusiastic travelers,
booster-type editors and eager business promoters. Their hopes
were bolstered by several years of above-normal rainfall in the
late 1860s and early 1870s. The concept that "Rain Follows the
Plough" was broadcast in chamber-of-commerce style by agricultural improvement societies and business enterprises. This
was the "Garden Myth"—that planting trees and crops on the
dry plains would result in increased rainfall in a self-perpetuating
manner. The climate pendulum, however, underwent several
swings from adequate to inadequate rainfall until a nadir was
reached in the late 1880s and early 1890s, resulting in disaster for
the many cattle ranchers and the abandonment of farming in
much of western Kansas and western Nebraska.

The occupation of the central plains by farmers, the west- 23
ern plains by cattlemen, the mountains by miners, and the Pacific
Northwest by lumbermen brought more adequate knowledge of
the actual climates of these regions. The filling in of the nation's
climatological charts was completed about 1890, when the avail-
ability of free land ended and the frontier was considered closed.

THE SOUTHERN CALIFORNIA HEALTH MYTH

During the first 30 years of American settlement Southern 24
California remained a frontier country with ranching and agriculture dominating the economy. The last two decades of the century, however, brought a change. Promoters and developers exploited the region's prime natural attraction, a beneficent

climate, to make it the health frontier of the United States. Its favorable features were widely promoted in a tidal wave of publicity, and hordes of Easterners responded by migrating to the promised land in search of restored health. Thanks to man's ingenuity, the barren outlands had suddenly become habitable and even attractive.

During the decades from 1850 to 1880, native Angelenos 25 might have been forgiven for doubting their climate would turn out to be the most promising feature of the region. Damaging floods occurred in 1862 and 1868, devastating droughts came in 1862–64 and 1876–77 and a long spell of recurrent cold weather in the late 1870s and early 1880s set many still-standing date records for coldness. In addition, a destructive earthquake struck in 1857 and every year there were "tremblos."

Despite the lack of knowledge of the effect of California's 26 climate on disease, publicity for the region's salubrity soon poured forth. A pamphlet entitled, *Southern California: The Italy of America,* claimed for the area the "only perfect climate in the world and the grandest scenery under the sun." The *Los Angeles Star* in 1872 carried an article, "Land of Glorious Sunsets," which was considered by historian Oscar O. Winther (in 1946) as "the opening trumpet blast of a climate promotion campaign that has not ended."

Concerted efforts to attract visitors and settlers became an 27 increasingly active industry in the 1880s. The local Chamber of Commerce was careful to point out that not all parts of California enjoyed the salubrious climate claimed for the southern region. The results soon became apparent. A great boom in real estate and business developed in the mid-1880s, similar to those previously experienced in other sections of the western frontier country.

In the 1890s, climate continued to be the principal pitch of 28 promotion agencies. In 1892, the Southern California Information Bureau asserted: "...we sell the climate at so much an acre and throw in the land." To a complaint that the region had nothing to sell except climate, one enthusiast declared: "That's right, and we sell it, too—$10 for an acre of land, $490 an acre for the climate."

The health angle and longevity prospects were emphasized 29
in the promotional publications of the 1890s. Dr. Peter C. Re-
mondino stated the extreme claim for the region in his book, *The
Mediterranean Shores of America: Southern California:* "from
my personal observations, I can say that at least an extra ten
years' lease on life is gained by a removal to this coast from the
Eastern States; not ten years to be added with its extra weight of
age and infirmity, but ten years more with additional benefit of
feeling ten years younger during the time."

They came at first by the thousands, and finally by the mil- 30
lions; today more than 15 million people live in Southern California where a century ago there were only 32,000.

Ironically, the concentration of population with attendant 31
urban sprawl and congested freeways affected the climate in a
way none of its promoters of the late 1800s foresaw. The effu-
sions of millions of combustion engines, trapped in the area's
natural basins by the almost daily inversions in the lower atmosphere, have created smog conditions detrimental to health.

ALASKAN CLIMYTHOLOGY

The bill for $7,200,000 to pay for Alaska "loosed a storm in 32
the House of Representatives. I shall not attempt to say whether
it was a hurricane or tornado, but it was accompanied by a lot of
wind, by a great flood—a flood of oratory and some verbal thunder," declared Senator Ernest Gruening at a meeting of the
American Meteorological Society at the University of Alaska on
June 27, 1962. The former Russian colony was portrayed as "a
frozen waste with a savage climate, where little or nothing could
grow, and where few could or would live."

Typical of the statements of these pioneer climythologists 33
was that of Benjamin F. Loan of St. Louis, who declared:

"...the acquisition of this inhospitable and barren waste 34
will never add a dollar to the wealth of our country or furnish any
homes to our people. It is utterly worthless....To suppose that
anyone would leave the United States...to seek a home...in the
regions of perpetual snow is simply to suppose such a person insane."

Another climatic pessimist, Representative Orange Ferris 35
of Glens Falls, New York, asserted that Alaska "is a barren and
unproductive region covered with ice and snow" and "will never
be populated by an enterprising people."

A representative from New York, Dennis McCarthy of Syr- 36
acuse, cited "reports that every foot of the soil of Alaska is frozen from five to six feet in depth" and ventured that his colleagues would soon hear that Greenland was on the market.

And the minority report of the House Committee on For- 37
eign Relations, in a scathing denunciation, declared Alaska "had
no capacity as an agricultural country...no value as a mineral
country....its timber generally of poor quality and growing upon
inaccessible mountains....its fur trade...of insignificant value,
and, will speedily come to an end....the fisheries of doubtful
value....in a climate unfit for the habitation of civilized men."

Today, Alaska supports a population of more than one half 38
million people and an annual economy worth more than $9 billion.

1987

Reflections on Horror Movies
Robert Brustein

Although horror movies have recently been enjoying a 1
vogue, they have always been perennial supporting features
among Grade B and C fare. The popularity of the form is no
doubt partly explained by its ability to engage the spectator's
feelings without making any serious demand on his mind. In addition, however, horror movies covertly embody certain underground assumptions about science which reflect popular opinions.

The horror movies I am mainly concerned with I have di- 2
vided into three major categories: Mad Doctor, Atomic Beast
and Interplanetary Monster. They do not exhaust all the types

but they each contain two essential characters, the Scientist and the Monster, towards whom the attitudes of the movies are in a revealing state of change.

The Mad Doctor series is by far the most long lived of the 3 three. It suffered a temporary decline in the Forties when Frankenstein, Dracula, and the Wolfman (along with their countless offspring) were first loaned out as straight men to Abbott and Costello, and then set out to graze in the parched pastures of the cheap all-night movie houses, but it has recently demonstrated its durability in a group of English remakes and a Teen-age Monster craze. These films find their roots in certain European folk myths. Dracula was inspired by an ancient Balkan superstition about vampires, the Werewolf is a Middle European folk myth recorded, among other places, in the Breton *lais* of Marie de France, and even Frankenstein, though out of Mary Shelley by the Gothic tradition, has a medieval prototype in the Golem, a monster the Jews fashioned from clay and earth to free them from oppression. The spirit of these films is still medieval, combining a vulgar religiosity with folk superstitions. Superstition now, however, has been crudely transferred from magic and alchemy to creative science, itself a form of magic to the untutored mind. The devil of the Vampire and Werewolf myths, who turned human beings into baser animals, today has become a scientist, and the metamorphosis is given a technical name—it is a "regression" into an earlier state of evolution. The alchemist and devil-conjuring scholar, Dr. Faustus, gives way to Dr. Frankenstein, the research physician, while the magic circle, the tetragrammaton, and the full moon are replaced by test tubes, complicated electrical apparatus, and Bunsen burners.

Frankenstein, like Faustus, defies God by exploring areas 4 where humans are not meant to trespass. In Mary Shelley's book (it is subtitled *A Modern Prometheus*), Frankenstein is a latter-day Faustus, a superhuman creature whose aspiration embodies the expansiveness of his age. In the movies, however, Frankenstein loses his heroic quality and becomes a lunatic monomaniac, so obsessed with the value of his work that he no longer cares whether his discovery proves a boon or a curse to mankind. When the mad doctor, his eyes wild and inflamed, bends over his intricate equipment, pouring in a little of this and a little of that, the spectator is confronted with an immoral being whose mental superiority is only a measure of his madness. Like the popular image of the theoretical scientist engaged in basic research ("Basic research," says Charles Wilson, "is science's attempt to prove the grass is green"), he succeeds only in creating something badly which nature has already made well. The Frankenstein monster is a parody of man. Ghastly in appearance, clumsy in movement, criminal in behavior, imbecilic of mind, it is superior only in physical strength and resistance to destruction. The scientist has fashioned it in the face of divine disapproval (the heavens disgorge at its birth)—not to mention the disapproval of friends and frightened townspeople—and it can lead only to trouble.

For Dr. Frankenstein, however, the monster symbolizes 5 the triumph of his intellect over the blind morality of his enemies and it confirms him in the ultimate soundness of his thought ("They thought I was mad, but this proves who is the superior being"). When it becomes clear that his countrymen are unimpressed by his achievement and regard him as a menace to society, the monster becomes the agent of his revenge. As it ravages the countryside and terrorizes the inhabitants, it embodies and expresses the scientist's own lust and violence. It is an extension of his own mad soul, come to life not in a weak and ineffectual body but in a body of formidable physical power. (In a movie like *Dr. Jekyll and Mr. Hyde,* the identity of monster and doctor is even clearer; Mr. Hyde, the monster, is the aggressive and libidinous element in the benevolent Dr. Jekyll's personality.) The rampage of the monster is the rampage of mad, unrestrained science which inevitably turns on the scientist, destroying him too. As the lava bubbles over the sinking head of the monster, the crude moral of the film frees itself from the horror and is asserted. Experimental science (and by extension knowledge itself) is superfluous, dangerous, and unlawful, for in exploring the unknown, it leads man to usurp God's creative power. Each of these films is a victory for obscurantism, flattering the spectator into believing that his intellectual inferiority is a sign that he is loved by God.

The Teen-age Monster films, a very recent phenomenon, 6

amend the assumptions of these horror movies in a startling manner. Their titles—*I Was a Teenage Werewolf, I Was a Teenage Frankenstein, Blood of Dracula,* and *Teenage Monster*—(some wit awaits one called *I Had a Teenage Monkey on My Back*)—suggest a Hollywood prank, but they are deadly serious, mixing the conventions of early horror movies with the ingredients of adolescent culture. The doctor, significantly enough, is no longer a fringe character whose madness can be inferred from the rings around his eyes and his wild hair but a respected member of society, a high-school chemistry teacher (*Blood of Dracula*) or a psychoanalyst (*Teenage Werewolf*) or a visiting lecturer from Britain (*Teenage Frankenstein*). Although he gives the appearance of benevolence—he pretends to help teen-agers with their problems—behind this facade he hides evil experimental designs. The monster, on the other hand, takes on a more fully developed personality. He is a victim who begins inauspiciously as an average, though emotionally troubled, adolescent and ends, through the influence of the doctor, as a voracious animal. The monster as teen-ager becomes the central character in the film and the teen-age audience is expected to identify and sympathize with him.

In *I Was a Teenage Werewolf,* the hero is characterized as   7
brilliant but erratic in his studies and something of a delinquent. At the suggestion of his principal, he agrees to accept therapy from an analyst helping maladjusted students. The analyst gets the boy under his control and, after injecting him with a secret drug, turns him into a werewolf. Against his will he murders a number of his contemporaries. When the doctor refuses to free him from this curse, he kills him and is himself killed by the police. In death, his features relax into the harmless countenance of an adolescent.

The crimes of the adolescent are invariably committed   8
against other youths (the doctor has it in for teen-agers) and are always connected with those staples of juvenile culture, sex and violence. The advertising displays show the male monsters, dressed in leather jackets and blue jeans, bending ambiguously over the diaphanously draped body of a luscious young girl while the female teen-age vampire of *Blood of Dracula,* her nails long

and her fangs dripping, is herself half-dressed and lying on top of a struggling male (whether to rape or murder him is not clear). The identification of sex and violence is further underlined by the promotion blurbs: "In her eyes DESIRE! in her veins—the blood of a MONSTER!" (*Blood of Dracula*); "A Teenage Titan on a Lustful Binge that Paralyzed a Town with Fear" (*Teenage Monster*). It is probable that these crimes are performed less reluctantly than is suggested and that the adolescent spectator is more thrilled than appalled by this "lustful binge" which captures the attention of the adult community. The acquisition of power and prestige through delinquent sexual and aggressive activity is a familiar juvenile fantasy (the same distributors exploit it more openly in films like *Reform School Girl* and *Drag-Strip Girl*), one which we can see frequently acted out by delinquents in our city schools. In the Teen-age Monster films, however, the hero is absolved of his aggressive and libidinous impulses. Although he both feels and acts on them, he can attribute the responsibility to the mad scientist who controls his behavior. What these films seem to be saying, in their underground manner, is that behind the harmless face of the high-school chemistry teacher and the intellectual countenance of the psychoanalyst lies the warped authority responsible for teen-age violence. The adolescent feels victimized by society—turned into a monster by society—and if he behaves in a delinquent manner, society and not he is to blame. Thus, we can see one direction in which the hostility for experimental research, explicit in the Mad Doctor films, can go—it can be transmuted into hatred of adult authority itself.

Or it can go underground, as in the Atomic Beast movies. 9 The Mad Doctor movies, in exploiting the supernatural, usually locate their action in Europe (often a remote Bavarian village) where wild fens, spectral castles, and ominous graveyards provide the proper eerie background. The Atomic Beast movies depend for their effect on the contemporary and familiar and there is a corresponding change in locale. The monster (or "thing" as it is more often called) appears now in a busy American city—usually Los Angeles to save the producer money—where average men walk about in business suits. The thing terrorizes not only the hero, the heroine, and a few anonymous (and expend-

able) characters in Tyrolean costumes, but the entire world. Furthermore, it has lost all resemblance to anything human. It appears as a giant ant (*Them!*), a prehistoric animal (*Beast from
Twenty Thousand Fathoms*), an outsized grasshopper (*Beginning
of the End*) or a monstrous spider (*Tarantula*). Although these
films, in their deference to science fiction, seem to smile more
benignly on scientific endeavor, they are unconsciously closer to
the anti-theoretical biases of the Mad Doctor series than would
first appear.

All these films are similarly plotted, so the plot of *Begin-* 10
ning of the End will serve as an example of the whole genre. The
scene opens on a pair of adolescents necking in their car off a
desert road. Their attention is caught by a weird clicking sound,
the boy looks up in horror, the girl screams, the music stings and
the scene fades. In the next scene, we learn that the car has been
completely demolished and its occupants have disappeared. The
police, totally baffled, are conducting fruitless investigations
when word comes that a small town nearby has been destroyed
in the same mysterious way. Enter the young scientist hero. Ex-
amining the wreckage of the town, he discovers a strange fluid
which when analyzed proves to have been manufactured by a giant grasshopper. The police ridicule his conclusions and are instantly attacked by a fleet of these grasshoppers, each fifteen feet
high, which wipe out the entire local force and a few state troop-
ers. Interrupting a perfunctory romance with the heroine, the scientist flies to Washington to alert the nation. He describes the
potential danger to a group of bored politicians and yawning big
brass, but they remain skeptical until word comes that the things
have reached Chicago and are crushing buildings and eating the
occupants. The scientist is then put in charge of the army and air
force. Although the military men want to evacuate the city and
drop an atomic bomb on it, the scientist devises a safer method
of destroying the creatures and proceeds to do so through exemplary physical courage and superior knowledge of their behavior.
The movie ends on a note of foreboding: have the things been
completely exterminated?

Externally, there seem to be very significant changes in- 11
deed, especially in the character of the scientist. No longer fang-

toothed, long-haired, and subject to delirious ravings (Bela Lugosi, John Carradine, Basil Rathbone), the doctor is now a highly admired member of society, muscular, handsome, and heroic (John Agar). He is invariably wiser, more reasonable, and more humane than the bone-headed bureaucrats and trigger-happy brass that compose the members of his "team," and he even has sexual appeal, a quality which Hollywood's eggheads have never enjoyed before. The scientist-hero, however, is not a very convincing intellectual. Although he may use technical, polysyllabic language when discussing his findings, he always yields gracefully to the admonition to "tell us in our own words, Doc" and proves that he can speak as simply as you or I; in the crisis, in fact, he is almost monosyllabic. When the chips are down, he loses his glasses (a symbol of his intellectualism) and begins to look like everyone else. The hero's intellect is part of his costume and makeup, easily shed when heroic action is demanded. That he is always called upon not only to outwit the thing but to wrestle with it as well (in order to save the heroine) indicates that he is in constant danger of tripping over the thin boundary between specialist and average Joe.

The fact remains that there is a new separation between the 12 scientist and the monster. Rather than being an extension of the doctor's evil will, the monster functions completely on its own, creating havoc through its predatory nature. We learn through charts, biological film, and the scientist's patient explanations that ants and grasshoppers are not the harmless little beasties they appear but actually voracious insects who need only the excuse of size to prey upon humanity. The doctor, rather than allying himself with the monster in its rampage against our cities, is in strong opposition to it, and reverses the pattern of the Mad Doctor films by destroying it.

And yet, if the individual scientist is absolved of all respon- 13 sibility for the "thing," science somehow is not. These films suggest an uneasiness about science which, though subtle and unpremeditated, reflects unconscious American attitudes. These attitudes are sharpened when we examine the genesis of the thing for, though it seems to rise out of nowhere, it is invariably caused by a scientific blunder. The giant ants of *Them!*, for example, result from a nuclear explosion which caused a mutation in the species; another fission test has awakened, in *Beast from Twenty Thousand Fathoms*, a dinosaur encrusted in polar ice-caps; the spider of *Tarantula* grows in size after having been in-jected with radioactive isotopes, and escapes during a fight in the lab between two scientists; the grasshoppers of *Beginning of the End* enlarge after crawling into some radioactive dust carelessly left about by a researcher. We are left with a puzzling substate-ment: science destroys the thing but scientific experimentation has created it.

I think we can explain this equivocal attitude when we ac- 14 knowledge that the thing "which is too horrible to name," which owes its birth to an atomic or nuclear explosion, which begins in a desert or frozen waste and moves from there to cities, and which promises ultimately to destroy the world, is probably a crude symbol for the bomb itself. The scientists we see repre-sented in these films are unlike the Mad Doctors in another more fundamental respect: they are never engaged in basic research. The scientist uses his knowledge in a purely defensive manner, like a specialist working on rocket interception or a physician trying to cure a disease. The isolated theoretician who tinkers cu-riously in his lab (and who invented the atomic bomb) is never shown, only the practical working scientist who labors to undo the harm. The thing's destructive rampage against cities, like the rampage of the Frankenstein monster, is the result of too much cleverness, and the consequences for all the world are only too apparent.

These consequences are driven home more powerfully in 15 movies like *The Incredible Shrinking Man* and *The Amazing Co-lossal Man* where the audience gets the opportunity to identify closely with the victims of science's reckless experimentation. The hero of the first movie is an average man who, through con-tact with fallout while on his honeymoon, begins to shrink away to nothing. As he proceeds to grow smaller, he finds himself in much the same dilemma as the other heroes of the *Atomic Beast* series: he must do battle with (now) gigantic insects in order to survive. Scientists can do nothing to save him—after a while they can't even find him—so as he dwindles into an atomic particle he finally turns to God for whom "there is no zero." The inevitable sequel, *The Amazing Colossal Man,* reverses the dilemma. The hero grows to enormous size through the premature explosion of a plutonium bomb. Size carries with it the luxury of power but the hero cannot enjoy his new stature. He feels like a freak and his body is proceeding to outgrow his brain and heart. Although the scientists labor to help him and even succeed in reducing an elephant to the size of a cat, it is too late; the hero has gone mad, demolished Las Vegas and fallen over Boulder Dam. The victimization of man by theoretical science has become, in these two movies, less of a suggestion and more of a fact.

In the Interplanetary Monster movies, Hollywood handles the public's ambivalence towards science in a more obvious way, by splitting the scientist in two. Most of these movies feature both a practical scientist who wishes to destroy the invader and a theoretical scientist who wants to communicate with it. In *The Thing,* for example, we find billeted among a group of more altruistic average-Joe colleagues with crew cuts an academic long-haired scientist of the Dr. Frankenstein type. When the evil thing (a highly evolved vegetable which, by multiplying itself, threatens to take over the world) descends in a flying saucer, this scientist tries to perpetuate its life in order "to find out what it knows." He is violently opposed in this by the others who take the occasion to tell him that such amoral investigation produced the atomic bomb. But he cannot be reasoned with and almost wrecks the entire party. After both he and the thing are destroyed, the others congratulate themselves on remaining safe, though in the dark. In *Forbidden Planet* (a sophisticated thriller inspired in part by Shakespeare's *Tempest*), the good and evil elements in science are represented, as in *Dr. Jekyll and Mr. Hyde,* by the split personality of the scientist. He is urbane and benevolent (Walter Pidgeon plays the role) and is trying to realize an ideal community on the far-off planet he has discovered. Although he has invented a robot (Ariel) who cheerfully performs man's baser tasks, we learn that he is also responsible, though unwittingly, for a terrible invisible force (Caliban) overwhelming in its destructiveness. While he sleeps, the aggressive forces in his libido activate a dynamo he has been tinkering with which gives them enormous power to kill those the doctor unconsciously resents. Thus, Freudian psychology is evoked to endow the scientist with guilt. At the end, he accepts his guilt and sacrifices his life in order to combat the being he has created.

The Interplanetary Monster series sometimes reverses the 17 central situation of most horror films. We often find the monster controlling the scientist and forcing him to do its evil will. In *It Conquered the World* (the first film to capitalize on Sputnik and Explorer), the projection of a space satellite proves to be a mistake, for it results in the invasion of America by a monster from Venus. The monster takes control of the scientist who, embittered by the indifference of the masses towards his ideas, mistakenly thinks the monster will free men from stupidity. This muddled egghead finally discovers the true intentions of the monster and destroys it, dying himself in the process. In *The Brain from Planet Arous,* a hideous brain inhabits the mind of a nuclear physicist with the intention of controlling the universe. As the physical incarnation of the monster, the scientist is at the mercy of its will until he can free himself of its influence. The monster's intellect, like the intellect of the Mad Doctor, is invariably superior, signified graphically by its large head and small body (in the last film named it is nothing but Brain). Like the Mad Doctor, its superior intelligence is always accompanied by moral depravity and an unconscionable lust for power. If the monster is to be destroyed at all, this will not be done by matching wits with it but by finding some chink in its armor. The chink quite often is a physical imperfection: in *War of the Worlds,* the invading Martians are stopped, at the height of their victory, by their vulnerability to the disease germs of earth. Before this Achilles heel is discovered, however, the scientist is controlled to do evil, and with the monster and the doctor in collaboration again, even in this qualified sense, the wheel has come full circle.

The terror of most of these films, then, stems from the 18 matching of knowledge with power, always a source of fear for Americans—when Nietzsche's Superman enters comic book culture he loses his intellectual and spiritual qualities and becomes a muscle man. The muscle man, even with X-ray vision, poses no threat to the will, but muscle in collaboration with mind is generally thought to have a profound effect on individual destinies.

The tendency to attribute everything that happens in the heavens, from flying saucers to Florida's cold wave, to science and the bomb ("Why don't they stop," said an old lady on the bus behind me the other day, "they don't know what they're doing") accounts for the extreme ways in which the scientist is regarded in our culture: either as a protective savior or as a destructive blunderer. It is little wonder that America exalts the physician (and the football player) and ignores the physicist. These issues, the issues of the great debate over scientific education and basic research, assert themselves crudely through the unwieldy monster and the Mad Doctor. The films suggest that the academic scientist, in exploring new areas, has laid the human race open to devastation either by human or interplanetary enemies—the doctor's madness, then, is merely a suitable way of expressing a conviction that the scientist's idle curiosity has shaken itself loose from prudence or principle. There is obviously a sensitive moral problem involved here, one which needs more articulate treatment than the covert and superstitious way it is handled in horror movies. That the problem is touched there at all is evidence of how profoundly it has stirred the American psyche.

1958

Cinematypes
Susan Allen Toth

Aaron takes me only to art films. That's what I call them, anyway: strange movies with vague poetic images I don't always understand, long dreamy movies about a distant Technicolor past, even longer black-and-white movies about the general meaninglessness of life. We do not go unless at least one reputable critic has found the cinematography superb. We went to *The Devil's Eye,* and Aaron turned to me in the middle and said, "My God, this is *funny*." I do not think he was pleased.

When Aaron and I go to the movies, we drive our cars sep- 2
arately and meet by the box office. Inside the theater he sits ten-
tatively in his seat, ready to move if he can't see well, poised to
leave if the film is disappointing. He leans away from me, careful
not to touch the bare flesh of his arm against the bare flesh of
mine. Sometimes he leans so far I am afraid he may be touching
the woman on his other side. If the movie is very good, he leans
forward, too, peering between the heads of the couple in front of
us. The light from the screen bounces off his glasses; he gleams
with intensity, sitting there on the edge of his seat, watching the
screen. Once I tapped him on the arm so I could whisper a comment in his ear. He jumped.

After *Belle de Jour* Aaron said he wanted to ask me if he 3
could stay overnight. "But I can't," he shook his head mournfully before I had a chance to answer, "because I know I never
sleep well in strange beds." Then he apologized for asking. "It's
just that after a film like that," he said, "I feel the need to assert
myself."

Pete takes me only to movies that he thinks have redeeming 4
social value. He doesn't call them "films." They tend to be
about poverty, war, injustice, political corruption, struggling
unions in the 1930s, and the military-industrial complex. Pete
doesn't like propaganda movies, though, and he doesn't like to
be too depressed, either. We stayed away from *The Sorrow and
the Pity;* it would be, he said, just too much. Besides, he assured
me, things are never that hopeless. So most of the movies we see
are made in Hollywood. Because they are always topical, these
movies offer what Pete calls "food for thought." When we saw
Coming Home, Pete's jaw set so firmly with the first half-hour
that I knew we would end up at Poppin' Fresh Pies afterward.

When Pete and I go to the movies, we take turns driving so 5
no one owes anyone else anything. We leave the car far from the
theater so we don't have to pay for a parking space. If it's raining
or snowing, Pete offers to let me off at the door, but I can tell
he'll feel better if I go with him while he finds a spot, so we share
the walk too. Inside the theater Pete will hold my hand when I
get scared if I ask him. He puts my hand firmly on his knee and

covers it completely with his own hand. His knee never twitches. After a while, when the scary part is past, he loosens his hand slightly and I know that is a signal to take mine away. He sits companionably close, letting his jacket just touch my sweater, but he does not infringe. He thinks I ought to know he is there if I need him.

One night, after *The China Syndrome,* I asked Pete if he 6 wouldn't like to stay for a second drink, even though it was past midnight. He thought a while about that, considering my offer from all possible angles, but finally he said no. Relationships today, he said, have a tendency to move too quickly.

Sam likes movies that are entertaining. By that he means 7 movies that Will Jones in the *Minneapolis Tribune* loved and either *Time* or *Newsweek* rather liked; also movies that do not have sappy love stories, are not musicals, do not have subtitles, and will not force him to think. He does not go to movies to think. He liked *California Suite* and *The Seduction of Joe Tynan,* though the plots, he said, could have been zippier. He saw it all coming too far in advance, and that took the fun out. He doesn't like to know what is going to happen. "I just want my brain to be tickled," he says. It is very hard for me to pick out movies for Sam.

When Sam takes me to the movies, he pays for everything. 8 He thinks that's what a man ought to do. But I buy my own popcorn, because he doesn't approve of it; the grease might smear his flannel slacks. Inside the theater, Sam makes himself comfortable. He takes off his jacket, puts one arm around me, and all during the movie he plays with my hand, stroking my palm, beating a small tattoo on my wrist. Although he watches the movie intently, his body operates on instinct. Once I inclined my head and kissed him lightly just behind his ear. He beat a faster tattoo on my wrist, quick and musical, but he didn't look away from the screen.

When Sam takes me home from the movies, he stands out- 9 side my door and kisses me long and hard. He would like to come in, he says regretfully, but his steady girlfriend in Duluth wouldn't like it. When the *Tribune* gives a movie four stars, he has to save it to see with her. Otherwise her feelings might be hurt.

I go to some movies by myself. On rainy Sunday afternoons 10
I often sneak into a revival house or a college auditorium for old
Technicolor musicals, *Kiss Me Kate, Seven Brides for Seven
Brothers, Calamity Jane,* even, once, *The Sound of Music.*
Wearing saggy jeans so I can prop my feet on the seat in front, I
sit toward the rear where no one can see me. I eat large handfuls
of popcorn with double butter. Once the movie starts, I feel completely at home. Howard Keel and I are old friends; I grin back at
him on the screen. I know the sound tracks by heart. Sometimes
when I get really carried away I hum along with Kathryn Gray-
son, remembering how I once thought I would fill out a formal
like that. I am rather glad now I never did. Skirts whirl, feet tap,
acrobatic young men perform impossible feats, and then the camera dissolves into a dream sequence I know I can comfortably
follow. It is not, thank God, Bergman.

If I can't find an old musical, I settle for Hepburn and 11
Tracy, vintage Grant or Gable, on adventurous days Claudette
Colbert or James Stewart. Before I buy my ticket I make sure it
will all end happily. If necessary, I ask the girl at the box office.
I have never seen *Stella Dallas* or *Intermezzo*. Over the years I
have developed other peccadilloes: I will, for example, see anything that is redeemed by Thelma Ritter. At the end of *Daddy
Long Legs* I wait happily for the scene when Fred Clark, no
longer angry, at last pours Thelma a convivial drink. They smile
at each other, I smile at them, I feel they are smiling at me. In the
movies I go to by myself, the men and women always like each
other.

1980

6

Comparison and Contrast

Grant and Lee: A Study in Contrasts
Bruce Catton

When Ulysses S. Grant and Robert E. Lee met in the parlor 1 of a modest house at Appomattox Court House, Virginia, on April 9, 1865, to work out the terms for the surrender of Lee's Army of Northern Virginia, a great chapter in American life came to a close, and a great new chapter began.

These men were bringing the Civil War to its virtual finish. 2 To be sure, other armies had yet to surrender, and for a few days the fugitive Confederate government would struggle desperately and vainly, trying to find some way to go on living now that its chief support was gone. But in effect it was all over when Grant and Lee signed the papers. And the little room where they wrote out the terms was the scene of one of the poignant, dramatic contrasts in American history.

They were two strong men, these oddly different generals, 3 and they represented the strengths of two conflicting currents that, through them, had come into final collision.

Back of Robert E. Lee was the notion that the old aristo- 4 cratic concept might somehow survive and be dominant in American life.

Lee was tidewater Virginia, and in his background were 5

225

family, culture, and tradition...the age of chivalry transplanted to a New World which was making its own legends and its own myths. He embodied a way of life that had come down through the age of knighthood and the English country squire. America was a land that was beginning all over again, dedicated to nothing much more complicated than the rather hazy belief that all men had equal rights, and should have an equal chance in the world. In such a land Lee stood for the feeling that it was somehow of advantage to human society to have a pronounced inequality in the social structure. There should be a leisure class, backed by ownership of land; in turn, society itself should be keyed to the land as the chief source of wealth and influence. It would bring forth (according to this ideal) a class of men with a strong sense of obligation to the community; men who lived not to gain advantage for themselves, but to meet the solemn obligations which had been laid on them by the very fact that they were privileged. From them the country would get its leadership; to them it could look for the higher values—of thought, of conduct, of personal deportment—to give it strength and virtue.

Lee embodied the noblest elements of this aristocratic 6 ideal. Through him, the landed nobility justified itself. For four years, the Southern states had fought a desperate war to uphold the ideals for which Lee stood. In the end, it almost seemed as if the Confederacy fought for Lee; as if he himself was the Confederacy...the best thing that the way of life for which the Confederacy stood could ever have to offer. He had passed into legend before Appomattox. Thousands of tired, underfed, poorly clothed Confederate soldiers, long-since past the simple enthusiasm of the early days of the struggle, somehow considered Lee the symbol of everything for which they had been willing to die. But they could not quite put this feeling into words. If the Lost Cause, sanctified by so much heroism and so many deaths, had a living justification, its justification was General Lee.

Grant, the son of a tanner on the Western frontier, was ev- 7 erything Lee was not. He had come up the hard way, and embodied nothing in particular except the eternal toughness and sinewy fiber of the men who grew up beyond the mountains. He was one of a body of men who owed reverence and obeisance to no one, who were self-reliant to a fault, who cared hardly anything for the past but who had a sharp eye for the future.

These frontier men were the precise opposites of the tide- 8 water aristocrats. Back of them, in the great surge that had taken people over the Alleghenies and into the opening Western country, there was a deep, implicit dissatisfaction with a past that had settled into grooves. They stood for democracy, not from any reasoned conclusion about the proper ordering of human society, but simply because they had grown up in the middle of democracy and knew how it worked. Their society might have privileges, but they would be privileges each man had won for himself. Forms and patterns meant nothing. No man was born to anything, except perhaps to a chance to show how far he could rise. Life was competition.

Yet along with this feeling had come a deep sense of be- 9 longing to a national community. The Westerner who developed a farm, opened a shop or set up in business as a trader, could hope to prosper only as his own community prospered—and his community ran from the Atlantic to the Pacific and from Canada down to Mexico. If the land was settled, with towns and highways and accessible markets, he could better himself. He saw his fate in terms of the nation's own destiny. As its horizons expanded, so did his. He had, in other words, an acute dollars-and-cents stake in the continued growth and development of his country.

And that, perhaps, is where the contrast between Grant and 10 Lee becomes most striking. The Virginia aristocrat, inevitably, saw himself in relation to his own region. He lived in a static society which could endure almost anything except change. Instinctively, his first loyalty would go to the locality in which that society existed. He would fight to the limit of endurance to defend it, because in defending it he was defending everything that gave his own life its deepest meaning.

The Westerner, on the other hand, would fight with an 11 equal tenacity for the broader concept of society. He fought so because everything he lived by was tied to growth, expansion, and a constantly widening horizon. What he lived by would survive or fall with the nation itself. He could not possibly stand by unmoved in the face of an attempt to destroy the Union. He would combat it with everything he had, because he could only see it as an effort to cut the ground out from under his feet.

So Grant and Lee were in complete contrast, representing 12 two diametrically opposed elements in American life. Grant was the modern man emerging; beyond him, ready to come on the stage, was the great age of steel and machinery, of crowded cities and a restless, burgeoning vitality. Lee might have ridden down from the old age of chivalry, lance in hand, silken banner fluttering over his head. Each man was the perfect champion of his cause, drawing both his strengths and his weaknesses from the people he led.

Yet it was not all contrast, after all. Different as they 13 were—in background, in personality, in underlying aspiration— these two great soldiers had much in common. Under everything else, they were marvelous fighters. Furthermore, their fighting qualities were really very much alike.

Each man had, to begin with, the great virtue of utter te- 14 nacity and fidelity. Grant fought his way down the Mississippi Valley in spite of acute personal discouragement and profound military handicaps. Lee hung on in the trenches at Petersburg after hope itself had died. In each man there was an indomitable quality...the born fighter's refusal to give up as long as he can still remain on his feet and lift his two fists.

Daring and resourcefulness they had, too; the ability to 15 think faster and move faster than the enemy. These were the qualities which gave Lee the dazzling campaigns of Second Manassas and Chancellorsville and won Vicksburg for Grant.

Lastly, and perhaps greatest of all, there was the ability, at 16 the end, to turn quickly from war to peace once the fighting was over. Out of the way these two men behaved at Appomattox came the possibility of a peace of reconciliation. It was a possibility not wholly realized, in the years to come, but which did, in the end, help the two sections to become one nation again...after a war whose bitterness might have seemed to make such a reunion wholly impossible. No part of either man's life became him more than the part he played in their brief meeting in the McLean house at Appomattox. Their behavior there put all succeeding generations of Americans in their debt. Two great Americans, Grant and Lee—very different, yet under everything very much alike. Their encounter at Appomattox was one of the great moments of American history.

1958

On Permission to Write
Cynthia Ozick

I hate everything that does not relate to literature, conversations bore me (even when they relate to literature), to visit people bores me, the joys and sorrows of my relatives bore me to my soul. Conversation takes the importance, the seriousness, the truth, out of everything I think.

Franz Kafka, from his diary, 1918

In a small and depressing city in a nearby state there lives a young man (I will call him David) whom I have never met and with whom I sometimes correspond. David's letters are voluminous, vehemently bookish, and—in obedience to literary modernism—without capitals. When David says "I," he writes "i." This does not mean that he is insecure in his identity or that he suffers from a weakness of confidence—David cannot be characterized by thumbnail psychologizing. He is like no one else (except maybe Jane Austen). He describes himself mostly as poor and provincial, as in Balzac, and occasionally as poor and black. He lives alone with his forbearing and bewildered mother in a flat "with imaginary paintings on the walls in barren rooms," writes stories and novels, has not yet published, and appears to spend his days hauling heaps of books back and forth from the public library.

He has read, it seems, everything. His pages are masses of flashy literary allusions—nevertheless entirely lucid, witty, learned, and sane. David is not *exactly* a crank who writes to writers, although he is probably a bit of that too. I don't know how he gets his living, or whether his letters romanticize either his poverty (he reports only a hunger for books) or his passion (ditto); still, David is a free intellect, a free imagination. It is possible that he hides his manuscripts under a blotter, Jane-Austenly, when his mother creeps mutely in to collect his discarded socks. (A week's worth, perhaps, curled on the floor next to Faulkner and Updike and Cummings and *Tristram Shandy*. Of the latter he remarks: "a worthy book. dare any man get offspring on less?")

On the other hand, David wants to be noticed. He wants to   3
be paid attention to. Otherwise, why would he address charming letters to writers (I am not the only one) he has never met? Like Joyce in "dirty provincial Dublin," he says, he means to announce his "inevitable arrival on the mainland." A stranger's eyes, even for a letter, is a kind of publication. David, far from insisting on privacy, is a would-be public man. It may be that he pants after fame. And yet in his immediate position—his secret literary life, whether or not he intends it to remain secret—there is something delectable. He thirsts to read, so he reads; he thirsts to write, so he writes. He is in the private cave of his freedom, an eremite, a solitary; he orders his mind as he pleases. In this condition he is prolific. He writes and writes. Ah, he is poor and provincial, in a dim lost corner of the world. But his lonely place (a bare cubicle joyfully tumbling with library books) and his lonely situation (the liberty to be zealous) have given him the permission to write. To be, in fact, prolific.

I am not like David. I am not poor, or provincial (except in   4
the New York way), or unpublished, or black. (David, the sovereign of his life, invents an aloofness from social disabilities, at least in his letters, and I have not heard him mythologize "negritude"; he admires poets for their words and cadences.) But all this is not the essential reason I am not like David. I am not like him because I do not own his permission to write freely, and zealously, and at will, and however I damn please; and abundantly; and always.

There is this difference between the prolific and the non-   5 prolific: the prolific have arrogated to themselves the permission to write.

By permission I suppose I ought to mean *inner* permission. 6 Now "inner permission" is a phrase requiring high caution: it was handed to me by a Freudian dogmatist, a writer whose energy and confidence depend on regular visits to his psychoanalyst. In a useful essay called "Art and Neurosis," Lionel Trilling warns against the misapplication of Freud's dictum that "we are all ill, i.e., neurotic," and insists that a writer's productivity derives from "the one part of him that is healthy, by any conceivable definition of health...that which gives him the power to conceive, to plan, to work, and to bring his work to a conclusion." The capacity to write, in short, comes from an uncharted space over which even all-prevailing neurosis can have no jurisdiction or dominion. "The use to which [the artist] puts his power...may be discussed with reference to his particular neurosis," Trilling concedes; yet Trilling's verdict is finally steel: "But its essence is irreducible. It is, as we say, a gift."

If permission to write (and for a writer this is exactly equal 7 to the power to write) is a gift, then what of the lack of permission? Does the missing "Go ahead" mean neurosis? I am at heart one of those hapless pre-moderns who believe that the light bulb is the head of a demon called forth by the light switch, and that Freud is a German word for pleasure; so I am not equipped to speak about principles of electricity or psychoanalysis. All the same, it seems to me that the electrifying idea of inward obstacle—neurosis—is not nearly so often responsible for low productivity as we are told. Writer's permission is not something that is switched off by helpless forces inside the writer, but by social currents—human beings and their ordinary predilections and prejudices—outside. If David writes freely and others don't, the reason might be that, at least for a while, David has kidnapped himself beyond the pinch of society. He is Jane Austen with her hidden manuscript momentarily slipped out from under the blotter; he is Thoreau in his cabin. He is a free man alone in a room with imaginary pictures on the walls, reading and writing in a private rapture.

There are some writers who think of themselves as sha- 8
mans, dervishes of inspiration, divinely possessed ecstatics—
writers who believe with Emerson that the artist "has cast off the
common motives of humanity and has ventured to trust himself
for a taskmaster": himself above everyone. Emerson it is who
advises writers to aspire, through isolation, to "a simple
purpose...as strong as iron necessity is to others," and who—in
reply to every contingency—exhorts, "O father, O mother, O
wife, O brother, O friend, I have lived with you after appear-
ances hitherto. Henceforward I am the truth's." These shaman-
writers, with their cult of individual genius and romantic egoism,
may be self-glamorizing holy madmen, but they are not maniacs;
they know what is good for them, and what is good for them is
fences. You cannot get near them, whatever your need or demand. O father, O mother, O wife, O brother, O friend, they will
tell you—*beat it*. They call themselves caviar, and for the general
their caviar is a caveat.

Most writers are more modest than this, and more reason- 9
able, and don't style themselves as unbridled creatures celes-
tially privileged and driven. They know that they are citizens like
other citizens, and have simply chosen a profession, as others
have. These are the writers who go docilely to gatherings where
they are required to marvel at every baby; who yield slavishly to
the ukase that sends them out for days at a time to scout a sam-
ovar for the birthday of an elderly great-uncle; who pretend to
overnight guests that they are capable of sitting at the breakfast
table without being consumed by print; who craftily let on to in-
laws that they are diligent cooks and sheltering wives, though
they would sacrifice a husband to a hurricane to fetch them a
typewriter ribbon; and so on. In short, they work at appear-
ances, trust others for taskmasters, and do not insist too rigor-
ously on whose truth they will live after. And they are honorable
enough. In company, they do their best to dress like everyone
else: if they are women they will tolerate panty hose and high-
heeled shoes, if they are men they will show up in a three-piece
suit; but in either case they will be concealing the fact that during
any ordinary row of days they sleep in their clothes. In the same
company they lend themselves, decade after decade, to the ex-

pectation that they will not lay claim to unusual passions, that they will believe the average belief, that they will take pleasure in the average pleasure. Dickens, foreseeing the pain of relinquishing his pen at a time not of his choosing, reportedly would not accept an invitation. "Thank God for books," Auden said, "as an alternative to conversation." Good-citizen writers, by contrast, year after year decline no summons, refuse no banquet, turn away from no tedium, willingly enter into every anecdote and brook the assault of any amplified band. They will put down their pens for a noodle pudding.

And with all this sterling obedience, this strenuous courtli- 10 ness and congeniality, this anxious flattery of unspoken coercion down to the third generation, something goes wrong. One dinner in twenty years is missed. Or no dinner at all is missed, but an "attitude" is somehow detected. No one is fooled; the cordiality is pronounced insincere, the smile a fake, the goodwill a dud, the talk a fib, the cosseting a cozening. These sweating citizen-writers are in the end always found out and accused. They are accused of elitism. They are accused of snobbery. They are accused of loving books and bookishness more feelingly than flesh and blood.

Edith Wharton, in her cool and bitter way, remarked of 11 the literary life that "in my own family it created a kind of restraint that grew with the years. None of my relations ever spoke to me of my books, either to praise or to blame—they simply ignored them;...the subject was avoided as if it were a kind of family disgrace, which might be condoned but could not be forgotten."

Good-citizen writers are not read by their accusers; per- 12 haps they cannot be. "If I succeed," said Conrad, "you shall find there according to your deserts: encouragement, consolation, fear, charm—all you demand—and, perhaps, also that glimpse of truth for which you have forgotten to ask." But some never demand, or demand less. "If you simplified your style," a strict but kindly aunt will advise, "you might come up to par," and her standard does not exempt Conrad.

The muse-inspired shaman-writers are never called snobs, 13 for the plain reason that no strict but kindly aunt will ever get within a foot of any of them. But the good-citizen writers—by virtue of their very try at citizenship—are suspect and resented. Their work will not be taken for work. They will always be condemned for not being interchangeable with nurses or salesmen or schoolteachers or accountants or brokers. They will always be found out. They will always be seen to turn longingly after a torn peacock's tail left over from a fugitive sighting of paradise. They will always have hanging from a back pocket a telltale shred of idealism, or a cache of a few grains of noble importuning, or, if nothing so grandly quizzical, then a single beautiful word, in Latin or Hebrew; or else they will tip their hand at the wedding feast by complaining meekly of the raging horn that obliterates the human voice; or else they will forget not to fall into Montaigne over the morning toast; or else they will embarrass everyone by oafishly banging on the kettle of history; or else, while the room fills up with small talk, they will glaze over and inwardly chant "This Lime-Tree Bower My Prison"; or else—but never mind. What is not understood is not allowed. These citizen-pretenders will never be respectable. They will never come up to par. They will always be blamed for their airs. They will always be charged with superiority, disloyalty, coldness, want of family feeling. They will always be charged with estranging their wives, husbands, children. They will always be called snob.

They will never be granted the permission to write as serious writers are obliged to write: fanatically, obsessively, consumingly, torrentially, above all comically—and for life.   14

And therefore: enviable blissful provincial prolific lonesome David!   15

1984

Football Red and Baseball Green
Murray Ross

The 1970 Superbowl, the final game of the professional   1
football season, drew a larger television audience than either the
moonwalk or Tiny Tim's wedding. This revelation is one way of
indicating just how popular spectator sports are in this country.
Americans, or American men anyway, seem to care about the
games they watch as much as the Elizabethans cared about their
plays, and I suspect for some of the same reasons. There is, in
sport, some of the rudimentary drama found in popular theater:
familiar plots, type characters, heroic and comic action spiced
with new and unpredictable variations. And common to watching
both activities is the sense of participation in a shared tradition
and in shared fantasies. If it is true that sport exploits these fantasies without significantly transcending them, it seems no less
satisfying for all that.

It is my guess that sport spectating involves something   2
more than the vicarious pleasures of identifying with athletic
prowess. I suspect that each sport contains a fundamental myth
which it elaborates for its fans, and that our pleasure in watching
such games derives in part from belonging briefly to the mythic
world which the game and its players bring to life. I am especially interested in baseball and football because they are so popular and so uniquely *American;* they began here and unlike basketball they have not been widely exported. Thus whatever can
be said, mythically, about these games would seem to apply directly and particularly to our own culture.

Baseball's myth may be the easier to identify since we have   3
a greater historical perspective on the game. It was an instant
success during the Industrialization, and most probably it was a
reaction to the squalor, the faster pace and the dreariness of the
new conditions. Baseball was old fashioned right from the start;
it seems conceived in nostalgia, in the resuscitation of the Jeffer-
sonian dream. It established an artificial rural environment, one
removed from the toil of an urban life, which spectators could be

admitted to and temporarily breathe in. Baseball is a *pastoral* sport, and I think the game can be best understood as this kind of art. For baseball does what all good pastoral does—it creates an atmosphere in which everything exists in harmony.

Consider, for instance, the spatial organization of the game.   4
A kind of controlled openness is created by having everything fan out from home plate, and the crowd sees the game through an arranged perspective that is rarely violated. Visually this means that the game is always seen as a constant, rather calm whole, and that the players and the playing field are viewed in relationship to each other. Each player has a certain position, a special area to tend, and the game often seems to be as much a dialogue between the fielders and the field as it is a contest between the players themselves: will that ball get through the hole? Can that outfielder run under that fly? As a moral genre pastoral asserts the virtue of communion with nature. As a competitive game, baseball asserts that the team which best relates to the playing field (by hitting the ball in the right places) will be the team which wins.

I suspect baseball's space has a subliminal function too, for   5
topographically it is a sentimental mirror of older America. Most of the game is played between the pitcher and the hitter in the extreme corner of the playing area. This is the busiest, most sophisticated part of the ball park, where something is always happening, and from which all subsequent action depends. From this urban corner we move to a supporting infield, active but a little less crowded, and from there we come to the vast stretches of the outfield. As is traditional in American lore danger increases with distance, and the outfield action is often the most spectacular in the game. The long throw, the double off the wall, the leaping catch—these plays take place in remote territory, and they belong, like most legendary feats, to the frontier.

Having established its landscape, pastoral art operates to   6
eliminate any references to that bigger, more disturbing, more real world it has left behind. All games are to some extent insulated from the outside by having their own rules, but baseball has a circular structure as well which furthers its comfortable feeling of self-sufficiency. By this I mean that every motion of extension

is also one of return—a ball hit outside is a *home* run, a full circle. Home—familiar, peaceful, secure—it is the beginning and
end of everything. You must go out and you must come back, for
only the completed movement is registered.

Time is a serious threat to any form of pastoral. The genre   7
poses a timeless world of perpetual spring, and it does its best to
silence the ticking of clocks which remind us that in time the
green world fades into winter. One's sense of time is directly related to what happens in it, and baseball is so structured as to
stretch out and ritualize whatever action it contains. Dramatic
moments are few, and they are almost always isolated by the
routine texture of normal play. It is certainly a game of climax
and drama, but it is perhaps more a game of repeated and predictable action: the foul balls, the walks, the pitcher fussing
around on the mound, the lazy fly ball to centerfield. This is, I
think, as it should be, for baseball exists as an alternative to a
world of too much action, struggle and change. It is a merciful
release from a more grinding and insistent tempo, and its time, as
William Carlos Williams suggests, makes a virtue out of idleness
simply by providing it:

> The crowd at the ball game
>
> is moved uniformly
>
> by a spirit of uselessness
>
> which delights them...

Within this expanded and idle time the baseball fan is at lib-   8
erty to become a ceremonial participant and a lover of style. Because the action is normalized, how something is done becomes
as important as the action itself. Thus baseball's most delicate
and detailed aspects are often, to the spectator, the most interesting. The pitcher's windup, the anticipatory crouch of the in-
fielders, the quick waggle of the bat as it poises for the pitch—
these subtle miniature movements are as meaningful as the home
runs and the strikeouts. It somehow matters in baseball that all
the tiny rituals are observed: the shortstop must kick the dirt and
the umpire must brush the plate with his pocket broom. In a

sense baseball is largely a continuous series of small gestures, and I think it characteristic that the game's most treasured moment came when Babe Ruth pointed to the place where he subsequently hit a home run.

Baseball is a game where the little things mean a lot, and 9 this, together with its clean serenity, its open space, and its ritualized action is enough to place it in a world of yesterday. Baseball evokes for us a past which may never have been ours, but which we believe was, and certainly that is enough. In the Second World War, supposedly, we fought for "Baseball, Mom and Apple Pie," and considering what baseball means that phrase is a good one. We fought then for the right to believe in a green world of tranquillity and uninterrupted contentment, where the little things would count. But now the possibilities of such a world are more remote, and it seems that while the entertainment of such a dream has an enduring appeal, it is no longer sufficient for our fantasies. I think this may be why baseball is no longer our preeminent national pastime, and why its myth is being replaced by another more appropriate to the new realities (and fantasies) of our time.

Football, especially professional football, is the embodi- 10 ment of a newer myth, one which in many respects is opposed to baseball's. The fundamental difference is that football is not a pastoral game; it is a heroic one. One way of seeing the difference between the two is by the juxtaposition of Babe Ruth and Jim Brown, both legendary players in their separate genres. Ruth, baseball's most powerful hitter, was a hero maternalized (his name), an epic figure destined for a second immortality as a candy bar. His image was impressive but comfortable and altogether human: round, dressed in a baggy uniform, with a schoolboy's cap and a bat which looked tiny next to him. His spindly legs supported a Santa sized torso, and this comic disproportion would increase when he was in motion. He ran delicately, with quick, very short steps, since he felt that stretching your stride slowed you down. This sort of superstition is typical of baseball players, and typical too is the way in which a personal quirk or mannerism mitigates their awesome skill and makes them poignant and vulnerable.

There was nothing funny about Jim Brown. His muscular 11
and almost perfect physique was emphasized further by the uniform which armored him. Babe Ruth had a tough face, but boy-
ish and innocent; Brown was an expressionless mask under the
helmet. In action he seemed invincible, the embodiment of speed
and power in an inflated human shape. One can describe Brown
accurately only with superlatives, for as a player he was a kind of
Superman, undisguised.

Brown and Ruth are caricatures, yet they represent their 12
games. Baseball is part of a comic tradition which insists that its
participants be humans, while football, in the heroic mode, asks
that its players be more than that. Football converts men into
gods, and suggests that magnificence and glory are as desirable as
happiness. Football is designed, therefore, to impress its audience
rather differently than baseball, as I think comparison will show.

As a pastoral game, baseball attempts to close the gap be- 13
tween the players and the crowd. It creates the illusion, for instance, that with a lot of hard work, a little luck, and possibly
some extra talent, the average spectator might well be playing;
not watching. For most of us can do a few of the things the ball-
players do: catch a pop-up, field a ground ball, and maybe get a
hit once in a while. Chance is allotted a good deal of play in the
game. There is no guarantee, for instance, that a good pitch will
not be looped over the infield, or that a solidly batted ball will
turn into a double play. In addition to all of this, almost every fan
feels he can make the manager's decision for him, and not entirely without reason. Baseball's statistics are easily calculated
and rather meaningful; and the game itself, though a subtle one,
is relatively lucid and comprehensible.

As a heroic game football is not concerned with a shared 14
community of near-equals. It seeks almost the opposite relationship between its spectators and players, one which stresses the
distance between them. We are not allowed to identify directly
with Jim Brown any more than we are with Zeus, because to do
so would undercut his stature as something more than human.
The players do much of the distancing themselves by their own
excesses of speed, size and strength. When Bob Brown, the giant
all pro tackle says that he could "block King Kong all day," we

look at him and believe. But the game itself contributes to the players' heroic isolation. As George Plimpton has graphically illustrated in *Paper Lion,* it is almost impossible to imagine yourself in a professional football game without also considering your imminent humiliation and possible injury. There is scarcely a single play that the average spectator could hope to perform adequately, and there is even a difficulty in really understanding what is going on. In baseball what happens is what meets the eye, but in football each action is the result of eleven men acting simultaneously against eleven other men, and clearly this is too much for the eye to totally comprehend. Football has become a game of staggering complexity, and coaches are now wired in to several "spotters" during the games so that they too can find out what is happening.

If football is distanced from its fans by its intricacy and its 15 "superhuman" play, it nonetheless remains an intense spectacle. Baseball, as I have implied, dissolves time and urgency in a green expanse, thereby creating a luxurious and peaceful sense of leisure. As is appropriate to a heroic enterprise, football reverses this procedure and converts space into time. The game is ideally played in an oval stadium, not in a "park," and the difference is the elimination of perspective. This makes football a perfect television game, because even at first hand it offers a flat, perpetually moving foreground (wherever the ball is). The eye in baseball viewing opens up; in football it zeroes in. There is no democratic vista in football, and spectators are not asked to relax, but to concentrate. You are encouraged to watch the drama, not a medley of ubiquitous gestures, and you are constantly reminded that this event is taking place in time. The third element in baseball is the field; in football this element is the clock. Traditionally heroes do reckon with time, and football players are no exceptions. Time in football is wound up inexorably until it reaches the breaking point in the last minutes of a close game. More often than not it is the clock which emerges as the real enemy, and it is the sense of time running out that regularly produces a pitch of tension uncommon in baseball.

A further reason for football's intensity, surely, is that the 16 game is played like a war. The idea is to win by going through, around or over the opposing team and the battle lines, quite literally, are drawn on every play. Violence is somewhere at the heart of the game, and the combat quality is reflected in football's army language ("blitz," "trap," "zone," "bomb," "trenches," etc.). Coaches often sound like generals when they discuss their strategy. Woody Hayes of Ohio State, for instance, explains his quarterback option play as if it had been conceived in the Pentagon: "You know," he says, "the most effective kind of warfare is siege. You have to attack on broad fronts. And that's all the option is—attacking on a broad front. You know General Sherman ran an option right through the South."

Football like war is an arena for action, and like war football leaves little room for personal style. It seems to be a game which projects "character" more than personality, and for the most part football heroes, publicly, are a rather similar lot. They tend to become personifications rather than individuals, and, with certain exceptions, they are easily read emblematically as embodiments of heroic qualities such as "strength," "confidence," "perfection," etc.—cliches really, but forceful enough when represented by the play of a Dick Butkus, a Johnny Unitas or a Bart Starr. Perhaps this simplification of personality results in part from the heroes' total identification with their mission, to the extent that they become more characterized by their work than by what they intrinsically "are." At any rate football does not make allowances for the idiosyncrasies that baseball actually seems to encourage, and as a result there have been few football players as uniquely crazy or human as, say, Casey Stengel or Dizzy Dean.

A further reason for the underdeveloped qualities of football personalities, and one which gets us to the heart of the game's modernity, is that football is very much a game of modern technology. Football's action is largely interaction, and the game's complexity requires that its players mold themselves into a perfectly coordinated unit. Jerry Kramer, the veteran guard and author of *Instant Replay,* writes how Lombardi would work to develop such integration:

> He makes us execute the same plays over and over, a hundred times, two hundred times, until we do every little thing automatically. He works to make the kickoff team perfect, the punt-return team perfect, the field-goal team

perfect. He ignores nothing. Technique, technique,
technique, over and over and over, until we feel like we're
going crazy. But we win.

Mike Garratt, the halfback, gives the player's version: 19

After a while you train your mind like a computer—put
the ideas in, digest it, and the body acts accordingly.

As the quotations imply, pro football is insatiably preoccu- 20
pied with the smoothness and precision of play execution, and
most coaches believe that the team which makes the fewest mistakes will be the team that wins. Individual identity thus comes
to be associated with the team or unit that one plays for to a
much greater extent than in baseball. To use a reductive analogy,
it is the difference between *Bonanza* and *Mission Impossible*.
Ted Williams is mostly Ted Williams, but Bart Starr is mostly the
Green Bay Packers. The latter metaphor is a precise one, since
football heroes stand out not because of purely individual acts,
but because they epitomize the action and style of the groups
they are connected to. Kramer cites the obvious if somewhat
self-glorifying historical precedent: "Perhaps," he writes,
"we're living in Camelot." Ideally a football team should be
what Camelot was supposed to have been, a group of men who
function as equal parts of a larger whole, entirely dependent on
each other for their total meaning....

Football's collective pattern is only one aspect of the way 21
in which it seems to echo our contemporary environment. The
game, like our society, can be thought of as a cluster of people
living under great tension in a state of perpetual flux. The potential for sudden disaster or triumph is as great in football as it is in
our own age, and although there is something ludicrous in equat-
ing interceptions with assassinations and long passes with moon-
shots, there is also something valid and appealing in the analo-
gies. It seems to me that football does successfully reflect those
salient and common conditions which affect us all, and it does so
with the end of making us feel better about them and our lot. For
one thing, it makes us feel that something can be connected in all
this chaos; out of the accumulated pile of bodies something can

emerge—a runner breaks into the clear or a pass finds its way to a receiver. To the spectator plays such as these are human and dazzling. They suggest to the audience what it has hoped for (and been told) all along, that technology is still a tool and not a master. Fans get living proof of this every time a long pass is completed; they see at once that it is the result of careful planning, perfect integration and an effective "pattern," but they see too that it is human and that what counts as well is man, his desire, his natural skill and his "grace under pressure." Football metaphysically yokes heroic action and technology together by violence to suggest that they are mutually supportive. It's a doubtful proposition, but given how we live it has its attractions.

Football, like the space program, is a game in the grand   22 manner, yet it is a rather sober sport and often seems to lack that positive, comic vision of which baseball's pastoral is a part. It is a winter game, as those fans who saw the Minnesota Vikings play the Detroit Lions last Thanksgiving were graphically reminded. The two teams played in a blinding snowstorm, and except for the small flags in the corners of the end zones, and a patch of mud wherever the ball was downed, the field was totally obscured. Even through the magnified television lenses the players were difficult to identify; you saw only huge shapes come out of the gloom, thump against each other and fall in a heap. The movement was repeated endlessly and silently in a muffled stadium, interrupted once or twice by a shot of a bare-legged girl who fluttered her pom-poms in the cold. The spectacle was by turns pathetic, compelling and absurd; a kind of theater of oblivion....

A final note. It is interesting that the heroic and pastoral   23 conventions which underlie our most popular sports are almost classically opposed. The contrasts are familiar: city vs. country, aspiration vs. contentment, activity vs. peace and so on. Judging from the rise of professional football we seem to be slowly relinquishing that unfettered rural vision of ourselves that baseball so beautifully mirrors, and we have come to cast ourselves in a genre more reflective of a nation confronted by constant and unavoidable challenges. Right now, like the Elizabethans, we seem to share both heroic and pastoral yearnings, and we reach out to both. Perhaps these divided needs account in part for the enormous attention we as a nation now give to spectator sports. For sport provides one place, at least, where we can have our football and our baseball too.

1971

Two Views of the Mississippi
Mark Twain

Now when I had mastered the language of this water, and had come to know every trifling feature that bordered the great river as familiarly as I knew the letters of the alphabet, I had made a valuable acquisition. But I had lost something, too. I had lost something which could never be restored to me while I lived. All the grace, the beauty, the poetry, had gone out of the majestic river! I still keep in mind a certain wonderful sunset which I witnessed when steamboating was new to me. A broad expanse of the river was turned to blood; in the middle distance the red hue brightened into gold, through which a solitary log came floating black and conspicuous; in one place a long, slanting mark lay sparkling upon the water; in another the surface was broken by boiling, tumbling rings, that were as many-tinted as an opal; where the ruddy flush was faintest, was a smooth spot that was covered with graceful circles and radiating lines, ever so delicately traced; the shore on our left was densely wooded, and the somber shadow that fell from this forest was broken in one place by a long, ruffled trail that shone like silver; and high above the forest wall a clean-stemmed dead tree waved a single leafy bough that glowed like a flame in the unobstructed splendor that was flowing from the sun. There were graceful curves, reflected images, woody heights, soft distances; and over the whole scene, far and near, the dissolving lights drifted steadily, enriching it every passing moment with new marvels of coloring.

I stood like one bewitched. I drank it in, in a speechless 2 rapture. The world was new to me, and I had never seen anything like this at home. But as I have said, a day came when I began to cease from noting the glories and the charms which the moon and the sun and the twilight wrought upon the river's face; another day came when I ceased altogether to note them. Then, if that sunset scene had been repeated, I should have looked upon it without rapture, and should have commented upon it, inwardly, after this fashion: "This sun means that we are going to have wind to-morrow; that floating log means that the river is rising, small thanks to it; that slanting mark on the water refers to a bluff reef which is going to kill somebody's steamboat one of these nights, if it keeps on stretching out like that; those tumbling 'boils' show a dissolving bar and a changing channel there; the lines and circles in the slick water over yonder are a warning that that troublesome place is shoaling up dangerously; that silver streak in the shadow of the forest is the 'break' from a new snag, and he has located himself in the very best place he could have found to fish for steamboats; that tall dead tree, with a single living branch, is not going to last long, and then how is a body ever going to get through this blind place at night without the friendly old landmark?"

No, the romance and beauty were all gone from the river. 3 All the value any feature of it had for me now was the amount of usefulness it could furnish toward compassing the safe piloting of a steamboat. Since those days, I have pitied doctors from my heart. What does the lovely flush in a beauty's cheek mean to a doctor but a "break" that ripples above some deadly disease? Are not all her visible charms sown thick with what are to him the signs and symbols of hidden decay? Does he ever see her beauty at all, or doesn't he simply view her professionally, and comment upon her unwholesome condition all to himself? And doesn't he sometimes wonder whether he has gained most or lost most by learning his trade?

1883

The Rewards of Living a Solitary Life
May Sarton

    The other day an acquaintance of mine, a gregarious and 1
charming man, told me he had found himself unexpectedly alone
in New York for an hour or two between appointments. He went
to the Whitney and spent the "empty" time looking at things in
solitary bliss. For him it proved to be a shock nearly as great as
falling in love to discover that he could enjoy himself so much
alone.

    What had he been afraid of, I asked myself? That, suddenly 2
alone, he would discover that he bored himself, or that there
was, quite simply, no self there to meet? But having taken the
plunge, he is now on the brink of adventure; he is about to be
launched into his own inner space, space as immense, unexplored and sometimes frightening as outer space to the astronaut.
His every perception will come to him with a new freshness and,
for a time, seem startlingly original. For anyone who can see
things for himself with a naked eye becomes, for a moment or
two, something of a genius. With another human being present
vision becomes double vision, inevitably. We are busy wondering, what does my companion see or think of this, and what do I
think of it? The original impact gets lost, or diffused.

    "Music I heard with you was more than music." Exactly. 3
And therefore music *itself* can only be heard alone. Solitude is
the salt of personhood. It brings out the authentic flavor of every
experience.

    "Alone one is never lonely: the spirit adventures, walking/ 4
In a quiet garden, in a cool house, abiding single there."

    Loneliness is most acutely felt with other people, for with 5
others, even with a lover sometimes, we suffer from our differences of taste, temperament, mood. Human intercourse often demands that we soften the edge of perception, or withdraw at the
very instant of personal truth for fear of hurting, or of being in-
appropriately present, which is to say naked, in a social situation. Alone we can afford to be wholly whatever we are, and to
feel whatever we feel absolutely. That is a great luxury!

For me the most interesting thing about a solitary life, and 6
mine has been that for the last twenty years, is that it becomes
increasingly rewarding. When I can wake up and watch the sun
rise over the ocean, as I do most days, and know that I have an
entire day ahead, uninterrupted, in which to write a few pages,
take a walk with my dog, lie down in the afternoon for a long
think (why does one think better in a horizontal position?), read
and listen to music, I am flooded with happiness.

I am lonely only when I am overtired, when I have worked 7
too long without a break, when for the time being I feel empty
and need filling up. And I am lonely sometimes when I come
back home after a lecture trip, when I have seen a lot of people
and talked a lot, and am full to the brim with experience that
needs to be sorted out.

Then for a little while the house feels huge and empty, and 8
I wonder where my self is hiding. It has to be recaptured slowly by
watering the plants, perhaps, and looking again at each one as
though it were a person, by feeding the two cats, by cooking a meal.

It takes a while, as I watch the surf blowing up in fountains 9
at the end of the field, but the moment comes when the world falls
away, and the self emerges again from the deep unconscious,
bringing back all I have recently experienced to be explored and
slowly understood, when I can converse again with my hidden
powers, and so grow, and so be renewed, till death do us part.

1946

Viewing vs. Reading
Marie Winn

Until the television era a young child's access to symbolic 1
representations of reality was limited. Unable to read, he entered
the world of fantasy primarily by way of stories told to him or
read to him from a book. But rarely did such "literary" experi-

ences take up a significant proportion of a child's waking time; even when a willing reader or storyteller was available, an hour or so a day was more time than most children spent ensconced in the imagination of others. And when the pretelevision child *did* enter those imaginary worlds, he always had a grown-up escort along to interpret, explain, and comfort, if need be. Before he learned to read, it was difficult for the child to enter the fantasy world alone.

For this reason the impact of television was undoubtedly   2 greater on preschoolers and pre-readers than on any other group. By means of television, very young children were able to enter and spend sizable portions of their waking time in a secondary world of incorporeal people and intangible things, unaccompanied, in too many cases, by an adult guide or comforter. School-age children fell into a different category. Because they could read, they had other opportunities to leave reality behind. For these children television was merely *another* imaginary world.

But since reading, once the school child's major imagina-   3 tive experience, has now been virtually eclipsed by television, the television experience must be compared with the reading experience to try to discover whether they are, indeed, similar activities fulfilling similar needs in a child's life.

WHAT HAPPENS WHEN YOU READ

It is not enough to compare television watching and reading   4 from the viewpoint of quality. Although the quality of the material available in each medium varies enormously, from junky books and shoddy programs to literary masterpieces and fine, thoughtful television shows, the *nature* of the two experiences is different and that difference significantly affects the impact of the material taken in.

Few people besides linguistics students and teachers of   5 reading are aware of the complex mental manipulations involved in the reading process. Shortly after learning to read, a person assimilates the process into his life so completely that the words in books seem to acquire an existence almost equal to the objects or acts they represent. It requires a fresh look at a printed page to recognize that those symbols that we call letters of the alphabet are completely abstract shapes bearing no inherent "meaning" of their own. Look at an "o," for instance, or a "k." The "o" is a curved figure; the "k" is an intersection of three straight lines. Yet it is hard to divorce their familiar figures from their sounds, though there is nothing "o-ish" about an "o" or "k-ish" about a "k." A reader unfamiliar with the Russian alphabet will find it easy to look at the symbol "ш" and see it as an abstract shape; a Russian reader will find it harder to detach that symbol from its sound, *shch*. And even when trying to consider "k" as an abstract symbol, we cannot see it without the feeling of a "k" sound somewhere between the throat and the ears, a silent pronunciation of "k" that occurs the instant we see the letter.

That is the beginning of reading: we learn to transform abstract figures into sounds, and groups of symbols into the combined sounds that make up the words of our language. As the mind transforms the abstract symbols into sounds and the sounds into words, it "hears" the words, as it were, and thereby invests them with meanings previously learned in the spoken language. Invariably, as the skill of reading develops, the meaning of each word begins to seem to dwell within those symbols that make up the word. The word "dog," for instance, comes to bear some relationship with the real animal. Indeed, the word "dog" seems to *be* dog in a certain sense, to possess some of the qualities of a dog. But it is only as a result of a swift and complex series of mental activities that the word "dog" is transformed from a series of meaningless squiggles into an idea of something real. This process goes on smoothly and continuously as we read, and yet it becomes no less complex. The brain must carry out all the steps of decoding and investing with meaning each time we read; but it becomes more adept at it as the skill develops, so that we lose the sense of struggling with symbols and meanings that children have when they first learn to read. 6

But not merely does the mind *hear* words in the process of reading; it is important to remember that reading involves images as well. For when the reader sees the word "dog" and under- 7

stands the idea of "dog," an image representing a dog is conjured up as well. The precise nature of this "reading image" is
little understood, nor is there agreement about what relation it
bears to visual images taken in directly by the eyes. Nevertheless
images necessarily color our reading, else we would perceive no
meaning, merely empty words. The great difference between
these "reading images" and the images we take in when viewing
television is this: we *create* our own images when reading, based
upon our own life experiences and reflecting our own individual
needs, while we must accept what we receive when watching
television images. This aspect of reading, which might be called
"creative" in the narrow sense of the word, is present during all
reading experiences, regardless of *what* is being read. The reader
"creates" his own images as he reads, almost as if he were creating his own, small, inner television program. The result is a
nourishing experience for the imagination. As Bruno Bettelheim
notes, "Television captures the imagination but does not liberate
it. A good book at once stimulates and frees the mind."

Television images do not go through a complex symbolic   8
transformation. The mind does not have to decode and manipulate during the television experience. Perhaps this is a reason
why the visual images received directly from a television set are
strong, stronger, it appears, than the images conjured up mentally while reading. But ultimately they satisfy less. A ten-year-
old child reports on the effects of seeing television dramatiza-
tions of books he has previously read: "The TV people leave a
stronger impression. Once you've seen a character on TV, he'll
always look like that in your mind, even if you made a different
picture of him in your mind before, when you read the book
yourself." And yet, as the same child reports, "the thing about a
book is that you have so much freedom. You can make each
character look exactly the way you want him to look. You're
more in control of things when you read a book than when you
see something on TV."

It may be that television-bred children's reduced opportu-   9
nities to indulge in this "inner picture-making" accounts for the
curious inability of so many children today to adjust to nonvisual
experiences. This is commonly reported by experienced teachers

who bridge the gap between the pretelevision and the television eras.

"When I read them a story without showing them pictures, 10 the children always complain—'I can't see.' Their attention flags," reports a first-grade teacher. "They'll begin to talk or wander off. I have to really work to develop their visualizing skills. I tell them that there's nothing to see, that the story is coming out of my mouth, and that they can make their own pictures in their 'mind's eye.' They get better at visualizing, with practice. But children never needed to learn how to visualize before television, it seems to me."

VIEWING VS. READING: CONCENTRATION

Because reading demands complex mental manipulations, a 11 reader is required to concentrate far more than a television viewer. An audio expert notes that "with the electronic media it is openness [that counts]. Openness permits auditory and visual stimuli more direct access to the brain…someone who is taught to concentrate will fail to perceive many patterns of information conveyed by the electronic stimuli."

It may be that a predisposition toward concentration, ac- 12 quired, perhaps, through one's reading experiences, makes one an inadequate television watcher. But it seems far more likely that the reverse situation obtains: that a predisposition toward "openness" (which may be understood to mean the opposite of focal concentration), acquired through years and years of television viewing, has influenced adversely viewers' ability to concentrate, to read, to write clearly—in short, to demonstrate any of the verbal skills a literate society requires.

PACE

A comparison between reading and viewing may be made 13 in respect to the pace of each experience, and the relative control a person has over that pace, for the pace may influence the ways one uses the material received in each experience. In addition, the pace of each experience may determine how much it intrudes upon other aspects of one's life.

The pace of reading, clearly, depends entirely upon the 14 reader. He may read as slowly or as rapidly as he can or wishes to read. If he does not understand something, he may stop and reread it, or go in search of elucidation before continuing. The reader can accelerate his pace when the material is easy or less than interesting, and slow down when it is difficult or enthralling. If what he reads is moving, he can put down the book for a few moments and cope with his emotions without fear of losing anything.

The pace of the television experience cannot be controlled 15 by the viewer; only its beginning and end are within his control as he clicks the knob on and off. He cannot slow down a delightful program or speed up a dreary one. He cannot "turn back" if a word or phrase is not understood. The program moves inexorably forward, and what is lost or misunderstood remains so.

Nor can the television viewer readily transform the material 16 he receives into a form that might suit his particular emotional needs, as he invariably does with material he reads. The images move too quickly. He cannot use his own imagination to invest the people and events portrayed on television with the personal meanings that would help him understand and resolve relationships and conflicts in his own life; he is under the power of the imagination of the show's creators. In the television experience the eyes and ears are overwhelmed with the immediacy of sights and sounds. They flash from the television set just fast enough for the eyes and ears to take them in before moving on quickly to the new pictures and sounds...so as *not to lose the thread*.

Not to lose the thread...it is this need, occasioned by the 17 irreversible direction and relentless velocity of the television experience, that not only limits the workings of the viewer's imagination, but also causes television to intrude into human affairs far more than reading experiences can ever do. If someone enters the room while one is watching television—a friend, a relative, a child, someone, perhaps, one has not seen for some time—one must continue to watch or one will lose the thread. The greetings must wait, for the television program will not. A book, of course, can be set aside, with a pang of regret, perhaps, but with no sense of permanent loss.

A grandparent describes a situation that is, by all reports, 18 not uncommon:

"Sometimes when I come to visit the girls, I'll walk into 19 their room and they're watching a TV program. Well, I know they love me, but it makes me feel *bad* when I tell them hello, and they say, without even looking up, 'Wait a minute...we have to see the end of this program.' It hurts me to have them care more about that machine and those little pictures than about being glad to see me. I know that they probably can't help it, but still...."

Can they help it? Ultimately the power of a television 20 viewer to release himself from his viewing in order to attend to human demands arising in the course of his viewing is not altogether a function of the pace of the program. After all, the viewer might *choose* to operate according to human priorities rather than electronic dictatorship. He might quickly decide "to hell with this program" and simply stop watching when a friend entered the room or a child needed attention.

He might...but the hypnotic power of television makes it 21 difficult to shift one's attention away, makes one desperate not to lose the thread of the program....

THE BASIC BUILDING BLOCKS

There is another difference between reading and television 22 viewing that must affect the response to each experience. This is the relative acquaintance of readers and viewers with the fundamental elements of each medium. While the reader is familiar with the basic building blocks of the reading medium, the television viewer has little acquaintance with those of the television medium.

As a person reads, he has his own writing experience to fall 23 back upon. His understanding of what he reads, and his feelings about it, are necessarily affected, and deepened, by his possession of writing as a means of communicating. As a child begins to learn reading, he begins to acquire the rudiments of writing. That these two skills are always acquired together is important and not coincidental. As the child learns to read words, he needs to understand that a word is something he can write himself, though his muscle control may temporarily prevent him from writing it clearly. That he wields such power over the words he is struggling to decipher makes the reading experience a satisfying one right from the start.

A young child watching television enters a realm of materi- 24
als completely beyond his control—and understanding. Though the images that appear on the screen may be reflections of familiar people and things, they appear as if by magic. The child cannot create similar images, nor even begin to understand how those flickering, electronic shapes and forms come into being. He takes on a far more powerless and ignorant role in front of the television set than in front of a book.

There is no doubt that many young children have a con- 25
fused relationship to the television medium. When a group of preschool children were asked, "How do kids get to be on your TV?" only 22 percent of them showed any real comprehension of the nature of the television images. When asked, "Where do the people and kids and things go when your TV is turned off?" only 20 percent of the three-year-olds showed the smallest glimmer of understanding. Although there was an increase in comprehension among the four-year-olds, the authors of the study note that "even among the older children the vast majority still did not grasp the nature of television pictures."

The child's feelings of power and competence are nour- 26
ished by another feature of the reading experience that does not obtain for television: the nonmechanical, easily accessible, and easily transportable nature of reading matter. The child can always count on a book for pleasure, though the television set may break down at a crucial moment. The child may take a book with him wherever he goes, to his room, to the park, to his friend's house, to school to read under his desk: he can *control* his use of books and reading materials. The television set is stuck in a certain place; it cannot be moved easily. It certainly cannot be casually transported from place to place by a child. The child must not only watch television wherever the set is located, but he

must watch certain programs at certain times, and is powerless to change what comes out of the set and when it comes out.

In this comparison of reading and television experiences a picture begins to emerge that quite confirms the commonly held notion that reading is somehow "better" than television viewing. Reading involves a complex form of mental activity, trains the mind in concentration skills, develops the powers of imagination and inner visualization; the flexibility of its pace lends itself to a better and deeper comprehension of the material communicated. Reading engrosses, but does not hypnotize or seduce the reader from his human responsibilities. Reading is a two-way process: the reader can also write; television viewing is a one-way street: the viewer cannot create television images. And books are ever available, ever controllable. Television controls.

1977

Conservatives and Liberals

Ralph Waldo Emerson

The two parties which divide the state, the party of Conservatism and that of Innovation, are very old, and have disputed the possession of the world ever since it was made. This quarrel is the subject of civil history. The conservative party established the reverend hierarchies and monarchies of the most ancient world. The battle of patrician and plebeian, of parent state and colony, of old usage and accommodation to new facts, of the rich and the poor, reappears in all countries and times. The war rages not only in battle-fields, in national councils, and ecclesiastical synods, but agitates every man's bosom with opposing advantages every hour. On rolls the old world meantime, and now one, now the other gets the day, and still the fight renews itself as if for the first time, under new names and hot personalities.

Such an irreconcilable antagonism, of course, must have a 2
correspondent depth of seat in the human constitution. It is the
opposition of Past and Future, of Memory and Hope, of the Understanding and the Reason. It is the primal antagonism, the appearance in trifles of the two poles of nature.

There is a fragment of old fable which seems somehow to 3
have been dropped from the current mythologies, which may deserve attention, as it appears to relate to this subject.

Saturn grew weary of sitting alone, or with none but the 4
great Uranus or Heaven beholding him, and he created an oyster. Then he would act again, but he made nothing more, but
went on creating the race of oysters. Then Uranus cried, "a new
work, O Saturn! the old is not good again."

Saturn replied, "I fear. There is not only the alternative of 5
making and not making, but also of unmaking. Seest thou the
great sea, how it ebbs and flows? So is it with me; my power
ebbs; and if I put forth my hands, I shall not do, but undo. Therefore I do what I have done; I hold what I have got; and so I resist
Night and Chaos."

"O Saturn," replied Uranus. "Thou canst not hold thine 6
own, but by making more. Thy oysters are barnacles and cock-
les, and with the next flowing of the tide, they will be pebbles
and sea foam."

"I see," rejoins Saturn, "thou art in league with Night, 7
thou art become an evil eye: thou spakest from love; now thy
words smite me with hatred. I appeal to Fate, must there not be
rest?"—"I appeal to Fate also," said Uranus, "must there not
be motion?"—But Saturn was silent and went on making oysters
for a thousand years.

After that, the word of Uranus came into his mind like a ray 8
of the sun, and he made Jupiter; and then he feared again; and
nature froze, the things that were made went backward, and to
save the world, Jupiter slew his father Saturn.

This may stand for the earliest account of a conversation on 9
politics between a Conservative and a Radical, which has come
down to us. It is ever thus. It is the counteraction of the centripetal and the centrifugal forces. Innovation is the salient energy;
Conservatism the pause on the last movement. "That which is

was made by God," saith Conservatism. "He is leaving that, he is entering this other;" rejoins Innovation.

There is always a certain meanness in the argument of con- 10 servatism, joined with a certain superiority in its fact. It affirms because it holds. Its fingers clutch the fact, and it will not open its eyes to see a better fact. The castle, which conservatism is set to defend, is the actual state of things, good and bad. The project of innovation is the best possible state of things. Of course, conservatism always has the worst of the argument, is always apologizing, pleading a necessity, pleading that to change would be to deteriorate; it must saddle itself with the mountainous load of all the violence and vice of society, must deny the possibility of good, deny ideas, and suspect and stone the prophet; whilst innovation is always in the right, triumphant, attacking, and sure of final success. Conservatism stands on man's incontestable limitations; reform on his indisputable infinitude; conservatism on circumstance; liberalism on power; one goes to make an adroit member of the social frame; the other to postpone all things to the man himself; conservatism is debonair and social; reform is individual and imperious. We are reformers in spring and summer, in autumn and winter we stand by the old; reformers in the morning, conservers at night. Reform is affirmative, conservatism negative; conservatism goes for comfort, reform for truth. Conservatism is more candid to behold another's worth; reform more disposed to maintain and increase its own. Conservatism makes no poetry, breathes no prayer, has no invention; it is all memory. Reform has no gratitude, no prudence, no husbandry. It makes a great difference to your figure and to your thought, whether your foot is advancing or receding. Conservatism never puts the foot forward; in the hour when it does that, it is not establishment, but reform. Conservatism tends to universal seeming and treachery, believes in a negative fate; believes that men's temper governs them; that for me, it avails not to trust in principles; they will fail me; I must bend a little; it distrusts nature; it thinks there is a general law without a particular application,— law for all that does not include any one. Reform in its antagonism inclines to asinine resistance, to kick with hoofs; it runs to egotism and bloated self-conceit; it runs to a bodiless pretension, to unnatural refining and elevation, which ends in hypocrisy and sensual reaction.

And so whilst we do not go beyond general statements, it 11 may be safely affirmed of these two metaphysical antagonists, that each is a good half, but an impossible whole. Each exposes the abuses of the other, but in a true society, in a true man, both must combine. Nature does not give the crown of its approbation, namely, Beauty, to any action or emblem or actor but to one which combines both these elements; not to the rock which resists the waves from age to age, nor to the wave which lashes incessantly the rock, but the superior beauty is with the oak which stands with its hundred arms against the storms of a century and grows every year like a sapling; or the river which ever flowing, yet is found in the same bed from age to age; or, greatest of all, the man who has subsisted for years amid the changes of nature, yet has distanced himself, so that when you remember what he was, and see what he is, you say, what strides! what a disparity is here!

1841

7

Example and Illustration

Backwater Cuisine
Ann Hodgman

I realize that she's dead and that there are some toes you just don't step on in this culture, but the fact remains: Janis Joplin wasn't really a good singer. If she were to come back today as a food, she'd be some kind of awful regional dish. *So earthy!* the foodies would bellow. *So quirkily honest, so down-home! Such a powerful antidote to our synthetic, overcivilized lives!*

"Like white hot dogs?" pipes up a little boy from my hometown, Rochester, New York. Yes, sonny, exactly like them. White hots—which taste like ordinary dogs and look even nastier—are a perfect example of *real* regional cuisine. Not the kind of regional dish Paul Prudhomme makes for Craig Claiborne's birthday, but the kind that arrivistes like me pretend they've never tasted.

No, really, I'm happy to be from Rochester, birthplace of Zab's Backyard Hots. We're very proud of Zab's. We think they make a lovely present for the folks downstate.

White hots are made from ham, pork, beef, veal, mustard, paprika and other spices. At the same time, say their creators mysteriously, they contain *no seasonings*. What are spices if not seasoning? And anyway, why brag about selling unseasoned

259

food? "We wanted to make sure that three hours later you're not belching," explains company president Don Zabkar helpfully. (Maybe *seasonings* is a Rochester euphemism for *garlic,* the way *sick* is a traveler's euphemism for—well, you know.) There's an advertising slogan in there somewhere, I feel sure. "*Three hours after Zab's White Hots, you're still not belching!*"

But why should I feel ashamed? At least white hots contain 5 no variety meats, whereas the most famous regional protein from Pennsylvania—scrapple—seems to be made of little else. It's silly to be concerned about this, of course. Meat is meat, whether it's tucked demurely away under a rib or right out there next to the eye. In any case, Ingredient Concern seems a little starry-eyed in these days of ozone depletion. Still, it gives me some pleasure to realize that some of the ingredients in dog food are considered a little too...chichi to be used in scrapple.

My decade-old memory of opening a can of dog food to find 6 an unprocessed pig's snout still makes me fly into the air, but according to the *Times,* things like snouts give scrapple a false elegance. Some scrapple makers, the paper says, "break further with tradition by enriching their scrapple with such parts as snouts, ears and tails, parts that would formerly have been served on their own." It seems that all real scrapple needs is "useless pork parts, neckbones, backs, skins and livers." And, of course, buckwheat, which is what makes the mixture so nice and gray.

O-*kay!* Let's fry some up! I have a plastic-wrapped block of 7 Parks scrapple here that my husband has forbidden me to cook or even open in front of him. I can hardly blame him; this is perhaps the ugliest food I've ever seen, despite the fact that it does contain those fancy pig snouts. Sidewalk-colored, it's flecked with white blobs and translucent bits of gristle that bounce back when palpated through the plastic. If you look closely, you can see tiny yellow dots throughout, and those pink things....I'm sorry, but I can't bring myself to cut the package open. (I'm treading close enough to Mystery Meat jokes as it is.)

Parks scrapple is made not in Pennsylvania but in Balti- 8 more, which is home to some pretty repellent regional dishes itself. One of these is roast turkey with sauerkraut. I don't object to sauerkraut, but am I alone in thinking it's supposed to go with things like white hots? I guess so. "I just couldn't live without my sauerkraut on Thanksgiving," claims a Baltimore woman who—like other Baltimoreans that I've spoken to—obstinately refuses to admit there's anything disgusting about holiday kraut. "It's no worse than cranberry sauce," says a friend of mine, probably crossing her fingers as she speaks.

I hear you're supposed to start with canned sauerkraut. 9 (This part is fine with me. The recipe for fresh sauerkraut in *The Joy of Cooking* tells you to remove the scum daily.) You add some water and a ham hock and cook it for, I swear, ten hours. "It stinks up the house," my friend says proudly. But doesn't sauerkraut get soggy—soggier, I mean—when it's cooked that long? "But it doesn't get *tangy* enough unless you cook it for a long time!"

They don't stop there, though: Baltimore Thanksgivings 10 also include hominy, starch's uncanny imitation of large-curd cottage cheese. But I don't mean to talk only about Thanksgiving—not when another Baltimore specialty is beef kidney stew on waffles.

Speaking of waffles, how about some breakfast? Let's 11 switch to my hometown-in-law, Kansas City, which has few culinary lapses except when it tries to get European. True, it sometimes takes blood-and-guts cooking too far—the Hen House sells chicken hearts in cardboard vats the size of those stupefyingly large tubs of movie popcorn—but I think we've all had enough variety protein for today. For the most part, Kansas City's food mistakes are rare.

There's one exception: T. J. Cinnamons Bakery rolls and 12 sticky buns.

It's not only that T. J. Cinnamons sounds like the name of 13 a rascally li'l cartoon character soon to be licensed to Hallmark. It's not only that the rolls are individually packed in Styrofoam containers so that you keep thinking, *A Big Mac is in there,* despite yourself. It's not only that T. J. Cinnamons franchises sell soft drinks, forcing you to imagine what it would be like to wash down a pecan sticky bun with Sprite.

It's the rolls themselves. Although the top half is like a dry, 14 raisinless raisin bread, the bottom half is drenched, squishy, literally oozing melted butter and sugar. (Maybe things would even out if you turned the rolls upside down for a few days.) When you order a cinnamon roll, they ask, "Do you want icing with that?" and when you say yes, they squeeze big lines of it all over the top. When you order a pecan sticky bun, they scrape up extra stickum from the bottom of the pan and spread it on the pecans. I know, I know—it sounds great. But bear in mind that the rolls weigh something like *half a pound apiece*. These people want us to die.

Well, I'm full—how 'bout you? Let's talk about huevos rancheros and fried pies and chili with spaghetti and jelly omelets another time. Meanwhile, I'll just be glad that I don't live in a region.   15

1987

Why Don't We Complain?
William F. Buckley, Jr.

It was the very last coach and the only empty seat on the   1
entire train, so there was no turning back. The problem was to breathe. Outside, the temperature was below freezing. Inside the railroad car the temperature must have been about 85 degrees. I took off my overcoat, and a few minutes later my jacket, and noticed that the car was flecked with the white shirts of the passengers. I soon found my hand moving to loosen my tie. From one end of the car to the other, as we rattled through Westchester County, we sweated; but we did not moan.

I watched the train conductor appear at the head of the car.   2
"Tickets, all tickets, please!" In a more virile age, I thought, the passengers would seize the conductor and strap him down on a seat over the radiator to share the fate of his patrons. He shuffled down the aisle, picking up tickets, punching commutation cards.

No one addressed a word to him. He approached my seat, and I drew a deep breath of resolution. "Conductor," I began with a considerable edge to my voice....Instantly the doleful eyes of my seatmate turned tiredly from his newspaper to fix me with a resentful stare: what question could be so important as to justify my sibilant intrusion into his stupor? I was shaken by those eyes. I am incapable of making a discreet fuss, so I mumbled a question about what time we were due in Stamford (I didn't even ask whether it would be before or after dehydration could be expected to set in), got my reply, and went back to my newspaper and to wiping my brow.

The conductor had nonchalantly walked down the gauntlet of eighty sweating American freemen, and not one of them had asked him to explain why the passengers in that car had been consigned to suffer. There is nothing to be done when the temperature *outdoors* is 85 degrees, and indoors the air conditioner has broken down; obviously when that happens there is nothing to do, except perhaps curse the day that one was born. But when the temperature outdoors is below freezing, it takes a positive act of will on somebody's part to set the temperature *indoors* at 85. Somewhere a valve was turned too far, a furnace overstocked, a thermostat maladjusted: something that could easily be remedied by turning off the heat and allowing the great outdoors to come indoors. All this is so obvious. What is not obvious is what has happened to the American people. 3

It isn't just the commuters, whom we have come to visualize as a supine breed who have got on to the trick of suspending their sensory faculties twice a day while they submit to the creeping dissolution of the railroad industry. It isn't just they who have given up trying to rectify irrational vexations. It is the American people everywhere. 4

A few weeks ago at a large movie theatre I turned to my wife and said, "The picture is out of focus." "Be quiet," she answered. I obeyed. But a few minutes later I raised the point again, with mounting impatience. "It will be all right in a minute," she said apprehensively. (She would rather lose her eyesight than be around when I make one of my infrequent scenes.) I waited. It was *just* out of focus—not glaringly out, but 5 out. My vision is 20-20, and I assume that is the vision, adjusted, of most people in the movie house. So, after hectoring my wife throughout the first reel, I finally prevailed upon her to admit that it *was* off, and very annoying. We then settled down, coming to rest on the presumption that: a) someone connected with the management of the theatre must soon notice the blur and make the correction; or b) that someone seated near the rear of the house would make the complaint in behalf of those of us up front; or c) that—any minute now—the entire house would explode into catcalls and foot stamping, calling dramatic attention to the irksome distortion.

What happened was nothing. The movie ended, as it had begun *just* out of focus, and as we trooped out, we stretched our faces in a variety of contortions to accustom the eye to the shock of normal focus. 6

I think it is safe to say that everybody suffered on that occasion. And I think it is safe to assume that everyone was expecting someone else to take the initiative in going back to speak to the manager. And it is probably true even that if we had supposed the movie would run right through the blurred image, someone surely would have summoned up the purposive indignation to get up out of his seat and file his complaint. 7

But notice that no one did. And the reason no one did is because we are all increasingly anxious in America to be unobtrusive, we are reluctant to make our voices heard, hesitant about claiming our rights; we are afraid that our cause is unjust, or that if it is not unjust, that it is ambiguous; or if not even that, that it is too trivial to justify the horrors of a confrontation with Authority; we will sit in an oven or endure a racking headache before undertaking a head-on, I'm-here-to-tell-you complaint. That tendency to passive compliance, to a heedless endurance, is something to keep one's eyes on—in sharp focus. 8

I myself can occasionally summon the courage to complain, but I cannot, as I have intimated, complain softly. My own instinct is so strong to let the thing ride, to forget about it—to expect that someone will take the matter up, when the grievance is collective, in my behalf—that it is only when the provocation is at a very special key, whose vibrations touch simultaneously a 9

complexus of nerves, allergies, and passions, that I catch fire and
find the reserves of courage and assertiveness to speak up. When
that happens, I get quite carried away. My blood gets hot, my
brow wet, I become unbearably and unconscionably sarcastic
and bellicose; I am girded for a total showdown.

Why should that be? Why could not I (or anyone else) on 10
that railroad coach have said simply to the conductor, "Sir"—I
take that back: that sounds sarcastic—"Conductor, would you
be good enough to turn down the heat? I am extremely hot. In
fact, I tend to get hot every time the temperature reaches 85
degr—" Strike that last sentence. Just end it with the simple
statement that you are extremely hot, and let the conductor infer
the cause.

Every New Year's Eve I resolve to do something about the 11
Milquetoast in me and vow to speak up, calmly, for my rights,
and for the betterment of our society, on every appropriate occasion. Entering last New Year's Eve I was fortified in my resolve because that morning at breakfast I had had to ask the
waitress three times for a glass of milk. She finally brought it—
after I had finished my eggs, which is when I don't want it any
more. I did not have the manliness to order her to take the milk
back, but settled instead for a cowardly sulk, and ostentatiously
refused to drink the milk—though I later paid for it—rather than
state plainly to the hostess, as I should have, why I had not
drunk it, and would not pay for it.

So by the time the New Year ushered out the Old, riding in 12
on my morning's indignation and stimulated by the gastric juices
of resolution that flow so faithfully on New Year's Eve, I rendered my vow. Henceforward I would conquer my shyness, my
despicable disposition to supineness. I would speak out like a
man against the unnecessary annoyances of our time.

Forty-eight hours later, I was standing in line at the ski re- 13
pair store in Pico Peak, Vermont. All I needed, to get on with my
skiing, was the loan, for one minute, of a small screwdriver, to
tighten a loose binding. Behind the counter in the workshop were
two men. One was industriously engaged in servicing the complicated requirements of a young lady at the head of the line, and
obviously he would be tied up for quite a while. The other—

"Jiggs," his workmate called him—was a middle-aged man, who sat in a chair puffing a pipe, exchanging small talk with his working partner. My pulse began its telltale acceleration. The minutes ticked on. I stared at the idle shopkeeper, hoping to shame him into action, but he was impervious to my telepathic reproof and continued his small talk with his friend, brazenly insensitive to the nervous demands of six good men who were raring to ski.

Suddenly my New Year's Eve resolution struck me. It was 14 now or never. I broke from my place in line and marched to the counter. I was going to control myself. I dug my nails into my palms. My effort was only partially successful.

"If you are not too busy," I said icily, "would you mind 15 handing me a screwdriver?"

Work stopped and everyone turned his eyes on me, and I 16 experienced that mortification I always feel when I am the center of centripetal shafts of curiosity, resentment, perplexity.

But the worst was yet to come. "I am sorry, sir," said Jiggs 17 deferentially, moving the pipe from his mouth. "I am not supposed to move. I have just had a heart attack." That was the signal for a great whirring noise that descended from heaven. We looked, stricken, out the window, and it appeared as though a cyclone had suddenly focused on the snowy courtyard between the shop and the ski lift. Suddenly a gigantic army helicopter materialized, and hovered down to a landing. Two men jumped out of the plane carrying a stretcher, tore into the ski shop, and lifted the shopkeeper onto the stretcher. Jiggs bade his companion goodby, was whisked out the door, into the plane, up to the heavens, down—we learned—to a near-by army hospital. I looked up manfully—into a score of man-eating eyes. I put the experience down as a reversal.

As I write this, on an airplane, I have run out of paper and 18 need to reach into my briefcase under my legs for more. I cannot do this until my empty lunch tray is removed from my lap. I arrested the stewardess as she passed empty-handed down the aisle on the way to the kitchen to fetch the lunch trays for the passengers up forward who haven't been served yet. "Would you please take my tray?" "Just a *moment*, sir!" she said, and marched on sternly. Shall I tell her that since she is headed for the kitchen *anyway,* it could not delay the feeding of the other passengers by more than two seconds necessary to stash away my empty tray? Or remind her that not fifteen minutes ago she spoke unctuously into the loudspeaker the words undoubtedly devised by the airline's highly paid public relations counselor: "If there is anything I or Miss French can do for you to make your trip more enjoyable, *please* let us—" I have run out of paper.

I think the observable reluctance of the majority of Ameri- 19 cans to assert themselves in minor matters is related to our increased sense of helplessness in an age of technology and centralized political and economic power. For generations, Americans who were too hot, or too cold, got up and did something about it. Now we call the plumber, or the electrician, or the furnace man. The habit of looking after our own needs obviously had something to do with the assertiveness that characterized the American family familiar to readers of American literature. With the technification of life goes our direct responsibility for our material environment, and we are conditioned to adopt a position of helplessness not only as regards the broken air conditioner, but as regards the overheated train. It takes an expert to fix the former, but not the latter; yet these distinctions, as we withdraw into helplessness, tend to fade away.

Our notorious political apathy is a related phenomenon. 20 Every year, whether the Republican or the Democratic Party is in office, more and more power drains away from the individual to feed vast reservoirs in far-off places; and we have less and less say about the shape of events which shape our future. From this alienation of personal power comes the sense of resignation with which we accept the political dispensations of a powerful government whose hold upon us continues to increase.

An editor of a national weekly news magazine told me a 21 few years ago that as few as a dozen letters of protest against an editorial stance of his magazine was enough to convene a plenipotentiary meeting of the board of editors to review policy. "So few people complain, or make their voices heard," he explained to me, "that we assume a dozen letters represent the inarticulated views of thousands of readers." In the past ten years, he said, the volume of mail has noticeably decreased, even though the circulation of his magazine has risen.

When our voices are finally mute, when we have finally 22 suppressed the natural instinct to complain, whether the vexation is trivial or grave, we shall have become automatons, incapable of feeling. When Premier Khrushchev first came to this country late in 1959 he was primed, we are informed, to experience the bitter resentment of the American people against his tyranny, against his persecutions, against the movement which is responsible for the great number of American deaths in Korea, for billions in taxes every year, and for life everlasting on the brink of disaster; but Khrushchev was pleasantly surprised, and reported back to the Russian people that he had been met with overwhelming cordiality (read: apathy), except, to be sure, for "a few fascists who followed me around with their wretched posters, and should be horsewhipped."

I may be crazy, but I say there would have been lots more 23 posters in a society where train temperatures in the dead of winter are not allowed to climb to 85 degrees without complaint.

1961

Does America Still Exist?
Richard Rodriguez

For the children of immigrant parents the knowledge comes 1 easier. America exists everywhere in the city—on billboards, frankly in the smell of French fries and popcorn. It exists in the pace: traffic lights, the assertions of neon, the mysterious bong-bong-bong through the atriums of department stores. America exists as the voice of the crowd, a menacing sound—the high nasal accent of American English.

When I was a boy in Sacramento (California, the fifties), people would ask me, "Where you from?" I was born in this country, but I knew the question meant to decipher my darkness, my looks.

My mother once instructed me to say, "I am an American of American descent." By the time I was nine or ten, I wanted to say, but dared not reply, "I am an American."

Immigrants come to America and, against hostility or mere loneliness, they recreate a homeland in the parlor, tacking up postcards or calendars of some impossible blue—lake or sea or sky. Children of immigrant parents are supposed to perch on a hyphen between two countries. Relatives assume the achievement as much as anyone. Relatives are, in any case, surprised when the child begins losing old ways. One day at the family picnic the boy wanders away from their spiced food and faceless stories to watch other boys play baseball in the distance.

There is sorrow in the American memory, guilty sorrow for having left something behind—Portugal, China, Norway. The American story is the story of immigrant children and of their children—children no longer able to speak to grandparents. The memory of exile becomes inarticulate as it passes from generation to generation, along with wedding rings and pocket watches—like some mute stone in a wad of old lace. Europe. Asia. Eden.

But, it needs to be said, if this is a country where one stops being Vietnamese or Italian, this is a country where one begins to be an American. America exists as a culture and a grin, a faith and a shrug. It is clasped in a handshake, called by a first name.

As much as the country is joined in a common culture, however, Americans are reluctant to celebrate the process of assimilation. We pledge allegiance to diversity. America was born Protestant and bred Puritan, and the notion of community we share is derived from a seventeenth-century faith. Presidents and the pages of ninth-grade civics readers yet proclaim the orthodoxy: We are gathered together—but as individuals, with separate pasts, distinct destinies. Our society is as paradoxical as a Puritan congregation: We stand together, alone.

Americans have traditionally defined themselves by what they refused to include. As often, however, Americans have

struggled, turned in good conscience at last to assert the great
Protestant virtue of tolerance. Despite outbreaks of nativist
frenzy, America has remained an immigrant country, open and
true to itself.

Against pious emblems of rural America—soda fountain,   9
Elks hall, Protestant church, and now shopping mall—stands the
cold-hearted city, crowded with races and ambitions, curious
laughter, much that is odd. Nevertheless, it is the city that has
most truly represented America. In the city, however, the millions of singular lives have had no richer notion of wholeness to
describe them than the idea of pluralism.

"Where you from?" the American asks the immigrant   10
child. "Mexico," the boy learns to say.

Mexico, the country of my blood ancestors, offers formal   11
contrast to the American achievement. If the United States was
formed by Protestant individualism, Mexico was shaped by a medieval Catholic dream of one world. The Spanish journeyed to
Mexico to plunder, and they may have gone, in God's name,
with an arrogance peculiar to those who intend to convert. But
through the conversion, the Indian converted the Spaniard. A
new race was born, the *mestizo,* wedding European to Indian.
José Vasconcelos, the Mexican philosopher, has celebrated this
New World creation, proclaiming it the "cosmic race."

Centuries later, in a San Francisco restaurant, a Mexican-   12
American lawyer of my acquaintance says, in English, over
salade niçoise, that he does not intend to assimilate into gringo
society. His claim is echoed by a chorus of others (Italian-
Americans, Greeks, Asians) in this era of ethnic pride. The melting pot has been retired, clanking, into the museum of quaint disgrace, alongside Aunt Jemima and the Katzenjammer Kids. But
resistance to assimilation is characteristically American. It only
makes clear how inevitable the process of assimilation actually is.

For generations, this has been the pattern. Immigrant par-   13
ents have sent their children to school (simply, they thought) to
acquire the "skills" to survive in the city. The child returned
home with a voice his parents barely recognized or understood,
couldn't trust, and didn't like.

In Eastern cities—Philadelphia, New York, Boston, Balti-   14 more—class after class gathered immigrant children to women (usually women) who stood in front of rooms full of children, changing children. So also for me in the 1950s. Irish-Catholic nuns. California. The old story. The hyphen tipped to the right, away from Mexico and toward a confusing but true American identity.

I speak now in the chromium American accent of my gram- 15 mar school classmates—Billy Reckers, Mike Bradley, Carol Schmidt, Kathy O'Grady....I believe I became like my classmates, became German, Polish, and (like my teachers) Irish. And because assimilation is always reciprocal, my classmates got something of me. (I mean sad eyes; belief in the Indian Virgin; a taste for sugar skulls on the Feast of the Dead.) In the blending, we became what our parents could never have been, and we carried America one revolution further.

"Does America still exist?" Americans have been asking 16 the question for so long that to ask it again only proves our continuous link. But perhaps the question deserves to be asked with urgency—now. Since the black civil rights movement of the 1960s, our tenuous notion of a shared public life has deteriorated notably.

The struggle of black men and women did not eradicate rac- 17 ism, but it became the great moment in the life of America's conscience. Water hoses, bulldogs, blood—the images, rendered black, white, rectangular, passed into living rooms.

It is hard to look at a photograph of a crowd taken, say, in 18 1890 or in 1930 and not notice the absence of blacks. (It becomes an impertinence to wonder if America *still* exists.)

In the sixties, other groups of Americans learned to cham- 19 pion their rights by analogy to the black civil rights movement. But the heroic vision faded. Dr. Martin Luther King Jr. had spoken with Pauline eloquence of a nation that would unite Christian and Jew, old and young, rich and poor. Within a decade, the struggles of the 1960s were reduced to a bureaucratic competition for little more than pieces of a representational pie. The quest for a portion of power became an end in itself. The metaphor for the American city of the 1970s was a committee: one black, one woman, one person under thirty....

If the small town had sinned against America by too neatly 20 defining who could be an American, the city's sin was a romantic secession. One noticed the romanticism in the antiwar movement—certain demonstrators who demonstrated a lack of tact or desire to persuade and seemed content to play secular protestants. One noticed the romanticism in the competition among members of "minority groups" to claim the status of Primary Victim. To Americans unconfident of their common identity, minority standing became a way of asserting individuality. Middle-class Americans—men and women clearly not the primary victims of social oppression—brandished their suffering with exuberance.

The dream of a single society probably died with *The Ed Sullivan Show*. The reality of America persists. Teenagers pass through big-city high schools banded in racial groups, their collars turned up to a uniform shrug. But then they graduate to jobs at the phone company or in banks, where they end up working alongside people unlike themselves. Typists and tellers walk out together at lunchtime. 21

It is easier for us as Americans to believe the obvious fact of our separateness—easier to imagine the black and white Americas prophesied by the Kerner report (broken glass, street fires)—than to recognize the reality of a city street at lunchtime. Americans are wedded by proximity to a common culture. The panhandler at one corner is related to the pamphleteer at the next who is related to the banker who is kin to the Chinese old man wearing an MIT sweatshirt. In any true national history, Thomas Jefferson begets Martin Luther King Jr. who begets the Gray Panthers. It is because we lack a vision of ourselves entire—the city street is crowded and we are each preoccupied with finding our own way home—that we lack an appropriate hymn. 22

Under my window now passes a little white girl softly rehearsing to herself a Motown obbligato. 23

1984

I Remember...

Joyce Maynard

We got our TV set in 1959, when I was 5. So I can barely 1
remember life without television. I have spent 20,000 hours of
my life in front of the set. Not all of my contemporaries watched
so much, but many did, and what's more, we watched the same
programs, heard the same commercials, were exposed to the
same end-of-show lessons. So there is, among this generation of
television children, a shared history, a tremendous fund of common experience. These massive doses of TV have not affected
all of us in an identical way, and it would be risky to draw broad
conclusions. But if a sociologist were—rashly—to try to uncover
some single most important influence on this generation, which
has produced Patty Hearst and Alice Cooper and the Jesus
movement and the peace movement; if he were searching for the
roots of 1960's psychedelia and 1970's apathy, he would do well
to look first at television.

My own motives are less ambitious. I know, simply, that a 2
rerun of *I Love Lucy* or *Father Knows Best,* the theme music
from *Dr. Kildare* or the sad, whistling refrain from *Lassie* can
make me stand, frozen, before the set. It is as if I, and not
Timmy Martin, had been stuck in an abandoned mine shaft during a thunderstorm, as if I, and not Lucy Ricardo, had dropped a
diamond ring somewhere in the batter of a seven-layer cake. I
didn't so much *watch* those shows when I was little; I let them
wash over me. Now I study them like a psychiatrist on his own
couch, looking hungrily for some clue inside the TV set to explain the person I have become.

I was not a dull or energyless child, or neglected by my par- 3
ents. Our house was full of books and paints, and sometimes I
did choose to draw or ride my bike. But the picture of my childhood that comes to mind is one of a dimly lit room in a small
New Hampshire town and a girl listening, leaden-eyed, to some
talk-show rendition of "I Left My Heart in San Francisco." It is
a picture of myself at age 8, wise to the ways of "Vegas," the

timing of standup comics, the marriages of Zsa Zsa Gabor, the advertising slogans of Bufferin and Fab.

And what did all this television watching teach me? Well, I   4
rarely swallowed the little pellets of end-of-show morals pre-sented in the television shows I watched (that crime does not pay, that one must always obey one's parents). But I observed something of the way the world works: that life is easier if one fits in with the established conventions; that everything is easier if one has a pretty face.

And in the process of acquiring those melancholy truths I   5
picked up an embarrassingly large fund of knowledge that is to-tally unusable (except, perhaps, ironically, on some television game show). I can hum Perry Mason's theme song or give the name of the actress who played Donna Reed's best friend. I would happily trade that knowledge for the facility with piano or ballet I might have had if I'd spent those television hours prac-ticing music and dance instead. But something else I gained from television should be less lightly dismissed. I guess it is a sense of knowing America, not simply its vulgarities but its strengths as well: the rubber face of Lucille Ball, the lovableness of Ameri-cans on *Candid Camera,* an athlete's slow-motion grace in an in-stant replay on *Monday Night Football.*

So many hours of television I watched—hundreds of bank   6
robberies, touch-and-go operations and barroom fights, millions of dollars' worth of refrigerators awarded to thousands of house-wives who kissed dozens of game-show moderators—and yet the list of individual programs I remember is very short. One is the Beatles' appearance, the winter I was 10, on *The Ed Sullivan Show.* I remember the on-camera shooting of Lee Oswald, and the face of Jacqueline Kennedy at her husband's funeral. A few particularly marvelous episodes of the old *Dick Van Dyke Show* stand out: Laura Petrie getting her toe stuck in the bathroom fau-cet; Rob imagining that he's going bald. One or two *I Love Lucy, Andy Griffith* shows, a Miss America contestant who sang a number from "The Sound of Music"—dressed like a nun—and then whipped off her habit to reveal a spangled bathing suit. I re-member a special five-part *Dr. Kildare* segment in which a team of doctors had to choose five patients for a lifesaving kidney ma-chine out of eight candidates. I remember getting up at midnight

to watch Neil Armstrong land on the moon—expecting to be awed, but falling asleep instead.

My strongest memories are of one series and one character. 7
Not the best, but the one that formed me more than any other, that haunts me still, and left its mark on a good-sized part of a generation: *Leave It to Beaver*. I watched that show every day after school (fresh from my own failures) and studied it, like homework, because the Cleaver family was so steady and normal—and my own was not—and because the boys had so many friends, played basketball, drank sodas, *fit in*. Watching that series and other family situation comedies was almost like taking a course in how to be an American.

I loved my father, but I longed secretly for a "Dad" like 8
Ward Cleaver, who puttered in a work shed, building bookcases and oiling hinges, one who spent his Saturday afternoons playing golf or mowing the lawn or dipping his finger into cake batter whipped up by a mother in a frilly apron who spent her time going to PTA meetings and playing bridge with "the girls." Wally Cleaver, the older brother, was one of those boys destined to be captain of every team he plays on. But Beaver had his problems—often he was uncoordinated, gullible, less than perfectly honest, tricked by his older brother's friends, made fun of. He lost library books and haircut money. Once he sent away for a "free" accordion and suddenly found himself wildly in debt. Of course he got caught—he always did. I remember him so clearly, as familiar to me as a brother.

Occasionally I go to college campuses. Some student in the 9
audience always mentions Beaver Cleaver, and when the name is spoken, a satisfied murmur can be heard in the crowd. Somebody—a stranger, in his 20s now—wrote to say he watches *Beaver* reruns every morning. He just wanted to share memories of the show with me and recall favorite episodes. We were not readers, after all, this stranger and I. We have no great literary tradition behind us. Our heritage is television. Wally and Beaver Cleaver were our Tom Sawyer and Huck Finn.

There's something terribly sad about this need to remi- 10
nisce, and the lack of real stories, true experiences, to reminisce about. Partly it is that we grew up in the '60s, when life was soft, and partly that we grew up with television, which made life

softer. We had Vietnam, of course, and civil-rights battles, and a brief threat of nuclear attack that led neighbors, down the block, to talk of building a fallout shelter. But I remember the large events, like the Kennedy and King assassinations, the space launches and the war, as I experienced them through television. I watched it all from a goose-down-filled easy chair with a plate of oatmeal cookies on my lap—on television.

We grew up to be observers, not participants, to respond to 11 action, not initiate it. And I think finally, it was this lack of real hardship (when we lacked for nothing else) that was our greatest hardship and that led so many among this television generation to seek out some kind of artificial pain. Some of us, for a time at least, gave up matching skirt-and-sweater sets for saffron-colored Hare Krishna robes; some gave up parents and clean-cut fiances for the romance of poverty and the excitement of crime. Rebellion like that is not so much inspired by television violence as it is brought about by television banality: it is a response not to *The Man from U.N.C.L.E.* but to *Father Knows Best*. One hears it said that hatred of an idea is closer to love than to indifference. Large and angry rejections of the bourgeois, the conventional—the Beaver Cleaver life—aren't so surprising, coming from a generation that grew up admiring those things so much.

Television smartened us up, expanded our minds, and then 12 proceeded to fill them with the only kinds of knowledge it had to offer: names of Las Vegas nightclubs, brands of detergent, players of bit parts. And knowledge—accurate or not—about life: marriage as we learned about it from Ozzie and Harriet. Justice as practiced by Matt Dillon. Politics as revealed to us on the 6 o'clock news.

Anguished, frustrated and enraged by a decade of war in 13 Vietnam as we saw it on the news, we became part of the news ourselves—with peace marches, rallies in the streets. But only briefly; we were easily discouraged, quick to abandon hope for change and to lose interest. That, also, comes from a television-watching childhood, I think: a short attention span, and a limpness, an inertia, acquired from too many hours spent in the easy chair, never getting up except to change the channels.

1975

A Few Kind Words for Superstition
Robertson Davies

In grave discussions of "the renaissance of the irrational" 1
in our time, superstition does not figure largely as a serious challenge to reason or science. Parapsychology, UFO's, miracle
cures, transcendental meditation and all the paths to instant enlightenment are condemned, but superstition is merely deplored.
Is it because it has an unacknowledged hold on so many of us?

Few people will admit to being superstitious; it implies na- 2
ïveté or ignorance. But I live in the middle of a large university,
and I see superstition in its four manifestations, alive and flour-
ishing among people who are indisputably rational and learned.

You did not know that superstition takes four forms? Theo- 3
logians assure us that it does. First is what they call Vain Obser-
vances, such as not walking under a ladder, and that kind of
thing. Yet I saw a deeply learned professor of anthropology, who
had spilled some salt, throwing a pinch of it over his left shoulder; when I asked him why, he replied, with a wink, that it was
"to hit the Devil in the eye." I did not question him further about
his belief in the Devil: but I noticed that he did not smile until I
asked him what he was doing.

The second form is Divination, or consulting oracles. An- 4
other learned professor I know, who would scorn to settle a
problem by tossing a coin (which is a humble appeal to Fate to
declare itself), told me quite seriously that he had resolved a matter related to university affairs by consulting the *I Ching*. And why
not? There are thousands of people on this continent who appeal
to the *I Ching,* and their general level of education seems to ab-
solve them of superstition. Almost, but not quite. The *I Ching,* to
the embarrassment of rationalists, often gives excellent advice.

The third form is Idolatry, and universities can show plenty 5
of that. If you have ever supervised a large examination room,
you know how many jujus, lucky coins and other bringers of luck
are placed on the desks of the candidates. Modest idolatry, but
what else can you call it?

The fourth form is Improper Worship of the True God. A 6

while ago, I learned that every day, for several days, a $2 bill (in Canada we have $2 bills, regarded by some people as unlucky) had been tucked under a candlestick on the altar of a college chapel. Investigation revealed that an engineering student, worried about a girl, thought that bribery of the Deity might help. When I talked with him, he did not think he was pricing God cheap, because he could afford no more. A reasonable argument, but perhaps God was proud that week, for the scientific oracle went against him.

Superstition seems to run, a submerged river of crude religion, below the surface of human consciousness. It has done so for as long as we have any chronicle of human behavior, and although I cannot prove it, I doubt if it is more prevalent today than it has always been. Superstition, the theologians tell us, comes from the Latin *supersisto,* meaning to stand in terror of the Deity. Most people keep their terror within bounds, but they cannot root it out, nor do they seem to want to do so.   7

The more the teaching of formal religion declines, or takes a sociological form, the less God appears to great numbers of people as a God of Love, resuming his older form of a watchful, minatory power, to be placated and cajoled. Superstition makes its appearance, apparently unbidden, very early in life, when children fear that stepping on cracks in the sidewalk will bring ill fortune. It may persist even among the greatly learned and devout, as in the case of Dr. Samuel Johnson, who felt it necessary to touch posts that he passed in the street. The psychoanalysts have their explanation, but calling a superstition a compulsion neurosis does not banish it.   8

Many superstitions are so widespread and so old that they must have risen from a depth of the human mind that is indifferent to race or creed. Orthodox Jews place a charm on their doorposts; so do (or did) the Chinese. Some peoples of Middle Europe believe that when a man sneezes, his soul, for that moment, is absent from his body, and they hasten to bless him, lest the soul be seized by the Devil. How did the Melanesians come by the same idea? Superstition seems to have a link with some body of belief that far antedates the religions we know—religions which have no place for such comforting little ceremonies and charities.   9

People who like disagreeable historical comparisons recall   10 that when Rome was in decline, superstition proliferated wildly, and that something of the same sort is happening in our Western world today. They point to the popularity of astrology, and it is true that sober newspapers that would scorn to deal in love philters carry astrology columns and the fashion magazines count them among their most popular features. But when has astrology not been popular? No use saying science discredits it. When has the heart of man given a damn for science?

Superstition in general is linked to man's yearning to know 11 his fate, and to have some hand in deciding it. When my mother was a child, she innocently joined her Roman Catholic friends in killing spiders on July 11, until she learned that this was done to ensure heavy rain the day following, the anniversary of the Battle of Boyne, when the Orangemen would hold their parade. I knew an Italian, a good scientist, who watched every morning before leaving his house, so that the first person he met would not be a priest or a nun, as this would certainly bring bad luck.

I am not one to stand aloof from the rest of humanity in this 12 matter, for when I was a university student, a gypsy woman with a child in her arms used to appear every year at examination time, and ask a shilling of anyone who touched the Lucky Baby; that swarthy infant cost me four shillings altogether, and I never failed an examination. Of course, I did it merely for the joke—or so I thought then. Now, I am humbler.

1978

Were Dinosaurs Dumb?
Stephen Jay Gould

When Muhammad Ali flunked his army intelligence test, he 1 quipped (with a wit that belied his performance on the exam): "I only said I was the greatest; I never said I was the smartest." In our metaphors and fairy tales, size and power are almost always balanced by a want of intelligence. Cunning is the refuge of the little guy. Think of Br'er Rabbit and Br'er Bear; David smiting Goliath with a slingshot; Jack chopping down the beanstalk. Slow wit is the tragic flaw of a giant.

The discovery of dinosaurs in the nineteenth century pro- 2 vided, or so it appeared, a quintessential case for the negative correlation of size and smarts. With their pea brains and giant bodies, dinosaurs became a symbol of lumbering stupidity. Their extinction seemed only to confirm their flawed design.

Dinosaurs were not even granted the usual solace of a gi- 3 ant—great physical prowess. God maintained a discreet silence about the brains of behemoth, but he certainly marveled at its strength: "Lo, now, his strength is in his loins, and his force is in the navel of his belly. He moveth his tail like a cedar.... His bones are as strong pieces of brass; his bones are like bars of iron [Job 40:16–18]." Dinosaurs, on the other hand, have usually been reconstructed as slow and clumsy. In the standard illustration, *Brontosaurus* wades in a murky pond because he cannot hold up his own weight on land.

Popularizations for grade school curricula provide a good 4 illustration of prevailing orthodoxy. I still have my third grade copy (1948 edition) of Bertha Morris Parker's *Animals of Yesterday*, stolen, I am forced to suppose, from P.S. 26, Queens (sorry Mrs. McInerney). In it, boy (teleported back to the Jurassic) meets brontosaur:

> It is huge, and you can tell from the size of its head that it must be stupid.... This giant animal moves about very slowly as it eats. No wonder it moves slowly! Its huge feet are very heavy, and its great tail is not easy to pull around. You are not surprised that the thunder lizard likes to stay in the water so that the water will help it hold up its huge body.... Giant dinosaurs were once the lords of the earth. Why did they disappear? You can probably guess part of the answer—their bodies were too large for their brains. If their bodies had been smaller, and their brains larger, they might have lived on.

Dinosaurs have been making a strong comeback of late, in 5 this age of "I'm OK, you're OK." Most paleontologists are now willing to view them as energetic, active, and capable animals. The *Brontosaurus* that wallowed in its pond a generation ago is now running on land, while pairs of males have been seen twining their necks about each other in elaborate sexual combat for access to females (much like the neck wrestling of giraffes). Modern anatomical reconstructions indicate strength and agility, and many paleontologists now believe that dinosaurs were warmblooded....

The idea of warmblooded dinosaurs has captured the public imagination and received a torrent of press coverage. Yet another vindication of dinosaurian capability has received very little attention, although I regard it as equally significant. I refer to the issue of stupidity and its correlation with size. The revisionist interpretation, which I support in this column, does not enshrine dinosaurs as paragons of intellect, but it does maintain that they were not small brained after all. They had the "right-sized" brains for reptiles of their body size.

I don't wish to deny that the flattened, minuscule head of large-bodied *Stegosaurus* houses little brain from our subjective, top-heavy perspective, but I do wish to assert that we should not expect more of the beast. First of all, large animals have relatively smaller brains than related, small animals. The correlation of brain size with body size among kindred animals (all reptiles, all mammals, for example) is remarkably regular. As we move from small to large animals, from mice to elephants or small lizards to Komodo dragons, brain size increases, but not so fast as body size. In other words, bodies grow faster than brains, and large animals have low ratios of brain weight to body weight. In fact, brains grow only about two-thirds as fast as bodies. Since we have no reason to believe that large animals are consistently stupider than their smaller relatives, we must conclude that large animals require relatively less brain to do as well as smaller animals. If we do not recognize this relationship, we are likely to underestimate the mental power of very large animals, dinosaurs in particular.

Second, the relationship between brain and body size is not identical in all groups of vertebrates. All share the same rate of relative decrease in brain size, but small mammals have much larger brains than small reptiles of the same body weight. This discrepancy is maintained at all larger body weights, since brain size increases at the same rate in both groups—two-thirds as fast as body size.

Put these two facts together—all large animals have rela-   9 tively small brains, and reptiles have much smaller brains than mammals at any common body weight—and what should we expect from a normal, large reptile? The answer, of course, is a brain of very modest size. No living reptile even approaches a middle-sized dinosaur in bulk, so we have no modern standard to serve as a model for dinosaurs.

Fortunately, our imperfect fossil record has, for once, not   10 severely disappointed us in providing data about fossil brains. Superbly preserved skulls have been found for many species of dinosaurs, and cranial capacities can be measured. (Since brains do not fill craniums in reptiles, some creative, although not unreasonable, manipulation must be applied to estimate brain size from the hole within a skull.) With these data, we have a clear test for the conventional hypothesis of dinosaurian stupidity. We should agree, at the outset, that a reptilian standard is the only proper one—it is surely irrelevant that dinosaurs had smaller brains than people or whales. We have abundant data on the relationship of brain and body size in modern reptiles. Since we know that brains increase two-thirds as fast as bodies as we move from small to large living species, we can extrapolate this rate to dinosaurian sizes and ask whether dinosaur brains match what we would expect of living reptiles if they grew so large.

Harry Jerison studied the brain sizes of ten dinosaurs and   11 found that they fell right on the extrapolated reptilian curve. Dinosaurs did not have small brains; they maintained just the right-sized brains for reptiles of their dimensions. So much for Ms. Parker's explanation of their demise.

Jerison made no attempt to distinguish among various kinds   12 of dinosaurs; ten species distributed over six major groups scarcely provide a proper basis for comparison. Recently, James A. Hopson of the University of Chicago gathered more data and made a remarkable and satisfying discovery.

Hopson needed a common scale for all dinosaurs. He there-   13 fore compared each dinosaur brain with the average reptilian brain we would expect at its body weight. If the dinosaur falls on the standard reptilian curve, its brain receives a value of 1.0 (called an encephalization quotient, or EQ—the ratio of actual brain to expected brain for a standard reptile of the same body weight). Dinosaurs lying above the curve (more brain than expected in a standard reptile of the same body weight) receive values in excess of 1.0, while those below the curve measure less than 1.0.

Hopson found that the major groups of dinosaurs can be ranked by increasing values of average EQ. This ranking corresponds perfectly with inferred speed, agility and behavioral complexity in feeding (or avoiding the prospect of becoming a meal). The giant sauropods, *Brontosaurus* and its allies, have the lowest EQ's—0.20 to 0.35. They must have moved fairly slowly and without great maneuverability. They probably escaped predation by virtue of their bulk alone, much as elephants do today. The armored ankylosaurs and stegosaurs come next with EQ's of 0.52 to 0.56. These animals, with their heavy armor, probably relied largely upon passive defense, but the clubbed tail of ankylosaurs and the spiked tail of stegosaurs imply some active fighting and increased behavioral complexity. 14

The ceratopsians rank next at about 0.7 to 0.9. Hopson remarks: "The larger ceratopsians, with their great horned heads, relied on active defensive strategies and presumably required somewhat greater agility than the tail-weaponed forms, both in fending off predators and in intraspecific combat bouts. The smaller ceratopsians, lacking true horns, would have relied on sensory acuity and speed to escape from predators." The ornithopods (duckbills and their allies) were the brainiest herbivores, with EQ's from 0.85 to 1.5. They relied upon "acute senses and relatively fast speeds" to elude carnivores. Flight seems to require more acuity and agility than standing defense. Among ceratopsians, small, hornless, and presumably fleeing *Protoceratops* had a higher EQ than great three-horned *Triceratops*. 15

Carnivores have higher EQ's than herbivores, as in modern vertebrates. Catching a rapidly moving or stoutly fighting prey demands a good deal more upstairs than plucking the right kind of plant. The giant theropods (*Tyrannosaurus* and its allies) vary 16 from 1.0 to nearly 2.0. Atop the heap, quite appropriately at its small size, rests the little coelurosaur *Stenonychosaurus* with an EQ well above 5.0. Its actively moving quarry, small mammals and birds perhaps, probably posed a greater challenge in discovery and capture than *Triceratops* afforded *Tyrannosaurus*.

I do not wish to make a naive claim that brain size equals 17 intelligence or, in this case, behavioral range and agility (I don't know what intelligence means in humans, much less in a group of extinct reptiles). Variation in brain size within a species has precious little to do with brain power (humans do equally well with 900 or 2,500 cubic centimeters of brain). But comparison across species, when the differences are large, seems reasonable. I do not regard it as irrelevant to our achievements that we so greatly exceed koala bears—much as I love them—in EQ. The sensible ordering among dinosaurs also indicates that even so coarse a measure as brain size counts for something.

If behavioral complexity is one consequence of mental 18 power, then we might expect to uncover among dinosaurs some signs of social behavior that demand coordination, cohesiveness, and recognition. Indeed we do, and it cannot be accidental that these signs were overlooked when dinosaurs labored under the burden of a falsely imposed obtuseness. Multiple trackways have been uncovered, with evidence for more than twenty animals traveling together in parallel movement. Did some dinosaurs live in herds? At the Davenport Ranch sauropod trackway, small footprints lie in the center and larger ones at the periphery. Could it be that some dinosaurs traveled much as some advanced herbivorous mammals do today, with large adults at the borders sheltering juveniles in the center?

In addition, the very structures that seemed most bizarre 19 and useless to older paleontologists—the elaborate crests of hadrosaurs, the frills and horns of ceratopsians, and the nine inches of solid bone above the brain of *Pachycephalosaurus*—now appear to gain a coordinated explanation as devices for sexual display and combat. Pachycephalosaurs may have engaged in head-butting contests much as mountain sheep do today. The crests of some hadrosaurs are well designed as resonating chambers; did they engage in bellowing matches? The ceratopsian horn and frill may have acted as sword and shield in the battle for mates. Since such behavior is not only intrinsically complex, but also implies an elaborate social system, we would scarcely expect to find it in a group of animals barely muddling through at a moronic level.

But the best illustration of dinosaurian capability may well 20 be the fact most often cited against them—their demise. Extinction, for most people, carries many of the connotations attributed to sex not so long ago—a rather disreputable business, frequent in occurrence, but not to anyone's credit, and certainly not to be discussed in proper circles. But, like sex, extinction is an ineluctable part of life. It is the ultimate fate of all species, not the lot of unfortunate and ill-designed creatures. It is no sign of failure.

The remarkable thing about dinosaurs is not that they be- 21 came extinct, but that they dominated the earth for so long. Dinosaurs held sway for 100 million years while mammals, all the while, lived as small animals in the interstices of their world. After 70 million years on top, we mammals have an excellent track record and good prospects for the future, but we have yet to display the staying power of dinosaurs.

People, on this criterion, are scarcely worth mentioning—5 22 million years perhaps since *Australopithecus,* a mere 50,000 for our own species, *Homo sapiens.* Try the ultimate test within our system of values: Do you know anyone who would wager a substantial sum, even at favorable odds, on the proposition that *Homo sapiens* will last longer than *Brontosaurus?*

1980

The Patterns of Eating
Peter Farb and George Armelagos

Among the important societal rules that represent one com- 1 ponent of cuisine are table manners. As a socially instilled form of conduct, they reveal the attitudes typical of a society. Changes in table manners through time, as they have been documented for western Europe, likewise reflect fundamental changes in human relationships. Medieval courtiers saw their table manners as distinguishing them from crude peasants; but by modern standards, the manners were not exactly refined. Feudal lords used their unwashed hands to scoop food from a common bowl and they passed around a single goblet from which all drank. A finger or two would be extended while eating, so as to be kept free of grease and thus available for the next course, or for dipping into spices and condiments—possibly accounting for today's "polite" custom of extending the finger while holding a spoon or small fork. Soups and sauces were commonly drunk by lifting the bowl to the mouth; several diners frequently ate from the same bread trencher. Even lords and nobles would toss gnawed bones back into the common dish, wolf down their food, spit onto the table (preferred conduct called for spitting under it), and blew their noses into the tablecloth.

By about the beginning of the sixteenth century, table manners began to move in the direction of today's standards. The importance attached to them is indicated by the phenomenal success of a treatise, *On Civility in Children*, by the philosopher Erasmus, which appeared in 1530; reprinted more than thirty times in the next six years, it also appeared in numerous translations. Erasmus' idea of good table manners was far from modern, but it did represent an advance. He believed, for example, that an upper class diner was distinguished by putting only three fingers of one hand into the bowl, instead of the entire hand in the manner of the lower class. Wait a few moments after being seated before you dip into it, he advises. Do not poke around in your dish, but take the first piece you touch. Do not put chewed food from the mouth back on your plate; instead, throw it under the table or behind your chair.

By the time of Erasmus, the changing table manners reveal a fundamental shift in society. People no longer ate from the same dish or drank from the same goblet, but were divided from one another by a new wall of constraint. Once the spontaneous, direct, and informal manners of the Middle Ages had been repressed, people began to feel shame. Defecation and urination were now regarded as private activities; handkerchiefs came into use for blowing the nose; nightclothes were now worn, and bedrooms were set apart as private areas. Before the sixteenth century, even nobles ate in their vast kitchens; only then did a special room designated for eating come into use away from the bloody sides of meat, the animals about to be slaughtered, and the bustling servants. These new inhibitions became the essence of "civilized" behavior, distinguishing adults from children, the upper classes from the lower, and Europeans from the "savages" then being discovered around the world. Restraint in eating habits became more marked in the centuries that followed. By about 1800, napkins were in common use, and before long they were placed on the thighs rather than wrapped around the neck; coffee and tea were no longer slurped out of the saucer; bread was genteelly broken into small pieces with the fingers rather than cut into large chunks with a knife.

Numerous paintings that depict meals—with subjects such as the Last Supper, the wedding at Cana, or Herod's feast—show what dining tables looked like before the seventeenth century. Forks were not depicted until about 1600 (when Jacopo Bassano painted one in a Last Supper), and very few spoons were shown. At least one knife is always depicted—an especially large one when it is the only one available for all the guests—but small individual knives were often at each place. Tin disks or oval pieces of wood had already replaced the bread trenchers. This change in eating utensils typified the new table manners in Europe. (In many other parts of the world, no utensils at all were used. In the Near East, for example, it was traditional to bring food to the mouth with the fingers of the right hand, the left being unacceptable because it was reserved for wiping the buttocks.) Utensils were employed in part because of a change in the attitude toward meat. During the Middle Ages, whole sides of meat, or even an entire dead animal, had been brought to the table and then carved in view of the diners. Beginning in the seventeenth century, at first in France but later elsewhere, the practice began to go out of fashion. One reason was that the family was ceasing to be a production unit that did its own slaughtering; as that function was transferred to specialists outside the home, the family became essentially a consumption unit. In addition, the size of the family was decreasing, and consequently whole animals, or even large parts of them, were uneconomical. The cuisines of Europe reflected these social and economic changes. The animal origin of meat dishes was concealed by the arts of preparation. Meat itself became distasteful to look upon, and carving was moved out of sight to the kitchen. Comparable changes had already taken place in Chinese cuisine, with meat being cut up beforehand, unobserved by the diners. England was an exception to the change in Europe, and in its former colonies—the United States, Canada, Australia, and South Africa—the custom has persisted of bringing a joint of meat to the table to be carved.

Once carving was no longer considered a necessary skill   5
among the well-bred, changes inevitably took place in the use of the knife, unquestionably the earliest utensil used for manipulating food. (In fact, the earliest English cookbooks were not so much guides to recipes as guides to carving meat.) The attitude of diners toward the knife, going back to the Middle Ages and the Renaissance, had always been ambivalent. The knife served as a utensil, but it offered a potential threat because it was also a weapon. Thus taboos were increasingly placed upon its use: It was to be held by the point with the blunt handle presented; it was not to be placed anywhere near the face; and most important, the uses to which it was put were sharply restricted. It was not to be used for cutting soft foods such as boiled eggs or fish, or round ones such as potatoes, or to be lifted from the table for courses that did not need it. In short, good table manners in Europe gradually removed the threatening aspect of the knife from social occasions. A similar change had taken place much earlier in China when the warrior was supplanted by the scholar as a cultural model. The knife was banished completely from the table in favor of chopsticks, which is why the Chinese came to regard Europeans as barbarians at their table who "eat with swords."

The fork in particular enabled Europeans to separate them-   6
selves from the eating process, even avoiding manual contact with their food. When the fork first appeared in Europe, toward the end of the Middle Ages, it was used solely as an instrument for lifting chunks from the common bowl. Beginning in the six-

teenth century, the fork was increasingly used by members of the upper classes—first in Italy, then in France, and finally in Germany and England. By then, social relations in western Europe had so changed that a utensil was needed to spare diners from the "uncivilized" and distasteful necessity of picking up food and putting it into the mouth with the fingers. The addition of the fork to the table was once said to be for reasons of hygiene, but this cannot be true. By the sixteenth century people were no longer eating from a common bowl but from their own plates, and since they also washed their hands before meals, their fingers were now every bit as hygienic as a fork would have been. Nor can the reason for the adoption of the fork be connected with the wish not to soil the long ruff that was worn on the sleeve at the time, since the fork was also adopted in various countries where ruffs were not then in fashion.

Along with the appearance of the fork, all table utensils be- 7
gan to change and proliferate from the sixteenth century onward. Soup was no longer eaten directly from the dish, but each diner used an individual spoon for that purpose. When a diner wanted a second helping from the serving dish, a ladle or a fresh spoon was used. More and more special utensils were developed for each kind of food: soup spoons, oyster forks, salad forks, two-tined fondue forks, blunt butter knives, special utensils for various desserts and kinds of fruit, each one differently shaped, of a different size, with differently numbered prongs and with blunt or serrated edges. The present European pattern eventually emerged, in which each person is provided with a table setting of as many as a dozen utensils at a full-course meal. With that, the separation of the human body from the taking of food became virtually complete. Good table manners dictated that even the cobs of maize were to be held by prongs inserted in each end, and the bones of lamb chops covered by ruffled paper pantalettes. Only under special conditions—as when Western people consciously imitate an earlier stage in culture at a picnic, fish fry, cookout, or campfire—do they still tear food apart with their fingers and their teeth, in a nostalgic reenactment of eating behaviors long vanished.

Today's neighborhood barbecue recreates a world of shar- 8

ing and hospitality that becomes rarer each year. We regard as a curiosity the behavior of hunters in exotic regions. But every year millions of North Americans take to the woods and lakes to kill a wide variety of animals—with a difference, of course: What hunters do for survival we do for sport (and also for proof of masculinity, for male bonding, and for various psychological rewards). Like hunters, too, we stuff ourselves almost whenever food is available. Nibbling on a roasted ear of maize gives us, in addition to nutrients, the satisfaction of participating in culturally simpler ways. A festive meal, however, is still thought of in Victorian terms, with the dominant male officiating over the roast, the dominant female apportioning vegetables, the extended family gathered around the table, with everything in its proper place—a revered picture, as indeed it was so painted by Norman Rockwell, yet one that becomes less accurate with each year that passes.

1980

8

Cause and Effect

How Do You Know It's Good?

Marya Mannes

Suppose there were no critics to tell us how to react to a 1
picture, a play, or a new composition of music. Suppose we wandered innocent as the dawn into an art exhibition of unsigned paintings. By what standards, by what values would we decide whether they were good or bad, talented or untalented, successes or failures? How can we ever know that what we think is right?

For the last fifteen or twenty years the fashion in criticism 2
or appreciation of the arts has been to deny the existence of any valid criteria and to make the words "good" or "bad" irrelevant, immaterial, and inapplicable. There is no such thing, we are told, as a set of standards, first acquired through experience and knowledge and later imposed on the subject under discussion. This has been a popular approach, for it relieves the critic of the responsibility of judgment and the public of the necessity of knowledge. It pleases those resentful of disciplines, it flatters the empty-minded by calling them open-minded, it comforts the confused. Under the banner of democracy and the kind of equality which our forefathers did *not* mean, it says, in effect, "Who are you to tell us what *is* good or bad?" This is the same cry used so long and so effectively by the producers of mass media who

291

insist that it is the public, not they, who decides what it wants to hear and see, and that for a critic to say that *this* program is bad and *this* program is good is purely a reflection of personal taste. Nobody recently has expressed this philosophy more succinctly than Dr. Frank Stanton, the highly intelligent president of CBS television. At a hearing before the Federal Communications Commission, this phrase escaped him under questioning: "One man's mediocrity is another man's good program."

There is no better way of saying "No values are absolute." There is another important aspect to this philosophy of *laissez faire:* It is the fear, in all observers of all forms of art, of guessing wrong. This fear is well come by, for who has not heard of the contemporary outcries against artists who later were called great? Every age has its arbiters who do not grow with their times, who cannot tell evolution from revolution or the difference between frivolous faddism, amateurish experimentation, and profound and necessary change. Who wants to be caught *flagrante delicto* with an error of judgment as serious as this? It is far safer, and certainly easier, to look at a picture or a play or a poem and to say "This is hard to understand, but it may be good," or simply to welcome it as a new form. The word "new"—in our country especially—has magical connotations. What is new must be good; what is old is probably bad. And if a critic can describe the new in language that nobody can understand, he's safer still. If he has mastered the art of saying nothing with exquisite complexity, nobody can quote him later as saying anything.

But all these, I maintain, are forms of abdication from the responsibility of judgment. In creating, the artist commits himself; in appreciating, you have a commitment of your own. For after all, it is the audience which makes the arts. A climate of appreciation is essential to its flowering, and the higher the expectations of the public, the better the performance of the artist. Conversely, only a public ill-served by its critics could have accepted as art and as literature so much in these last years that has been neither. If anything goes, everything goes; and at the bottom of the junkpile lie the discarded standards too.

But what are these standards? How do you get them? How

do you know they're the right ones? How can you make a clear pattern out of so many intangibles, including that greatest one, the very private I?

Well for one thing, it's fairly obvious that the more you 6 read and see and hear, the more equipped you'll be to practice that art of association which is at the basis of all understanding and judgment. The more you live and the more you look, the more aware you are of a consistent pattern—as universal as the stars, as the tides, as breathing, as night and day—underlying everything. I would call this pattern and this rhythm an order. Not order—*an* order. Within it exists an incredible diversity of forms. Without it lies chaos—the wild cells of destruction—sickness. It is in the end up to you to distinguish between the diversity that is health and the chaos that is sickness, and you can't do this without a process of association that can link a bar of Mozart with the corner of a Vermeer painting, or a Stravinsky score with a Picasso abstraction; or that can relate an aggressive act with a Franz Kline painting and a fit of coughing with a John Cage composition.

There is no accident in the fact that certain expressions of 7 art live for all time and that others die with the moment, and although you may not always define the reasons, you can ask the questions. What does an artist say that is timeless; how does he say it? How much is fashion, how much is merely reflection? Why is Sir Walter Scott so hard to read now, and Jane Austen not? Why is baroque right for one age and too effulgent for another?

Can a standard of craftsmanship apply to art of all ages, or 8 does each have its own, and different, definitions? You may have been aware, inadvertently, that craftsmanship has become a dirty word these years because, again, it implies standards—something done well or done badly. The result of this convenient avoidance is a plenitude of actors who can't project their voices, singers who can't phrase their songs, poets who can't communicate emotion, and writers who have no vocabulary—not to speak of painters who can't draw. The dogma now is that craftsmanship gets in the way of expression. You can do better if you don't know *how* you do it, let alone *what* you're doing.

I think it is time you helped reverse this trend by trying to re- 9 discover craft: the command of the chosen instrument, whether it is a brush, a word, or a voice. When you begin to detect the difference between freedom and sloppiness, between serious experimentation and egotherapy, between skill and slickness, between strength and violence, you are on your way to separating the sheep from the goats, a form of segregation denied us for quite a while. All you need to restore it is a small bundle of standards and a Geiger counter that detects fraud, and we might begin our tour of the arts in an area where both are urgently needed: contemporary painting.

I don't know what's worse: to have to look at acres of bad 10 art to find the little good, or to read what the critics say about it all. In no other field of expression has so much double-talk flourished, so much confusion prevailed, and so much nonsense been circulated: further evidence of the close interdependence between the arts and the critical climate they inhabit. It will be my pleasure to share with you some of this double-talk so typical of our times.

Item one: preface for a catalogue of an abstract painter: 11

"Time-bound meditation experiencing a life; sincere with 12 plastic piety at the threshold of hallowed arcana; a striving for pure ideation giving shape to inner drive; formalized patterns where neural balances reach a fiction." End of quote. Know what this artist paints like now?

Item two: a review in the *Art News:*   13

"...a weird and disparate assortment of material, but the 14 monstrosity which bloomed into his most recent cancer of aggregations is present in some form everywhere...." Then, later, "A gluttony of things and processes terminated by a glorious constipation."

Item three, same magazine, review of an artist who welds 15 automobile fragments into abstract shapes:

"Each fragment...is made an extreme of human exasperation, 16 torn at and fought all the way, and has its rightness of form as if by accident. *Any technique that requires order or discipline would just be the human ego.* No, these must be egoless, uncontrolled, undesigned and different enough to give you a bang— fifty miles an hour around a telephone pole...."

"Any technique that requires order or discipline would just 17 be the human ego." What does he mean—"just be"? What are they really talking about? Is this journalism? Is it criticism? Or is it that other convenient abdication from standards of performance and judgment practiced by so many artists and critics that they, like certain writers who deal only in sickness and depravity, "reflect the chaos about them"? Again, whose chaos? Whose depravity?

I had always thought that the prime function of art was to 18 create order *out* of chaos—again, not the order of neatness or rigidity or convention or artifice, but the order of clarity by which one will and one vision could draw the essential truth out of apparent confusion. I still do. It is not enough to use parts of a car to convey the brutality of the machine. This is as slavishly representative, and just as easy, as arranging dried flowers under glass to convey nature.

Speaking of which, i.e., the use of real materials (burlap, 19 old gloves, bottletops) in lieu of pigment, this is what one critic had to say about an exhibition of Assemblage at the Museum of Modern Art last year:

> Spotted throughout the show are indisputable works of art, accounting for a quarter or even a half of the total display. But the remainder are works of non-art, anti-art, and art substitutes that are the aesthetic counterparts of the social deficiencies that land people in the clink on charges of vagrancy. These aesthetic bankrupts...have no legitimate ideological roof over their heads and not the price of a square intellectual meal, much less a spiritual sandwich, in their pockets.

I quote these words of John Canaday of *The New York* 20 *Times* as an example of the kind of criticism which puts responsibility to an intelligent public above popularity with an intellectual coterie. Canaday has the courage to say what he thinks and the capacity to say it clearly: two qualities notably absent from his profession.

Next to art, I would say that appreciation and evaluation in 21 the field of music is the most difficult. For it is rarely possible to judge a new composition at one hearing only. What seems confusing or fragmented at first might well become clear and organic a third time. Or it might not. The only salvation here for the listener is, again, an instinct born of experience and association which allows him to separate intent from accident, design from experimentation, and pretense from conviction. Much of contemporary music is, like its sister art, merely a reflection of the composer's own fragmentation: an absorption in self and symbols at the expense of communication with others. The artist, in short, says to the public: If you don't understand this, it's because you're dumb. I maintain that you are not. You may have to go part way or even halfway to meet the artist, but if you must go the whole way, it's his fault, not yours. Hold fast to that. And remember it too when you read new poetry, that estranged sister of music.

> A multitude of causes, unknown to former times, are now acting with a combined force to blunt the discriminating powers of the mind, and, unfitting it for all voluntary exertion, to reduce it to a state of almost savage torpor. The most effective of these causes are the great national events which are daily taking place and the increasing accumulation of men in cities, where the uniformity of their occupations produces a craving for extraordinary incident, which the rapid communication of intelligence hourly gratifies. To this tendency of life and manners, the literature and theatrical exhibitions of the country have conformed themselves.

This startlingly applicable comment was written in the year 22 1800 by William Wordsworth in the preface to his "Lyrical Ballads"; and it has been cited by Edwin Muir in his recently published book "The Estate of Poetry." Muir states that poetry's effective range and influence have diminished alarmingly in the modern world. He believes in the inherent and indestructible qualities of the human mind and the great and permanent objects that act upon it, and suggests that the audience will increase when "poetry loses what obscurity is left in it by attempting greater themes, for great themes have to be stated clearly." If you keep that firmly in mind and resist, in Muir's words, "the vast dissemination of secondary objects that isolate us from the natural world," you have gone a long way toward equipping yourself for the examination of any work of art.

When you come to theatre, in this extremely hasty tour of 23 the arts, you can approach it on two different levels. You can bring to it anticipation and innocence, giving yourself up, as it were, to the life on the stage and reacting to it emotionally, if the play is good, or listlessly, if the play is boring; a part of the audience organism that expresses its favor by silence or laughter and its disfavor by coughing and rustling. Or you can bring to it certain critical faculties that may heighten, rather than diminish, your enjoyment.

You can ask yourselves whether the actors are truly in their 24 parts or merely projecting themselves; whether the scenery helps or hurts the mood; whether the playwright is honest with himself, his characters, and you. Somewhere along the line you can learn to distinguish between the true creative act and the false arbitrary gesture; between fresh observation and stale cliché; between the avant-garde play that is pretentious drivel and the avant-garde play that finds new ways to say old truths.

Purpose and craftsmanship—end and means—these are the 25 keys to your judgment in all the arts. What is this painter trying to say when he slashes a broad band of black across a white canvas and lets the edges dribble down? Is it a statement of violence? Is it a self-portrait? If it is *one* of these, has he made you believe it? Or is this a gesture of the ego or a form of therapy? If it shocks you, what does it shock you into?

And what of this tight little painting of bright flowers in a 26 vase? Is the painter saying anything new about flowers? Is it different from a million other canvases of flowers? Has it any life, any meaning, beyond its statement? Is there any pleasure in its forms or texture? The question is not whether a thing is abstract or representational, whether it is "modern" or conventional. The question, inexorably, is whether it is good. And this is a decision which only you, on the basis of instinct, experience, and association, can make for yourself. It takes independence and courage. It involves, moreover, the risk of wrong decision and the humility, after the passage of time, of recognizing it as such. As we grow and change and learn, our attitudes can change too, and what we once thought obscure or "difficult" can later emerge as coherent and illuminating. Entrenched prejudices, obdurate opinions are as sterile as no opinions at all.

Yet standards there are, timeless as the universe itself. And 27 when you have committed yourself to them, you have acquired a passport to that elusive but immutable realm of truth. Keep it with you in the forests of bewilderment. And never be afraid to speak up.

1962

The Villain in the Atmosphere
Isaac Asimov

The villain in the atmosphere is carbon dioxide.   1

It does not seem to be a villain. It is not very poisonous and   2
it is present in the atmosphere in so small a quantity that it does us no harm. For every 1,000,000 cubic feet of air there are only 340 cubic feet of carbon dioxide—only 0.034 percent.

What's more, that small quantity of carbon dioxide in the   3
air is essential to life. Plants absorb carbon dioxide and convert it into their own tissues, which serve as the basic food supply for all of animal life (including human beings, of course). In the process, they liberate oxygen, which is also necessary for all animal life.

But here is what this apparently harmless and certainly es-   4
sential gas is doing to us:

The sea level is rising very slowly from year to year. The   5
high tides tend to be progressively higher, even in quiet weather, and storms batter at breakwaters more and more effectively, erode the beaches more savagely, batter houses farther inland.

In all likelihood, the sea level will continue to rise and do so   6
at a greater rate in the course of the next hundred years. This means that the line separating ocean from land will retreat inland

everywhere. It will do so only slightly where high land abuts the ocean. In those places, however, where there are low-lying coastal areas (where a large fraction of humanity lives) the water will advance steadily and inexorably and people will have to retreat inland.

Virtually all of Long Island will become part of the shallow offshore sea bottom, leaving only a line of small islands running east to west, marking off what had been the island's highest points. Eventually the sea will reach a maximum of two hundred feet above the present water level, and will be splashing against the windows along the twentieth floors of Manhattan's skyscrapers. Naturally the Manhattan streets will be deep under water, as will the New Jersey shoreline and all of Delaware. Florida, too, will be gone, as will much of the British Isles, the northwestern European coast, the crowded Nile valley, and the low-lying areas of China, India, and the Soviet Union. 7

It is not only that people will be forced to retreat by the millions and that many cities will be drowned, but much of the most productive farming areas of the world will be lost. Although the change will not be overnight, and though people will have time to leave and carry with them such of their belongings as they can, there will not be room in the continental interiors for all of them. As the food supply plummets with the ruin of farming areas, starvation will be rampant and the structure of society may collapse under the unbearable pressures. 8

And all because of carbon dioxide. But how does that come about? What is the connection? 9

It begins with sunlight, to which the various gases of the atmosphere (including carbon dioxide) are transparent. Sunlight, striking the top of the atmosphere, travels right through miles of it to reach the Earth's surface, where it is absorbed. In this way, the Earth is warmed. 10

The Earth's surface doesn't get too hot, because at night the Earth's heat radiates into space in the form of infrared radiation. As the Earth gains heat by day and loses it by night, it maintains an overall temperature balance to which Earthly life is well-adapted. 11

However, the atmosphere is not quite as transparent to in- 12

frared radiation as it is to visible light. Carbon dioxide in particular tends to be opaque to that radiation. Less heat is lost at
night, for that reason, than would be lost if carbon dioxide were
not present in the atmosphere. Without the small quantity of that
gas present, the Earth would be distinctly cooler on the whole,
perhaps a bit uncomfortably cool.

This is called the ''greenhouse effect'' of carbon dioxide. It 13
is so called because the glass of greenhouses lets sunshine in but
prevents the loss of heat. For that reason it is warm inside a
greenhouse on sunny days even when the temperature is low.

We can be thankful that carbon dioxide is keeping us com- 14
fortably warm, but the concentration of carbon dioxide in the atmosphere is going up steadily and that is where the villainy
comes in. In 1958, when the carbon dioxide of the atmosphere
first began to be measured carefully, it made up only 0.0316 percent of the atmosphere. Each year since, the concentration has
crept upward and it now stands at 0.0340 percent. It is estimated
that by 2020 the concentration will be about 0.0660 percent, or
nearly twice what it is now.

This means that in the coming decades, Earth's average 15
temperature will go up slightly. Winters will grow a bit milder on
the average and summers a bit hotter. That may not seem frightening. Milder winters don't seem bad, and as for hotter summers, we can just run our air-conditioners a bit more.

But consider this: If winters in general grow milder, less 16
snow will fall during the cold season. If summers in general grow
hotter, more snow will melt during the warm season. That means
that, little by little, the snow line will move away from the equa-
tor and toward the poles. The glaciers will retreat, the mountain
tops will grow more bare, and the polar ice caps will begin to
melt.

That might be annoying to skiers and to other devotees of 17
winter sports, but would it necessarily bother the rest of us? After all, if the snow line moves north, it might be possible to grow
more food in Canada, Scandinavia, the Soviet Union, and Pat-
agonia.

Still, if the cold weather moves poleward, then so do the 18
storm belts. The desert regions that now exist in subtropical ar-

eas will greatly expand, and fertile land gained in the north will be lost in the south. More may be lost than gained.

It is the melting of the ice caps, though, that is the worst 19 change. It is this which demonstrates the villainy of carbon dioxide.

Something like 90 percent of the ice in the world is to be 20 found in the huge Antarctica ice cap, and another 8 percent is in the Greenland ice cap. In both places the ice is piled miles high. If these ice caps begin to melt, the water that forms won't stay in place. It will drip down into the ocean and slowly the sea level will rise, with the results that I have already described.

Even worse might be in store, for a rising temperature 21 would manage to release a little of the carbon dioxide that is tied up in vast quantities of limestone that exist in the Earth's crust. It will also liberate some of the carbon dioxide dissolved in the ocean. With still more carbon dioxide, the temperature of the Earth will creep upward a little more and release still more carbon dioxide.

All this is called the "runaway greenhouse effect," and it 22 may eventually make Earth an uninhabitable planet.

But, as you can see, it is not carbon dioxide in itself that is 23 the source of the trouble; it is the fact that the carbon dioxide concentration in the atmosphere is steadily rising and seems to be doomed to continue rising. Why is that?

To blame are two factors. First of all, in the last few cen- 24 turies, first coal, then oil and natural gas, have been burned for energy at a rapidly increasing rate. The carbon contained in these fuels, which has been safely buried underground for many millions of years, is now being burned to carbon dioxide and poured into the atmosphere at a rate of many tons per day.

Some of that additional carbon dioxide may be absorbed by 25 the soil or by the ocean, and some might be consumed by plant life, but the fact is that a considerable fraction of it remains in the atmosphere. It must, for the carbon dioxide content of the atmosphere is going up year by year.

To make matters worse, Earth's forests have been disap- 26 pearing, slowly at first, but in the last couple of centuries quite rapidly. Right now it is disappearing at the rate of sixty-four acres per minute.

Whatever replaces the forest—grasslands or farms or scrub—produces plants that do not consume carbon dioxide at a rate equal to that of forest. Thus, not only is more carbon dioxide being added to the atmosphere through the burning of fuel, but as the forests disappear, less carbon dioxide is being subtracted from the atmosphere by plants.

But this gives us a new perspective on the matter. The carbon dioxide is not rising by itself. It is people who are burning the coal, oil, and gas, because of their need for energy. It is people who are cutting down the forests, because of their need for farmland. And the two are connected, for the burning of coal and oil is producing acid rain which helps destroy the forests. It is *people,* then, who are the villains.

What is to be done?

First, we must save our forests, and even replant them. From forests, properly conserved, we get wood, chemicals, soil retention, ecological health—and a slowdown of carbon dioxide increase.

Second, we must have new sources of fuel. There are, after all, fuels that do not involve the production of carbon dioxide. Nuclear fission is one of them, and if that is deemed too dangerous for other reasons, there is the forthcoming nuclear fusion, which may be safer. There is also the energy of waves, tides, wind, and the Earth's interior heat. Most of all, there is the direct use of solar energy.

All of this will take time, work, and money, to be sure, but all that time, work, and money will be invested in order to save our civilization and our planet itself.

After all, humanity seems to be willing to spend *more* time, work, and money in order to support competing military machines that can only destroy us all. Should we begrudge *less* time, work, and money in order to save us all?

1986

Pain Is Not the Ultimate Enemy

Norman Cousins

Americans are probably the most pain-conscious people on the face of the earth. For years we have had it drummed into us—in print, on radio, over television, in everyday conversation—that any hint of pain is to be banished as though it were the ultimate evil. As a result, we are becoming a nation of pill-grabbers and hypochondriacs, escalating the slightest ache into a searing ordeal. 1

We know very little about pain and what we don't know makes it hurt all the more. Indeed, no form of illiteracy in the United States is so widespread or costly as ignorance about pain— what it is, what causes it, how to deal with it without panic. Almost everyone can rattle off the names of at least a dozen drugs that can deaden pain from every conceivable cause—all the way from headaches to hemorrhoids. There is far less knowledge about the fact that about 90 percent of pain is self-limiting, that it is not always an indication of poor health, and that, most frequently, it is the result of tension, stress, worry, idleness, boredom, frustration, suppressed rage, insufficient sleep, overeating, poorly balanced diet, smoking, excessive drinking, inadequate exercise, stale air, or any of the other abuses encountered by the human body in modern society. 2

The most ignored fact of all about pain is that the best way to eliminate it is to eliminate the abuse. Instead, many people reach almost instinctively for the painkillers—aspirins, barbiturates, codeines, tranquilizers, sleeping pills, and dozens of other analgesics or desensitizing drugs. 3

Most doctors are profoundly troubled over the extent to which the medical profession today is taking on the trappings of a pain-killing industry. Their offices are overloaded with people who are morbidly but mistakenly convinced that something dreadful is about to happen to them. It is all too evident that the campaign to get people to run to a doctor at the first sign of pain has boomeranged. Physicians find it difficult to give adequate attention to patients genuinely in need of expert diagnosis and treatment because their time is soaked up by people who have 4 nothing wrong with them except a temporary indisposition or a psychogenic ache.

Patients tend to feel indignant and insulted if the physician 5 tells them he can find no organic cause for the pain. They tend to interpret the term "psychogenic" to mean that they are complaining of nonexistent symptoms. They need to be educated about the fact that many forms of pain have no underlying physical cause but are the result, as mentioned earlier, of tension, stress, or hostile factors in the general environment. Sometimes a pain may be a manifestation of "conversion hysteria"...the name given by Jean Charcot to physical symptoms that have their origins in emotional disturbances.

Obviously, it is folly for an individual to ignore symptoms 6 that could be a warning of a potentially serious illness. Some people are so terrified of getting bad news from a doctor that they allow their malaise to worsen, sometimes past the point of no return. Total neglect is not the answer to hypochondria. The only answer has to be increased education about the way the human body works, so that more people will be able to steer an intelligent course between promiscuous pill-popping and irresponsible disregard of genuine symptoms.

Of all forms of pain, none is more important for the individual 7 to understand than the "threshold" variety. Almost everyone has a telltale ache that is triggered whenever tension or fatigue reaches a certain point. It can take the form of a migraine-type headache or a squeezing pain deep in the abdomen or cramps or a pain in the lower back or even pain in the joints. The individual who has learned how to make the correlation between such threshold pains and their cause doesn't panic when they occur; he or she does something about relieving the stress and tension. Then, if the pain persists despite the absence of apparent cause, the individual will telephone the doctor.

If ignorance about the nature of pain is widespread, ignorance 8 about the way pain-killing drugs work is even more so. What is not generally understood is that many of the vaunted pain-killing drugs conceal the pain without correcting the underlying condition. They deaden the mechanism in the body that alerts the brain to the fact that something may be wrong. The body can pay a high price for suppression of pain without regard to its basic cause.

Professional athletes are sometimes severely disadvantaged 9 by trainers whose job it is to keep them in action. The more famous the athlete, the greater the risk that he or she may be subjected to extreme medical measures when injury strikes. The star baseball pitcher whose arm is sore because of a torn muscle or tissue damage may need sustained rest more than anything else. But his team is battling for a place in the World Series; so the trainer or team doctor, called upon to work his magic, reaches for a strong dose of Butazolidine or other powerful pain suppressants. Presto, the pain disappears! The pitcher takes his place on the mound and does superbly. That could be the last game, however, in which he is able to throw a ball with full strength. The drugs didn't repair the torn muscle or cause the damaged tissue to heal. What they did was to mask the pain, enabling the pitcher to throw hard, further damaging the torn muscle. Little wonder that so many star athletes are cut down in their prime, more the victims of overzealous treatment of their injuries than of the injuries themselves.

The king of all painkillers, of course, is aspirin. The U.S. 10 Food and Drug Administration permits aspirin to be sold without prescription, but the drug, contrary to popular belief, can be dangerous and, in sustained doses, potentially lethal. Aspirin is self-administered by more people than any other drug in the world. Some people are aspirin-poppers, taking ten or more a day. What they don't know is that the smallest dose can cause internal bleeding. Even more serious perhaps is the fact that aspirin is antagonistic to collagen, which has a key role in the formation of connective tissue. Since many forms of arthritis involve disintegration of the connective tissue, the steady use of aspirin can actually intensify the underlying arthritic condition.

Aspirin is not the only pain-killing drug, of course, that is 11 known to have dangerous side effects. Dr. Daphne A. Roe, of Cornell University, at a medical meeting in New York City in 1974, presented startling evidence of a wide range of hazards associated with sedatives and other pain suppressants. Some of these drugs seriously interfere with the ability of the body to metabolize food properly, producing malnutrition. In some instances, there is also the danger of bone-marrow depression, interfering with the ability of the body to replenish its blood supply.

Pain-killing drugs are among the greatest advances in the 12 history of medicine. Properly used, they can be a boon in alleviating suffering and in treating disease. But their indiscriminate and promiscuous use is making psychological cripples and chronic ailers out of millions of people. The unremitting barrage of advertising for pain-killing drugs, especially over television, has set the stage for a mass anxiety neurosis. Almost from the moment children are old enough to sit upright in front of a television screen, they are being indoctrinated into the hypochondriac's clamorous and morbid world. Little wonder so many people fear pain more than death itself.

It might be a good idea if concerned physicians and edu- 13 cators could get together to make knowledge about pain an important part of the regular school curriculum. As for the populace at large, perhaps some of the same techniques used by public-service agencies to make people cancer-conscious can be used to counteract the growing terror of pain and illness in general. People ought to know that nothing is more remarkable about the human body than its recuperative drive, given a modicum of respect. If our broadcasting stations cannot provide equal time for responses to the pain-killing advertisements, they might at least set aside a few minutes each day for common-sense remarks on the subject of pain. As for the Food and Drug Administration, it might be interesting to know why an agency that has energetically warned the American people against taking vitamins without prescriptions is doing so little to control over-the-counter sales each year of billions of pain-killing pills, some of which can do more harm than the pain they are supposed to suppress.

1979

My Wood
E. M. Forster

A few years ago I wrote a book which dealt in part with the   1
difficulties of the English in India. Feeling that they would have
had no difficulties in India themselves, the Americans read the
book freely. The more they read it the better it made them feel,
and a cheque to the author was the result. I bought a wood with
the cheque. It is not a large wood—it contains scarcely any trees,
and it is intersected, blast it, by a public footpath. Still, it is the
first property that I have owned, so it is right that other people
should participate in my shame, and should ask themselves, in accents that will vary in horror, this very important question: What is
the effect of property upon the character? Don't let's touch economics; the effect of private ownership upon the community as a
whole is another question—a more important question, perhaps,
but another one. Let's keep to psychology. If you own things,
what's their effect on you? What's the effect on me of my wood?

In the first place, it makes me feel heavy. Property does   2
have this effect. Property produces men of weight, and it was
a man of weight who failed to get into the Kingdom of Heaven.
He was not wicked, that unfortunate millionaire in the parable,
he was only stout; he stuck out in front, not to mention behind, and as he wedged himself this way and that in the crys-
talline entrance and bruised his well-fed flanks, he saw beneath him a comparatively slim camel passing through the eye
of a needle and being woven into the robe of God. The Gospels
all through couple stoutness and slowness. They point out
what is perfectly obvious, yet seldom realized: that if you have
a lot of things you cannot move about a lot, that furniture requires dusting, dusters require servants, servants require insurance stamps, and the whole tangle of them makes you think
twice before you accept an invitation to dinner or go for a
bathe in the Jordan. Sometimes the Gospels proceed further
and say with Tolstoy that property is sinful; they approach the
difficult ground of asceticism here, where I cannot follow

them. But as to the immediate effects of property on people, they just show straightforward logic. It produces men of weight. Men of weight cannot, by definition, move like the lightning from the East unto the West, and the ascent of a fourteen-stone bishop into a pulpit is thus the exact antithesis of the coming of the Son of Man. My wood makes me feel heavy.

In the second place, it makes me feel it ought to be larger. 3

The other day I heard a twig snap in it. I was annoyed at 4 first, for I thought that someone was blackberrying, and depreciating the value of the undergrowth. On coming nearer, I saw it was not a man who had trodden on the twig and snapped it, but a bird, and I felt pleased. My bird. The bird was not equally pleased. Ignoring the relation between us, it took fright as soon as it saw the shape of my face, and flew straight over the boundary hedge into a field, the property of Mrs. Henessy, where it sat down with a loud squawk. It had become Mrs. Henessy's bird. Something seemed grossly amiss here, something that would not have occurred had the wood been larger. I could not afford to buy Mrs. Henessy out, I dared not murder her, and limitations of this sort beset me on every side. Ahab did not want that vineyard—he only needed it to round off his property, preparatory to plotting a new curve—and all the land around my wood has become necessary to me in order to round off the wood. A boundary protects. But—poor little thing—the boundary ought in its turn to be protected. Noises on the edge of it. Children throw stones. A little more, and then a little more, until we reach the sea. Happy Canute! Happier Alexander! And after all, why should even the world be the limit of possession? A rocket containing a Union Jack, will, it is hoped, be shortly fired at the moon. Mars. Sirius. Beyond which...But these immensities ended by saddening me. I could not suppose that my wood was the destined nucleus of universal dominion—it is so very small and contains no mineral wealth beyond the blackberries. Nor was I comforted when Mrs. Henessy's bird took alarm for the second time and flew clean away from us all, under the belief that it belonged to itself.

In the third place, property makes its owner feel that he 5 ought to do something to it. Yet he isn't sure what. A restlessness comes over him, a vague sense that he has a personality to express—the same sense which, without any vagueness, leads the artist to an act of creation. Sometimes I think I will cut down such trees as remain in the wood, at other times I want to fill up the gaps between them with new trees. Both impulses are pretentious and empty. They are not honest movements towards money-making or beauty. They spring from a foolish desire to express myself and from an inability to enjoy what I have got. Creation, property, enjoyment form a sinister trinity in the human mind. Creation and enjoyment are both very very good, yet they are often unattainable without a material basis, and at such moments property pushes itself in as a substitute, saying, "Accept me instead—I'm good enough for all three." It is not enough. It is, as Shakespeare said of lust, "The expense of spirit in a waste of shame": it is "Before, a joy proposed; behind, a dream." Yet we don't know how to shun it. It is forced on us by our economic system as the alternative to starvation. It is also forced on us by an internal defect in the soul, by the feeling that in property may lie the germs of self-development and of exquisite or heroic deeds. Our life on earth is, and ought to be, material and carnal. But we have not yet learned to manage our materialism and carnality properly; they are still entangled with the desire for ownership, where (in the words of Dante) "Possession is one with loss."

And this brings us to our fourth and final point: the black- 6
berries.

Blackberries are not plentiful in this meagre grove, but they 7
are easily seen from the public footpath which traverses it, and all too easily gathered. Foxgloves, too—people will pull up the foxgloves, and ladies of an educational tendency even grub for toadstools to show them on the Monday in class. Other ladies, less educated, roll down the bracken in the arms of their gentlemen friends. There is paper, there are tins. Pray, does my wood belong to me or doesn't it? And, if it does, should I not own it best by allowing no one else to walk there? There is a wood near Lyme Regis, also cursed by a public footpath, where the owner has not hesitated on this point. He has built high stone walls each side of the path, and has spanned it by bridges, so that the public circulate like termites while he gorges on the blackberries unseen. He

really does own his wood, this able chap. Dives in Hell did pretty well, but the gulf dividing him from Lazarus could be traversed by vision, and nothing traverses it here. And perhaps I shall come to this in time. I shall wall in and fence out until I really taste the sweets of property. Enormously stout, endlessly avaricious, pseudo-creative, intensely selfish, I shall weave upon my forehead the quadruple crown of possession until those nasty Bolshies come and take it off again and thrust me aside into the outer darkness.

1936

Watching the Grasshopper Get the Goodies

Ellen Goodman

I don't usually play the great American game called Categories. There are already too many ways to divide us into opposing teams, according to age, race, sex and favorite flavors. Every time we turn around, someone is telling us that the whole country is made up of those who drive pick-up trucks and those who do not, and then analyzing what this means in terms of the Middle East.   1

Still, it occurs to me that if we want to figure out why people are angry right now, it's not a bad idea to see ourselves as a nation of planners and nonplanners. It's the planners these days who are feeling penalized, right down to their box score at the bank.   2

The part of us which is most visibly and vocally infuriated by inflation, for example, isn't our liberal or conservative side but, rather, our planning side. Inflation devastates our attempts to control our futures—to budget and predict and expect. It particularly makes fools out of the people who saved then to buy   3 now. To a certain extent, it rewards instant gratification and makes a joke out of our traditional notions of preparation.

It is no news bulletin that the people who dove over their 4 heads into the real-estate market a few years ago are now generally better off than those who dutifully decided to save up for a larger down payment. With that "larger down payment" they can now buy two double-thick rib lambchops and a partridge in a pear tree.

But inflation isn't the only thing that leaves the planners 5 feeling betrayed. There are other issues that find them actively pitched against the nonplanners.

We all know families who saved for a decade to send their 6 kids to college. A college diploma these days costs about the same amount as a Mercedes-Benz. Of course, the Mercedes lasts longer and has a higher trade-in value. But the most devoted parent can be infuriated to discover that a neighboring couple who spent its income instead of saving is now eligible for college financial aid, while they are not. To the profligate go the spoils.

This can happen anywhere on the economic spectrum. 7 There is probably only one mother in the annals of the New York welfare rolls to save up a few thousand dollars in hopes of getting off aid. But she would have been better off spending it. When she was discovered this year, the welfare department took the money back. She, too, was penalized for planning.

In these crimped times, the Planned Parents of the Purse 8 are increasingly annoyed at other parents—whether they are unwed or on welfare or just prolific. For the first time in my own town, you can hear families with few children complaining out loud at the tax bill for the public schooling of families with many children.

One man I heard even suggesting charging tuition for the 9 third child. He admitted, "It's not a very generous attitude, I know. But I'm not feeling very generous these days." He is suffering from planner's warts.

At the same time I've talked with friends whose parents 10 prepared, often with financial difficulty, for their "old age" and illness. They feel sad when this money goes down a nursing home drain, but furious when other people who didn't save get this same care for free.

Now we are all aware that if many people don't plan their 11 economic lives, it may be because they can't. It does no one any good to keep the cashless out of college, to stash the old and poor into elderly warehouses, to leave the "extra" children illiterate. We do want to help others, but we also want our own efforts to make a difference.

There is nothing that grates a planner more than seeing a 12 nonplanner profit. It's as if the ant had to watch the grasshopper get the goodies.

Our two notions about what's fair end up on opposite sides. 13 It isn't fair if the poor get treated badly, and it isn't fair if those who work and save, plan and postpone aren't given a better shake. We want the winners to be the deserving. Only there is no divining rod for the deserving.

The hard part is to create policies that are neither unkind 14 nor insane. It is, after all, madness not to reward the kind of behavior we want to encourage. If we want the ranks of the planners to increase in this massive behavior-modification program called society, we have to give them the rewards, instead of the outrage.

1981

Nuclear Holocaust
Jonathan Schell

Part of the horror of thinking about a holocaust lies in the 1 fact that it leads us to supplant the human world with a statistical world; we seek a human truth and come up with a handful of figures. The only source that gives us a glimpse of that human truth is the testimony of the survivors of the Hiroshima and Nagasaki bombings. Because the bombing of Hiroshima has been more thoroughly investigated than the bombing of Nagasaki, and therefore more information about it is available, I shall restrict myself to a brief description of that catastrophe.

On August 6, 1945, at 8:16 A.M., a fission bomb with a yield 2 of twelve and a half kilotons was detonated about nineteen hundred feet above the central section of Hiroshima. By present-day standards, the bomb was a small one, and in today's arsenals it would be classed among the merely tactical weapons. Nevertheless, it was large enough to transform a city of some three hundred and forty thousand people into hell in the space of a few seconds. "It is no exaggeration," the authors of "Hiroshima and Nagasaki" tell us, "to say that the whole city was ruined instantaneously." In that instant, tens of thousands of people were burned, blasted, and crushed to death. Other tens of thousands suffered injuries of every description or were doomed to die of radiation sickness. The center of the city was flattened, and every part of the city was damaged. The trunks of bamboo trees as far away as five miles from ground zero—the point on the ground directly under the center of the explosion—were charred. Almost half the trees within a mile and a quarter were knocked down. Windows nearly seventeen miles away were broken. Half an hour after the blast, fires set by the thermal pulse and by the collapse of the buildings began to coalesce into a firestorm, which lasted for six hours. Starting about 9 A.M. and lasting until late afternoon, a "black rain" generated by the bomb (otherwise, the day was fair) fell on the western portions of the city, carrying radioactive fallout from the blast to the ground. For four hours at midday, a violent whirlwind, born of the strange meteorological conditions produced by the explosion, further devastated the city. The number of people who were killed outright or who died of their injuries over the next three months is estimated to be a hundred and thirty thousand. Sixty-eight percent of the buildings in the city were either completely destroyed or damaged beyond repair, and the center of the city was turned into a flat, rubble-strewn plain dotted with the ruins of a few of the sturdier buildings.

In the minutes after the detonation, the day grew dark, as 3 heavy clouds of dust and smoke filled the air. A whole city had

fallen in a moment, and in and under its ruins were its people.
Among those still living, most were injured, and of these most
were burned or had in some way been battered or had suffered
both kinds of injury. Those within a mile and a quarter of ground
zero had also been subjected to intense nuclear radiation, often
in lethal doses. When people revived enough from their uncon-
sciousness or shock to see what was happening around them,
they found that where a second before there had been a city getting ready to go about its daily business on a peaceful, warm August morning, now there was a heap of debris and corpses and a
stunned mass of injured humanity. But at first, as they awakened
and tried to find their bearings in the gathering darkness, many
felt cut off and alone. In a recent volume of recollections by survivors called "Unforgettable Fire," in which the effects of the
bombing are rendered in drawings as well as in words, Mrs.
Haruko Ogasawara, a young girl on that August morning, recalls
that she was at first knocked unconscious. She goes on to write:

> How many seconds or minutes had passed I could not tell,
> but, regaining consciousness, I found myself lying on the
> ground covered with pieces of wood. When I stood up in a
> frantic effort to look around, there was darkness. Terribly
> frightened, I thought I was alone in a world of death, and
> groped for any light. My fear was so great I did not think
> anyone would truly understand. When I came to my
> senses, I found my clothes in shreds, and I was without
> my wooden sandals.

Soon cries of pain and cries for help from the wounded   4
filled the air. Survivors heard the voices of their families and
their friends calling out in the gloom. Mrs. Ogasawara writes:

> Suddenly, I wondered what had happened to my mother
> and sister. My mother was then forty-five, and my sister
> five years old. When the darkness began to fade, I found
> that there was nothing around me. My house, the next
> door neighbor's house, and the next had all vanished. I
> was standing amid the ruins of my house. No one was
> around. It was quiet, very quiet—an eerie moment. I
> discovered my mother in a water tank. She had fainted.

Crying out, "Mama, Mama," I shook her to bring her
back to her senses. After coming to, my mother began to
shout madly for my sister: "Eiko! Eiko!"

I wondered how much time had passed when there were
cries of searchers. Children were calling their parents'
names, and parents were calling the names of their
children. We were calling desperately for my sister and
listening for her voice and looking to see her. Suddenly,
Mother cried "Oh Eiko!" Four or five meters away, my
sister's head was sticking out and was calling my
mother....Mother and I worked desperately to remove the
plaster and pillars and pulled her out with great effort. Her
body had turned purple from the bruises, and her arm was
so badly wounded that we could have placed two fingers
in the wound.

Others were less fortunate in their searches and rescue at- 5
tempts. In "Unforgettable Fire," a housewife describes a scene
she saw:

A mother, driven half-mad while looking for her child, was
calling his name. At last she found him. His head looked
like a boiled octopus. His eyes were half-closed, and his
mouth was white, pursed, and swollen.

Throughout the city, parents were discovering their 6
wounded or dead children, and children were discovering their
wounded or dead parents. Kikuno Segawa recalls seeing a little
girl with her dead mother:

A woman who looked like an expectant mother was dead.
At her side, a girl of about three years of age brought
some water in an empty can she had found. She was
trying to let her mother drink from it.

The sight of people in extremities of suffering was ubiqui- 7
tous. Kinzo Nishida recalls:

While taking my severely wounded wife out to the
riverbank by the side of the hill of Nakahiro-machi, I was
horrified, indeed, at the sight of a stark naked man
standing in the rain with his eyeball in his palm. He looked

to be in great pain, but there was nothing that I could do
for him.

Many people were astonished by the sheer sudden absence   8
of the known world. The writer Yoko Ota later wrote:

> I just could not understand why our surroundings had
> changed so greatly in one instant....I thought it might
> have been something which had nothing to do with the
> war—the collapse of the earth, which it was said would
> take place at the end of the world, and which I had read
> about as a child.

And a history professor who looked back at the city after   9
the explosion remarked later, "I saw that Hiroshima had disappeared."

As the fires sprang up in the ruins, many people, having   10
found injured family members and friends, were now forced to
abandon them to the flames or to lose their own lives in the firestorm. Those who left children, husbands, wives, friends, and
strangers to burn often found these experiences the most awful
of the entire ordeal. Mikio Inoue describes how one man, a professor, came to abandon his wife:

> It was when I crossed Miyuki Bridge that I saw Professor
> Takenaka, standing at the foot of the bridge. He was
> almost naked, wearing nothing but shorts, and he had a
> ball of rice in his right hand. Beyond the streetcar line, the
> northern area was covered by red fire burning against the
> sky. Far away from the line, Ote-machi was also a sea of
> fire.
>
> That day, Professor Takenaka had not gone to Hiroshima
> University, and the A-bomb exploded when he was at
> home. He tried to rescue his wife, who was trapped under
> a roofbeam, but all his efforts were in vain. The fire was
> threatening him also. His wife pleaded, "Run away,
> dear!" He was forced to desert his wife and escape from
> the fire. He was now at the foot of Miyuki Bridge.
>
> But I wonder how he came to hold that ball of rice in his
> hand. His naked figure, standing there before the flames

with that ball of rice, looked to me as a symbol of the
modest hopes of human beings.

In "Hiroshima," John Hersey describes the flight of a   11
group of German priests and their Japanese colleagues through a
burning section of the city:

> The street was cluttered with parts of houses that had slid
> into it, and with fallen telephone poles and wires. From
> every second or third house came the voices of people
> buried and abandoned, who invariably screamed, with
> formal politeness, "*Tasukete kure!* Help, if you please!"
> The priests recognized several ruins from which these
> cries came as the homes of friends, but because of the fire
> it was too late to help.

And thus it happened that throughout Hiroshima all the ties   12
of affection and respect that join human beings to one another
were being pulled and rent by the spreading firestorm. Soon processions of the injured—processions of a kind that had never
been seen before in history—began to file away from the center
of the city toward its outskirts. Most of the people suffered from
burns, which had often blackened their skin or caused it to sag
off them. A grocer who joined one of these processions has described them in an interview with Robert Jay Lifton which appears in his book "Death in Life":

> They held their arms bent [forward]...and their skin—not
> only on their hands but on their faces and bodies, too—
> hung down....If there had been only one or two such
> people...perhaps I would not have had such a strong
> impression. But wherever I walked, I met these
> people....Many of them died along the road. I can still
> picture them in my mind—like walking ghosts. They didn't
> look like people of this world.

The grocer also recalls that because of people's injuries   13
"you couldn't tell whether you were looking at them from in
front or in back." People found it impossible to recognize one
another. A woman who at the time was a girl of thirteen, and suffered disfiguring burns on her face, has recalled, "My face was

so distorted and changed that people couldn't tell who I was. After a while I could call others' names but they couldn't recognize me." In addition to being injured, many people were vomiting—an early symptom of radiation sickness. For many, horrifying and unreal events occurred in a chaotic jumble. In "Unforgettable Fire," Torako Hironaka enumerates some of the things that she remembers:

1. Some burned work-clothes.

2. People crying for help with their heads, shoulders, or the soles of their feet injured by fragments of broken window glass. Glass fragments were scattered everywhere.

3. [A woman] crying, saying "Aigo! Aigo!" (a Korean expression of sorrow).

4. A burning pine tree.

5. A naked woman.

6. Naked girls crying, "Stupid America!"

7. I was crouching in a puddle, for fear of being shot by a machine gun. My breasts were torn.

8. Burned down electric power lines.

9. A telephone pole had burned and fallen down.

10. A field of watermelons.

11. A dead horse.

12. What with dead cats, pigs, and people, it was just a hell on earth.

Physical collapse brought emotional and spiritual collapse 14 with it. The survivors were, on the whole, listless and stupefied. After the escapes, and the failures to escape, from the firestorm, a silence fell over the city and its remaining population. People suffered and died without speaking or otherwise making a sound. The processions of the injured, too, were soundless. Dr. Michihiko Hachiya has written in his book, "Hiroshima Diary":

Those who were able walked silently toward the suburbs in the distant hills, their spirits broken, their initiative gone. When asked whence they had come, they pointed to the city and said, "That way," and when asked where they were going, pointed away from the city and said, "This way." They were so broken and confused that they moved and behaved like automatons.

Their reactions had astonished outsiders, who reported with amazement the spectacle of long files of people holding stolidly to a narrow, rough path when close by was a smooth, easy road going in the same direction. The outsiders could not grasp the fact that they were witnessing the exodus of a people who walked in the realm of dreams.

Those who were still capable of action often acted in an absurd or an insane way. Some of them energetically pursued tasks that had made sense in the intact Hiroshima of a few minutes before but were now utterly inappropriate. Hersey relates that the German priests were bent on bringing to safety a suitcase, containing diocesan accounts and a sum of money, that they had rescued from the fire and were carrying around with them through the burning city. And Dr. Lifton describes a young soldier's punctilious efforts to find and preserve the ashes of a burned military code book while people around him were screaming for help. Other people simply lost their minds. For example, when the German priests were escaping from the firestorm, one of them, Father Wilhelm Kleinsorge, carried on his back a Mr. Fukai, who kept saying that he wanted to remain where he was. When Father Kleinsorge finally put Mr. Fukai down, he started running. Hersey writes:

Father Kleinsorge shouted to a dozen soldiers, who were standing by the bridge, to stop him. As Father Kleinsorge started back to get Mr. Fukai, Father LaSalle called out, "Hurry! Don't waste time!" So Father Kleinsorge just requested the soldiers to take care of Mr. Fukai. They said they would, but the little, broken man got away from them, and the last the priests could see of him, he was running back toward the fire.

In the weeks after the bombing, many survivors began to 16
notice the appearance of petechiae—small spots caused by hem-
orrhages—on their skin. These usually signalled the onset of the
critical stage of radiation sickness. In the first stage, the victims
characteristically vomited repeatedly, ran a fever, and developed
an abnormal thirst. (The cry "Water! Water!" was one of the few
sounds often heard in Hiroshima on the day of the bombing.)
Then, after a few hours or days, there was a deceptively hopeful
period of remission of symptoms, called the latency period,
which lasted from about a week to about four weeks. Radiation
attacks the reproductive function of cells, and those that reproduce most frequently are therefore the most vulnerable. Among
these are the bone-marrow cells, which are responsible for the
production of blood cells. During the latency period, the count of
white blood cells, which are instrumental in fighting infections,
and the count of platelets, which are instrumental in clotting,
drop precipitously, so the body is poorly defended against infec-
tion and is liable to hemorrhaging. In the third, and final, stage,
which may last for several weeks, the victim's hair may fall out
and he may suffer from diarrhea and may bleed from the intestines, the mouth, or other parts of the body, and in the end he
will either recover or die. Because the fireball of the Hiroshima
bomb did not touch the ground, very little ground material was
mixed with the fission products of the bomb, and therefore very
little local fallout was generated. (What fallout there was descended in the black rain.) Therefore, the fatalities from radiation
sickness were probably all caused by the initial nuclear radiation,
and since this affected only people within a radius of a mile and
a quarter of ground zero, most of the people who received lethal
doses were killed more quickly by the thermal pulse and the blast
wave. Thus, Hiroshima did not experience the mass radiation
sickness that can be expected if a weapon is ground-burst. Since
the Nagasaki bomb was also burst in the air, the effect of widespread lethal fallout on large areas, causing the death by radiation sickness of whole populations in the hours, days, and weeks
after the blast, is a form of nuclear horror that the world has not
experienced.

In the months and years following the bombing of Hi- 17

roshima, after radiation sickness had run its course and most of the injured had either died of their wounds or recovered from them, the inhabitants of the city began to learn that the exposure to radiation they had experienced would bring about a wide variety of illnesses, many of them lethal, throughout the lifetimes of those who had been exposed. An early sign that the harm from radiation was not restricted to radiation sickness came in the months immediately following the bombing, when people found that their reproductive organs had been temporarily harmed, with men experiencing sterility and women experiencing abnormalities in their menstrual cycles. Then, over the years, other illnesses, including cataracts of the eye and leukemia and other forms of cancer, began to appear in larger than normally expected numbers among the exposed population. In all these illnesses, correlations have been found between nearness to the explosion and incidence of the disease. Also, fetuses exposed to the bomb's radiation in utero exhibited abnormalities and developmental retardation. Those exposed within the mile-and-a-quarter radius were seven times as likely as unexposed fetuses to die in utero, and were also seven times as likely to die at birth or in infancy. Surviving children who were exposed in utero tended to be shorter and lighter than other children, and were more often mentally retarded. One of the most serious abnormalities caused by exposure to the bomb's radiation was microcephaly—abnormal smallness of the head, which is often accompanied by mental retardation. In one study, thirty-three cases of microcephaly were found among a hundred and sixty-nine children exposed in utero.

What happened at Hiroshima was less than a millionth part **18** of a holocaust at present levels of world nuclear armament. The more than millionfold difference amounts to more than a difference in magnitude; it is also a difference in kind. The authors of "Hiroshima and Nagasaki" observe that "an atomic bomb's massive destruction and indiscriminate slaughter involves the sweeping breakdown of all order and existence—in a word, the collapse of society itself," and that therefore "the essence of atomic destruction lies in the totality of its impact on man and society." This is true also of a holocaust, of course, except that the totalities in question are now not single cities but nations, eco-systems, and the earth's ecosphere. Yet with the exception of fallout, which was relatively light at Hiroshima and Nagasaki (because both the bombs were air-burst), the immediate devastation caused by today's bombs would be of a sort similar to the devastation in those cities. The immediate effects of a twenty-megaton bomb are not different in kind from those of a twelve-and-a-half-kiloton bomb; they are only more extensive.... Therefore, while the total effect of a holocaust is qualitatively different from the total effect of a single bomb, the experience of individual people in a holocaust would be, in the short term (and again excepting the presence of lethal fallout wherever the bombs were ground-burst), very much like the experience of individual people in Hiroshima. The Hiroshima people's experience, accordingly, is of much more than historical interest. It is a picture of what our whole world is always poised to become—a backdrop of scarcely imaginable horror lying just behind the surface of our normal life, and capable of breaking through into that normal life at any second. Whether we choose to think about it or not, it is an omnipresent, inescapable truth about our lives to-day that at every single moment each one of us may suddenly become the deranged mother looking for her burned child; the professor with the ball of rice in his hand whose wife has just told him "Run away, dear!" and died in the fires; Mr. Fukai running back into the firestorm; the naked man standing on the blasted plain that was his city, holding his eyeball in his hand; or, more likely, one of millions of corpses. For whatever our "modest hopes" as human beings may be, every one of them can be nullified by a nuclear holocaust.

One way to begin to grasp the destructive power of present-day nuclear weapons is to describe the consequences of the detonation of a one-megaton bomb, which possesses eighty times the explosive power of the Hiroshima bomb, on a large city, such as New York. Burst some eighty-five hundred feet above the Empire State Building, a one-megaton bomb would gut or flatten almost every building between Battery Park and 125th Street, or within a radius of four and four-tenths miles, or in an area of sixty-one square miles, and would heavily damage buildings be- 19 tween the northern tip of Staten Island and the George Washington Bridge, or within a radius of about eight miles, or in an area of about two hundred square miles. A conventional explosive delivers a swift shock, like a slap, to whatever it hits, but the blast wave of a sizable nuclear weapon endures for several seconds and "can surround and destroy whole buildings."...People, of course, would be picked up and hurled away from the blast along with the rest of the debris. Within the sixty-one square miles, the walls, roofs, and floors of any buildings that had not been flattened would be collapsed, and the people and furniture inside would be swept down onto the street. (Technically, this zone would be hit by various overpressures of at least five pounds per square inch. Overpressure is defined as the pressure in excess of normal atmospheric pressure.) As far away as ten miles from ground zero, pieces of glass and other sharp objects would be hurled about by the blast wave at lethal velocities. In Hiroshima, where buildings were low and, outside the center of the city, were often constructed of light materials, injuries from falling buildings were often minor. But in New York, where the buildings are tall and are constructed of heavy materials, the physical collapse of the city would certainly kill millions of people. The streets of New York are narrow ravines running between the high walls of the city's buildings. In a nuclear attack, the walls would fall and the ravines would fill up. The people in the buildings would fall to the street with the debris of the buildings, and the people in the street would be crushed by this avalanche of people and buildings. At a distance of two miles or so from ground zero, winds would reach four hundred miles an hour, and another two miles away they would reach a hundred and eighty miles an hour. Meanwhile, the fireball would be growing, until it was more than a mile wide, and rocketing upward, to a height of over six miles. For ten seconds, it would broil the city below. Anyone caught in the open within nine miles of ground zero would receive third-degree burns and would probably be killed; closer to the explosion, people would be charred and killed instantly....

If it were possible (as it would not be) for someone to stand 20 at Fifth Avenue and Seventy-second Street (about two miles from ground zero) without being instantly killed, he would see the following sequence of events. A dazzling white light from the fireball would illumine the scene, continuing for perhaps thirty seconds. Simultaneously, searing heat would ignite everything flammable and start to melt windows, cars, buses, lampposts, and everything else made of metal or glass. People in the street would immediately catch fire, and would shortly be reduced to heavily charred corpses. About five seconds after the light appeared, the blast wave would strike, laden with the debris of a now nonexistent midtown. Some buildings might be crushed, as though a giant fist had squeezed them on all sides, and others might be picked up off their foundations and whirled uptown with the other debris. On the far side of Central Park, the West Side skyline would fall from south to north. The four-hundred-mile-an-hour wind would blow from south to north, die down after a few seconds, and then blow in the reverse direction with diminished intensity. While these things were happening, the fireball would be burning in the sky for the ten seconds of the thermal pulse. Soon huge, thick clouds of dust and smoke would envelop the scene, and as the mushroom cloud rushed overhead (it would have a diameter of about twelve miles) the light from the sun would be blotted out, and day would turn to night. Within minutes, fires, ignited both by the thermal pulse and by broken gas mains, tanks of gas and oil, and the like, would begin to spread in the darkness, and a strong, steady wind would begin to blow in the direction of the blast. As at Hiroshima, a whirlwind might be produced, which would sweep through the ruins, and radioactive rain, generated under the meteorological conditions created by the blast, might fall. Before long, the individual fires would coalesce into a mass fire, which, depending largely on the winds, would become either a conflagration or a firestorm. In a conflagration, prevailing winds spread a wall of fire as far as there is any combustible material to sustain it; in a firestorm, a vertical updraft caused by the fire itself sucks the surrounding air in toward a central point, and the fires therefore converge in a single fire of extreme heat. A mass fire of either kind renders shelters useless by burning up all the oxygen in the air and creating toxic gases, so that anyone inside the shelters is asphyxiated, and also by heating the ground to such high temperatures that the shelters turn, in effect, into ovens, cremating the people inside them. In Dresden, several days after the firestorm raised there by Allied conventional bombing, the interiors of some bomb shelters were still so hot that when they were opened the inrushing air caused the contents to burst into flame. Only those who had fled their shelters when the bombing started had any chance of surviving. (It is difficult to predict in a particular situation which form the fires will take. In actual experience, Hiroshima suffered a firestorm and Nagasaki suffered a conflagration.)

In this vast theatre of physical effects, all the scenes of agony and death that took place at Hiroshima would again take place, but now involving millions of people rather than hundreds of thousands. Like the people of Hiroshima, the people of New York would be burned, battered, crushed, and irradiated in every conceivable way. The city and its people would be mingled in a smoldering heap. And then, as the fires started, the survivors (most of whom would be on the periphery of the explosion) would be driven to abandon to the flames those family members and other people who were unable to flee, or else to die with them. Before long, while the ruins burned, the processions of injured, mute people would begin their slow progress out of the outskirts of the devastated zone.... 21

If instead of being burst in the air the bomb were burst on or near the ground in the vicinity of the Empire State Building, the overpressure would be very much greater near the center of the blast area but the range hit by a minimum of five pounds per square inch of overpressure would be less. The range of the thermal pulse would be about the same as that of the air burst. The fireball would be almost two miles across, and would engulf midtown Manhattan from Greenwich Village nearly to Central Park. Very little is known about what would happen to a city that was inside a fireball, but one would expect a good deal of what was there to be first pulverized and then melted or vaporized. Any human beings in the area would be reduced to smoke and ashes; they would simply disappear. A crater roughly three blocks in diameter and two hundred feet deep would open up. In addition, 22 heavy radioactive fallout would be created as dust and debris from the city rose with the mushroom cloud and then fell back to the ground.... Exposure to radioactivity in human beings is measured in units called rems—an acronym for "roentgen equivalent in man." The roentgen is a standard measurement of gamma- and X-ray radiation, and the expression "equivalent in man" indicates that an adjustment has been made to take into account the differences in the degree of biological damage that is caused by radiation of different types. Many of the kinds of harm done to human beings by radiation—for example, the incidence of cancer and of genetic damage—depend on the dose accumulated over many years; but radiation sickness, capable of causing death, results from an "acute" dose, received in a period of anything from a few seconds to several days. Because almost ninety percent of the so-called "infinite-time dose" of radiation from fallout—that is, the dose from a given quantity of fallout that one would receive if one lived for many thousands of years—is emitted in the first week, the one-week accumulated dose is often used as a convenient measure for calculating the immediate harm from fallout. Doses in the thousands of rems, which could be expected throughout the city, would attack the central nervous system and would bring about death within a few hours. Doses of around a thousand rems, which would be delivered some tens of miles downwind from the blast, would kill within two weeks everyone who was exposed to them. Doses of around five hundred rems, which would be delivered as far as a hundred and fifty miles downwind (given a wind speed of fifteen miles per hour), would kill half of all exposed able-bodied young adults. At this level of exposure, radiation sickness proceeds in the three stages observed at Hiroshima. The plume of lethal fallout could descend, depending on the direction of the wind, on other parts of New York State and parts of New Jersey, Pennsylvania, Delaware, Maryland, Connecticut, Massachusetts, Rhode Island, Vermont, and New Hampshire, killing additional millions of people. The circumstances in heavily contaminated areas, in which millions of people were all declining together, over a period of weeks, toward painful deaths, are ones that, like so many of the consequences of nuclear explosions, have never been experienced.

A description of the effects of a one-megaton bomb on New 23
York City gives some notion of the meaning in human terms of a
megaton of nuclear explosive power, but a weapon that is more
likely to be used against New York is the twenty-megaton bomb,
which has one thousand six hundred times the yield of the Hiroshima bomb. The Soviet Union is estimated to have at least a
hundred and thirteen twenty-megaton bombs in its nuclear arsenal, carried by Bear intercontinental bombers. In addition, some
of the Soviet SS-18 missiles are capable of carrying bombs of this
size, although the actual yields are not known. Since the explosive power of the twenty-megaton bombs greatly exceeds the
amount necessary to destroy most military targets, it is reasonable to suppose that they are meant for use against large cities. If
a twenty-megaton bomb were air-burst over the Empire State
Building at an altitude of thirty thousand feet, the zone gutted or
flattened by the blast wave would have a radius of twelve
miles...reaching from the middle of Staten Island to the northern edge of the Bronx, the eastern edge of Queens, and well into
New Jersey, and the zone of heavy damage from the blast wave
(the zone hit by a minimum of two pounds of overpressure per
square inch) would have a radius of twenty-one and a half
miles...reaching to the southernmost tip of Staten Island, north
as far as southern Rockland County, east into Nassau County,
and west to Morris County, New Jersey. The fireball would be
about four and a half miles in diameter and would radiate the
thermal pulse for some twenty seconds. People caught in the
open twenty-three miles away from ground zero, in Long Island,
New Jersey, and southern New York State, would be burned to
death....People hundreds of miles away who looked at the burst
would be temporarily blinded and would risk permanent eye
injury....The mushroom cloud would be seventy miles in diameter. New York City and its suburbs would be transformed into a
lifeless, flat, scorched desert in a few seconds.

If a twenty-megaton bomb were ground-burst on the Em- 24
pire State Building, the range of severe blast damage would, as

with the one-megaton ground blast, be reduced, but the fireball...would cover Manhattan from Wall Street to northern Central Park and also parts of New Jersey, Brooklyn, and Queens, and everyone within it would be instantly killed, with most of them physically disappearing. Fallout would again be generated, this time covering thousands of square miles with lethal intensities of radiation. A fair portion of New York City and its incinerated population, now radioactive dust, would have risen into the mushroom cloud and would now be descending on the surrounding territory.... [I]f the wind carried the fallout onto populated areas, then this one bomb would probably doom upward of twenty million people, or almost ten percent of the population of the United States.

1982

The Iks

Lewis Thomas

The small tribe of Iks, formerly nomadic hunters and gatherers in the mountain valleys of northern Uganda, have become celebrities, literary symbols for the ultimate fate of disheartened, heartless mankind at large. Two disastrously conclusive things happened to them: the government decided to have a national park, so they were compelled by law to give up hunting in the valleys and become farmers on poor hillside soil, and then they were visited for two years by an anthropologist who detested them and wrote a book about them.

The message of the book is that the Iks have transformed themselves into an irreversibly disagreeable collection of unattached, brutish creatures, totally selfish and loveless, in response to the dismantling of their traditional culture. Moreover, this is what the rest of us are like in our inner selves, and we will all turn into Iks when the structure of our society comes all unhinged.

The argument rests, of course, on certain assumptions   3 about the core of human beings, and is necessarily speculative. You have to agree in advance that man is fundamentally a bad lot, out for himself alone, displaying such graces as affection and compassion only as learned habits. If you take this view, the story of the Iks can be used to confirm it. These people seem to be living together, clustered in small, dense villages, but they are really solitary, unrelated individuals with no evident use for each other. They talk, but only to make ill-tempered demands and cold refusals. They share nothing. They never sing. They turn the children out to forage as soon as they can walk, and desert the elders to starve whenever they can, and the foraging children snatch food from the mouths of the helpless elders. It is a mean society.

They breed without love or even casual regard. They defe-   4 cate on each other's doorsteps. They watch their neighbors for signs of misfortune, and only then do they laugh. In the book they do a lot of laughing, having so much bad luck. Several times they even laughed at the anthropologist, who found this especially repellent (one senses, between the lines, that the scholar is not himself the world's luckiest man). Worse, they took him into the family, snatched his food, defecated on his doorstep, and hooted dislike at him. They gave him two bad years.

It is a depressing book. If, as he suggests, there is only Ik-   5 ness at the center of each of us, our sole hope for hanging onto the name of humanity will be in endlessly mending the structure of our society, and it is changing so quickly and completely that we may never find the threads in time. Meanwhile, left to ourselves alone, solitary, we will become the same joyless, zestless, untouching lone animals.

But this may be too narrow a view. For one thing, the Iks   6 are extraordinary. They are absolutely astonishing, in fact. The anthropologist has never seen people like them anywhere, nor have I. You'd think, if they were simply examples of the common essence of mankind, they'd seem more recognizable. Instead, they are bizarre, anomalous. I have known my share of peculiar, difficult, nervous, grabby people, but I've never encountered any genuinely, consistently detestable human beings in all my life. The Iks sound more like abnormalities, maladies.

I cannot accept it. I do not believe that the Iks are repre- 7
sentative of isolated, revealed man, unobscured by social habits. I believe their behavior is something extra, something laid on. This unremitting, compulsive repellence is a kind of complicated ritual. They must have learned to act this way; they copied it, somehow.

I have a theory, then. The Iks have gone crazy. 8

The solitary Ik, isolated in the ruins of an exploded culture, 9
has built a new defense for himself. If you live in an unworkable society you can make up one of your own, and this is what the Iks have done. Each Ik has become a group, a one-man tribe on its own, a constituency.

Now everything falls into place. This is why they do seem, 10
after all, vaguely familiar to all of us. We've seen them before. This is precisely the way groups of one size or another, ranging from committees to nations, behave. It is, of course, this aspect of humanity that has lagged behind the rest of evolution, and this is why the Ik seems so primitive. In his absolute selfishness, his incapacity to give anything away, no matter what, he is a successful committee. When he stands at the door of his hut, shouting insults at his neighbors in a loud harangue, he is a city addressing another city.

Cities have all the Ik characteristics. They defecate on door- 11
steps, in rivers and lakes, their own or anyone else's. They leave rubbish. They detest all neighboring cities, give nothing away. They even build institutions for deserting elders out of sight.

Nations are the most Iklike of all. No wonder the Iks seem 12
familiar. For total greed, rapacity, heartlessness, and irresponsibility there is nothing to match a nation. Nations, by law, are solitary, self-centered, withdrawn into themselves. There is no such thing as affection between nations, and certainly no nation ever loved another. They bawl insults from their doorsteps, defecate into whole oceans, snatch all the food, survive by detestation, take joy in the bad luck of others, celebrate the death of others, live for the death of others.

That's it, and I shall stop worrying about the book. It 13
does not signify that man is a sparse, inhuman thing at his center. He's all right. It only says what we've always known and
never had enough time to worry about, that we haven't yet
learned how to stay human when assembled in masses. The Ik,
in his despair, is acting out this failure, and perhaps we should
pay closer attention. Nations have themselves become too
frightening to think about, but we might learn some things by
watching these people.

1974

Art and the State in South Africa
Nadine Gordimer

I once wrote that the best way to write was to do so as if 1
one were already dead: afraid of no one's reactions, answerable
to no one for one's views. I still think that is the way to write.
Insofar as no one forces a writer to visualize an "audience" (unless he has one eye on the bank), to imagine who it is who is going to be moved, shocked, delighted, incensed or perhaps illumi-
nated by the piece of work in hand, it is possible to keep to this
ideal of a writer's freedom. But in the circumstances of political
and social pressure applicable to writers under consideration at
our conference, this basis of the writer's basic freedom is belea-
guered from without and psychologically threatened from within.

In the society in which I live and work—apartheid South 2
Africa—the legal framework of censorship affects the work even
of dead writers, so there's no freedom to be gained there, in my
dictum of writing as if from beyond the grave. A banned work
remains banned, even if the writer is no longer living, just as it
does in the case of the exiled writer, who is alive but civically
"dead" in his own country.

Censorship of literature is procured chiefly by two statutes,   3
the Internal Security Act of 1950 and the Publications Act No. 42
of 1974. Together those statutes aim to insure that the South African reader is deprived not only of sexually titillating magazines,
books and films but also of serious works that question, radically, the institutions and practices of a society based on racial
discrimination. Together those statutes are designed to preserve
political orthodoxy according to the ruling color and class by iso-
lating the public from radical political thought and contemporary
literary trends.

The Internal Security Act is aimed at suppressing overtly   4
political writing, but its legislative tentacles have also stran-
gled a substantial body of creative writing, since in the words
of Thomas Mann, in some eras and some countries, "politics
is fate," and imaginative writing has always been occupied, in
one interpretation or another, with human fate. The Internal
Security Act functions as a censor by providing for the banning of both publications *and* writers. In the first instance, the
act authorizes the banning of any publication that expresses
views "calculated to further the achievement of any of the objects of communism." That "any" means that the precepts of
human rights common to the spectrum of progressive thought,
from liberalism to communism, are lumped together, along with
the actual advocacy of violent overthrow of the state, under the
general heading of subversion.

It was under this act that the moderate, wide-circulation   5
black daily newspaper the *World* was banned in 1977. The rele-
vant clause invoked stated that the newspaper had served "as a
means for expressing views or conveying information the publication of which is calculated to endanger the security of the State
or the maintenance of public order." What the *World* had indeed
been publishing was an accurate account of the actions and state
of mind of the black population of South Africa, and of Soweto in
particular, in the year of school boycotts that followed the black
children's and students' uprising against second-class education in
1976, and in the labor unrest which gathered momentum in 1977.

Other provisions of the act have the power to impose a ban   6
not merely on a single publication such as the *World* but on *all*

the utterances as well as the writings of certain individuals. Persons whose views may not be quoted at all in South Africa in terms of Section II of the act fall into several categories. First, members of organizations outlawed under the Internal Security Act; second, persons banned by the Minister of Justice, under Section 9, from attending gatherings, on the ground that they have engaged in activities that further the achievement of any of the objects of communism. In the 1960s, a whole generation of black South African writers living abroad were listed under a third category, which bans former residents of South Africa who, again in the opinion of the Minister of Justice, "advocate or engage in activities abroad calculated to further the achievement of any of the objects of communism." The writers include Alex La Guma, Dennis Brutus, Ezekiel Mphahlele and the late Can Themba. Of them, only the works of Mphahlele, with the passage of time and his return to South Africa under a restricted academic dispensation, have been released from this ban. A few white writers in exile, notably Albie Sachs and Mary Benson, are prevented from being read in South Africa by a similar type of ban.

With the rise, during the 1970s, of the Black Consciousness 7 movement, with its emphasis on the cultural arm of the black struggle for human rights, a number of young black writers and aspiring writers have been prevented from publishing their work because they are banned under Section 9, which forbids their attendance at gatherings. A ban of this nature would seem to have little to do with writers, since they don't do their writing at public gatherings. But these young writers see their literary activity as an integral part of their political activity. Most are active as speakers at political meetings and as poets or short-story writers at home. If the ban that prevents them from attending gatherings usually is imposed not because of anything they have written but because of their platform or organizational activity, or the part they have played in boycotts or strikes, nevertheless that ban falls upon their writings, since it implies that nothing they say or write may be quoted or published. Thus, a fairy tale or a love poem by one of these writers may not be published any more than a political statement one of them may have made.

Other writers are silenced by a ban in the first category of 8

Section II because they are or are alleged to be members of organizations outlawed under the Internal Security Act. Since 1976, this has meant the Christian Institute, a non-racial radical church organization, as well as the various Black Consciousness movements and, of course, the mass liberatory movements of the 1950s and 1960s—the A.N.C. (African National Congress) and P.A.C. (Pan-African Congress). Among individuals recently banned are Zwelakhe Sisulu (prominent journalist and son of Walter Sisulu, a great A.N.C. leader imprisoned with Nelson Mandela on Robben Island), Phil Mtimkulu, Joe Thloloe, Charles Ngakula, Mathatha Tsedu, Mari Subramoney, Vuyisile Mdleleni, all journalists and/or writers. Amanda Kwadi was detained for some weeks and released just before I left South Africa a month ago.

Needless to say, South Africa's infamous practice of deten- **9** tion without trial has effectively silenced various black writers, sometimes for long periods. Of those who have been brought to trial, few have been charged on the evidence of their writings, with the notable exception of the famous SASO (South African Students Organization) trial in the 1970s, when the chief evidence was plays and poems written by some of the accused. Yet all detained writers without exception are prevented from writing; some, released without ever having been charged with any offense, are nevertheless served with bans upon their release, which then silence them outside prison as well. All prohibitions under the Internal Security Act are characterized by the absoluteness of their terms and by the arbitrary nature of their imposition.

The Publications Act of 1974 replaces the Publications and **10** Entertainments Act of 1963, which banned not only books by South African writers but also books by Edmund Wilson, Mary McCarthy, Philip Roth and John Updike, in addition to those by writers one might expect, such as Eldridge Cleaver and Franz Fanon. Under the old legislation, writers were banned by a Publications Control Board, but they had a right to appeal to South Africa's Supreme Court. Although relatively few appeals against the board's decisions were brought into court, a number of its decisions were reversed by the Supreme Court. This led to the present Publications Act, which excludes the right of appeal to the court. Under this act, Kurt Vonnegut is one of the most recent American writers to join the list of foreign writers banned in South Africa.

The 1974 act established a government-appointed Director- 11 ate of Publications, which is responsible for the overall administration of the act. The directorate appoints committees which are given the task of deciding whether publications, objects, films and public entertainment referred to them by the directorate are "undesirable" within the meaning of the act. Appeals can be made only to the Appeal Board set up by the directorate itself.

"Undesirability" is defined thus: 12

A publication, object, film or public entertainment is 13 deemed undesirable if it:

is indecent or obscene or is offensive or harmful to public 14 morals;

is blasphemous or is offensive to the religious convictions 15 or feelings of any section of the inhabitants of the Republic;

if it is harmful to the relations between any sections of the 16 inhabitants of the Republic;

if it is prejudicial to the safety of the State, the general wel- 17 fare or the peace and good order of the State.

In the application of the act, it is laid down that "particular 18 regard" is to be paid to "the constant endeavor of the population of the Republic of South Africa to uphold a Christian view of life"—this in a population where there exist the claims of traditional African, Moslem, Hindu and Jewish religious and secular moralities. Moreover, for the purpose of determining undesirability, the motive of the author is irrelevant. A work may be found undesirable if *any part of it* is undesirable—a principle that reached its apogee when a Gore Vidal novel was banned on the ground that one passage compared the Holy Trinity to male genitalia.

The production and distribution of works declared undesir- 19 able is a criminal offense. Sexual candor aside, the most dangerous ground the writer treads is in the area of open or implied criticism of the institutions of state (in particular the police and defense), the administration of justice and the politico-legal apparatus of so-called separate development for people of different colors; in the sympathetic treatment of black liberation movements and radical opponents of the status quo; and in explicit accounts of interracial sexual relations. More and more in the last five years, sympathetic or even simply honest treatment of black liberation movements and the activities of all other radical opponents, of all colors, of the union between capitalism and racial oppression in South Africa have increasingly become the areas to which censorship reacts most strongly.

Under the strictures of these repressive acts, how does a **20** writer work?

In the twenty years since censorship was introduced in **21** South Africa, writers' attitudes have changed to meet it in different ways, and in relation to the different contexts of their lives in a grossly unequal society.

At the beginning, black writers were little interested in cen- **22** sorship. White writers were concerned with the one area where apartheid limited the lives of black and white alike, but black writers saw the suppression of freedom of expression as the least tangible and therefore the least of the different aspects of oppression experienced in their daily lives. Without freedom to sell their labor, without freedom of movement, without freedom of association—in a phrase, "with the passbook in their pockets"— the risk of having a book banned seemed trivial. At the beginning of the 1960s, it was difficult to get black intellectuals to sign protests against censorship. But after the banning of the black mass movements with their populist appeal, the renaissance of the black spirit of liberation was cupped in the hands of young blacks who saw, in a police state situation where overt political consciousness-raising was impossible, the importance of cultural consciencization. They looked to writers to imbue the new generation with a sense of identity and pride in that identity through song and story rather than taboo political doctrine. They saw those writers, as I have already said, as the cultural fist of liberation. It was then that censorship no longer seemed irrelevant. This coincided, roughly, with a hardening in the attitude of progressive white writers, who changed their tactic of, in a sense, co-operating with the hated censorship by appealing when a book was banned to the tactic of noncooperation with any functions of censorship. The principle of "publish and be damned" ran up its flag.

That principle has been implemented, to a surprising ex- 23 tent, by the formation of small publishing houses, mainly by people who are themselves writers. These publishers, unlike the rich British publishers operating as a fossilized colonial outpost in South Africa, were prepared to lose the little money they had if a book should be banned from sale, in the hope that at least some copies would be circulated before the ax fell. That is the way many books reach readers in South Africa today, and the way in which writers tread the dangerous ground of subjects I have referred to.

Conscious and unconscious self-censorship and stylistic de- 24 fenses are questions with which I have already dealt. There remains to be said that as the situation in South Africa has become more and more crisis-ridden, painful and dangerous, the fear that prompted self-censorship has been cast out. And so something of the writer's innate freedom has been regained.

1983

9

Analogy

The Myth of the Cave
Plato

And now, I said, let me show in a figure how far our na- 1
ture is enlightened or unenlightened:—Behold! human beings
living in an underground den, which has a mouth open toward
the light and reaching all along the den; here they have been
from their childhood, and have their legs and necks chained so
that they cannot move, and can only see before them, being
prevented by the chains from turning round their heads.
Above and behind them a fire is blazing at a distance, and between the fire and the prisoners there is a raised way; and you
will see, if you look, a low wall built along the way, like the
screen which marionette players have in front of them, over
which they show the puppets.

I see. 2

And do you see, I said, men passing along the wall carrying 3
all sorts of vessels, and statues and figures of animals made of
wood and stone and various materials, which appear over the
wall? Some of them are talking, others silent.

You have shown me a strange image, and they are strange 4
prisoners.

Like ourselves, I replied; and they see only their own shad- 5 ows, or the shadows of one another, which the fire throws on the opposite wall of the cave?

True, he said; how could they see anything but the shadows 6 if they were never allowed to move their heads?

And of the objects which are being carried in like manner 7 they would only see the shadows?

Yes, he said. 8

And if they were able to converse with one another, would 9 they not suppose that they were naming what was actually before them?

Very true. 10

And suppose further that the prison had an echo which 11 came from the other side, would they not be sure to fancy when one of the passers-by spoke that the voice which they heard came from the passing shadow?

No question, he replied. 12

To them, I said, the truth would be literally nothing but the 13 shadows of the images.

That is certain. 14

And now look again, and see what will naturally follow if 15 the prisoners are released and disabused of their error. At first, when any of them is liberated and compelled suddenly to stand up and turn his neck round and walk and look toward the light, he will suffer sharp pains; the glare will distress him, and he will be unable to see the realities of which in his former state he had seen the shadows; and then conceive some one saying to him, that what he saw before was an illusion, but that now, when he is approaching nearer to being and his eye is turned toward more real existence, he has a clearer vision—what will be his reply? And you may further imagine that his instructor is pointing to the objects as they pass and requiring him to name them—will he not be perplexed? Will he not fancy that the shadows which he formerly saw are truer than the objects which are now shown to him?

Far truer. 16

And if he is compelled to look straight at the light, will he 17 not have a pain in his eyes which will make him turn away to take refuge in the objects of vision which he can see, and which

he will conceive to be in reality clearer than the things which are
now being shown to him?

True, he said.   18

And suppose once more, that he is reluctantly dragged up a 19
steep and rugged ascent, and held fast until he is forced into the
presence of the sun himself, is he not likely to be pained and irritated? When he approaches the light his eyes will be dazzled,
and he will not be able to see anything at all of what are now
called realities.

Not all in a moment, he said.   20

He will require to grow accustomed to the sight of the up- 21
per world. And first he will see the shadows best, next the reflections of men and other objects in the water, and then the objects
themselves; then he will gaze upon the light of the moon and the
stars and the spangled heaven; and he will see the sky and the stars
by night better than the sun or the light of the sun by day?

Certainly.   22

Last of all he will be able to see the sun, and not mere re- 23
flections of him in the water, but he will see him in his own
proper place, and not in another; and he will contemplate him as
he is.

Certainly.   24

He will then proceed to argue that this is he who gives the 25
season and the years, and is the guardian of all that is in the visible world, and in a certain way the cause of all things which he
and his fellows have been accustomed to behold?

Clearly, he said, he would first see the sun and then reason 26
about him.

And when he remembered his old habitation, and the wis- 27
dom of the den and his fellow-prisoners, do you not suppose that
he would felicitate himself on the change, and pity them?

Certainly, he would.   28

And if they were in the habit of conferring honors among 29
themselves on those who were quickest to observe the passing
shadows and to remark which of them went before, and which
followed after, and which were together; and who were therefore
best able to draw conclusions as to the future, do you think that

he would care for such honors and glories, or envy the possess-
ors of them? Would he not say with Homer,

Better to be the poor servant of a poor master,

and to endure anything, rather than think as they do and live after their manner?

Yes, he said, I think that he would rather suffer anything 30
than entertain these false notions and live in this miserable
manner.

Imagine once more, I said, such a one coming suddenly out 31
of the sun to be replaced in his old situation; would he not be
certain to have his eyes full of darkness?

To be sure, he said.   32

And if there were a contest, and he had to compete in mea- 33
suring the shadows with the prisoners who had never moved out
of the den, while his sight was still weak, and before his eyes had
become steady (and the time which would be needed to acquire
this new habit of sight might be very considerable), would he not
be ridiculous? Men would say of him that up he went and down
he came without his eyes; and that it was better not even to think
of ascending; and if any one tried to loose another and lead him
up to the light, let them only catch the offender, and they would
put him to death.

No question, he said.   34

This entire allegory, I said, you may now append, dear 35
Glaucon, to the previous argument; the prison-house is the world
of sight, the light of the fire is the sun, and you will not misap-
prehend me if you interpret the journey upwards to be the ascent
of the soul into the intellectual world according to my poor belief, which, at your desire, I have expressed—whether rightly or
wrongly God knows. But, whether true or false, my opinion is
that in the world of knowledge the idea of good appears last of
all, and is seen only with an effort; and, when seen, is also inferred to be the universal author of all things beautiful and right,
parent of light and of the lord of light in this visible world, and
the immediate source of reason and truth in the intellectual; and

that this is the power upon which he who would act rationally either in public or private life must have his eye fixed.

I agree, he said, as far as I am able to understand you.   36

Moreover, I said, you must not wonder that those who at- 37 tain to this beatific vision are unwilling to descend to human affairs; for their souls are ever hastening into the upper world where they desire to dwell; which desire of theirs is very natural, if our allegory may be trusted.

Yes, very natural.   38

And is there anything surprising in one who passes from di- 39 vine contemplations to the evil state of man, misbehaving himself in a ridiculous manner; if, while his eyes are blinking and before he has become accustomed to the surrounding darkness, he is compelled to fight in courts of law, or in other places, about the images or the shadows of images of justice, and is endeavoring to meet the conceptions of those who have never yet seen absolute justice?

Anything but surprising, he replied.   40

Any one who has common sense will remember that the be- 41 wilderments of the eyes are of two kinds, and arise from two causes, either from coming out of the light or from going into the light, which is true of the mind's eye, quite as much as of the bodily eye; and he who remembers this when he sees any one whose vision is perplexed and weak, will not be too ready to laugh; he will first ask whether that soul of man has come out of the brighter life, and is unable to see because unaccustomed to the dark, or having turned from darkness to the day is dazzled by excess of light. And he will count the one happy in his condition and state of being, and he will pity the other; or, if he have a mind to laugh at the soul which comes from below into the light, there will be more reason in this than in the laugh which greets him who returns from above out of the light into the den.

That, he said, is a very just distinction.   42

ca. 373 B.C.

Body Ritual among the Nacirema
Horace Miner

The anthropologist has become so familiar with the diver- 1
sity of ways in which different peoples behave in similar situa-
tions that he is not apt to be surprised by even the most exotic
customs. In fact, if all of the logically possible combinations of
behavior have not been found somewhere in the world, he is apt
to suspect that they must be present in some yet undescribed
tribe. This point has, in fact, been expressed with respect to clan
organization by Murdock.[1] In this light, the magical beliefs and
practices of the Nacirema present such unusual aspects that it
seems desirable to describe them as an example of the extremes
to which human behavior can go.

Professor Linton first brought the ritual of the Nacirema to 2
the attention of anthropologists twenty years ago, but the culture
of this people is still very poorly understood. They are a North
American group living in the territory between the Canadian
Cree, the Yaqui and Tarahumare of Mexico, and the Carib and
Arawak of the Antilles.[2] Little is known of their origin, although
tradition states that they came from the east....

Nacirema culture is characterized by a highly developed 3
market economy which has evolved in a rich natural habitat.
While much of the people's time is devoted to economic pur-
suits, a large part of the fruits of these labors and a considerable
portion of the day are spent in ritual activity. The focus of this
activity is the human body, the appearance and health of which
loom as a dominant concern in the ethos of the people. While
such a concern is certainly not unusual, its ceremonial aspects
and associated philosophy are unique.

The fundamental belief underlying the whole system ap- 4

[1] American anthropologist George Peter Murdock (b. 1897), authority on primitive cultures.

[2] Native American tribes formerly inhabiting the Saskatchewan region of Canada, the Sonora region of Mexico, and the West Indies.

pears to be that the human body is ugly and that its natural tendency is to debility and disease. Incarcerated in such a body, man's only hope is to avert these characteristics through the use of the powerful influences of ritual and ceremony. Every household has one or more shrines devoted to this purpose. The more powerful individuals in the society have several shrines in their houses and, in fact, the opulence of a house is often referred to in terms of the number of such ritual centers it possesses. Most houses are of wattle and daub construction, but the shrine rooms of the more wealthy are walled with stone. Poorer families imitate the rich by applying pottery plaques to their shrine walls.

While each family has at least one such shrine, the rituals 5 associated with it are not family ceremonies but are private and secret. The rites are normally only discussed with children, and then only during the period when they are being initiated into these mysteries. I was able, however, to establish sufficient rapport with the natives to examine these shrines and to have the rituals described to me.

The focal point of the shrine is a box or chest which is built 6 into the wall. In this chest are kept the many charms and magical potions without which no native believes he could live. These preparations are secured from a variety of specialized practitioners. The most powerful of these are the medicine men, whose assistance must be rewarded with substantial gifts. However, the medicine men do not provide the curative potions for their clients, but decide what the ingredients should be and then write them down in an ancient and secret language. This writing is understood only by the medicine men and by the herbalists who, for another gift, provide the required charm.

The charm is not disposed of after it has served its purpose, 7 but is placed in the charm-box of the household shrine. As these magical materials are specific for certain ills, and the real or imagined maladies of the people are many, the charm-box is usually full to overflowing. The magical packets are so numerous that people forget what their purposes were and fear to use them again. While the natives are very vague on this point, we can only assume that the idea in retaining all the old magical materials is that their presence in the charm-box, before which the body rituals are conducted, will in some way protect the worshipper.

Beneath the charm-box is a small font. Each day every **8** member of the family, in succession, enters the shrine room, bows his head before the charm-box, mingles different sorts of holy water in the font, and proceeds with a brief rite of ablution. The holy waters are secured from the Water Temple of the community, where the priests conduct elaborate ceremonies to make the liquid ritually pure.

In the hierarchy of magical practitioners, and below the **9** medicine men in prestige, are specialists whose designation is best translated "holy-mouth-men." The Nacirema have an almost pathological horror of and fascination with the mouth, the condition of which is believed to have a supernatural influence on all social relationships. Were it not for the rituals of the mouth, they believe that their teeth would fall out, their gums bleed, their jaws shrink, their friends desert them, and their lovers reject them. They also believe that a strong relationship exists between oral and moral characteristics. For example, there is a ritual ablution of the mouth for children which is supposed to improve their moral fiber.

The daily body ritual performed by everyone includes a **10** mouth-rite. Despite the fact that these people are so punctilious about care of the mouth, this rite involves a practice which strikes the uninitiated stranger as revolting. It was reported to me that the ritual consists of inserting a small bundle of hog hairs into the mouth, along with certain magical powders, and then moving the bundle in a highly formalized series of gestures.

In addition to the private mouth-rite, the people seek out a **11** holy-mouth-man once or twice a year. These practitioners have an impressive set of paraphernalia, consisting of a variety of augers, awls, probes, and prods. The use of these objects in the exorcism of the evils of the mouth involves almost unbelievable ritual torture of the client. The holy-mouth-man opens the client's mouth and, using the above mentioned tools, enlarges any holes which decay may have created in the teeth. Magical materials are put into these holes. If there are not naturally occurring holes in the teeth, large sections of one or more teeth are gouged out so that the supernatural substance can be applied. In the client's view, the purpose of these ministrations is to arrest decay and to draw friends. The extremely sacred and traditional character of the rite is evident in the fact that the natives return to the holy-mouth-men year after year, despite the fact that their teeth continue to decay.

It is to be hoped that, when a thorough study of the Nacir- 12 ema is made, there will be careful inquiry into the personality structure of these people. One has but to watch the gleam in the eye of a holy-mouth-man, as he jabs an awl into an exposed nerve, to suspect that a certain amount of sadism is involved. If this can be established, a very interesting pattern emerges, for most of the population shows definite masochistic tendencies. It was to these that Professor Linton referred in discussing a distinctive part of the daily body ritual which is performed only by men. This part of the rite involves scraping and lacerating the surface of the face with a sharp instrument. Special women's rites are performed only four times during each lunar month, but what they lack in frequency is made up in barbarity. As part of this ceremony, women bake their heads in small ovens for about an hour. The theoretically interesting point is that what seems to be a preponderantly masochistic people have developed sadistic specialists.

The medicine men have an imposing temple, or latipso, in 13 every community of any size. The more elaborate ceremonies required to treat very sick patients can only be performed at this temple. These ceremonies involve not only the thaumaturge but a permanent group of vestal maidens who move sedately about the temple chambers in distinctive costume and headdress.

The latipso ceremonies are so harsh that it is phenomenal 14 that a fair proportion of the really sick natives who enter the temple ever recover. Small children whose indoctrination is still incomplete have been known to resist attempts to take them to the temple because "that is where you go to die." Despite this fact, sick adults are not only willing but eager to undergo the protracted ritual purification, if they can afford to do so. No matter how ill the supplicant or how grave the emergency, the guardians of many temples will not admit a client if he cannot give a rich gift to the custodian. Even after one has gained admission and survived the ceremonies, the guardians will not permit the neophyte to leave until he makes still another gift.

The supplicant entering the temple is first stripped of all his 15 or her clothes. In everyday life the Nacirema avoids exposure of his body and its natural functions. Bathing and excretory acts are performed only in the secrecy of the household shrine, where they are ritualized as part of the body-rites. Psychological shock results from the fact that body secrecy is suddenly lost upon entry into the latipso. A man, whose own wife has never seen him in an excretory act, suddenly finds himself naked and assisted by a vestal maiden while he performs his natural functions into a sacred vessel. This sort of ceremonial treatment is necessitated by the fact that the excreta are used by a diviner to ascertain the course and nature of the client's sickness. Female clients, on the other hand, find their naked bodies are subjected to the scrutiny, manipulation and prodding of the medicine men.

Few supplicants in the temple are well enough to do any- 16 thing but lie on their hard beds. The daily ceremonies, like the rites of the holy-mouth-men, involve discomfort and torture. With ritual precision, the vestals awaken their miserable charges each dawn and roll them about on their beds of pain while performing ablutions, in the formal movements of which the maidens are highly trained. At other times they insert magic wands in the supplicant's mouth or force him to eat substances which are supposed to be healing. From time to time the medicine men come to their clients and jab magically treated needles into their flesh. The fact that these temple ceremonies may not cure, and may even kill the neophyte, in no way decreases the people's faith in the medicine men.

There remains one other kind of practitioner, known as a 17 "listener." This witchdoctor has the power to exorcise the devils that lodge in the heads of people who have been bewitched. The Nacirema believe that parents bewitch their own children. Mothers are particularly suspected of putting a curse on children while teaching them the secret body rituals. The counter-magic of the witchdoctor is unusual in its lack of ritual. The patient simply tells the "listener" all his troubles and fears, beginning with the earliest difficulties he can remember. The memory displayed by the Nacirema in these exorcism sessions is truly remarkable. It is not uncommon for the patient to bemoan the rejection he felt upon being weaned as a babe, and a few individuals even see their troubles going back to the traumatic effects of their own birth.

In conclusion, mention must be made of certain practices 18 which have their base in native esthetics but which depend upon the pervasive aversion to the natural body and its functions. There are ritual fasts to make fat people thin and ceremonial feasts to make thin people fat. Still other rites are used to make women's breasts larger if they are small, and smaller if they are large. General dissatisfaction with breast shape is symbolized in the fact that the ideal form is virtually outside the range of human variation. A few women afflicted with almost inhuman hyper-mammary development are so idolized that they make a hand-some living by simply going from village to village and permitting the natives to stare at them for a fee.

Reference has already been made to the fact that excretory 19 functions are ritualized, routinized, and relegated to secrecy. Natural reproductive functions are similarly distorted. Inter-course is taboo as a topic and scheduled as an act. Efforts are made to avoid pregnancy by the use of magical materials or by limiting intercourse to certain phases of the moon. Conception is actually very infrequent. When pregnant, women dress so as to hide their condition. Parturition takes place in secret, without friends or relatives to assist, and the majority of women do not nurse their infants.

Our review of the ritual life of the Nacirema has certainly 20 shown them to be a magic-ridden people. It is hard to understand how they have managed to exist so long under the burdens which they have imposed upon themselves. But even such exotic cus-toms as these take on real meaning when they are viewed with the insight provided by Malinowski when he wrote:

"Looking from far and above, from our high places of 21 safety in the developed civilization, it is easy to see all the cru-dity and irrelevance of magic. But without its power and guid-ance early man could not have mastered his practical difficulties as he has done, nor could man have advanced to the higher stages of civilization.''

1956

Transfiguration
Annie Dillard

I live on northern Puget Sound, in Washington State, alone. 1
I have a gold cat, who sleeps on my legs, named Small. In the morning I joke to her blank face, Do you remember last night? Do you remember? I throw her out before breakfast, so I can eat.

There is a spider, too, in the bathroom, with whom I keep a 2
sort of company. Her little outfit always reminds me of a certain moth I helped to kill. The spider herself is of uncertain lineage, bulbous at the abdomen and drab. Her six-inch mess of a web works, works somehow, works miraculously, to keep her alive and me amazed. The web itself is in a corner behind the toilet, connecting tile wall to tile wall and floor, in a place where there is, I would have thought, scant traffic. Yet under the web are sixteen or so corpses she has tossed to the floor.

The corpses appear to be mostly sow bugs, those little ar- 3
madillo creatures who live to travel flat out in houses, and die round. There is also a new shred of earwig, three old spider skins crinkled and clenched, and two moth bodies, wingless and huge and empty, moth bodies I drop to my knees to see.

Today the earwig shines darkly and gleams, what there is of 4
him: a dorsal curve of thorax and abdomen, and a smooth pair of cerci by which I knew his name. Next week, if the other bodies are any indication, he will be shrunken and gray, webbed to the floor with dust. The sow bugs beside him are hollow and empty of color, fragile, a breath away from brittle fluff. The spider skins

lie on their sides, translucent and ragged, their legs drying in knots. And the moths, the empty moths, stagger against each other, headless, in a confusion of arching strips of chitin like peeling varnish, like a jumble of buttresses for cathedral domes, like nothing resembling moths, so that I should hesitate to call them moths, except that I have had some experience with the figure Moth reduced to a nub.

Two summers ago I was camping alone in the Blue Ridge   5
Mountains in Virginia. I had hauled myself and gear up there to read, among other things, James Ramsey Ullman's *The Day on Fire,* a novel about Rimbaud that had made me want to be a writer when I was sixteen; I was hoping it would do it again. So I read, lost, every day sitting under a tree by my tent, while warblers swung in the leaves overhead and bristle worms trailed their inches over the twiggy dirt at my feet; and I read every night by candlelight, while barred owls called in the forest and pale moths massed round my head in the clearing, where my light made a ring.

Moths kept flying into the candle. They would hiss and re-   6
coil, lost upside down in the shadows among my cooking pans. Or they would singe their wings and fall, and their hot wings, as if melted, would stick to the first thing they touched—a pan, a lid, a spoon—so that the snagged moths could flutter only in tiny arcs, unable to struggle free. These I could release by a quick flip with a stick; in the morning I would find my cooking stuff gilded with torn flecks of moth wings, triangles of shiny dust here and there on the aluminum. So I read, and boiled water, and replenished candles, and read on.

One night a moth flew into the candle, was caught, burnt   7
dry, and held. I must have been staring at the candle, or maybe I looked up when a shadow crossed my page; at any rate, I saw it all. A golden female moth, a biggish one with a two-inch wing-span, flapped into the fire, dropped her abdomen into the wet wax, stuck, flamed, frazzled and fried in a second. Her moving wings ignited like tissue paper, enlarging the circle of light in the clearing and creating out of the darkness the sudden blue sleeves of my sweater, the green leaves of jewelweed by my side, the ragged red trunk of a pine. At once the light contracted again and

the moth's wings vanished in a fine, foul smoke. At the same time her six legs clawed, curled, blackened, and ceased, disappearing utterly. And her head jerked in spasms, making a spattering noise; her antennae crisped and burned away and her heaving mouth parts crackled like pistol fire. When it was all over, her head was, so far as I could determine, gone, gone the long way of her wings and legs. Had she been new, or old? Had she mated and laid her eggs, had she done her work? All that was left was the glowing horn shell of her abdomen and thorax—a fraying, partially collapsed gold tube jammed upright in the candle's round pool.

And then this moth-essence, this spectacular skeleton, began to act as a wick. She kept burning. The wax rose in the moth's body from her soaking abdomen to her thorax to the jagged hole where her head should be, and widened into flame, a saffron-yellow flame that robed her to the ground like any immolating monk. That candle had two wicks, two flames of identical height, side by side. The moth's head was fire. She burned for two hours, until I blew her out.   8

She burned for two hours without changing, without bending or leaning—only glowing within, like a building fire glimpsed through silhouetted walls, like a hollow saint, like a flame-faced virgin gone to God, while I read by her light, kindled, while Rimbaud in Paris burnt out his brains in a thousand poems, while night pooled wetly at my feet.   9

And that is why I believe those hollow crisps on the bathroom floor are moths. I think I know moths, and fragments of moths, and chips and tatters of utterly empty moths, in any state. How many of you, I asked the people in my class, which of you want to give your lives and be writers? I was trembling from coffee, or cigarettes, or the closeness of faces all around me. (Is this what we live for? I thought; is this the only final beauty: the color of any skin in any light, and living, human eyes?) All hands rose to the question. (You, Nick? Will you? Margaret? Randy? Why do I want them to mean it?) And then I tried to tell them what the choice must mean: you can't be anything else. You must go at your life with a broadax.... They had no idea what I was saying. (I have two hands, don't   10

I? And all this energy, for as long as I can remember. I'll do it
in the evenings, after skiing, or on the way home from the
bank, or after the children are asleep....) They thought I was
raving again. It's just as well.

I have three candles here on the table which I disentangle   11
from the plants and light when visitors come. Small usually
avoids them, although once she came too close and her tail
caught fire; I rubbed it out before she noticed. The flames move
light over everyone's skin, draw light to the surface of the faces
of my friends. When the people leave I never blow the candles
out, and after I'm asleep they flame and burn.

1977

"But a Watch in the Night": A Scientific Fable
James C. Rettie

Out beyond our solar system there is a planet called Coper-   1
nicus. It came into existence some four or five billion years before the birth of our Earth. In due course of time it became inhabited by a race of intelligent men.

About 750 million years ago the Copernicans had developed   2
the motion picture machine to a point well in advance of the
stage that we have reached. Most of the cameras that we now
use in motion picture work are geared to take twenty-four pictures per second on a continuous strip of film. When such film is
run through a projector, it throws a series of images on the
screen and these change with a rapidity that gives the visual impression of normal movement. If a motion is too swift for the human eye to see it in detail, it can be captured and artificially
slowed down by means of the slow-motion camera. This one is
geared to take many more shots per second—ninety-six or even

more than that. When the slow motion film is projected at the normal speed of twenty-four pictures per second, we can see just how the jumping horse goes over a hurdle.

What about motion that is too slow to be seen by the human eye? That problem has been solved by the use of the time-lapse camera. In this one, the shutter is geared to take only one shot per second, or one per minute, or even one per hour—depending upon the kind of movement that is being photographed. When the time-lapse film is projected at the normal speed of twenty-four pictures per second, it is possible to see a bean sprout growing up out of the ground. Time-lapse films are useful in the study of many types of motion too slow to be observed by the unaided, human eye.

The Copernicans, it seems, had time-lapse cameras some 757 million years ago and they also had superpowered telescopes that gave them a clear view of what was happening upon this Earth. They decided to make a film record of the life history of Earth and to make it on the scale of one picture per year. The photography has been in progress during the last 757 million years.

In the near future, a Copernican interstellar expedition will arrive upon our Earth and bring with it a copy of the time-lapse film. Arrangements will be made for showing the entire film in one continuous run. This will begin at midnight of New Year's Eve and continue day and night without a single stop until midnight of December 31. The rate of projection will be twenty-four pictures per second. Time on the screen will thus seem to move at the rate of twenty-four years per second; 1440 years per minute; 86,400 years per hour; approximately two million years per day; and sixty-two million years per month. The normal lifespan of individual man will occupy about three seconds. The full period of earth history that will be unfolded on the screen (some 757 million years) will extend from what the geologists call Pre-Cambrian times up to the present. This will, by no means, cover the full time-span of the earth's geological history but it will embrace the period since the advent of living organisms.

During the months of January, February, and March the picture will be desolate and dreary. The shape of the land masses and the oceans will bear little or no resemblance to those that we know. The violence of geological erosion will be much in evidence. Rains will pour down on the land and promptly go booming down to the seas. There will be no clear streams anywhere except where the rains fall upon hard rock. Everywhere on the steeper ground the stream channels will be filled with boulders hurled down by rushing waters. Raging torrents and dry stream beds will keep alternating in quick succession. High mountains will seem to melt like so much butter in the sun. The shifting of land into the seas, later to be thrust up as new mountains, will be going on at a grand scale.

Early in April there will be some indication of the presence of single-celled living organisms in some of the warmer and sheltered coastal waters. By the end of the month it will be noticed that some of these organisms have become multicellular. A few of them, including the Trilobites, will be encased in hard shells. **7**

Toward the end of May, the first vertebrates will appear, but they will still be aquatic creatures. In June about 60 per cent of the land area that we know as North America will be under water. One broad channel will occupy the space where the Rocky Mountains now stand. Great deposits of limestone will be forming under some of the shallower seas. Oil and gas deposits will be in process of formation—also under shallow seas. On land there will still be no sign of vegetation. Erosion will be rampant, tearing loose particles and chunks of rock and grinding them into sand and silt to be spewed out by the streams into bays and estuaries. **8**

About the middle of July the first land plants will appear and take up the tremendous job of soil building. Slowly, very slowly, the mat of vegetation will spread, always battling for its life against the power of erosion. Almost foot by foot, the plant life will advance, lacing down with its root structures whatever pulverized rock material it can find. Leaves and stems will be giving added protection against the loss of the soil foothold. The increasing vegetation will pave the way for the land animals that will live upon it. **9**

Early in August the seas will be teeming with fish. This will be what geologists call the Devonian period. Some of the races of **10** these fish will be breathing by means of lung tissue instead of through gill tissues. Before the month is over, some of the lung fish will go ashore and take on a crude lizard-like appearance. Here are the first amphibians.

In early September the insects will put in their appearance. 11 Some will look like huge dragonflies and will have a wing spread of 24 inches. Large portions of the land masses will now be covered with heavy vegetation that will include the primitive spore-propagating trees. Layer upon layer of this plant growth will build up, later to appear as the coal deposits. About the middle of this month, there will be evidence of the first seed-bearing plants and the first reptiles. Heretofore, the land animals will have been amphibians that could reproduce their kind only by depositing a soft egg mass in quiet waters. The reptiles will be shown to be freed from the aquatic bond because they can reproduce by means of a shelled egg in which the embryo and its nurturing liquids are sealed and thus protected from destructive evaporation. Before September is over, the first dinosaurs will be seen—creatures destined to dominate the animal realm for about 140 million years and then to disappear.

In October there will be series of mountain uplifts along 12 what is now the eastern coast of the United States. A creature with feathered limbs—half bird and half reptile in appearance—will take itself into the air. Some small and rather unpretentious animals will be seen to bring forth their young in a form that is a miniature replica of the parents and to feed these young on milk secreted by mammary glands in the female parent. The emergence of this mammalian form of animal life will be recognized as one of the great events in geologic time. October will also witness the high water mark of the dinosaurs—creatures ranging in size from that of the modern goat to monsters like Brontosaurus that weighed some 40 tons. Most of them will be placid vegetarians, but a few will be hideous-looking carnivores, like Allosaurus and Tyrannosaurus. Some of the herbivorous dinosaurs will be clad in bony armor for protection against their flesh-eating comrades.

November will bring pictures of a sea extending from the 13 Gulf of Mexico to the Arctic in space now occupied by the

Rocky Mountains. A few of the reptiles will take to the air on
bat-like wings. One of these, called Pteranodon, will have a
wingspread of 15 feet. There will be a rapid development of the
modern flowering plants, modern trees, and modern insects. The
dinosaurs will disappear. Toward the end of the month there will
be a tremendous land disturbance in which the Rocky Mountains
will rise out of the sea to assume a dominating place in the North
American landscape.

As the picture runs on into December it will show the mam- 14
mals in command of the animal life. Seed-bearing trees and
grasses will have covered most of the land with a heavy mantle
of vegetation. Only the areas newly thrust up from the sea will be
barren. Most of the streams will be crystal clear. The turmoil of
geologic erosion will be confined to localized areas. About December 25 will begin the cutting of the Grand Canyon of the Colorado River. Grinding down through layer after layer of sedimen-
tary strata, this stream will finally expose deposits laid down in
Pre-Cambrian times. Thus in the walls of that canyon will appear
geological formations dating from recent times to the period
when the Earth had no living organisms upon it.

The picture will run on through the latter days of December 15
and even up to its final day with still no sign of mankind. The
spectators will become alarmed in the fear that man has somehow been left out. But not so; sometimes about noon on December 31 (one million years ago) will appear a stooped, massive
creature of man-like proportions. This will be Pithecanthropus,
the Java ape man. For tools and weapons he will have nothing
but crude stone and wooden clubs. His children will live a precarious existence threatened on the one side by hostile animals
and on the other by tremendous climatic changes. Ice sheets—in
places 4000 feet deep—will form in the northern parts of North
America and Eurasia. Four times this glacial ice will push southward to cover half the continents. With each advance the plant
and animal life will be swept under or pushed southward. With
each recession of the ice, life will struggle to reestablish itself in
the wake of the retreating glaciers. The woolly mammoth, the
musk ox, and the caribou all will fight to maintain themselves

near the ice line. Sometimes they will be caught and put into cold storage—skin, flesh, blood, bones and all.

The picture will run on through supper time with still very 16 little evidence of man's presence on the earth. It will be about 11 o'clock when Neanderthal man appears. Another half hour will go by before the appearance of Cro-Magnon man living in caves and painting crude animal pictures on the walls of his dwelling. Fifteen minutes more will bring Neolithic man, knowing how to chip stone and thus produce sharp cutting edges for spears and tools. In a few minutes more it will appear that man has domesticated the dog, the sheep and, possibly, other animals. He will then begin the use of milk. He will also learn the arts of basket weaving and the making of pottery and dugout canoes.

The dawn of civilization will not come until about five or 17 six minutes before the end of the picture. The story of the Egyptians, the Babylonians, the Greeks, and the Romans will unroll during the fourth, the third, and the second minute before the end. At 58 minutes and 43 seconds past 11:00 PM (just 1 minute and 17 seconds before the end) will come the beginning of the Christian era. Columbus will discover the new world 20 seconds before the end. The Declaration of Independence will be signed just 7 seconds before the final curtain comes down.

In those few moments of geologic time will be the story of 18 all that has happened since we became a nation. And what a story it will be! A human swarm will sweep across the face of the continent and take it away from the...red men. They will change it far more radically than it has ever been changed before in a comparable time. The great virgin forests will be seen going down before ax and fire. The soil, covered for eons by its protective mantle of trees and grasses, will be laid bare to the ravages of water and wind erosion. Streams that had been flowing clear will, once again, take up a load of silt and push it toward the seas. Humus and mineral salts, both vital elements of productive soil, will be seen to vanish at a terrifying rate. The railroads and highways and cities that will spring up may divert attention, but they cannot cover up the blight of man's recent activities. In great sections of Asia, it will be seen that man must utilize cow dung and every scrap of available straw or grass for fuel to cook his food. The forests that once provided wood for this purpose will be gone without a trace. The use of these agricultural wastes for fuel, in place of returning them to the land, will be leading to increasing soil impoverishment. Here and there will be seen a dust storm darkening the landscape over an area a thousand miles across. Man-creatures will be shown counting their wealth in terms of bits of printed paper representing other bits of a scarce but comparatively useless yellow metal that is kept buried in strong vaults. Meanwhile, the soil, the only real wealth that can keep mankind alive on the face of this earth is savagely being cut loose from its ancient moorings and washed into the seven seas.

We have just arrived upon this earth. How long will we stay? [19]

1950

The Cosmic Prison
Loren Eiseley

"A name is a prison, God is free," once observed the Greek poet Nikos Kazantzakis. He meant, I think, that valuable though language is to man, it is by very necessity limiting, and creates for man an invisible prison. Language implies boundaries. A word spoken creates a dog, a rabbit, a man. It fixes their nature before our eyes; henceforth their shapes are, in a sense, our own creation. They are no longer part of the unnamed shifting architecture of the universe. They have been transfixed as if by sorcery, frozen into a concept, a word. Powerful though the spell of human language has proven itself to be, it has laid boundaries upon the cosmos. [1]

No matter how far-ranging some of the mental probes that [2] man has philosophically devised, by his own created nature he is forced to hold the specious and emerging present and transform it into words. The words are startling in their immediate effectiveness, but at the same time they are always finally imprisoning because man has constituted himself a prison keeper. He does so out of no conscious intention, but because for immediate purposes he has created an unnatural world of his own, which he calls the cultural world, and in which he feels at home. It defines his needs and allows him to lay a small immobilizing spell upon the nearer portions of his universe. Nevertheless, it transforms that universe into a cosmic prison house which is no sooner mapped than man feels its inadequacy and his own.

He seeks then to escape, and the theory of escape involves 3 bodily flight. Scarcely had the first moon landing been achieved before one U.S. senator boldly announced: "We are the masters of the universe. We can go anywhere we choose." This statement was widely and editorially acclaimed. It is a striking example of the comfort of words, also of the covert substitutions and mental projections to which they are subject. The cosmic prison is not made less so by a successful journey of some two hundred and forty thousand miles in a cramped and primitive vehicle.

To escape the cosmic prison man is poorly equipped. He 4 has to drag portions of his environment with him, and his life span is that of a mayfly in terms of the distances he seeks to penetrate. There is no possible way to master such a universe by flight alone. Indeed such a dream is a dangerous illusion. This may seem a heretical statement, but its truth is self-evident if we try seriously to comprehend the nature of time and space that I sought to grasp when held up to view the fiery messenger that flared across the zenith in 1910. "Seventy-five years," my father had whispered in my ear, "seventy-five years and it will be racing homeward. Perhaps you will live to see it again. Try to remember."

And so I remembered. I had gained a faint glimpse of the 5 size of our prison house. Somewhere out there beyond a billion miles in space, an entity known as a comet had rounded on its track in the black darkness of the void. It was surging homeward toward the sun because it was an eccentric satellite of this solar system. If I lived to see it it would be but barely, and with the dimmed eyes of age. Yet it, too, in its long traverse, was but a flitting mayfly in terms of the universe the night sky revealed.

So relative is the cosmos we inhabit that, as we gaze upon 6 the outer galaxies available to the reach of our telescopes, we are placed in about the position that a single white blood cell in our bodies would occupy, if it were intelligently capable of seeking to understand the nature of its own universe, the body it inhabits. The cell would encounter rivers ramifying into miles of distance seemingly leading nowhere. It would pass through gigantic structures whose meaning it could never grasp—the brain, for example. It could never know there was an outside, a vast being on a scale it could not conceive of and of which it formed an infinitesimal part. It would know only the pouring tumult of the creation it inhabited, but of the nature of that great beast, or even indeed that it was a beast, it could have no conception whatever. It might examine the liquid in which it floated and decide, as in the case of the fall of Lucretius's atoms, that the pouring of obscure torrents had created its world.

It might discover that creatures other than itself swam in 7 the torrent. But that its universe was alive, had been born and was destined to perish, its own ephemeral existence would never allow it to perceive. It would never know the sun; it would explore only through dim tactile sensations and react to chemical stimuli that were borne to it along the mysterious conduits of the arteries and veins. Its universe would be centered upon a great arborescent tree of spouting blood. This, at best, generations of white blood cells by enormous labor and continuity might succeed, like astronomers, in charting.

They could never, by any conceivable stretch of the 8 imagination, be aware that their so-called universe was, in actuality, the prowling body of a cat or the more time-enduring body of a philosopher, himself engaged upon the same quest in a more gigantic world and perhaps deceived proportionately by greater vistas. What if, for example, the far galaxies man observes make up, across void spaces of which even we are atomically composed, some kind of enormous creature or cosmic snowflake whose exterior we will never see? We will know more than the phagocyte in our bodies, but no more than that limited creature can we climb out of our universe, or successfully enhance our size or longevity sufficiently to thrust our heads through the confines of the universe that terminates our vision.

Some further "outside" will hover elusively in our thought, 9 but upon its nature, or even its reality, we can do no more than speculate. The phagocyte might observe the salty turbulence of an eternal river system, Lucretius the fall of atoms creating momentary living shapes. We suspiciously sense, in the concept of the expanding universe derived from the primordial atom—the monobloc—some kind of oscillating universal heart. At the instant of its contraction we will vanish. It is not given us, nor can our science recapture, the state beyond the monobloc, nor whether we exist in the diastole of some inconceivable being. We know only a little more extended reality than the hypothetical creature below us. Above us may lie realms it is beyond our power to grasp.

1970

My Horse
Barry Lopez

It is curious that Indian warriors on the northern plains in 1 the nineteenth century, who were almost entirely dependent on the horse for mobility and status, never gave their horses names. If you borrowed a man's horse and went off raiding for other horses, however, or if you lost your mount in battle and then jumped on mine and counted coup on an enemy—well, those horses would have to be shared with the man whose horse you borrowed, and that coup would be mine, not yours. Because even if I gave him no name, he was my horse.

If you were a Crow warrior and I a young Teton Sioux out 2 after a warrior's identity and we came over a small hill somewhere in the Montana prairie and surprised each other, I could tell a lot about you by looking at your horse.

Your horse might have feathers tied in his mane, or in his 3 tail, or a medicine bag tied around his neck. If I knew enough about the Crow, and had looked at you closely, I might make some sense of the decoration, even guess who you were if you were well-known. If you had painted your horse I could tell even more, because we both decorated our horses with signs that meant the same things. Your white handprints high on his flanks would tell me you had killed an enemy in a hand-to-hand fight. Small horizontal lines stacked on your horse's foreleg, or across his nose, would tell me how many times you had counted coup. Horse hoof marks on your horse's rump, or three-sided boxes, would tell me how many times you had stolen horses. If there was a bright red square on your horse's neck I would know you were leading a war party and that there were probably others out there in the coulees behind you.

You might be painted all over as blue as the sky and cov- 4 ered with white dots, with your horse painted the same way. Maybe hailstorms were your power—or if I chased you a hailstorm might come down and hide you. There might be lightning bolts on the horse's legs and flanks, and I would wonder if you had lightning power, or a slow horse. There might be white circles around your horse's eyes to help him see better.

Or you might be like Crazy Horse, with no decoration, no 5 marks on your horse to tell me anything, only a small lightning bolt on your cheek, a piece of turquoise tied behind your ear.

You might have scalps dangling from your rein. 6

I could tell something about you by your horse. All this 7 would come to me in a few seconds. I might decide this was my moment and shout my war cry—*Hoka hey!* Or I might decide you were like the grizzly bear: I would raise my weapon to you in salute and go my way, to see you again when I was older.

I do not own a horse. I am attached to a truck, however, 8 and I have come to think of it in a similar way. It has no name; it never occurred to me to give it a name. It has little decoration; neither of us is partial to decoration. I have a piece of turquoise

in the truck because I had heard once that some of the south-
western tribes tied a small piece of turquoise in a horse's hock to
keep him from stumbling. I like the idea. I also hang sage in the
truck when I go on a long trip. But inside, the truck doesn't look
much different from others that look just like it on the outside. I
like it that way. Because I like my privacy.

For two years in Wyoming I worked on a ranch wrangling 9
horses. The horse I rode when I had to have a good horse was a
quarter horse and his name was Coke High. The name came with
him. At first I thought he'd been named for the soft drink. I'd
known stranger names given to horses by whites. Years later I
wondered if some deviate Wyoming cowboy wise to cocaine had
not named him. Now I think he was probably named after a
rancher, an historical figure of the region. I never asked the people who owned him for fear of spoiling the spirit of my inquiry.

We were running over a hundred horses on this ranch. 10
They all had names. After a few weeks I knew all the horses and
the names too. You had to. No one knew how to talk about the animals or put them in order or tell the wranglers what to do unless
they were using the names—Princess, Big Red, Shoshone, Clay.

My truck is named Dodge. The name came with it. I don't 11
know if it was named after the town or the verb or the man who
invented it. I like it for a name. Perfectly anonymous, like Rex for a
dog, or Old Paint. You can't tell anything with a name like that.

The truck is a van. I call it a truck because it's not a car and 12
because "van" is a suburban sort of consumer word, like "oxford loafer," and I don't like the sound of it. On the outside it
looks like any other Dodge Sportsman 300. It's a dirty tan color.
There are a few body dents, but it's never been in a wreck. I tore
the antenna off against a tree on a pinched mountain road. A boy
in Midland, Texas, rocked one of my rear view mirrors off. A
logging truck in Oregon squeeze-fired a piece of debris off the
road and shattered my windshield. The oil pan and gas tank are
pug-faced from high-centering on bad roads. (I remember a horse
I rode for a while named Targhee whose hocks were scarred
from tangles in barbed wire when he was a colt and who spooked
a lot in high grass, but these were not like "dents." They were
more like bad tires.)

I like to travel. I go mostly in the winter and mostly on two- **13**
lane roads. I've driven the truck from Key West to Vancouver,
British Columbia, and from Yuma to Long Island over the past
four years. I used to ride Coke High only about five miles every
morning when we were rounding up horses. Hard miles of twisting and turning. About six hundred miles a year. Then I'd turn
him out and ride another horse for the rest of the day. That's
what was nice about having a remuda. You could do all you had
to do and not take it all out on your best horse. Three car family.

My truck came with a lot of seats in it and I've never really **14**
known what to do with them. Sometimes I put the seats in and go
somewhere with a lot of people, but most of the time I leave
them out. I like riding around with that empty cavern of space
behind my head. I know it's something with a history to it, that
there's truth in it, because I always rode a horse the same way—
with empty saddle bags. In case I found something. The possibility
of finding something is half the reason for being on the road.

The value of anything comes to me in its use. If I am not **15**
using something it is of no value to me and I give it away. I
wasn't always that way. I used to keep everything I owned—just
in case. I feel good about the truck because it gets used. A lot.
To haul hay and firewood and lumber and rocks and garbage and
animals. Other people have used it to haul furniture and freezers
and dirt and recycled newspapers. And to move from one house
to another. When I lend it for things like that I don't look to get
anything back but some gas (if we're going to be friends). But if
you go way out in the country to a dump and pick up the things
you can still find out there (once a load of cedar shingles we sold
for $175 to an architect) I expect you to leave some of those
things around my place when you come back—if I need them.

When I think back, maybe the nicest thing I ever put in that **16**
truck was timber wolves. It was a long night's drive from Oregon
up into British Columbia. We were all very quiet about it; it was
like moving clouds across the desert.

Sometimes something won't fit in the truck and I think **17**
about improving it—building a different door system, for example. I am forever going to add better gauges on the dash and a

pair of driving lamps and a sunroof, but I never get around to doing any of it. I remember I wanted to improve Coke High once too, especially the way he bolted like a greyhound through patches of cottonwood on a river flat. But all I could do with him was to try to rein him out of it. Or hug his back.

Sometimes, road-stoned in a blur of country like southwest- 18 ern Wyoming or North Dakota, I talk to the truck. It's like wandering on the high plains under a summer sun, on plains where, George Catlin wrote, you were "out of sight of land." I say what I am thinking out loud, or point at things along the road. It's a crazy, sun-stroked sort of activity, a sure sign it's time to pull over, to go for a walk, to make a fire and have some tea, to lie in the shade of the truck.

I've always wanted to pat the truck. It's basic to the rela- 19 tionship. But it never works.

I remember when I was on the ranch, just at sunrise, after 20 I'd saddled Coke High, I'd be huddled down in my jacket smoking a cigarette and looking down into the valley, along the river where the other horses had spent the night. I'd turn to Coke and run my hand down his neck and slap-pat him on the shoulder to say I was coming up. It made a bond, an agreement we started the day with.

I've thought about that a lot with the truck, because we've 21 gone out together at sunrise on so many mornings. I've even fumbled around trying to do it. But metal won't give.

The truck's personality is mostly an expression of two 22 ideas: "with-you" and "alone." When Coke High was "with-you" he and I were the same animal. We could have cut a rooster out of a flock of chickens, we were so in tune. It's the same with the truck: rolling through Kentucky on a hilly two-lane road, three in the morning under a full moon and no traffic. Picture it. You roll like water.

There are other times when you are with each other but 23 there's no connection at all. Coke got that way when he was bored and we'd fight each other about which way to go around a tree. When the truck gets like that—"alone"—it's because it feels its Detroit fat-ass design dragging at its heart and making a fool out of it.

I can think back over more than a hundred nights I've slept 24 in the truck, sat in it with a lamp burning, bundled up in a parka, reading a book. It was always comfortable. A good place to wait out a storm. Like sleeping inside a buffalo.

The truck will go past 100,000 miles soon. I'll rebuild the 25 engine and put a different transmission in it. I can tell from magazine advertisements that I'll never get another one like it. Because every year they take more of the heart out of them. One thing that makes a farmer or a rancher go sour is a truck that isn't worth a shit. The reason you see so many old pickups in ranch country is because these are the only ones with any heart. You can count on them. The weekend rancher runs around in a new pickup with too much engine and not enough transmission and with the wrong sort of tires because he can afford anything, even the worst. A lot of them have names for their pickups too.

My truck has broken down, in out of the way places at the 26 worst of times. I've walked away and screamed the foulness out of my system and gotten the tools out. I had to fix a water pump in a blizzard in the Panamint Mountains in California once. It took all day with the Coleman stove burning under the engine block to keep my hands from freezing. We drifted into Beatty, Nevada, that night with it jury-rigged together with—I swear— baling wire, and we were melting snow as we went and pouring it in to compensate for the leaks.

There is a dent next to the door on the driver's side I put 27 there one sweltering night in Miami. I had gone to the airport to meet my wife, whom I hadn't seen in a month. My hands were so swollen with poison ivy blisters I had to drive with my wrists. I had shut the door and was locking it when the window fell off its runners and slid down inside the door. I couldn't leave the truck unlocked because I had too much inside I didn't want to lose. So I just kicked the truck a blow in the side and went to work on the window. I hate to admit kicking the truck. It's like kicking a dog, which I've never done.

Coke High and I had an accident once. We hit a badger hole 28 at a full gallop. I landed on my back and blacked out. When I came to, Coke High was about a hundred yards away. He stayed a hundred yards away for six miles, all the way back to the ranch.

I want to tell you about carrying those wolves, because it 29
was a fine thing. There were ten of them. We had four in the
truck with us in crates and six in a trailer. It was a five hundred
mile trip. We went at night for the cool air and because there
wouldn't be as much traffic. I could feel from the way the truck
rolled along that its heart was in the trip. It liked the wolves inside it, the sweet odor that came from the crates. I could feel that
same tireless wolf-lope developing in its wheels; it was like you
might never have to stop for gas, ever again.

The truck gets very self-focused when it works like this; its 30
heart is strong and it's good to be around it. It's good to be *with*
it. You get the same feeling when you pull someone out of a ditch.
Coke High and I pulled a Volkswagen out of the mud once, but
Coke didn't like doing it very much. Speed, not strength, was his
center. When the guy who owned the car thanked us and tried to
pat Coke, the horse snorted and swung away, trying to preserve
his distance, which is something a horse spends a lot of time on.

So does the truck.   31

Being distant lets the truck get its heart up. The truck has 32
been cold and alone in Montana at 38 below zero. It's climbed
horrible, eroded roads in Idaho. It's been burdened beyond over-
loading, and made it anyway. I've asked it to do these things because they build heart, and without heart all you have is a machine. You have nothing. I don't think people in Detroit know
anything at all about heart. That's why everything they build dies
so young.

One time in Arizona the truck and I came through one of 33
the worst storms I've ever been in, an outrageous, angry blizzard. But we went down the road, right through it. You couldn't
explain our getting through by the sort of tires I had on the truck,
or the fact that I had chains on, or was a good driver, or had a lot
of weight over my drive wheels or a good engine, because it was
more than this. It was a contest between the truck and the blizzard—and the truck wouldn't quit. I could have gone to sleep
and the truck would have just torn a road down Interstate 40 on
its own. It scared the hell out of me; but it gave me heart, too.

We came off the Mogollon Rim that night and out of the 34
storm and headed south for Phoenix. I pulled off the road to

sleep for a few hours, but before I did I got out of the truck. It was raining. Warm rain. I tied a short piece of red avalanche cord into the grill. I left it there for a long time, like an eagle feather on a horse's tail. It flapped and spun in the wind. I could hear it ticking against the grill when I drove.

When I have to leave that truck I will just raise up my left 35 arm—*Hoka hey!*—and walk away.

1975

The Perfect House
Farley Mowat

As I grew to know the People, so my respect for their in-   1 telligence and ingenuity increased. Yet it was a long time before I could reconcile my feelings of respect with the poor, shoddy dwelling places that they constructed. As with most Eskimos, the winter homes of the Ihalmiut are the snow-built domes we call igloos. (Igloo in Eskimo means simply "house" and thus an igloo can be built of wood or stone, as well as of snow.) But un-like most other Innuit, the Ihalmiut make snow houses which are cramped, miserable shelters. I think the People acquired the art of igloo construction quite recently in their history and from the coast Eskimos. Certainly they have no love for their igloos, and prefer the skin tents. This preference is related to the problem of fuel.

Any home in the arctic, in winter, requires some fuel if only   2 for cooking. The coast peoples make use of fat lamps, for they have an abundance of fat from the sea mammals they kill, and so they are able to cook in the igloo, and to heat it as well. But the Ihalmiut can ill afford to squander the precious fat of the deer, and they dare to burn only one tiny lamp for light. Willow must serve as fuel, and while willow burns well enough in a tent open at the peak to allow the smoke to escape, when it is burned in a snow igloo, the choking smoke leaves no place for human occupants.

So snow houses replace the skin tents of the Ihalmiut only 3 when winter has already grown old and the cold has reached the seemingly unbearable extremes of sixty or even seventy degrees below zero. Then the tents are grudgingly abandoned and snow huts built. From that time until spring no fires may burn inside the homes of the People, and such cooking as is attempted must be done outside, in the face of the blizzards and gales.

Yet though tents are preferred to igloos, it is still rather 4 hard to understand why....Great, gaping slits outline each hide on the frame of a tent. Such a home offers hardly more shelter than a thicket of trees, for on the unbroken sweep of the plains the winds blow with such violence that they drive the hard snow through the tents as if the skin walls did not really exist. But the People spend many days and dark nights in these feeble excuses for houses, while the wind rises like a demon of hatred and the cold comes as if it meant to destroy all life in the land.

In these tents there may be a fire; but consider this fire, this 5 smoldering handful of green twigs, dug with infinite labor from under the drifts. It gives heat only for a few inches out from its sullen coals so that it barely suffices to boil a pot of water in an hour or two. The eternal winds pour into the tent and dissipate what little heat the fire can spare from the cook-pots. The fire gives comfort to the Ihalmiut only through its appeal to the eyes.

However, the tent with its wan little fire is a more desirable 6 place than the snow house with no fire at all. At least the man in the tent can have a hot bowl of soup once in a while, but after life in the igloos begins, almost all food must be eaten while it is frozen to the hardness of rocks. Men sometimes take skin bags full of ice into the beds so that they can have water to drink, melted by the heat of their bodies. It is true that some of the People build cook shelters outside the igloos but these snow hearths burn very badly, and then only when it is calm. For the most part the winds prevent any outside cooking at all, and anyway by late winter the willow supply is so deeply buried under the drifts, it is almost impossible for men to procure it.

So you see that the homes of the Ihalmiut in winter are   7
hardly models of comfort. Even when spring comes to the land
the improvement in housing conditions is not great. After the
tents go up in the spring, the rains begin. During daylight it rains
with gray fury and the tents soak up the chill water until the hides
hang slackly on their poles while rivulets pour through the tent to
drench everything inside. At night, very likely, there will be frost
and by dawn everything not under the robes with the sleepers
will be frozen stiff.

With the end of the spring rains, the hot sun dries and   8
shrinks the hides until they are drum-taut, but the ordeal is not
yet over. Out of the steaming muskegs come the hordes of blood-
sucking and flesh-eating flies and these find that the Ihalmiut
tents offer no barrier to their invasion. The tents belong equally
to the People and to the flies, until midsummer brings an end to
the plague, and the hordes vanish.

My high opinion of the People was often clouded when I   9
looked at their homes. I sometimes wondered if the Ihalmiut
were as clever and as resourceful as I thought them to be. I had
been too long conditioned to think of home as four walls and a
roof, and so the obvious solution of the Ihalmiut housing problem escaped me for nearly a year. It took me that long to realize
that the People not only have good homes, but that they have devised the one perfect house.

The tent and the igloo are really only auxiliary shelters. The   10
real home of the Ihalmio is much like that of the turtle, for it is
what he carries about on his back. In truth it is the only house
that can enable men to survive on the merciless plains of the Bar-
rens. It has central heating from the fat furnace of the body, its
walls are insulated to a degree of perfection that we white men
have not been able to surpass, or even emulate. It is complete,
light in weight, easy to make and easy to keep in repair. It costs
nothing, for it is a gift of the land, through the deer. When I consider that house, my opinion of the astuteness of the Ihalmiut is
no longer clouded.

Primarily the house consists of two suits of fur, worn one   11
over the other, and each carefully tailored to the owner's dimen-

sions. The inner suit is worn with the hair of the hides facing inward and touching the skin while the outer suit has its hair turned out to the weather. Each suit consists of a pullover parka with a hood, a pair of fur trousers, fur gloves and fur boots. The double motif is extended to the tips of the fingers, to the top of the head, and to the soles of the feet where soft slippers of harehide are worn next to the skin.

The high winter boots may be tied just above the knee so 12 that they leave no entry for the cold blasts of the wind. But full ventilation is provided by the design of the parka. Both inner and outer parkas hang slackly to at least the knees of the wearer, and they are not belted in winter. Cold air does not rise, so that no drafts can move up under the parkas to reach the bare flesh, but the heavy, moisture-laden air from close to the body sinks through the gap between parka and trousers and is carried away. Even in times of great physical exertion, when the Ihalmio sweats freely, he is never in any danger of soaking his clothing and so inviting quick death from frost afterwards. The hides are not in contact with the body at all but are held away from the flesh by the soft resiliency of the deer hairs that line them, and in the space between the tips of the hair and the hide of the parka there is a constantly moving layer of warm air which absorbs all the sweat and carries it off.

Dressed for a day in the winter, the Ihalmio has this pro- 13 tection over all parts of his body, except for a narrow oval in front of his face—and even this is well protected by a long silken fringe of wolverine fur, the one fur to which the moisture of breathing will not adhere and freeze.

In the summer rain, the hide may grow wet, but the layer of 14 air between deerhide and skin does not conduct the water, and so it runs off and is lost while the body stays dry. Then there is the question of weight. Most white men trying to live in the winter arctic load their bodies with at least twenty-five pounds of clothing, while the complete deerskin home of the Innuit weighs about seven pounds. This, of course, makes a great difference in the mobility of the wearers. A man wearing tight-fitting and too bulky clothes is almost as helpless as a man in a diver's suit. But besides their light weight, the Ihalmiut clothes are tailored so that they are slack wherever muscles must work freely beneath them. There is ample space in this house for the occupant to move and to breathe, for there are no partitions and walls to limit his motions, and the man is almost as free in his movements as if he were naked. If he must sleep out, without shelter, and it is fifty below, he has but to draw his arms into his parka, and he sleeps nearly as well as he would in a double-weight eiderdown bag.

This is in winter, but what about summer? I have explained 15 how the porous hide nevertheless acts as a raincoat. Well, it does much more than that. In summer the outer suit is discarded and all clothing pared down to one layer. The house then offers effective insulation against heat entry. It remains surprisingly cool, for it is efficiently ventilated. Also, and not least of its many advantages, it offers the nearest thing to perfect protection against the flies. The hood is pulled up so that it covers the neck and the ears, and the flies find it nearly impossible to get at the skin underneath. But of course the Ihalmiut have long since learned to live with the flies, and they feel none of the hysterical and frustrating rage against them so common with us.

In the case of women's clothing, home has two rooms. The 16 back of the parka has an enlargement, as if it were made to fit a hunchback, and in this space, called the *amaut,* lives the unweaned child of the family. A bundle of remarkably absorbent sphagnum moss goes under his backside and the child sits stark naked, in unrestricted delight, where he can look out on the world and very early in life become familiar with the sights and the moods of his land. He needs no clothing of his own, and as for the moss—in that land there is an unlimited supply of soft sphagnum and it can be replaced in an instant.

When the child is at length forced to vacate this pleasant 17 apartment, probably by the arrival of competition, he is equipped with a one-piece suit of hides which looks not unlike the snow suits our children wear in the winter. Only it is much lighter, more efficient, and much less restricting. This first home of his own is a fine home for the Ihalmio child, and one that his white relatives would envy if they could appreciate its real worth.

This then is the home of the People. It is the gift of the land, 18
but mainly it is the gift of Tuktu.*

1952

The Myth of Sisyphus
Albert Camus

The gods had condemned Sisyphus to ceaselessly rolling a 1
rock to the top of a mountain, whence the stone would fall back
of its own weight. They had thought with some reason that there
is no more dreadful punishment than futile and hopeless labor.

If one believes Homer, Sisyphus was the wisest and most 2
prudent of mortals. According to another tradition, however, he
was disposed to practice the profession of highwayman. I see no
contradiction in this. Opinions differ as to the reasons why he became the futile laborer of the underworld. To begin with, he is
accused of a certain levity in regard to the gods. He stole their
secrets. Aegina, the daughter of Aesopus, was carried off by Jupiter. The father was shocked by that disappearance and complained to Sisyphus. He, who knew of the abduction, offered to
tell about it on condition that Aesopus would give water to the
citadel of Corinth. To the celestial thunderbolts he preferred the
benediction of water. He was punished for this in the underworld. Homer tells us also that Sisyphus had put Death in chains.
Pluto could not endure the sight of his deserted, silent empire.
He dispatched the god of war, who liberated Death from the
hands of her conqueror.

It is said also that Sisyphus, being near to death, rashly 3
wanted to test his wife's love. He ordered her to cast his unbur-
ied body into the middle of the public square. Sisyphus woke up
in the underworld. And there, annoyed by an obedience so con-

* the caribou

trary to human love, he obtained from Pluto permission to return
to earth in order to chastise his wife. But when he had seen again
the face of this world, enjoyed water and sun, warm stones and
the sea, he no longer wanted to go back to the infernal darkness.
Recalls, signs of anger, warnings were of no avail. Many years
more he lived facing the curve of the gulf, the sparkling sea, and
the smiles of earth. A decree of the gods was necessary. Mercury
came and seized the impudent man by the collar and, snatching
him from his joys, led him forcibly back to the underworld,
where his rock was ready for him.

You have already grasped that Sisyphus is the absurd hero.   4
He *is,* as much through his passions as through his torture. His
scorn of the gods, his hatred of death, and his passion for life
won him that unspeakable penalty in which the whole being is
exerted toward accomplishing nothing. This is the price that
must be paid for the passions of this earth. Nothing is told us
about Sisyphus in the underworld. Myths are made for the imagination to breathe life into them. As for this myth, one sees
merely the whole effort of a body straining to raise the huge
stone, to roll it and push it up a slope a hundred times over; one
sees the face screwed up, the cheek tight against the stone, the
shoulder bracing the clay-covered mass, the foot wedging it, the
fresh start with arms outstretched, the wholly human security of
two earth-clotted hands. At the very end of his long effort measured by skyless space and time without depth, the purpose is
achieved. Then Sisyphus watches the stone rush down in a few
moments toward that lower world whence he will have to push it
up again toward the summit. He goes back down to the plain.

It is during that return, that pause, that Sisyphus interests   5
me. A face that toils so close to stones is already stone itself! I
see that man going back down with a heavy yet measured step
toward the torment of which he will never know the end. That
hour like a breathing-space which returns as surely as his suffering, that is the hour of consciousness. At each of those moments
when he leaves the heights and gradually sinks toward the lairs of
the gods, he is superior to his fate. He is stronger than his rock.

If this myth is tragic, that is because its hero is conscious.   6

Where would his torture be, indeed, if at every step the hope of succeeding upheld him? The workman of today works every day in his life at the same tasks, and this fate is no less absurd. But it is tragic only at the rare moments when it becomes conscious. Sisyphus, proletarian of the gods, powerless and rebellious, knows the whole extent of his wretched condition: it is what he thinks of during his descent. The lucidity that was to constitute his torture at the same time crowns his victory. There is no fate that cannot be surmounted by scorn.

If the descent is thus sometimes performed in sorrow, it can 7 also take place in joy. This word is not too much. Again I fancy Sisyphus returning toward his rock, and the sorrow was in the beginning. When the images of earth cling too tightly to memory, when the call of happiness becomes too insistent, it happens that melancholy rises in man's heart: this is the rock's victory, this is the rock itself. The boundless grief is too heavy to bear. These are our nights of Gethsemane. But crushing truths perish from being acknowledged. Thus, Oedipus at the outset obeys fate without knowing it. But from the moment he knows, his tragedy begins. Yet at the same moment, blind and desperate, he realizes that the only bond linking him to the world is the cool hand of a girl. Then a tremendous remark rings out: "Despite so many ordeals, my advanced age and the nobility of my soul make me conclude that all is well." Sophocles' Oedipus, like Dostoevsky's Kirilov, thus gives the recipe for the absurd victory. Ancient wisdom confirms modern heroism.

One does not discover the absurd without being tempted to 8 write a manual of happiness. "What! by such narrow ways—?" There is but one world, however. Happiness and the absurd are two sons of the same earth. They are inseparable. It would be a mistake to say that happiness necessarily springs from the absurd discovery. It happens as well that the feeling of the absurd springs from happiness. "I conclude that all is well," says Oedipus, and that remark is sacred. It echoes in the wild and limited universe of man. It teaches that all is not, has not been, exhausted. It drives out of this world a god who had come into it with dissatisfaction and a preference for futile sufferings. It makes of fate a human matter, which must be settled among men.

All Sisyphus' silent joy is contained therein. His fate belongs to him. His rock is his thing. Likewise, the absurd man, when he contemplates his torment, silences all the idols. In the universe suddenly restored to its silence, the myriad wondering little voices of the earth rise up. Unconscious, secret calls, invitations from all the faces, they are the necessary reverse and price of victory. There is no sun without shadow, and it is essential to know the night. The absurd man says yes and his effort will henceforth be unceasing. If there is a personal fate, there is no higher destiny, or at least there is but one which he concludes is inevitable and despicable. For the rest, he knows himself to be the master of his days. At that subtle moment when man glances backward over his life, Sisyphus returning toward his rock, in that slight pivoting he contemplates that series of unrelated actions which becomes his fate, created by him, combined under his memory's eye and soon sealed by his death. Thus, convinced of the wholly human origin of all that is human, a blind man eager to see who knows that the night has no end, he is still on the go. The rock is still rolling.

I leave Sisyphus at the foot of the mountain! One always finds one's burden again. But Sisyphus teaches the higher fidelity that negates the gods and raises rocks. He too concludes that all is well. This universe henceforth without a master seems to him neither sterile nor futile. Each atom of that stone, each mineral flake of that night-filled mountain, in itself forms a world. The struggle itself toward the heights is enough to fill a man's heart. One must imagine Sisyphus happy.

1955

10

Argument

A Modest Proposal
Jonathan Swift

It is a melancholy object to those who walk through this great town or travel in the country, when they see the streets, the roads, and cabin doors, crowded with beggars of the female sex, followed by three, four, or six children, all in rags and importuning every passenger for an alms. These mothers, instead of being able to work for their honest livelihood, are forced to employ all their time in strolling to beg sustenance for their helpless infants: who as they grow up either turn thieves for want of work, or leave their dear native country to fight for the pretender in Spain, or sell themselves to the Barbadoes.

I think it is agreed by all parties that this prodigious number of children in the arms, or on the backs, or at the heels of their mothers, and frequently of their fathers, is in the present deplorable state of the kingdom a very great additional grievance; and, therefore, whoever could find out a fair, cheap, and easy method of making these children sound, useful members of the commonwealth, would deserve so well of the public as to have his statue set up for a preserver of the nation.

But my intention is very far from being confined to provide only for the children of professed beggars; it is of a much greater extent, and shall take in the whole number of infants at a certain age who are born of parents in effect as little able to support them as those who demand our charity in the streets.

As to my own part, having turned my thoughts for many   4
years upon this important subject, and maturely weighed the several schemes of our projectors, I have always found them grossly mistaken in their computation. It is true, a child just dropped from its dam may be supported by her milk for a solar year, with little other nourishment; at most not above the value of 2s., which the mother may certainly get, or the value in scraps, by her lawful occupation of begging; and it is exactly at one year old that I propose to provide for them in such a manner as instead of being a charge upon their parents or the parish, or wanting food and raiment for the rest of their lives, they shall on the contrary contribute to the feeding, and partly to the clothing, of many thousands.

There is likewise another great advantage in my scheme,   5
that it will prevent those voluntary abortions, and that horrid practice of women murdering their bastard children, alas! too frequent among us! sacrificing the poor innocent babes I doubt more to avoid the expense than the shame, which would move tears and pity in the most savage and inhuman breast.

The number of souls in this kingdom being usually reck-   6
oned one million and a half, of these I calculate there may be about 200,000 couple whose wives are breeders; from which number I subtract 30,000 couple who are able to maintain their own children (although I apprehend there cannot be so many, under the present distress of the kingdom); but this being granted, there will remain 170,000 breeders. I again subtract 50,000 for those women who miscarry, or whose children die by accident or disease within the year. There only remain 120,000 children of poor parents annually born. The question therefore is, how this number shall be reared and provided for? which, as I have already said, under the present situation of affairs, is utterly impossible by all the methods hitherto proposed. For we can neither employ them in handicraft or agriculture; we neither build houses (I mean live in the country) nor cultivate land; they can very seldom pick up a livelihood by stealing, till they arrive at six

years old, except where they are of towardly parts; although I confess they learn the rudiments much earlier; during which time they can, however, be properly looked upon only as probationers; as I have been informed by a principal gentleman in the county of Cavan, who protested to me that he never knew above one or two instances under the age of six, even in a part of the kingdom so renowned for the quickest proficiency in that art.

I am assured by our merchants, that a boy or a girl before 7 twelve years old is no saleable commodity; and even when they come to this age they will not yield above 31. or 31.2s. 6d. at most on the exchange; which cannot turn to account either to the parents or kingdom, the charge of nutriment and rags having been at least four times that value.

I shall now therefore humbly propose my own thoughts, 8 which I hope will not be liable to the least objection.

I have been assured by a very knowing American of my ac- 9 quaintance in London, that a young healthy child well nursed is at a year old a most delicious, nourishing, and wholesome food, whether stewed, roasted, baked, or broiled; and I make no doubt that it will equally serve in a fricassee or a ragout.

I do therefore humbly offer it to public consideration that of 10 the 120,000 children already computed, 20,000 may be reserved for breed, whereof only one-fourth part to be males; which is more than we allow to sheep, black cattle, or swine; and my reason is, that these children are seldom the fruits of marriage, a circumstance not much regarded by our savages; therefore one male will be sufficient to serve four females. That the remaining 100,000 may, at a year old, be offered in sale to the persons of quality and fortune through the kingdom; always advising the mother to let them suck plentifully in the last month, so as to render them plump and fat for a good table. A child will make two dishes at an entertainment for friends; and when the family dines alone, the fore or hind quarter will make a reasonable dish, and seasoned with a little pepper or salt will be very good boiled on the fourth day, especially in winter.

I have reckoned upon a medium that a child just born will 11 weigh 12 pounds, and in a solar year, if tolerably nursed, will increase to 28 pounds.

I grant this food will be somewhat dear, and therefore very 12
proper for landlords, who, as they have already devoured most
of the parents, seem to have the best title to the children.

Infant's flesh will be in season throughout the year, but 13
more plentiful in March, and a little before and after: for we are
told by a grave author, an eminent French physician, that fish
being a prolific diet, there are more children born in Roman
Catholic countries about nine months after Lent than at any
other season; therefore, reckoning a year after Lent, the markets
will be more glutted than usual, because the number of popish
infants is at least three to one in this kingdom: and therefore it
will have one other collateral advantage, by lessening the number
of papists among us.

I have already computed the charge of nursing a beggar's 14
child (in which list I reckon all cottagers, laborers, and four-fifths
of the farmers) to be about 2s. per annum, rags included; and I
believe no gentleman would repine to give 10s. for the carcass of
a good fat child, which, as I have said, will make four dishes of
excellent nutritive meat, when he has only some particular friend
or his own family to dine with him. Thus the squire will learn to
be a good landlord, and grow popular among the tenants; the
mother will have 8s. net profit, and be fit for work till she produces another child.

Those who are more thrifty (as I must confess the times re- 15
quire) may flay the carcass; the skin of which artificially dressed
will make admirable gloves for ladies, and summer boots for fine
gentlemen.

As to our city of Dublin, shambles may be appointed for 16
this purpose in the most convenient parts of it, and butchers we
may be assured will not be wanting: although I rather recommend buying the children alive, and dressing them hot from the
knife as we do roasting pigs.

A very worthy person, a true lover of his country, and 17
whose virtues I highly esteem, was lately pleased in discoursing
on this matter to offer a refinement upon my scheme. He said
that many gentlemen of this kingdom, having of late destroyed
their deer, he conceived that the want of venison might be well
supplied by the bodies of young lads and maidens, not exceeding
fourteen years of age nor under twelve; so great a number of

both sexes in every country being now ready to starve for want of work and service; and these to be disposed of by their parents, if alive, or otherwise by their nearest relations. But with due deference to so excellent a friend and so deserving a patriot, I cannot be altogether in his sentiments; for as to the males, my American acquaintance assured me from frequent experience that their flesh was generally tough and lean, like that of our schoolboys by continual exercise, and their taste disagreeable; and to fatten them would not answer the charge. Then as to the females, it would, I think, with humble submission be a loss to the public, because they soon would become breeders themselves: and besides, it is not improbable that some scrupulous people might be apt to censure such a practice (although indeed very unjustly), as a little bordering upon cruelty; which, I confess, has always been with me the strongest objection against any project, how well soever intended.

But in order to justify my friend, he confessed that this expedient was put into his head by the famous Psalmanazar, a native of the island Formosa, who came from thence to London about twenty years ago: and in conversation told my friend, that in his country when any young person happened to be put to death, the executioner sold the carcass to persons of quality as a prime dainty; and that in his time the body of a plump girl of fifteen, who was crucified for an attempt to poison the emperor, was sold to his imperial majesty's prime minister of state, and other great mandarins of the court, in joints from the gibbet, at 400 crowns. Neither indeed can I deny, that if the same use were made of several plump young girls in this town, who without one single groat to their fortunes cannot stir without a chair, and appear at the playhouse and assemblies in foreign fineries which they never will pay for, the kingdom would not be the worse. **18**

Some persons of a desponding spirit are in great concern about that vast number of poor people, who are aged, diseased, or maimed, and I have been desired to employ my thoughts what course may be taken to ease the nation of so grievous an encumbrance. But I am not in the least pain upon that matter, because it is very well known that they are every day dying and rotting by cold and famine, and filth and vermin, as fast as can be reasonably expected. And as to the young laborers, they are now in as **19** hopeful a condition: they cannot get work, and consequently pine away for want of nourishment, to a degree that if at any time they are accidentally hired to common labor, they have not strength to perform it; and thus the country and themselves are happily delivered from the evils to come.

I have too long digressed, and therefore shall return to my 20 subject. I think the advantages by the proposal which I have made are obvious and many, as well as of the highest importance.

For first, as I have already observed, it would greatly 21 lessen the number of papists, with whom we are yearly overrun, being the principal breeders of the nation as well as our most dangerous enemies; and who stay at home on purpose to deliver the kingdom to the Pretender, hoping to take their advantage by the absence of so many good Protestants, who have chosen rather to leave their country than stay at home and pay tithes against their conscience to an Episcopal curate.

Secondly, The poor tenants will have something valuable of 22 their own, which by law may be made liable to distress and help to pay their landlord's rent, their corn and cattle being already seized, and money a thing unknown.

Thirdly, Whereas the maintenance of 100,000 children 23 from two years old and upward, cannot be computed at less than 10s. a-piece per annum, the nation's stock will be thereby increased £50,000 per annum, beside the profit of a new dish introduced to the tables of all gentlemen of fortune in the kingdom who have any refinement in taste. And the money will circulate among ourselves, the goods being entirely of our own growth and manufacture.

Fourthly, The constant breeders beside the gain of 8s. ster- 24 ling per annum by the sale of their children, will be rid of the charge of maintaining them after the first year.

Fifthly, This food would likewise bring great custom to tav- 25 erns, where the vintners will certainly be so prudent as to procure the best receipts for dressing it to perfection, and consequently have their houses frequented by all the fine gentlemen, who justly value themselves upon their knowledge in good eating; and a skilful cook who understands how to oblige his guests, will contrive to make it as expensive as they please.

Sixthly, This would be a great inducement to marriage, 26
which all wise nations have either encouraged by rewards or enforced by laws and penalties. It would increase the care and ten-
derness of mothers toward their children, when they were sure of
a settlement for life to the poor babes, provided in some sort by
the public, to their annual profit instead of expense. We should
see an honest emulation among the married women, which of
them would bring the fattest child to the market. Men would become as fond of their wives during the time of their pregnancy as
they are now of their mares in foal, their cows in calf, their sows
when they are ready to farrow; nor offer to beat or kick them (as
is too frequent a practice) for fear of a miscarriage.

Many other advantages might be enumerated. For instance, 27
the addition of some thousand carcasses in our exportation of
barreled beef, the propagation of swine's flesh, and improvement
in the art of making good bacon, so much wanted among us by
the great destruction of pigs, too frequent at our table; which are
no way comparable in taste or magnificence to a well-grown, fat,
yearling child, which roasted whole will make a considerable figure at a lord mayor's feast or any other public entertainment. But
this and many others I omit, being studious of brevity.

Supposing that 1,000 families in this city would be constant 28
customers for infants' flesh, besides others who might have it at
merry-meetings, particularly at weddings and christenings, I
compute that Dublin would take off annually about 20,000 carcasses; and the rest of the kingdom (where probably they will be
sold somewhat cheaper) the remaining 80,000.

I can think of no one objection that will possibly be raised 29
against this proposal, unless it should be urged that the number
of people will be thereby much lessened in the kingdom. This I
freely own, and it was indeed one principal design in offering it to
the world. I desire the reader will observe, that I calculate my
remedy for this one individual kingdom of Ireland and for no
other that ever was, is, or I think ever can be upon earth. Therefore let no man talk to me of other expedients: of taxing our ab-
sentees at 5s. a pound: of using neither clothes nor household
furniture except what is of our own growth and manufacture: of
utterly rejecting the materials and instruments that promote for-

eign luxury: of curing the expensiveness of pride, vanity, idleness, and gaming in our women: of introducing a vein of parsimony, prudence, and temperance: of learning to love our country, in the want of which we differ even from Laplanders and the inhabitants of Topinamboo: of quitting our animosities and factions, nor acting any longer like the Jews, who were murdering one another at the very moment their city was taken: of being a little cautious not to sell our country and conscience for nothing: of teaching landlords to have at least one degree of mercy toward their tenants: lastly, of putting a spirit of honesty, industry, and skill into our shopkeepers; who, if a resolution could now be taken to buy only our native goods, would immediately unite to cheat and exact upon us in the price, the measure, and the goodness, nor could ever yet be brought to make one fair proposal of just dealing, though often and earnestly invited to it.

Therefore I repeat, let no man talk to me of these and the like 30 expedients, till he has at least some glimpse of hope that there will be ever some hearty and sincere attempt to put them in practice.

But as to myself, having been wearied out for many years 31 with offering vain, idle, visionary thoughts, and at length utterly despairing of success, I fortunately fell upon this proposal; which, as it is wholly new, so it has something solid and real, of no expense and little trouble, full in our own power, and whereby we can incur no danger in disobliging England. For this kind of commodity will not bear exportation, the flesh being of too tender a consistence to admit a long continuance in salt, although perhaps I could name a country which would be glad to eat up our whole nation without it.

After all, I am not so violently bent upon my own opinion 32 as to reject any offer proposed by wise men, which shall be found equally innocent, cheap, easy, and effectual. But before something of that kind shall be advanced in contradiction to my scheme, and offering a better, I desire the author or authors will be pleased maturely to consider two points. First, as things now stand, how they will be able to find food and raiment for 100,000 useless mouths and backs. And secondly, there being a round million of creatures in human figure throughout this kingdom, whose subsistence put into a common stock would leave them in debt 2,000,000*l*. sterling, adding those who are beggars by profession to the bulk of farmers, cottagers, and laborers, with the wives and children who are beggars in effect; I desire those politicians who dislike my overture, and may perhaps be so bold as to attempt an answer, that they will first ask the parents of these mortals, whether they would not at this day think it a great happiness to have been sold for food at a year old in the manner I prescribe, and thereby have avoided such a perpetual scene of misfortunes as they have since gone through by the oppression of landlords, the impossibility of paying rent without money or trade, the want of common sustenance, with neither house nor clothes to cover them from the inclemencies of the weather, and the most inevitable prospect of entailing the like or greater miseries upon their breed for ever.

I profess, in the sincerity of my heart, that I have not the 33 least personal interest in endeavoring to promote this necessary work, having no other motive than the public good of my country, by advancing our trade, providing for infants, relieving the poor, and giving some pleasure to the rich. I have no children by which I can propose to get a single penny; the youngest being nine years old, and my wife past childbearing.

1714

The Great Person-Hole Cover Debate: A Modest Proposal for Anyone Who Thinks the Word "He" Is Just Plain Easier...

Lindsy Van Gelder

I wasn't looking for trouble. What I was looking for, actu- 1
ally, was a little tourist information to help me plan a camping
trip to New England.

But there it was, on the first page of the 1979 edition of the 2

State of Vermont *Digest of Fish and Game Laws and Regulations:* a special message of welcome from one Edward F. Kehoe, commissioner of the Vermont Fish and Game Department, to the reader and would-be camper, *i.e.,* me.

This person (*i.e.,* me) is called "the sportsman."   3

"We have no 'sportswomen, sportspersons, sportsboys, or   4 sportsgirls,' " Commissioner Kehoe hastened to explain, obviously anticipating that some of us sportsfeminists might feel a bit overlooked. "But," he added, "we are pleased to report that we do have many great sportsmen who are women, as well as young people of both sexes."

It's just that the Fish and Game Department is trying to   5 keep things "simple and forthright" and to respect "long-standing tradition." And anyway, we really ought to be flattered, "sportsman" being "a meaningful title being earned by a special kind of dedicated man, woman, or young person, as opposed to just any hunter, fisherman, or trapper."

I have heard this particular line of reasoning before. In fact,   6 I've heard it so often that I've come to think of it as The Great Person-Hole Cover Debate, since gender-neutral manholes are invariably brought into the argument as evidence of the lengths to which humorless, Newspeak-spouting feminists will go to destroy their mother tongue.

Consternation about woman-handling the language comes   7 from all sides. Sexual conservatives who see the feminist movement as a unisex plot and who long for the good olde days of *vive la différence,* when men were men and women were women, nonetheless do not rally behind the notion that the term "mankind" excludes women.

But most of the people who choke on expressions like   8 "spokesperson" aren't right-wing misogynists, and this is what troubles me. Like the undoubtedly well-meaning folks at the Vermont Fish and Game Department, they tend to reassure you right up front that they're only trying to keep things "simple" and to follow "tradition," and that some of their best men are women, anyway.

Usually they wind up warning you, with great sincerity,   9 that you're jeopardizing the worthy cause of women's rights by focusing on "trivial" side issues. I would like to know how anything that gets people so defensive and resistant can possibly be called "trivial," whatever else it might be.

The English language is alive and constantly changing. 10 Progress—both scientific and social—is reflected in our language, or should be.

Not too long ago, there was a product called "flesh- 11 colored" Band-Aids. The flesh in question was colored Caucasian. Once the civil rights movement pointed out the racism inherent in the name, it was dropped. I cannot imagine reading a thoughtful, well-intentioned company policy statement explaining that while the Band-Aids would continue to be called "flesh-colored" for old time's sake, black and brown people would now be considered honorary whites and were perfectly welcome to use them.

Most sensitive people manage to describe our national reli- 12 gious traditions as "Judeo-Christian," even though it takes a few seconds longer to say than "Christian." So why is it such a hardship to say "he or she" instead of "he"?

I have a modest proposal for anyone who maintains that 13 "he" is just plain easier: since "he" has been the style for several centuries now—and since it really includes everybody anyway, right?—it seems only fair to give "she" a turn. Instead of having to ponder over the intricacies of, say, "Congressman" versus "Congress person" versus "Representative," we can simplify things by calling them all "Congresswoman."

Other clarifications will follow: "a woman's home is her 14 castle..." "a giant step for all womankind"...."all women are created equal"...."Fisherwoman's Wharf."...

And don't be upset by the business letter that begins "Dear 15 Madam," fellas. It means you, too.

1980

The Farce Called "Grading"
Arthur E. Lean

A sustained effort should be made to throw out false inducements to learning. In one way or another most of these refer to our obsession with grades. A few colleges that have ended the grading system, like those truly brave ones that have thrown out faculty ranks, have shown what can be done. It is possible to interest students in intrinsic learning, once we rid ourselves of the ancient hobby of making book on each performance. Grades may be useful for checking the memory of items of fact or the solving of pat mathematical problems. As a system for evaluating attainment of broad educational aims, it remains a failure. Few teachers have any systematic idea of how to grade fairly. Grading is also the chief villain behind the scandal of college cheating.

Louis T. Benezet

I have long ago reached the conclusion that the marking system itself is damaging in its impact on the education of our children and youth, and that it should go the way of the hickory stick and dunce caps. It should be abandoned at all levels of education.

Ernest O. Melby

1   Of all the common practices in our schools, doubtless the most tyrannical and indefensible is our insistence on attempting to evaluate students' performance through a system of grades or "marks." The harm done by this practice is incalculable, but we persistently cling to it in spite of its obvious unworkability. Every person who has ever gone to school can cite numerous instances of unfairness and injustice caused by grading systems and practices, but for some strange reason we seem to assume it to be necessary and intrinsic to the process of formal education.

2   Some years ago, when numerical grading on a percentage basis was more common than today, several experiments were conducted in an attempt to determine how precisely teachers could evaluate students' written work. In one well-known study, in order to "prejudice the garden to roses," an *exact* subject was chosen—mathematics, of course, because in that field, as everybody knows, things are either right or wrong—and a panel of ex-

perienced mathematics teachers, recognized by their peers for their competence, was assembled to do the evaluating. Student papers in plane geometry were graded by these expert teachers, each using an identical copy so as to eliminate any persuasive effect of extraneous factors such as neatness. The result was, of course, that the grades assigned to exactly the same paper ranged all the way from the 90s down to the 40s and 50s. And this in an *exact* subject where answers are "either right or wrong"! Similar results were obtained in other comparable studies.

The shift to letter-grading with fewer distinctions (the familiar A, B, C, D, with either E or F to designate failure) has not really solved the problem; it has merely reduced the number of categories (whereupon, of course, we promptly proceed recidivistically to attach plus and minus signs—multiple ones if single ones will not suffice). And of course we *must* have an equivalency table to indicate that A includes the range 93–100 or 90–100, B 85–92 or 80–89, and so on down, refusing in our obstinacy to recognize the fatal inconsistency involved: is A 93 or 100 or something in between? How about 95? 98? 96.123456789? 3

During the hectic post–World War II days I was pressed into service to teach Freshman Composition (Expository Writing) at a large university. There were more than a hundred sections of this course, each with a maximum of twenty-five students. We used a book of readings as a basis for class discussion and weekly themes. In addition to class sessions, each student had a short fortnightly conference with his instructor to go over his work and discuss ways of improving his written expression. 4

One of the "full" professors in the English department was in charge of all the teaching in this course, and he regularly convened the instructors—some seventy or eighty of us—for purposes of coordination and standardization of instruction. Usually at these sessions we were given identical copies of an actual student theme which had been selected at random and duplicated exactly as originally submitted. We took thirty to forty minutes to read and evaluate this short theme, whereupon we wrote on it a grade and an evaluative comment. Having listed our names alphabetically on the blackboard, the professor in charge then called them one by one, and each instructor responded to his 5 name by stating the grade he had assigned to that theme. This grade was inscribed after his name on the blackboard.

Invariably the assigned grades on the same theme ranged 6 all the way from A (excellent) to E (failure). Those instructors who judged that theme to be in either of those extreme categories were then called upon to stand up and justify their grades. This they usually did with great earnestness and sincerity, albeit with increasing reluctance, for in the process their own personal biases, prejudices, and confusions were soon revealed for all to see. (It quickly became obvious to many neophyte instructors that C-minus was an inconspicuous, colorless grade which would not require them to expose themselves to the public justification-humiliation process.) Most of the assigned grades tended, of course, to cluster in the middle of the scale, but there were almost always some on the extremes. But not once did we stop to consider the *student* who must maintain a certain minimum grade-average to stay in school, and whose mark on that theme might be A or E depending on which instructor he has!

All of us are familiar with the classic examples of students' 7 submitting the same paper to different instructors (or even to the same instructor at different times!) and getting widely varying grades, of handing in obscure works of famous authors and getting them back marked "failure," and so on.

Grading tends to stigmatize and punish the less able stu- 8 dent, who may be trying very hard but, through no fault of his own, simply did not inherit much in the way of native intelligence.

In spite of the staggering amount of incontrovertible evi- 9 dence that grading not only does not accomplish its purpose but in reality inhibits and injures the educative process, we obstinately continue with this perverted practice.

After all, what is a "grade" supposed to be and do? Per- 10 haps we could get general agreement on the statement that it is a symbol purporting to express a measurement of academic achievement—an evaluation of the quality and quantity of learning. Now, in order to measure anything, we need a standard such as a ruler or tapeline for linear measurement, a scale for measuring weight, and so on. By using such standards I can determine that the desk at which I sit is thirty inches high, and that its surface measures twenty-eight inches by twenty inches. I put my portable typewriter on a scale and determine its weight to be nine pounds. I look at the thermometer on the wall and discover that room temperature is sixty-eight degrees Fahrenheit. Other people using the same standards would arrive at the same results; any variations would be infinitesimal and certainly negligible for practical purposes.

If all this be so, then what sense does it make for us to 11 speak of "giving" a grade to a student, or of his "earning" or "deserving" it? Do I "give" my desk a height of thirty inches? Does my typewriter "earn" a weight of nine pounds? Does this room "deserve" a temperature of sixty-eight degrees? Arrant nonsense, of course, but this ridiculous absurdity is exactly what we constantly do with our grading systems.

Compounding our criminal practices, we use grades for re- 12 ward and punishment. Recently a coed sued her university because she claimed that her failing grade in one course was "unfair" and resulted from an attempt "to discipline and punish her" for alleged wrongful conduct. She asserted that she had been found innocent by the university's disciplinary committee, but that the instructor and administrative superiors to whom she had appealed had refused to "raise the grade" to the B which she said she had "merited." And this occurred in an institution of what we fancifully call "higher learning"!

When students disobey instructions or otherwise transgress 13 (often unintentionally) we say to them, "Because of this, I am lowering your grade five points (or one letter)." Such behavior is surely the epitome of cynicism, and if our students display disquieting evidence of becoming increasingly cynical, we have ourselves and our indefensible practices largely to blame. With grades we *teach* them cynicism, to say nothing of lying, cheating, competitive throat-cutting, and other reprehensible practices.

"But," objects somebody, "after all, a grade is just a sort 14 of *estimate,* and most teachers try to be fair and accurate in their estimates." Yes; most teachers try to be fair and accurate, but all the time they know—at least, those who are honest with themselves know—that they are attempting the impossible. No self-

respecting teacher ever rests peacefully the night after turning in
a set of grades, for he knows that the "system" has made a char-
latan of him and he goes to bed hating himself for it. And as for
the estimate, let us not disregard the fact that an *absolute* pass-
or-fail system has no place for estimates. Is that 87 on your test
paper an estimate? If it is, then mightn't it really be 88, or 86, or
something else? Is that B-minus an estimate? No, indeed; when
the reports come out, when the averages and grade-points are
computed, when the failures are determined, when you are called
in and told that you've flunked out of school, there is no room for
estimates—this is a very *absolute* decision.

Incidentally, no teacher I know—myself included, God   15
wot—can explain the precise difference between a B-minus and a
C-plus, to say nothing of 60 and 59—or, for that matter, 60 and
59.999999999999.

"But," objects somebody else, "if grades are eliminated,   16
what can we substitute for them?" This inevitable question reminds me of the books that have been written on the subject of
how to stop smoking. Such a book can be written in one word:
Quit!

We have had this asinine practice of grading in schools for   17
so long that we unconsciously assume it to be necessary to the
learning process, but this is a manifestly false assumption.
Grades are one aspect of the artificial paraphernalia which we
have deliberately superimposed upon education—along with
courses, academic credit, "promotion," degrees, diplomas, cer-
tificates, commencement exercises, graduation, faculty rank,
and so on *ad infinitum, ad nauseam.*

We hold these minatory requirements over the students be-   18
cause we assume that most of them are naturally lazy, stupid
dolts who must somehow be coerced, cajoled, persuaded, threatened, strong-armed into learning what we have decided is "good
for them." Much of this required material is dull, boring, meaningless, and will be forgotten almost immediately; and the way it
is taught is even worse, but students realize that they must per-
force jump through the hoops in order to emerge finally with that
coveted degree, that beribboned diploma upon which our society
places such high value. What we invariably seem to forget is that

this superimposed academic apparatus is not at all intrinsic to learning—not at all a *sine qua non* of education, formal or informal. *It is there because we put it there.* Just because we're accustomed to it, let us not delude ourselves into assuming that it is essential, organic or integral; it isn't. But once it becomes an established system, students often shift their motivations and values and begin to "work for grades." And when we talk to them about "earning" and "deserving" marks, we are only compounding this felony.

There have been successful attempts to eliminate marks. 19 The Danish Folk High Schools and other brave experimental schools have gotten along very well without them. In place of report cards or transcripts covered with cabalistic symbols, written reports and parent-teacher (or parent-teacher-student) conferences are sometimes used to facilitate communication and understanding. For example, employers of young people find descriptive comments about such traits as dependability, resourcefulness, intelligence, honesty, ability to get along with others, and so on, much more meaningful than the conventional academic transcripts of prospective employees. If you were such an employer, would you prefer, on the one hand, a thoughtful evaluation from adults who have observed the young people closely over a period of time, or, on the other hand, an official piece of paper informing you about a C-minus in English history and a B-plus in college algebra?

Students themselves are so conditioned to grading that they 20 soon become willing dupes of the system. They go to their instructors and ask, "How am I doing in this course?" But in most cases they already *know* how they are doing—better than the instructor does—and the fact that they ask the question demonstrates the unreliability of the system.

Some years ago I found a small midwestern town in which 21 the editor of the local weekly newspaper regularly printed on its front pages the complete names and marks of all the children in that town's schools each time report cards were issued. This editor was obviously a sick man who needed immediate confinement in an institution, but his problem is illustrative of the pathology endemic to the practice of grading. Its elimination is more than I dare hope for in my lifetime.* But until the cancer is rooted out and destroyed we can hope for little real improvement in American education.

1976

The Penalty of Death

H. L. Mencken

Of the arguments against capital punishment that issue from uplifters, two are commonly heard most often, to wit:

1. That hanging a man (or frying him or gassing him) is a dreadful business, degrading to those who have to do it and revolting to those who have to witness it.

2. That it is useless, for it does not deter others from the same crime.

The first of these arguments, it seems to me, is plainly too weak to need serious refutation. All it says, in brief, is that the work of the hangman is unpleasant. Granted. But suppose it is? It may be quite necessary to society for all that. There are, indeed, many other jobs that are unpleasant, and yet no one thinks of abolishing them—that of the plumber, that of the soldier, that of the garbage-man, that of the priest hearing confessions, that of the sand-hog, and so on. Moreover, what evidence is there that any actual hangman complains of his work? I have heard none.

---

*As William Clark Trow observes, "Marks...deserve to be abolished. Anyone who has not lived his life in the ivory tower, however, knows that trying to abolish them would be like trying to abolish money."

Thomas J. Fleming notes that "the colossal confusion currently reigning in American education in regard to what teachers call 'evaluating pupil performance' and what more down-to-earth parents and kids call *marks* is our number-one school scandal."

On the contrary, I have known many who delighted in their ancient art, and practiced it proudly.

In the second argument of the abolitionists there is rather 3
more force, but even here, I believe, the ground under them is
shaky. Their fundamental error consists in assuming that the
whole aim of punishing criminals is to deter other (potential)
criminals—that we hang or electrocute A simply in order to so
alarm B that he will not kill C. This, I believe, is an assumption
which confuses a part with the whole. Deterrence, obviously, is
one of the aims of punishment, but it is surely not the only one.
On the contrary, there are at least a half dozen, and some are
probably quite as important. At least one of them, practically
considered, is *more* important. Commonly, it is described as revenge, but revenge is really not the word for it. I borrow a better
term from the late Aristotle: *katharsis*. *Katharsis*, so used,
means a salubrious discharge of emotions, a healthy letting off of
steam. A school-boy, disliking his teacher, deposits a tack upon
the pedagogical chair; the teacher jumps and the boy laughs. This
is *katharsis*. What I contend is that one of the prime objects of all
judicial punishments is to afford the same grateful relief (*a*) to the
immediate victims of the criminal punished, and (*b*) to the general body of moral and timorous men.

These persons, and particularly the first group, are con- 4
cerned only indirectly with deterring other criminals. The thing
they crave primarily is the satisfaction of seeing the criminal actually before them suffer as he made them suffer. What they
want is the peace of mind that goes with the feeling that accounts
are squared. Until they get that satisfaction they are in a state of
emotional tension, and hence unhappy. The instant they get it
they are comfortable. I do not argue that this yearning is noble; I
simply argue that it is almost universal among human beings. In
the face of injuries that are unimportant and can be borne without damage it may yield to higher impulses; that is to say, it may
yield to what is called Christian charity. But when the injury is
serious Christianity is adjourned, and even saints reach for their
sidearms. It is plainly asking too much of human nature to expect
it to conquer so natural an impulse. A keeps a store and has a
bookkeeper, B. B steals $700, employs it in playing at dice or

bingo, and is cleaned out. What is A to do? Let B go? If he does so he will be unable to sleep at night. The sense of injury, of injustice, of frustration will haunt him like pruritus. So he turns B over to the police, and they hustle B to prison. Thereafter A can sleep. More, he has pleasant dreams. He pictures B chained to the wall of a dungeon a hundred feet underground, devoured by rats and scorpions. It is so agreeable that it makes him forget his $700. He has got his *katharsis*.

The same thing precisely takes place on a larger scale when　5 there is a crime which destroys a whole community's sense of security. Every law-abiding citizen feels menaced and frustrated until the criminals have been struck down—until the communal capacity to get even with them, and more than even, has been dramatically demonstrated. Here, manifestly, the business of deterring others is no more than an afterthought. The main thing is to destroy the concrete scoundrels whose act has alarmed everyone, and thus made everyone unhappy. Until they are brought to book that unhappiness continues; when the law has been executed upon them there is a sigh of relief. In other words, there is *katharsis*.

I know of no public demand for the death penalty for ordi-　6 nary crimes, even for ordinary homicides. Its infliction would shock all men of normal decency of feeling. But for crimes involving the deliberate and inexcusable taking of human life, by men openly defiant of all civilized order—for such crimes it seems, to nine men out of ten, a just and proper punishment. Any lesser penalty leaves them feeling that the criminal has got the better of society—that he is free to add insult to injury by laughing. That feeling can be dissipated only by a recourse to *katharsis*, the invention of the aforesaid Aristotle. It is more effectively and economically achieved, as human nature now is, by wafting the criminal to realms of bliss.

The real objection to capital punishment doesn't lie against　7 the actual extermination of the condemned, but against our brutal American habit of putting it off so long. After all, every one of us must die soon or late, and a murderer, it must be assumed, is one who makes that sad fact the cornerstone of his metaphysic. But it is one thing to die, and quite another thing to lie for long months and even years under the shadow of death. No sane man would choose such a finish. All of us, despite the Prayer Book, long for a swift and unexpected end. Unhappily, a murderer, under the irrational American system, is tortured for what, to him, must seem a whole series of eternities. For months on end he sits in prison while his lawyers carry on their idiotic buffoonery with writs, injunctions, mandamuses, and appeals. In order to get his money (or that of his friends) they have to feed him with hope. Now and then, by the imbecility of a judge or some trick of juridic science, they actually justify it. But let us say that, his money all gone, they finally throw up their hands. Their client is now ready for the rope or the chair. But he must still wait for months before it fetches him.

That wait, I believe, is horribly cruel. I have seen more **8** than one man sitting in the death-house, and I don't want to see any more. Worse, it is wholly useless. Why should he wait at all? Why not hang him the day after the last court dissipates his last hope? Why torture him as not even cannibals would torture their victims? The common answer is that he must have time to make his peace with God. But how long does that take? It may be accomplished, I believe, in two hours quite as comfortably as in two years. There are, indeed, no temporal limitations upon God. He could forgive a whole herd of murderers in a millionth of a second. More, it has been done.

1926

The Declaration of Independence
Thomas Jefferson

In CONGRESS, July 4, 1776. The Unanimous Declaration of the Thirteen United States of America.

When in the Course of human events, it becomes necessary **1** for one people to dissolve the political bands which have connected them with another, and to assume among the powers of the earth, the separate and equal station to which the Laws of

Nature and of Nature's God entitle them, a decent respect to the opinions of mankind requires that they should declare the causes which impel them to the separation.

We hold these truths to be self-evident, that all men are cre- 2
ated equal, that they are endowed by their Creator with certain unalienable Rights, that among these are Life, Liberty and the pursuit of Happiness.

That to secure these rights, Governments are instituted 3
among Men, deriving their just powers from the consent of the governed.

That whenever any Form of Government becomes destruc- 4
tive of these ends, it is the Right of the People to alter or to abol-ish it, and to institute new Government, laying its foundation on such principles and organizing its powers in such form, as to them shall seem most likely to effect their Safety and Happiness. Prudence, indeed, will dictate that Governments long established should not be changed for light and transient causes; and accord-ingly all experience hath shewn, that mankind are more disposed to suffer, while evils are sufferable, than to right themselves by abolishing the forms to which they are accustomed. But when a long train of abuses and usurpations, pursuing invariably the same Object evinces a design to reduce them under absolute Despotism, it is their right, it is their duty, to throw off such Gov-ernment, and to provide new Guards for their future security.

Such has been the patient sufferance of these Colonies; and 5
such is now the necessity which constrains them to alter their former Systems of Government. The history of the present King of Great Britain is a history of repeated injuries and usurpations, all having in direct object the establishment of an absolute Tyr-anny over these States. To prove this, let Facts be submitted to a candid world.

He has refused his Assent to Laws, the most wholesome 6
and necessary for the public good.

He has forbidden his Governors to pass Laws of immediate 7
and pressing importance, unless suspended in their operation till his Assent should be obtained; and when so suspended, he has utterly neglected to attend to them.

He has refused to pass other Laws for the accommodation 8
of large districts of people, unless those people would relinquish

the right of Representation in the Legislature, a right inestimable to them and formidable to tyrants only.

He has called together legislative bodies at places unusual, 9 uncomfortable, and distant from the depository of their public Records, for the sole purpose of fatiguing them into compliance with his measures.

He has dissolved Representative Houses repeatedly, for op- 10 posing with manly firmness his invasions on the rights of people.

He has refused for a long time, after such dissolutions, to 11 cause others to be elected; whereby the Legislative powers, incapable of Annihilation, have returned to the People at large for their exercise; the State remaining in the mean time exposed to all the dangers of invasion from without, and convulsions within.

He has endeavoured to prevent the population of these 12 States; for that purpose obstructing the Laws for Naturalization of Foreigners; refusing to pass others to encourage their migrations hither, and raising the conditions of new Appropriations of Lands.

He has obstructed the Administration of Justice, by refus- 13 ing his Assent to Laws for establishing Judiciary powers.

He has made Judges dependent on his Will alone, for the ten- 14 ure of their offices, and the amount and payment of their salaries.

He has erected a multitude of New Offices, and sent hither 15 swarms of Officers to harass our people, and eat out their substance.

He has kept among us, in times of peace, Standing Armies 16 without the Consent of our legislatures.

He has affected to render the Military independent of and 17 superior to the Civil power.

He has combined with others to subject us to a jurisdiction 18 foreign to our constitution, and unacknowledged by our laws; giving his Assent to their Acts of pretended Legislation:

For Quartering large bodies of armed troops among us: 19

For Protecting them, by a mock Trial, from punishment for 20 any Murders which they should commit on the Inhabitants of these States:

For cutting off our Trade with all parts of the world: 21

For imposing Taxes on us without our Consent: 22

For depriving us in many cases, of the benefits of Trial by 23 Jury:

For transporting us beyond Seas to be tried for pretended 24 offenses:

For abolishing the free System of English Laws in a neigh- 25 bouring Province, establishing therein an Arbitrary government, and enlarging its Boundaries so as to render it at once an example and fit instrument for introducing the same absolute rule into these Colonies:

For taking away our Charters, abolishing our most valuable 26 Laws, and altering fundamentally the Forms of our Governments:

For suspending our own Legislatures, and declaring them- 27 selves invested with power to legislate for us in all cases whatsoever.

He has abdicated Government here, by declaring us out of 28 his Protection and waging War against us:

He has plundered our seas, ravaged our Coasts, burnt our 29 towns, and destroyed the lives of our people.

He is at this time transporting large Armies of foreign Mer- 30 cenaries to compleat the works of death, desolation and tyranny, already begun with circumstances of Cruelty & perfidy scarcely paralleled in the most barbarous ages, and totally unworthy the Head of a civilized nation.

He has constrained our fellow Citizens taken Captive on 31 the high Seas to bear Arms against their Country, to become the executioners of their friends and Brethren, or to fall themselves by their Hands.

He has excited domestic insurrections amongst us, and has 32 endeavoured to bring on the inhabitants of our frontiers, the merciless Indian Savages, whose known rule of warfare, is an undistinguished destruction of all ages, sexes and conditions. In every stage of these Oppressions We have Petitioned for Redress in the most humble terms: Our repeated Petitions have been answered only by repeated injury. A Prince, whose character is thus marked by every act which may define a Tyrant, is unfit to be the ruler of a free people. Nor have We been wanting in attentions to our British brethren. We have warned them from time to time of attempts by their legislature to extend an unwarrantable jurisdiction over us. We have reminded them of the circumstances of our emigration and settlement here. We have appealed to their native justice and magnanimity, and we have conjured them by the ties of our common kindred to disavow these usurpations, which, would inevitably interrupt our connections and correspondence. They too have been deaf to the voice of justice and of consanguinity. We must, therefore, acquiesce in the necessity, which denounces our Separation, and hold them, as we hold the rest of mankind, Enemies in War, in Peace Friends.

We, THEREFORE the Representatives of the UNITED STATES OF **33** AMERICA, in General Congress Assembled, appealing to the Supreme Judge of the world for the rectitude of our intentions, do, in the Name and by Authority of the good People of these Colonies, solemnly publish and declare, That these United Colonies are, and of Right ought to be FREE AND INDEPENDENT STATES: that they are Absolved from all Allegiance to the British Crown, and that all political connection between them and the State of Great Britain, is and ought to be totally dissolved; and that as Free and Independent States, they have full Power to levy War, conclude Peace, contract Alliances, establish Commerce, and to do all other Acts and Things which Independent States may of right do.

And for the support of this Declaration, with a firm reliance **34** on the protection of divine Providence, we mutually pledge to each other our Lives, our Fortunes and our sacred Honor.

1776

I Have a Dream
Martin Luther King, Jr.

Five score years ago, a great American, in whose symbolic **1** shadow we stand, signed the Emancipation Proclamation. This momentous decree came as a great beacon light of hope to millions of Negro slaves who had been seared in the flames of withering injustice. It came as a joyous daybreak to end the long night of captivity.

But one hundred years later, we must face the tragic fact   2 that the Negro is still not free. One hundred years later, the life of the Negro is still sadly crippled by the manacles of segregation and the chains of discrimination. One hundred years later, the Negro lives on a lonely island of poverty in the midst of a vast ocean of material prosperity. One hundred years later, the Negro is still languishing in the corners of American society and finds himself an exile in his own land. So we have come here today to dramatize an appalling condition.

In a sense we have come to our nation's capital to cash a   3 check. When the architects of our republic wrote the magnificent words of the Constitution and the Declaration of Independence, they were signing a promissory note to which every American was to fall heir. This note was a promise that all men would be guaranteed the unalienable rights of life, liberty, and the pursuit of happiness.

It is obvious today that America has defaulted on this   4 promissory note insofar as her citizens of color are concerned. Instead of honoring this sacred obligation, America has given the Negro people a bad check; a check which has come back marked "insufficient funds." But we refuse to believe that the bank of justice is bankrupt. We refuse to believe that there are insufficient funds in the great vaults of opportunity of this nation. So we have come to cash this check—a check that will give us upon demand the riches of freedom and the security of justice. We have also come to this hallowed spot to remind America of the fierce urgency of *now*. This is no time to engage in the luxury of cooling off or to take the tranquilizing drugs of gradualism. *Now* is the time to make real the promises of Democracy. *Now* is the time to rise from the dark and desolate valley of segregation to the sunlit path of racial justice. *Now* is the time to open the doors of opportunity to all of God's children. *Now* is the time to lift our nation from the quicksands of racial injustice to the solid rock of brotherhood.

It would be fatal for the nation to overlook the urgency of   5 the moment and to underestimate the determination of the Negro. This sweltering summer of the Negro's legitimate discontent will not pass until there is an invigorating autumn of freedom and equality. 1963 is not an end, but a beginning. Those who hope that the Negro needed to blow off steam and will now be content will have a rude awakening if the nation returns to business as usual. There will be neither rest nor tranquillity in America until the Negro is granted his citizenship rights. The whirlwinds of revolt will continue to shake the foundations of our nation until the bright day of justice emerges.

But there is something that I must say to my people who 6 stand on the warm threshold which leads into the palace of justice. In the process of gaining our rightful place we must not be guilty of wrongful deeds. Let us not seek to satisfy our thirst for freedom by drinking from the cup of bitterness and hatred. We must forever conduct our struggle on the high plane of dignity and discipline. We must not allow our creative protest to degenerate into physical violence. Again and again we must rise to the majestic heights of meeting physical force with soul force. The marvelous new militancy which has engulfed the Negro community must not lead us to a distrust of all white people, for many of our white brothers, as evidenced by their presence here today, have come to realize that their destiny is tied up with our destiny and their freedom is inextricably bound to our freedom. We cannot walk alone.

And as we walk, we must make the pledge that we shall 7 march ahead. We cannot turn back. There are those who are asking the devotees of civil rights, "When will you be satisfied?" We can never be satisfied as long as the Negro is the victim of the unspeakable horrors of police brutality. We can never be satisfied as long as our bodies, heavy with the fatigue of travel, cannot gain lodging in the motels of the highways and the hotels of the cities. We cannot be satisfied as long as the Negro's basic mobility is from a smaller ghetto to a larger one. We can never be satisfied as long as a Negro in Mississippi cannot vote and a Negro in New York believes he has nothing for which to vote. No, no, we are not satisfied, and we will not be satisfied until justice rolls down like waters and righteousness like a mighty stream.

I am not unmindful that some of you have come here out of **8** great trials and tribulations. Some of you have come fresh from narrow jail cells. Some of you have come from areas where your quest for freedom left you battered by the storms of persecution and staggered by the winds of police brutality. You have been the veterans of creative suffering. Continue to work with the faith that unearned suffering is redemptive.

Go back to Mississippi, go back to Alabama, go back to **9** South Carolina, go back to Georgia, go back to Louisiana, go back to the slums and ghettos of our northern cities, knowing that somehow this situation can and will be changed. Let us not wallow in the valley of despair.

I say to you today, my friends, that in spite of the difficul- **10** ties and frustrations of the moment I still have a dream. It is a dream deeply rooted in the American dream.

I have a dream that one day this nation will rise up and live **11** out the true meaning of its creed: "We hold these truths to be self-evident; that all men are created equal."

I have a dream that one day on the red hills of Georgia the **12** sons of former slaves and the sons of former slaveowners will be able to sit down together at the table of brotherhood.

I have a dream that one day even the state of Mississippi, a **13** desert state sweltering with the heat of injustice and oppression, will be transformed into an oasis of freedom and justice.

I have a dream that my four little children will one day live **14** in a nation where they will not be judged by the color of their skin but by the content of their character.

I have a dream today. **15**

I have a dream that one day the state of Alabama, whose **16** governor's lips are presently dripping with the words of interposition and nullification, will be transformed into a situation where little black boys and black girls will be able to join hands with little white boys and white girls and walk together as sisters and brothers.

I have a dream today. **17**

I have a dream that one day every valley shall be exalted, **18** every hill and mountain shall be made low, the rough places will be made plain, and the crooked places will be made straight, and the glory of the Lord shall be revealed, and all flesh shall see it together.

This is our hope. This is the faith with which I return to the 19 South. With this faith we will be able to hew out of the mountain of despair a stone of hope. With this faith we will be able to transform the jangling discords of our nation into a beautiful symphony of brotherhood. With this faith we will be able to work together, to pray together, to struggle together, to go to jail together, to stand up for freedom together, knowing that we will be free one day.

This will be the day when all of God's children will be able 20 to sing with new meaning

My country, 'tis of thee,
Sweet land of liberty,
  Of thee I sing:
Land where my fathers died,
Land of the pilgrims' pride,
From every mountain-side
  Let freedom ring.

And if America is to be a great nation this must become 21 true. So let freedom ring from the prodigious hilltops of New Hampshire. Let freedom ring from the mighty mountains of New York. Let freedom ring from the heightening Alleghenies of Pennsylvania!

Let freedom ring from the snowcapped Rockies of Colo- 22 rado!

Let freedom ring from the curvaceous peaks of California! 23

But not only that; let freedom ring from Stone Mountain of 24 Georgia!

Let freedom ring from Lookout Mountain of Tennessee!   25

Let freedom ring from every hill and molehill of Missis- 26 sippi. From every mountainside, let freedom ring.

When we let freedom ring, when we let it ring from every 27 village and every hamlet, from every state and every city, we will be able to speed up that day when all of God's children, black men and white men, Jews and Gentiles, Protestants and Catholics, will be able to join hands and sing in the words of the old

Negro spiritual, "Free at last! free at last! thank God almighty, we are free at last!"

1963

Eight Signposts to Salvation
Alan Paton

Does a ruling group change towards those it rules because 1 of considerations of justice? The answer is, almost certainly, no. Does it change because of internal and external pressures? Possibly, yes.

This second answer is not wholly encouraging. If the inter- 2 nal and external pressures become really dangerous, it may be too late to change. The people exerting the pressures may no longer care if you change. The time has come to destroy you. But the answer is not wholly discouraging. A ruling group may consent to change while it can still influence the situation. It may realise that the way to survival no longer lies in resistance to change. It may see the clouds on the horizon and know what they mean.

There is a not very nice picture that comes often to my 3 mind. A man lives in a house full of possessions. The poor and the angry and the dispossessed keep knocking at the door. Inside some members of his family urge him to open the door and others tell him that he must never open the door. Then comes the final imperious knock, and he knows at last that he must open. And when he opens, it is Death who is waiting for him.

And the man is me, my wife, our children; he is the White 4 man; above all he is the Afrikaner.

But I am not writing to spread gloom. I am writing espe- 5 cially for those inside the house who are telling the man to open the door. I am writing for White students and priests and newspapermen and trade unionists, for the young people of the United

Party and the National Party and the Progressive Party, for all those who are working for change in this implacable land.

Why on earth do they do it?   6

They do it because of those strange unweighable and im-   7
measurable things like hope and faith. And I admire them for it in this faithless world where for many nothing exists that cannot be weighed and measured, a world that believes in so little.

What a strange thing, to have been away from South Africa   8
for some months, from its threats and bannings and denial of passports, and its implacability, and then to want to get back to it again!

Some people would say: Of course, you want to get back to   9
your White comforts and privileges. Whatever truth there is in this it's not true enough. You want to get back because it's there that your life has meaning. You want to get back to those stubborn things which are the very stuff of your life. You want to get back to the students and the priests and the newspapermen. They make you feel you are alive more than all the sights of Paris and London and even Copenhagen.

These young White people, the Young Turks,[1] the young   10
UPs and Progs and Nats, what do they want?

Well, at least it is clear what a great many of them want.   11
They want nothing less than a new country. They have realised that White leadership and Anglo-Afrikaner solidarity and Afrikaner supremacy don't mean anything anymore. Nothing means anything at all if its architects and planners are all White.

I am no longer a party man, and I must confess my impa-   12
tience with those who think that any existing political party can possibly hold the best, wisest, most practicable solution for our problems, or can possibly know the best, wisest, most practicable way towards such a solution. Some of the computer-like arguments between party and party are exasperating. The house is burning down and the would-be saviours are arguing about what colour to choose for the buckets.

I don't expect younger White people to rush into a new   13
party. But I do expect them to drop these useless recriminations. They must not shun one another. One thing binds them together

[1] Verligte, or enlightened, members of the United Party.

that is greater than any loyalty to any party, and that is loyalty to their country and all its people.

Are there any things they might all agree about? I believe **14** so and here they are. But I do not dogmatise about them.

1. The days of White domination are over.

2. The days of unilateral White political decisions are over.

3. The progress of the homelands to political independence—however much may be left to be desired—is irreversible.

4. The possibility that all or most of the homelands will eventually form a Black Federation must be recognised.

5. The possibility that the Black Federation may itself offer to federate with 'White' South Africa must be recognised.

6. If it does not make this offer, or if the offer is refused, then the final extinction of 'White' South Africa will be assured.

7. The offer will not be made if 'White' South Africa is not prepared to begin the dismantling of the machinery of apartheid.

8. It is the political constitution of the future 'White' South Africa that is the supreme political question facing all White people, especially young White people. When I say 'young', I don't mean only students. I mean all who are young enough to know that we must change or die.

The problem of 'White' South Africa is that there are: **15**
Some four million Whites. **16**
Some two million Coloured people. **17**
Some 750,000 Asians. **18**
Some eight million Africans. **19**
According to Nationalist theory these eight million Africans **20** are 'temporary sojourners'. They really belong somewhere else. But at least six million are permanent residents, *except for the fact that no urban African has any real sense of permanence:*
Four million Whites therefore constitute a third of the pop- **21**

ulation of 'White' South Africa. The days of their domination are over. They are faced with the problem—the magnitude of which cannot be exaggerated—of constructing a social order in which justice will be done to all. And they cannot construct it unilaterally. Better wages, the quality of education, the quality of housing, the preservation of family life, all are important. But they are no longer gifts to be given by Whites to Blacks.

I beg to close with three questions to all White people who 22 understand that we change or die. Is there any future for apartheid in 'White' South Africa? Is Afrikaner-English co-operation good enough, and is Afrikaner-English-Coloured-Asian co-operation not only unattainable, but downright dangerous? Is there any place for the qualified franchise in 'White' South Africa, or is it only another of these unilateral gifts?

Change is in the air. It will come whether we White people 23 like it or not. It won't—it cannot—be completely safe, completely sure, completely satisfying. But it will be safer and surer and more satisfying if we take our share in bringing it about in the company of all our fellow South Africans.

1975

On Rabbits, Morality, Etc.
Walter Murdoch

I hope the compositor will be especially careful over the ti- 1 tle of this essay, and that the linotype will play no unseemly tricks. To guard against any accident, I must ask you to take notice that the word 'rabbits' is, or ought to be, followed by a comma, not an apostrophe. It would be most distressing if any innocent person were cheated into reading the article in the hope of learning something about rabbits' morality—a subject on which my ignorance is profound....When you come to think of it, it would not be a bad subject. The rabbit might be taken as a fine example of what we call race patriotism. His supreme ethical motive is the expansion of the race. He dreams of the day when the rabbit family shall inherit the earth from pole to pole. If we could imagine a rabbit singing, we may suppose his song would be something like 'Rule, Britannia', or 'Deutschland uber Alles'. He is careless of the single life; the individual is nothing to him, the race is all. 'Do what you will with me,' he says; 'trap me, poison me, skin me, pack me tight in tins, make my fur into a hat and my carcass into a pie—what does it matter so long as my race endures and spreads and burrows its way across kingdoms until all the earth is one huge rabbit-warren?' He is the perfect Imperialist—that, however, is not my subject today; nor any other day. It deserves to be treated, not in my halting prose, but in Homeric verse. It is a matter for an epic. Mine is a humbler theme.

2   A little while ago you may have noticed on the cable page of your morning paper the following item: 'The death is reported from London of Mr John R. Collison of Maidstone, Kent, who claimed to be the first person to introduce rabbits into Australia. He was 85 years of age.' A few days later the cables informed us that Mr Collison's claim to this distinction was disputed. 'Mr C. J. Thatcher contends that his father was responsible for having introduced rabbits into Australia.'

3   Now, to begin with, this conflict of claims is surely a somewhat curious and diverting spectacle. The idea of two men each 'claiming' to have been the first to introduce a deadly pest into a country hitherto free from it, has the charm of novelty. Mr C. J. Thatcher, ready to die in the last ditch defending his father's claim to have done more harm to Australia than anybody else, presents a singular example of filial devotion. It is as if a man went about boasting that one of his ancestors had the honour of bringing malaria into Europe. It is as if a man gave himself airs because his Uncle Henry, and nobody else, had started the recent bush-fires in Victoria. It is as if a statesman were to write a large book to prove that he, and he alone, had had the honour of starting the Great War.

4   As to the historic fact, I have no doubt that Mr C. J. Thatcher is in the right. In 1863, or thereabout, some Victoria

sportsmen, sighing like Alexander for more worlds to conquer, bethought them that the coursing of hares and rabbits was a luxury no civilized country ought to be without. So they applied to the Acclimatization Society; and the Society, thinking it rather a bright idea, wrote to its travelling agent in Great Britain, Mr Manning Thatcher, who soon got together a sufficient herd of rabbits and started for Australia in the sailing-ship *Relief*. Ship life seems to have disagreed with the rabbits; when Mr Thatcher reached Australia, not a single one of his rabbits was alive. But he, indomitable man, went straight back to England to get some more rabbits. His next attempt was again unsuccessful; and the next. Three times he started for Australia with a cargo of rabbits; three times he failed to bring a rabbit alive to port. Three times the gods strove to save Australia; but against determination like Mr Thatcher's the very gods do battle in vain. On his third journey he had kept a close watch on his charges and found out the cause of their extraordinary death-rate; he provided a remedy, and his fourth voyage was entirely successful. It was as if the gods had given up the struggle in disgust; Mr Thatcher landed without the loss of a rabbit.

Meanwhile, owing to the long delay, the aforesaid sportsmen seem to have lost interest. Mr Thatcher found that nobody wanted his rabbits. With a companion, he went about the country offering baskets of live rabbits for sale, but he did not sell enough to pay expenses. His stock of rabbits increased faster than he could sell them. One hot summer afternoon the two men decided that they had had enough of the tedious and unprofitable business; so they took all their rabbits out into the bush—and opened the baskets. 5

I happen to have in my possession an old newspaper containing a portrait of Mr Thatcher—and a thoroughly benevolent old gentleman he looks—also a picture of the medal presented by the Acclimatization Society to Mr Thatcher in recognition of his splendid achievement in the matter of rabbits. I presume Mr C. J. Thatcher possesses the original medal; probably it hangs in a conspicuous place in his drawing-room. It is a perfect example of the irony of history. 6

Why have I kept that old newspaper? Well, primarily, I 7

suppose, because I am interested in ethics, as we all are whether
we know it or not. Every one of us, every day, is passing moral
judgments, though not in the technical terms of the moralist. We
do not, in our daily conversation, talk much about virtue, or the
summum bonum, or the moral sense, or the categorical impera-
tive, or the hedonistic calculus, or our ethical ideals; at least, we
do talk about them continually, but not under those names. We
don't say of a man that he is a highly virtuous character; we say
he's a pretty decent sort of chap. We don't say that certain conduct is ethically indefensible; we say it's a bit over the fence. We
mean just the same. We are passing moral judgments.

And our underlying assumption is that it is quite easy to tell   8
a good action from a bad one, right conduct from wrong conduct.
And this common assumption is favoured by popular preachers
and writers, who tell us that we ought not to split straws about a
plain question, and that it is a simple thing to obey conscience,
that divinely-given faculty which tells us, infallibly, what we
ought to do and what we ought not to do. They speak as if this
conscience were a kind of moral sense of smell, by which we can
tell a good action from a bad one just as certainly as we can, in
the dark, tell a violet from a polecat. Well, I want to ask those
who hold such a comfortable doctrine a question which puzzles
me. Was Mr Thatcher's action, in introducing the rabbit into
Australia, a good action or a bad one?

Mere common sense will not give us the answer. It would   9
be hard to persuade common sense that an action which ruined
thousands of innocent people and made desolate vast tracts of
country, which struck a terrific blow at the agricultural and pastoral industries of a continent, can be described as a good action.
Neither will common sense blame Mr Thatcher for obeying orders. He is unquestionably to be praised for his zeal, his enthusiasm, his unconquerable persistence in what he thought to be an
admirable project. We have only to look at his portrait to see that
he was a man of high character, a man actuated by the best intentions. If intentions, as common sense tells us, are what really
distinguish right conduct from wrong, Mr Thatcher beyond doubt
acted rightly. What then?—will common sense admit that a man
may act rightly in doing a bad action? It sounds like a paradox. It

is certainly a puzzle; and if you never, in the course of your practical life, feel that you are puzzled by it, that can only be because
you never think.

We make a mistake, of course, when we think of 'an action'   10
as if it were a simple separate whole. Merely to open a basket, as
Mr Thatcher did, is a thing neither right nor wrong in itself; all
depends on what is inside the basket—depends, that is, on the
consequence of the basket's being opened. The immediate consequence, in this instance, was that the rabbits jumped out,
happy in their freedom; so far, the act had added to the sum of
happiness in the sentient world; so far, it was a good action. Ten
years later, it began to be of a darker colour, for its consequences had begun to develop.

Surely there never was a more fallacious saying than Ten-   11
nyson's:

And, because right is right, to follow right
Were wisdom in the scorn of consequence.

Half the disasters endured by the long-suffering human race have
been produced by good men who acted in the scorn of consequence. To do a thing without considering what the result of your
action will be is mere imbecility. The truth is with that other poet
who tells us that

...Of waves
Our life is, and our deeds are pregnant graves
Blown rolling from the sunset to the dawn.

An action must be considered with its consequences; with   12
the sum-total of its consequences. And as no human being will
live long enough to see the sum-total of the consequences of any
of his actions—for the ultimate consequence cannot be known
until time comes to an end—we can never say that a given action
is absolutely good or absolutely bad.

How then are we to choose between right and wrong con-   13
duct? Choose we must, somehow; 'life's business', as Browning
says, 'being just the terrible choice.' Some years ago, certain
persons wished to introduce into Western Australia a certain

kind of deer. It was pointed out, however, that this very species had been introduced into South Africa, had eaten farmers out of house and home, and had been in fact a greater plague than ever the rabbit was in Australia. The persons who were preparing to do this thing without inquiry into the consequence of similar procedure in other countries would have been guilty, had they had their way, not merely of a bad action, but of a wrong action. It would be of no use to plead that their intentions were good—we know what road is paved with good intentions. It would be of no use to tell us that their consciences had commended the act; it is a common and deadly fallacy, that a mysterious faculty called the conscience absolves us from the duty of finding out, to the best of our ability, the probable consequences of our action.... Consideration of Mr Thatcher and his basket of rabbits thus brings us round to the conclusion reached so many centuries ago by Socrates. Virtue is knowledge.

1970

ACKNOWLEDGEMENTS

American Friends Service Committee, "Struggle for Justice." From *Struggle for Justice, A Report on Crime and Punishment in America,* prepared for the American Friends Service Committee. Copyright ©1971 by Hill and Wang, Inc. Reprinted by permission of Hill & Wang, a division of Farrar, Straus & Giroux, Inc.

Maya Angelou, "Grandmother's Victory." From *I Know Why the Caged Bird Sings,* by Maya Angelou. Copyright ©1969 by Maya Angelou. Reprinted by permission of Random House, Inc.

Isaac Asimov, "The Villain in the Atmosphere." From *Past, Present, and Future.* Copyright ©1968 by Isaac Asimov. Reprinted by permission of the author.

James David Barber, "Presidential Character and How to Foresee It." From *The Presidential Character,* by James David Barber. Copyright ©1972 by James David Barber. Reprinted by permission of the author.

Bruno Bettelheim, "The Holocaust." From *Surviving and Other Essays,* by Bruno Bettelheim. Copyright ©1979 by Bruno Bettelheim and Trude Bettelheim as trustees. Reprinted by permission of Alfred A. Knopf, Inc.

Bruno Brustein, "Reflections on Horror Movies." Copyright ©1958 by Robert Brustein. Adapted by permission of Alfred A. Knopf, Inc., from *The Third Theatre,* by Robert Brustein.

William F. Buckley, Jr., "Why Don't We Complain?" First appeared in *Esquire.* Copyright ©1961 by William F. Buckley, Jr. Reprinted by permission of Wallace & Sheil Agency, Inc.

Albert Camus, "The Myth of Sisyphus." From *The Myth of Sisyphus and Other Essays,* by Albert Camus, translated by Justin O'Brien.

Copyright ©1955 by Alfred A. Knopf, Inc. Reprinted by permission of the publisher.

Rachel Carson, "The Grey Beginnings." From *The Sea Around Us,* Revised Edition, by Rachel L. Carson. Copyright ©1950, 1951, 1961 by Rachel L. Carson; renewed 1979 by Roger Christie. Reprinted by permission of Oxford University Press, Inc.

Bruce Catton, "Grant and Lee: A Study in Contrasts." From *The American Story*. Reprinted by permission of the U. S. Capitol Historical Society.

Norman Cousins, "Pain Is Not the Ultimate Enemy." From *Anatomy of an Illness, As Perceived by the Patient,* by Norman Cousins. Reprinted by permission of W. W. Norton & Company, Inc. Copyright ©1979 by W. W. Norton & Company, Inc.

Robertson Davies, "A Few Kind Words for Superstition." Reprinted by permission of the author.

Joan Didion, "The Metropolitan Cathedral in San Salvador." From *Salvador*. Copyright ©1983 by Joan Didion. Reprinted by permission of Simon & Schuster, Inc.

Annie Dillard, "Transfiguration." From *Holy The Firm*. Copyright ©1977 by Annie Dillard. Reprinted by permission of Harper & Row, Publishers, Inc.

Loren Eiseley, "The Cosmic Prison." From *Pyramid*. Copyright ©1970 by Loren Eiseley. Reprinted by permission of Simon & Schuster, Inc.

Joseph Epstein, "The Virtues of Ambition." From *Ambition: The Secret Passion,* by Joseph Epstein. Copyright ©1980 by Joseph Epstein. Reprinted by permission of the publisher, E. P. Dutton, a division of NAL Penguin, Inc.

Peter Farb and George Armelagos, "The Patterns of Eating." From *Consuming Passions,* by Peter Farb and George Armelagos. Copyright ©1980 by the Estate of Peter Farb. Reprinted by permission of Houghton Mifflin Company.

E. M. Forster, "My Wood." From *Abinger Harvest*. Copyright ©1936; renewed 1964 by Edward Morgan Forster. Reprinted by permission of Harcourt Brace Jovanovich, Inc., and by Edward Arnold Publishers, Ltd.

Peter Freundlich, "The Crime of the Tooth: Dentistry in the Chair." Copyright ©1987 by *Harper's* Magazine. All rights reserved. Reprinted from the September issue by special permission.

Euell Gibbons, "How to Cook a Carp." From *Stalking the Wild Asparagus*. Copyright ©1962 by Euell Gibbons. Reprinted by permission of Frida F. Gibbons.

William Golding, "Thinking as a Hobby." From *Holiday*. Copyright ©1961 by William Golding. Reprinted by permission of Curtis Brown, Ltd.

Ellen Goodman, "Watching the Grasshopper Get the Goodies." From *At Large*. Copyright ©1981 by The Washington Post Company. Reprinted by permission of Summit Books, a division of Simon & Schuster, Inc.

Nadine Gordimer, "Art and the State in South Africa." First appeared in *The Nation,* December 14, 1983. Copyright ©1983 *The Nation* magazine/The Nation Company, Inc. Reprinted by permission of *The Nation*.

Stephen Jay Gould, "Were Dinosaurs Dumb?" From *The Panda's Thumb: More Reflections in Natural History,* by Stephen Jay Gould, by permission of W. W. Norton & Company, Inc. Copyright ©1980 by Stephen Jay Gould.

Barbara Grizzuti Harrison, "Moral Ambiguity." From *Off Center: Essays*. Copyright ©1980 by Barbara Grizzuti Harrison. Reprinted by permission of Dial Press.

Luz Alicia Herrera, "Testimonies of Guatemalan Women." From *Revolution in Central America,* edited by the Stanford Central America Action Network. Copyright ©1983 by Westview Press. Reprinted by permission of the publisher. Excerpted and abridged from a translation by Maria Alice Jacob in *Latin American Perspectives,* Issues 25 and 26, Spring and Summer 1980, Vol. VII, Nos. 2 and 3.

Ann Hodgman, "Backwater Cuisine." First appeared in *Spy* magazine. September, 1987. Copyright ©1987 *Spy* magazine. Reprinted by permission of SPY magazine.

Richard Howey, "How to Write a Rotten Poem with Almost No Effort." First appeared in *The Plain Dealer*. Reprinted by permission of the author.

Langston Hughes, "Salvation." From *The Big Sea,* by Langston Hughes. Copyright ©1940 by Langston Hughes. Reprinted by permission of Farrar, Straus & Giroux, Inc.

Martin Luther King, Jr., "I Have a Dream." Copyright ©1963 by Martin Luther King, Jr. Reprinted by permission of Joan Daves.

Akira Kurosawa, "Crybaby." From *Something Like an Autobiography,* by Akira Kurosawa, translated by Audie E. Bock. Copyright ©1982 by Alfred A. Knopf, Inc. Reprinted by permission of the publisher.

Margaret Laurence, "Where the World Began." From *Heart of a Stranger,* by Margaret Laurence. Used by permission of the Canadian Publishers, McClelland & Stewart, Toronto. Copyright ©1976 by Margaret Laurence.

Arthur A. Lean, "The Farce Called 'Grading'." From *And Merely Teach: Irreverent Essays on the Mythology of Education,* 2nd ed. Copyright ©1968, 1976 by Arthur A. Lean. Reprinted by permission of Southern Illinois University Press.

William Least Heat Moon, "Tuesday Morning." From *Blue Highways: A Journey into America,* by William Least Heat Moon. Copyright ©1982 by William Least Heat Moon. Reprinted by permission of Little, Brown & Company.

Doris Lessing, "My Father." From *A Small Personal Voice.* Copyright ©1956, 1957, 1959, 1963, 1966, 1968, 1971, 1972, 1974 by Doris Lessing. Reprinted by permission of the author and her agents, James Brown Associates, Inc.

Barry Lopez, "My Horse." First appeared in *The North American Review,* Summer 1975. Copyright ©1975 by Barry Lopez. Reprinted by permission of Sterling Lord Literistic, Inc.

David Ludlum, "The Climythology of America." First appeared in *Weatherwise* magazine, October 1987. Copyright ©1987 by David M. Ludlum. Reprinted by permission of *Weatherwise* magazine and Heldref Publications, Inc.

Marya Mannes, "How Do You Know It's Good?" From *Glamour* magazine, November 1962. Copyright ©1962 by Marya Mannes. Reprinted by permission of David J. Blow.

Joyce Maynard, "I Remember...." This article first appeared in *TV Guide.* Copyright ©1975 by Joyce Maynard. Reprinted by permission of Robert Cornfield Literary Agency.

H. L. Mencken, "The Penalty of Death." From *A Mencken Chrestomathy.* Copyright ©1926 by Alfred A. Knopf, Inc. and renewed 1954 by H. L. Mencken. Reprinted by permission of Alfred A. Knopf, Inc.

Horace Miner, "Body Ritual among the Nacirema." From *American Anthropologist,* 1956. Copyright ©1956 by Horace Miner. Reprinted by permission of Horace Miner and the American Anthropological Association.

Jessica Mitford, "Behind the Formaldehyde Curtain." From *The American Way of Death.* Copyright ©1963, 1978 by Jessica Mitford. Reprinted by permission of Simon & Schuster, Inc.

Farley Mowat, "The Perfect House." From *People of the Deer.* Copyright ©1952, Farley Mowat Limited. Used by permission of the author.

Walter Murdoch, "On Rabbits, Morality, Etc." From *The Best of Wal-*

ter Murdoch: 72 Essays. Reprinted by permission of Angus & Robertson Publishers, Sydney, Australia.

George Orwell, "A Hanging." From *The Collected Essays, Journalism and Letters of George Orwell* (Vol. I: *An Age Like This: 1920-1940*). Copyright ©1968 by Sonia Brownell Orwell. Reprinted by permission of Harcourt, Brace, Jovanovich, Inc.; A. M. Heath & Company; the estate of Sonia Brownell Orwell; and Secker & Warburg, Ltd. First appeared in the *Adelphi,* 1931.

Cynthia Ozick, "On Permission to Write." First appeared as "Writers Domestic and Demonic" in *The New York Times Book Review,* March 25, 1984. Copyright ©1984 by The New York Times Company. Reprinted by permission.

Jo Goodwin Parker, "What Is Poverty?" From *America's Other Children: Public Schools Outside Suburbs,* by George Henderson. Copyright ©1971 by the University of Oklahoma Press. Reprinted by permission of George Henderson.

Alan Paton, "Eight Signposts to Salvation." From *Knocking at the Door: Shorter Writings,* edited by Colin Gardner. Copyright ©1975 by Alan Paton. Reprinted by permission of Simon & Schuster, Inc.

Alexander Petrunkevitch, "The Spider and the Wasp." First appeared in *Scientific American,* August 1952. Copyright ©1952 by Scientific American, Inc. All rights reserved. Reprinted with permission.

James C. Rettie, "'But a Watch in the Night': A Scientific Fable." From *Forever the Land,* edited by Russell and Kate Lord. Copyright ©1950 by James Rettie. Reprinted by permission of Harper & Row, Publishers.

Mordecai Richler, "Main Street." From *The Street: A Memoir.* Copyright ©1969 by Mordecai Richler. Reprinted by permission of International Creative Management. First published in *The New Republic.*

Erika Ritter, "Bicycles." Excerpt from *Urban Scrawl.* Copyright ©1984 by Erika Ritter. Reprinted by permission of Macmillan of Canada, A Division of Canada Publishing Corporation.

Richard Rodriguez, "Does America Still Exist?" First appeared in *Harper's,* March 1984. Copyright ©1984 by Richard Rodriguez. Reprinted by permission of Georges Borchardt, Inc. for Richard Rodriguez.

Murray Ross, "Football Red and Baseball Green." First appeared in *Chicago Review,* 1971. Copyright ©1971 by Murray Ross. Reprinted by permission of the author.

May Sarton, "The Rewards of Living a Solitary Life." Copyright ©1974 by The New York Times Company. Reprinted by permission.

Jonathan Schell, "Nuclear Holocaust." From *The Fate of the Earth.* Copyright ©1982 by Jonathan Schell. Reprinted by permission of Alfred A. Knopf, Inc. First published in *The New Yorker.*

Peter Schjeldahl, "Cyclone! Rising to the Fall." First appeared in *Harper's,* June 1988. Copyright ©1988 by Peter Schjeldahl. Reprinted by permission of the author.

Richard Selzer, "The Discus Thrower." First appeared in *Harper's,* 1977. Copyright ©1979 by David Goldman and Janet Selzer, trustees. Reprinted by permission of William Morrow & Co.

Susan Sontag, "Beauty." Original title: "Women's Beauty: Put Down or Power Source." Copyright ©1975 by Susan Sontag. Reprinted by permission of Farrar, Straus & Giroux, Inc.

Lewis Thomas, "The Iks." From *The Lives of a Cell.* Copyright ©1974 by Lewis Thomas. All rights reserved. Reprinted by permission of Viking Penguin, Inc.

Susan Alan Toth, "Cinematypes." Copyright ©1980 by Susan Allen Toth. Reprinted by permission of the author.

Lindsy Van Gelder, "The Great Person-Hole Cover Debate: A Modest Proposal for Anyone Who Thinks the Word 'He' Is Just Plain Easier...." First appeared in *Ms. Magazine,* April 1980. Reprinted by permission of the author.

Marie Winn, "Viewing vs. Reading." From *The Plug-In Drug,* by Marie Winn. Copyright ©1977 by Marie Winn. Reprinted by permission of Viking Penguin, Inc.

Tom Wolfe, "Pornoviolence." From *Mauve Gloves and Madmen, Clutter and Vine.* Copyright ©1967 by Tom Wolfe. Reprinted by permission of Farrar, Straus & Giroux, Inc.

Virginia Woolf, "The Death of the Moth." From *The Death of the Moth and Other Essays.* Copyright ©1942 by Harcourt Brace Jovanovich, Inc; renewed 1970 by Marjorie T. Parsons, executrix. Reprinted by permission of the publisher, the estate of Virginia Woolf, and The Hogarth Press Ltd.

William Zinsser, "The Transaction." From *On Writing Well,* Second Edition. Copyright ©1980 by William K. Zinsser. Reprinted by permission of the author.